SOCIO-ECONOMIC

Steps Towards a Fairer Future

Securing Economic Development, Social Equity and Sustainability

Seán Healy, Ann Leahy, Sandra Mallon
Michelle Murphy, and Brigid Reynolds

Social Justice Ireland   ·· ·· ·· ··

SOCIO-ECONOMIC REVIEW 2014

ISBN No. 978-1-907501-11-1

First Published April 2014

Published by
Social Justice Ireland
Arena House
Arena Road
Sandyford
Dublin 18

www.socialjustice.ie

Tel: 01- 2130724

e-mail: secretary@socialjustice.ie

TABLE OF CONTENTS

1

INTRODUCTION

Having exited the bailout in December 2013 and seen some improvement on a number of economic indicators in subsequent months many seem to believe that all is now well with Ireland. Some even predict a mini-boom and a quick 'return to normal' with employment growing, house prices rising and interest rates on Irish Government debt remaining at relatively low levels.

Irish and European policy-makers point to Ireland as a vindication of their policy approach and a model to be copied and emulated. A few years ago at the height of the Celtic Tiger, policy-makers in Ireland and the EU (most of them the same then as now) were trumpeting Ireland's prosperity as a vindication of their policy approach at that time and a model to be emulated. Sadly we now know their claims were wrong. Surely we should be sceptical about their assertions now.

There is an extraordinary reluctance to address the question of Ireland's future, in a comprehensive and inclusive way, to be specific about the kind of society to be built from the wreckage of recent years. While Government focuses almost exclusively on its oft-repeated mantra of building "the best small country in the world in which to do business", and most policy developments are justified on the basis of that target, there is little or no discussion of what Ireland should look like ten years from now, of how the common good and the well-being of this and future generations are to be promoted and attained in a fair and sustainable manner. Yet these are critical issues.

While there might be general agreement on eliminating poverty, unemployment and waiting lists (for housing or healthcare) there is little or no discussion on the steps to be taken if these and many other desirable outcomes are to be achieved. Being a good place in which to do business is of course a means towards these desirable ends. However, Ireland needs a great deal more than that; in particular it needs a robust public debate, involving all its people, to address these issues.

There are four key steps for such a debate to be worthwhile. It should:

1. Set out a detailed analysis and critique of the present situation;
2. Agree a vision for Ireland's future – clarifying where Ireland should be in 10 to 15 years' time;
3. Set out a comprehensive policy framework to address the challenges of moving towards this future; and
4. Identify a range of specific policy initiatives to be taken within this framework.

Failure to promote and engage in such a debate has cost Ireland dearly in recent decades. By failing to address such questions Ireland, in recent years has, for example, allowed the single biggest transfer of resources from low and middle income people to the rich and powerful in its history and accepted the false justifications that enabled this to happen. The main beneficiaries of this transfer have been parts of the corporate sector especially the bondholders and financial institutions who took little or no 'hit' for their gambling in Ireland's private banking sector. Other large corporates also benefitted as their privileged tax position continues to be protected and they are not asked to make any contribution towards Ireland's rescue and ongoing recovery and development.

At the same time, poverty rose, unemployment reached record levels, emigration escalated dramatically, waiting lists for social housing rose, child poverty, long-term unemployment and the numbers of working poor people all became entrenched parts of Ireland's reality. Public services were reduced significantly. Charges were introduced for many services while charges were increased in areas where they had previously existed. Funding for the community and voluntary sector was cut disproportionately at the very moment when the demand for their services was increasing. The fact that the poorest 10% of the population had seen the biggest proportionate fall in their income was more or less ignored.

Interestingly enough the situation across the EU is not much better. The European Commission's Social Protection Report for 2013 (published March 2014) shows the social situation worsening across the Union. It states:

> The latest figures on living and income conditions in the EU show that the EU is not making any progress towards achieving its Europe 2020 poverty and social exclusion target of lifting at least 20 million people from poverty and social exclusion by 2020. There are 6.7 million more people living in poverty or social exclusion since 2008, a total of 124.2 million people for the EU28 or close to 1 in 4 Europeans in 2012. Poverty and social exclusion has increased in more than 1/3 of the Member States in both 2011 and 2012. (European Commission Social Report, 2014: 7)

Ireland is one of those countries as we show in chapters 3 and 5 of this Review.

Social Justice Ireland fully acknowledges Ireland's difficult fiscal position in recent times. We also accept that Ireland must pay its way. However, we believe strongly that there were alternatives to the approach the Irish Government followed, alternatives that would have led to fewer job losses and greater protection of the vulnerable while rescuing the economy and moving Ireland towards a desirable and sustainable future.

The following chapters in this Socio-Economic Review address these issues. They set out

- Our detailed analysis and critique of the current situation;
- Our vision of Ireland's future;
- A policy framework within which Ireland could move towards a desirable and sustainable future;
- A range of specific policy proposals in the wide range of areas addressed.

Social Justice Ireland has long advocated a new guiding vision for Irish society; one based on the values of human dignity, equality, human rights, solidarity, sustainability and the pursuit of the common good. These values are at the core of the vision for a nation in which all men, women and children have what they require to live life with dignity and to fulfil their potential: including sufficient income; access to the services they need; and active inclusion in a genuinely participatory society.

These values matter. They are not minority views as is sometimes stated, but reflect the aspirations of the majority of Irish citizens. Indeed, in February 2014, 85% of the members of the Convention on the Constitution convened by the government voted to afford greater constitutional protection to Economic, Social and Cultural (ESC) rights. This included a recommendation to include explicit mention of rights to housing, social security, essential healthcare, the rights of people with disabilities, linguistic and cultural rights in the Irish Constitution. These are rights that *Social Justice Ireland* has argued for over many years.

To achieve our vision we have set out a policy framework that identifies five key policy areas for reform.[1]

---

[1]The authors have presented an earlier version of this framework in Healy et al. (2013).

- The first is **macroeconomic stability**, which requires a stabilisation of Ireland's debt levels, fiscal and financial stability and sustainable economic growth, and an immediate boost to investment, which has collapsed during the crisis. (Dealt with in chapters 2 and 4)

- The second is the need for a **just taxation** system, which would require an increase in the overall tax-take to the European average; such an increase must be implemented equitably and in a way that reduces income inequality. (These issues are dealt with in much greater detail in chapter 4).

- The third area is **social protection**, the strengthening of social services and social infrastructure, the prioritisation of employment, and a commitment to quantitative targets to reduce poverty. (Chapters 3 – on income distribution; 4 – taxation; 5 - work, unemployment and job creation; 6 - public services; 7 - housing and accommodation; 8 – healthcare; and 9 - education and educational disadvantage).

- The fourth area is that of the **governance** of our country, which requires new criteria in policy evaluation, the development of a rights-based approach, and the promotion of deliberative democracy. (Chapter 10).

- Fifth, policies must be adopted that create **a sustainable future**, through the introduction of measures to slow down climate change and protect the environment, the promotion of balanced regional development, and promotion of new economic and social indicators to measure performance alongside traditional national accounting measures such as GNP, GDP and GNI. (Chapters 11 – sustainability; 12 - rural development; and 13 -the global south).

It is time that Ireland started to think long-term, setting out the kind of sustainable, equitable and democratic society it wishes to build and how it proposes to reach that destination. All Irish people should be engaged in this process in a real and meaningful way, focused on building a world where people care for each other and for the natural world, with a commitment to building a compassionate society and a better future.

Social Justice Ireland offers this analysis and critique, this vision of the future and policy framework, together with its detailed proposals, as a contribution to the public debate that is urgently needed on the central question of what steps need to be taken if we are to move towards a fairer future.

2

FROM CRISIS TO VIABLE FUTURE PATHWAY

This *Socio-Economic Review* is published at a time when many Irish and European policymakers are holding up Ireland as a success story, as the first, and thus far, only country to emerge from the Troika's structural adjustment programme. The Presidents of both the German Bundesbank and the European Commission, and the Taoiseach, have all hailed Ireland's performance during, and exit from, the Troika financing programme as an example to be emulated.[2] To those who have advocated fiscal consolidation focused on reducing government expenditure as a response to the Eurozone crisis, and as a mechanism to reduce bond yields on government debt, the Irish exit seems a vindication. It is likely that the mantra used to justify this approach, the simple slogan of 'there is no alternative', will be used again to justify continued reductions in vital public expenditure and to continue a neo-liberal approach to economic and social policymaking (see Box 2.1), while repeating many of the mistakes made in the years leading up to the crisis.

Social Justice Ireland does not accept many of the assumptions that have informed much of the commentary in public and policy-making arenas in recent times. We believe that there are alternatives, and that it is now more important than ever that there be robust public debate about the policy choices facing Ireland in the years ahead, and the values upon which these choices are based. This requires the articulation of a new vision based on an understanding of the common good, and a renewed commitment to vindicate economic, cultural and social rights for all, so that every citizen, whatever their social or economic status, might be able to fulfil their potential in a flourishing society. Such an approach will demand a progressive change in the distribution of wealth, power and income in Irish society. Achieving this vision requires a radically different set of policies than those pursued during the 2008-2014 period.

---

[2]   http://www.bundesbank.de/Redaktion/EN/Interviews/2014_01_24_weidmann_irishtimes.html

In this chapter we will chart the broad outlines of an economic and social policy framework which guides the contributions to specific policy areas outlined in the *Socio-Economic Review*. We will first provide a brief history and context, Irish and European, to the continuing economic and social crisis in Ireland, and examine the new European and international institutional framework that will shape Irish economic policy in the coming years. Finally, we will present our own alternative policy framework, which proposes positive policy alternatives that can be pursued over the coming years.

2.1 The Irish Economic Crisis, 2008-2014

Ireland has experienced a prolonged recession since 2009, one of the deepest in the European Union in the present crisis. This has caused a rapid rise in unemployment, and the re-emergence of significant levels of emigration. This section will briefly provide our analysis of how and why the crisis emerged, and then explore the policy response to the crisis, and its effects.[3]

2.1.1 The Emergence of the Crisis, 1990s-2008

The Irish Context
During the 1990s, Ireland rapidly converged with EU-15 levels of GDP per capita and by the 2000s was surpassing the EU-15 average (see Chart 2.1). Rapid economic expansion facilitated budget surpluses for the first time since the 1960s, and both phenomena led to the rapid reduction of Ireland's real debt burden. Migration fell while both total employment and the size of the labour force grew rapidly, driven by increased demand and on the supply side by a demographically young population and the entry of women into the labour force (see Chart 2.2). In some areas of policymaking, Ireland adapted influential neo-liberal nostrums: capital and income taxes were rapidly reduced, particularly after 1997; public enterprises previously considered of strategic importance were privatised; housing provision became reliant on the debt-driven private sector; financial regulation was placed on a 'light-touch' model; industrial policy was based on attracting foreign direct investment through low corporate tax rates; and the International Financial Services Centre (IFSC) was created to take advantage of global financial liberalisation.

However, policy was also influenced by other factors, such as the need to maintain industrial peace and retain social cohesion. Social Partnership provided a framework in which otherwise excluded groups gained an input into public policy. Industrial peace was secured through national pay agreements. In the early 2000s, policymakers believed they could distribute the proceeds of growth through tax reductions and

---

[3] For a much more detailed outline of our understanding of how and why the crisis emerged cf. Healy et al (2013), *Ireland - A Narrative*, which is available on our website at www.socialjustice.ie

increases in social security payments. Ireland was hailed internationally as proof that a country could develop using neo-liberal economic policies and investment in education and training while retaining a social safety net.[4]

Chart 2.1 –GDP per capita at current market prices per head of population (EU-15=100), Ireland 1992-2012.

Chart 2.2 – Rate of Unemployment (Left Axis) and Employment Rate (Right Axis), Ireland 1992-2012.

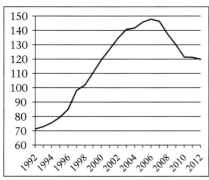

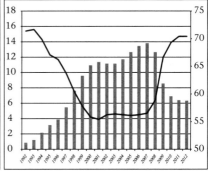

Source: AMECO (2014).   Source: AMECO (2014); Eurostat (2014).

The years leading up to the crisis were characterised by a credit-led, asset-price bubble in residential and commercial property. This was encouraged by ineffective planning regulations, a lack of resources for social and voluntary housing, and the failure of the National Spatial Strategy, which was designed to assure balanced regional development. Ireland's entry to the Eurozone also provided an impetus for credit expansion, as currency risk evaporated and the European Central Bank's (ECB) main refinancing rate was kept at a level – particularly between 2000 and 2005 - conducive to low-growth, low-inflation Germany and France. Irish policymakers did not appreciate the need to use fiscal, micro-prudential, housing and zoning policies as tools to address housing need, property-price bubbles, and to compensate for the loss of monetary policy upon entry to the Eurozone.

Credit outstanding advanced for home loans nearly trebled between March 2003 and September 2008, while credit advanced for construction and real estate expanded nearly fivefold in the same period (see Graph 2.4). To finance this lending the six domestic Irish banks dramatically expanded and altered their balance sheets, taking advantage of interbank lending provided by Eurozone and international banks, and by issuing debt securities (bonds). Debt securities rose from 0.1% (€71m) of Irish banking liabilities in December 1999 to 8.5% (€43.5bn) in May 2008, while deposits from non-Irish credit institutions rose from nearly 20% of liabilities to 30%

---

[4] http://www.nytimes.com/2005/06/29/opinion/29friedman.html?_r=0

(O'Connor et. al., 2012: 69). The combined balance sheet of the Irish banks rose nearly fivefold to over €500bn by September 2008.

Graph 2.3 – Index of GDP per capita at current market prices for selected Eurozone members (2002=100), 2003-2013

Graph 2.4 - Credit Outstanding to Irish Households and Firms (€bn), March 2003 – August 2013

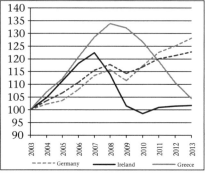

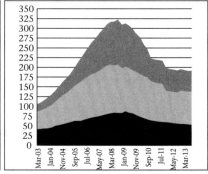

Source: AMECO (2014).   Source: Central Bank of Ireland (2014).

Irish policymakers were initially slow to realise the consequences of the liquidity problems that emerged in global financial markets in August 2007. Despite preparation following the bank run on Northern Rock in the UK, senior policymakers were taken by surprise in September 2008 when informed by the domestic Irish banks about large cash outflows, and the possible failure to meet maturing liabilities, given an inability to raise cash on the wholesale market. The Irish authorities - believing that Irish banks were solvent and requiring only liquidity support - issued a blanket guarantee which covered nearly 80% of the banks' existing liabilities, amounting to €400bn, owed by the Irish banks.[5]

This precipitous and unwise decision to socialise the banking debt accumulated throughout the bubble years surprised many of Ireland's European partners. Although the 'no bondholder left behind' approach was later affirmed as a Euro area policy by the European Central Bank, it was the failures of the Irish regulatory authorities that led to the banking crisis itself. The initial bank guarantee was a wholly Irish decision.

---

[5] The six domestic Irish banks were Allied Irish Banks, Bank of Ireland, Anglo Irish Bank, Irish Life and Permanent, Irish Nationwide Building Society and the Educational Building Society. There remains considerable confusion about the events leading up to and immediately after the bank guarantee was issued on the night of the 29th September. No definitive account of the events has yet emerged.

Box 2.1: Neoliberalism – what's in a word?

The term 'neo-liberalism' has become more widely used in popular debate since the economic crisis began. A speech by President Higgins which used the term attracted some opposition as it was interpreted as a political insult by some (O'Brien, 2013). Initially the term was used by a small group of radical economic thinkers such as Friedrich van Hayek and Milton Friedman to describe their own distinctive economic and social philosophy (Friedman, 1951; Stedman Jones, 2012). However, the term is increasingly used as a helpful analytic category used to describe a specific theory of government – not a theory of economics as is commonly imagined - and an associated economic and social policy agenda, and institutional framework. Indeed, President Higgins (2013) made this explicitly clear, distinguishing neoliberal doctrine from classical and neo-classical economics.

Finlayson (2013) has provided a useful précis of neo-liberalism as a governing philosophy which is based first on an 'economic' theory of human nature – that is, that human beings are rational and utility-maximising, and second, on the liberal principle that people should be left to do what they want, and how they want. Following these principles, price is seen as the key mechanism in transmitting information, allowing rational individuals make decisions and allocate resources; and following this, effective competition and competitive exchange is required for prices to be accurate. Finally, Finlayson argues that, due to these principals, neo-liberals do not hold a concept of the 'common good' in politics as they fear that government will act on a set of principles dictated by the common good, which will in turn make rational individual decision-making difficult.

Such a perspective is not necessarily anti-state, as is often implied. Rather, neoliberals advocate an enhanced role for market processes in many areas of social and economic life, which can often result in the rule of the state actually expanding as it takes up additional regulatory powers to ensure market competition and enforcement of rules. Associated with this is the widespread outsourcing and privatisation of government services, which doesn't actually reduce the scope of the government, but theoretically increases competition and thus more accurate – but not necessarily lower - pricing.

On a wider institutional but less precise basis, the term 'neoliberal' is used to describe the thrust of policy development from the 1970s on. This larger shift involved the liberalisation of capital flows, deregulation of finance and the concomitant growth of international capital flows and the power of international financial institutions and actors. In the Irish context, neo-liberal ideas in areas such as the role of finance and low levels of taxation were often simply accepted as 'common sense' rather than explicitly identified with a specific philosopher. It is hopefully clearer now that underlying policy approaches to areas such as banking regulation were neo-liberal beliefs in the superiority of the price mechanism and competition in leading to beneficial outcomes.

What are the reasons for the emergence of the crisis? Kelly (2010) consistently – years before the crisis itself - identified the proximate cause of a future recession: the misallocation of investment towards property created by a massive expansion of credit, and the subsequent collapse in property prices, and in turn, the value of the banking systems assets, which led to the insolvency of the banking institutions. In terms of the severity of the fiscal crisis, official reports highlighted the pro-cyclical structure of the Irish taxation system; for example, the report by the Governor of the Central Bank estimated that cyclical taxes (Corporation Tax, Stamp Duty and Capital Gains Tax) rose from accounting for 7% of the total tax take in 1987 to 30% in 2006 (Honohan, 2010: 29; Commission of Investigation into the Banking Sector in Ireland, 2011: 70; Regling & Watson, 2010: 27). These reports also highlighted the failures in financial regulation, under-capacity in key state institutions, and the collective behaviour of senior banking executives and boards, which allowed the massive expansion of credit.

Graph 2.5 – Public Social Expenditure as a % of GDP, 2007

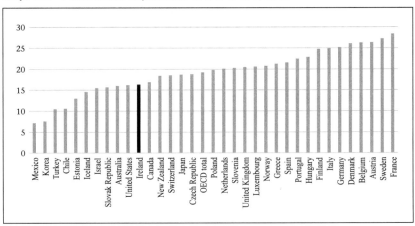

Source: OECD, 2011.

Excessive Government expenditure on social transfers has also been blamed for the emergence of the fiscal crisis. However, Irish social expenditure leading up to the crisis was below the OECD average (Graph 2.5), and the government was running budget surpluses and allowing the national debt to fall (Graph 2.7). On the tax and social contributions side Ireland maintained a relatively low tax-take of unstable composition, particularly in terms of the reliance on transactional taxes such as stamp duty and capital gains tax. Ireland also operated a range of tax reliefs which facilitated significant reductions in individuals' tax liabilities, particularly those on higher incomes (Collins & Walsh, 2011).

Indeed, Ireland's tax take as a percentage of GDP has remained one of the lowest in the European Union over the last fifteen years (see Graph 2.6). The dangerous mix of a relatively low-tax take and pro-cyclical composition was revealed when the property bubble burst, as the tax take from stamp duty and capital gains collapsed: in 2007, Capital Gains Tax (CGT) yielded €3,105m and Stamp Duty yielded €3,185m but by 2010 Capital Gains Tax yielded only €347m while Stamp Duty yielded only €960m. Government, and many commentators, had come to believe that Ireland could combine a low-tax model with increasing levels of social security provision.

Graph 2.6 – Receipts from Tax and Social Contributions as a % of GDP, Ireland, Denmark and EU-27 1995-2012

Graph 2.7 – Government Net Deficit/Surplus (left axis) and Gross public debt (right axis) as a % of GDP, Germany and Ireland, 1995-2008

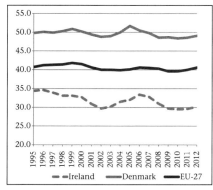

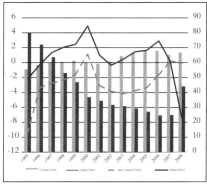

Source: Eurostat, 2014.

Source: AMECO, 2014.

Overall, Ireland's policy-making during this lead-up to the crisis was underpinned by a series of false assumptions and conclusions. These included:

i)   Economic growth was good in itself and the higher the rate of economic growth the better it would be for Ireland.

ii) Everyone would enjoy the benefits of economic growth, which would trickle down automatically.

iii) Infrastructure and social services at an EU-average level could be delivered with one of the lowest total tax-takes in the EU.

iv) The growing inequality and the widening gaps between those on higher incomes and those on lower incomes that followed from this approach to policy-development were not important because 'a rising tide lifts all boats'.

v)   Reducing taxes was far better than investing that money in developing and improving infrastructure and services; the sum of individual decisions would produce greater and more lasting prosperity than the collective decisions of the Irish people.

Arising from this series of false policy conclusions and false assumptions, there were many resulting policy failures. Among these were:

i)   Failure to take action to broaden the tax base by, for example:
  a. introducing a site-value tax.
  b. removing existing tax exemptions which have no demonstrated cost-benefit advantage.
ii) Failure to overcome infrastructure deficiencies, such as in broadband, public transport, primary health care, water, energy, social housing and waste.
iii) Failure to create a universal health service based on need.
iv) Failure to address income inequality.
v)   Failure to appropriately regulate the banking, financial and professional services sector.
vi) Failure to control the property bubble by providing affordable, quality housing for all.

The European Context

Rising defaults on subprime loans in the United States were the triggers for the Global Financial Crisis (GFC). Crotty (2009) has pointed to a fundamental cause in the underlying structural and theoretical weaknesses of a post-1980s 'New Financial Architecture' – created through financial deregulation - which accentuated asset price bubbles, concentrated risk and created incentives for financial institutions to become extremely leveraged. While deregulated global finance has often been stereotyped as an 'Anglo-Saxon' phenomenon, within the EU the liberalisation of the financial sector had also been pursued as good in itself and cross-border European financial flows were viewed as a benign result of monetary integration and capital liberalisation.

Blankenburg, King, Konzelmann and Wilkinson (2013) have described the way in which the GFC revealed the structural distinctions between the core and the periphery that had emerged within the Eurozone. The common currency removed exchange rate risks and led to a convergence of interest rates and yields on government debt. From this balance-of-payments view – of which Martin Wolf of the *Financial Times* is the most influential exponent - of the origins of the Eurozone crisis, current account deficits within the Eurozone were financed in Ireland and Spain by large private sector deficits mitigated by smaller public sector surpluses, while in Greece and Portugal a combination of private and public sector deficits emerged (Blankenburg, King, Konzelmann & Wilkinson, 2013: 464).

Graph 2.8 – Current Account as a % of GDP for selected Eurozone member-states, 2001-2008

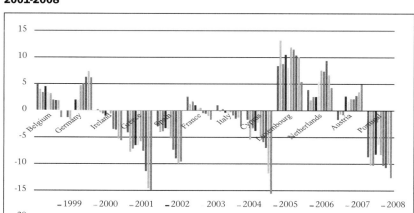

Source: Eurostat (2014).

Liberalised capital and financial markets facilitated lending by financial institutions within the core to financial institutions and states in the 'periphery'- sometimes through intermediaries - and in this way allowed the perpetuation of trade imbalances within the Eurozone, with the associated distinction between a current account surplus 'core' and a current account deficit 'periphery' (see Graph 2.8).

The European Commission (2012: 11) has recognised the emergence of current account imbalances within the Eurozone – and indeed the European Union – as a feature of the 2000s, noting that France, Britain and, to a lesser extent, Germany played an important role in intermediating financial flows, sometimes from non-EU countries, towards the deficit countries, contributing to 'credit-driven booms, reductions in savings and excessive investment in non-productive activities in the periphery, and excessive risk concentration in the financial systems of the core countries'.

The architects of the political economy of European Monetary Union (EMU) were focused on what they saw as the dangers of public debt and deficits: the European treaties prohibit bailouts (hence the structure of the financing given the programme countries), prohibit the ECB purchasing government debt in the primary market (i.e monetising debt) while the Stability and Growth Pact (SGP) was established to provide a framework to control public debt and deficits levels.

The ECB's sole mandate is to maintain price stability, rather than achieve full employment. The structure of the EMU created by the European treaties closely resembles the German tradition of *ordoliberalism* (or Freiburg School tradition): the creation of a strong rules-based legal and regulatory framework within which the free market is permitted to function, combined with an independent, technocratic central bank strongly committed to sound money. This model initially masked the distributional conflicts that could erupt within the EMU, both between capital and labour, and between nation-states. It also ignored the rapid rise in private debt that occurred in the periphery of the Eurozone, particularly Ireland and Spain.

Chart 2.9 – Public Debt as a % of GDP, selected Eurozone countries, 2001-2010

Chart 2.10 - Private debt in % of GDP, selected Eurozone countries, 2001-2010

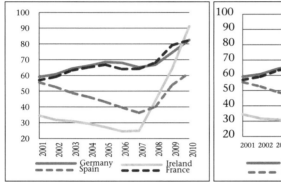
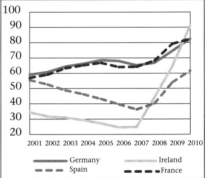

Source: AMECO (2014).   Source: Eurostat (2014).

During the early 1990s some commentators – particularly economist historians – expressed doubts about the viability of creating a common currency union along the model of the Eurozone (cf. Krugman, 1994: 182-187; von Hagen and Eichengreen, 1996; de Grauwe, 1992; Godley, 1992). Some economists argued that the Euro area was not, and is still not, an 'optimal currency union' (OCU). In practice, language and cultural barriers still restrict labour mobility – indeed, massive labour migrations would be extremely disruptive - and each member-state still retains distinctive economic institutions (see Mundell, 1961 for the original concept). Therefore, while economic recessions may remain local phenomena, countries are deprived of monetary policy tools, such as devaluation, which have traditionally been used to combat such recessions. Without those tools, the burden of adjustment would fall on wages and prices within a Eurozone member rather than on their currency, in a process sometimes called an 'internal devaluation'.

De Grauwe (1998) perceptively warned that 'excessive debt accumulation by the private sector can be equally, if not more, risky [than public sector debt]... this has escaped the attention of the founders of EMU, concerned as they were by the dangers of too much government debt'. By the end of 2008, the Eurozone was confronted by a banking sector whose underlying assets – for example, lending into the property sector in Ireland or Spain, or derivatives purchased from investment banks – were worth, or would be worth, far less than their face value. While many banks in the European 'core' were effectively bailed-out by the US government through its extensive nationalisations of European banks' counter-parties, and were heavily supported by the US Federal Reserve through its asset purchase programmes, they were still exposed to banks in the periphery.

2.1.2 The Response to the Crisis: Socialising debt, austerity and structural reform, 2008-2014

The European Response

Initially, in November 2008, EU member-states participated in expansionary fiscal policies in an attempt to mitigate the crisis. The Commission played a role in co-ordinating measures through a European Economic Recovery Plan, which played an important role in preventing the European economy contracting more than it would, arguably heading off another Great Depression. Germany, for example, produced a spending programme equal to nearly 3.3% of GDP spread over two years.

European governments reluctantly nationalised some of their more egregiously exposed financial institutions in September and October 2008. However, many governments, particularly in France and Germany, refused to acknowledge the solvency crisis their banking sectors faced. Lacking a European policy and legal framework on banking resolution, which would have provided for the winding up of a collapsed financial institution, the ECB argued that no bank should be allowed to default. The structure of inter-European lending – with 'core' banks and financial institutions holding bonds issued by, and deposits at, 'peripheral' banks, particularly Spanish ones, and 'peripheral' governments – meant that peripheral governments and citizens were required to re-capitalise domestic banks in the interest of protecting the position of foreign bondholders.

The ECB feared a 'contagion' resulting from a defaulting bank could collapse the European financial system. However, a concomitant commitment from 'core' countries to buttress their own financial institutions was not required. This 'no bondholder left behind' policy was a massive socialisation of the debt, which would fall on the citizens of the 'peripheral' countries, and potentially upon the citizens of the 'core' countries if they were required to offer assistance.

The Greek fiscal crisis emerged in 2009 when it became clear that the Greek state had falsified its level of national debt with the aid of US investment banks and others. When the true debt and deficit levels became known, Greek bond yields rose precipitously. European policymakers viewed the crisis as entirely a result of Greek profligacy and Greece, unable to finance itself through the government bond market, became the first country to enter an IMF/EU/ECB 'troika' financial aid programme. In return, the Troika demanded that Greece embark on an austerity programme, entailing fiscal consolidation and 'structural reforms' of the Greek state. Some of these were understandable, such as reform of the statistics agency. But others, such as labour market reform, merely increased job insecurity and unemployment. Two key characteristics of Greece's institutional problems were ignored: the high level of tax evasion amongst the country's elite and its high level of economic inequality, which is the greatest in the EU.

Despite repeated warnings from some prominent economists that the austerity programme would precipitate a deep depression and a profound social crisis, European policymakers and the IMF forged ahead. However, the latter at least recognised the impossibility of Greek recovery given the size of its debt burden. Eventually in February 2012, the ECB and German government came to an agreement and private sector involvement in a write-down of Greek public sector debt was secured. One of the results of this is that Greek government debt is now held entirely by international organisations, while future funding will likely rely on the official sector to roll over its existing government debt – that is, the European Union – until Greece regains access to something like market funding. The IMF (2013) offered some limited criticisms of the Greek programme, pointing at the lateness of other elements of the Troika in accepting the need for debt write-downs, and admitted that it underestimated the effects of fiscal consolidation on Greece.

Table 2.1 – Selected Timeline for Euro-crisis

Date

NOV-08	European Recovery Plan (1.5% of EU GDP) announced. **MAY-10** IMF/EU €110bn Programme for Greece, Finance Ministers announce creation of the EFSF. **SEP-10** EU Commission presents 'six-pack' rules to prevent excessive macroeconomic imbalances and deficits. **OCT-10** Agreement to establish a permanent crisis mechanism (the ESM). **NOV-10** IMF/EU €85bn Programme for Ireland. **MAR-11** Euro area leaders agree to lower interest rates on Greek loans and increase maturity of loans. **MAY-11** IMF/EU €78bn Programme for Portugal. **JUL-11** Second Greek Programme of €109bn (later €130bn) proposed, lowered interest rates on assistance loans and lengthened maturities. **AUG-11** ECB begins purchasing Italian and Spanish bonds in the secondary market. **SEP-11** European Council, Parliament and Commission agree final 'six-pack' legislation.
OCT-11	Mario Draghi begins term as President of the ECB, European Council Agreement on Greek PSI, agreement on the adoption of increased budgetary surveillance and fiscal compact, Greek PM announces referendum on debt deal

NOV-11	Greek PM cancels referendum, resigns and Greek coalition formed under pressure from EU leaders, Italian PM resigns and replaced by technocratic administration, European Commission proposes the 'two-pack', strengthening budgetary surveillance and monitoring. **DEC-11** 25 EU countries agree to new treaty on fiscal compact, sanctions for those who breach rules/ ECB extends range of collateral it accepts, trebles refinancing operations to 36 months to extend liquidity, €500bn take up of these Long-Term Refinancing Operations (LTRO). **FEB-12** New ESM treaty signed which ties ESM treaty to fiscal compact, final agreement on second rescue programme for Greece and higher level of write-downs for private investors. **MAR-12** Fiscal Compact treaty signed, ESM ceiling extended to €700bn. **JUN-12** Spain requests assistance from ESM to recapitalise banking sector. Euro area endorses banking union and possible retroactive recapitalisations and future recapitalisations by ESM. **JUL-12** President of ECB says ECB will 'do whatever it takes'.
AUG-12	ECB announces Outright Monetary Transactions (OMT), which involves possible interventions into short-term secondary government debt markets.
SEP-12	Finance Ministers of Germany, the Netherlands and Finland seem to rule out retroactive direct recapitalisations despite July 2012 agreement.
OCT-12	IMF admits fiscal multipliers have been under-estimated - implying fiscal consolidation had much greater contractionary effect than previously appreciated
FEB-12	Irish agreement with ECB on Anglo-Irish Promissory Notes
MAR-13	Cyprus announced deposit levy at behest of EU/IMF, introduces capital controls
DEC-13	Ireland exits the EU/IMF Programme

The nature of the Greek crisis has led to a common conception that the problems arising throughout the Eurozone have been fundamentally problems of public debt. However, this is misleading, as Ireland and Spain ran low deficits, and even surpluses, throughout early 2000s, as was noted above. The current large budget deficits are a result of the economic collapse in the peripheral countries, which is related to the overhang of private debt, and the interest payments on the bank debt taken on by governments. Efforts to address rising public debt through tax rises and expenditure cuts have not just failed; they have exacerbated the fall-out from private debt crises in the periphery. The creation of the European Financial Stability Facility (EFSF), which was used to fund the Greek, Irish and Portuguese programmes, and the European Stability Mechanism (ESM), a new permanent facility, were designed to facilitate public lending to the distressed EU members. However, these funds did not contain a provision of joint liability. Rather, each country's contribution to the EFSF and ESM is based on their GDP, and each country guarantees that portion of the subscription it provides.

Box 2.2: The 'Six Pack', 'Two Pack' and the Fiscal Compact

One of the results of the diagnosis of the financial crisis as a public finance crisis was the strengthening of the framework – the Stability and Growth Pack (SGP) - which governs member-states fiscal rules, increasing the surveillance and disciplining role of the European Commission. Additionally, the Commission was tasked with identifying and preventing macroeconomic imbalances, such as the persistent current account imbalances which built up during the early and mid-2000s. Despite opposition from the centre-left and left in the European Parliament, and the concerns expressed by French President Hollande, this framework will likely remain in place for some time and shape Irish fiscal policy over the next decade.

The legal framework is contained in the 'six pack' of five regulations and a directive, applying to the EU-28, the 'two pack' which applies to the Euro area member-states and increases monitoring by the European Commission – including submission of national budgets no later than 15 October – and the 'Fiscal Compact', an intergovernmental treaty (Britain and the Czech Republic did not sign it) which requires the direct transposition of the SGP measures into national law. The SGP rules state that government deficits must be 3% or less; government debt to GDP ratio must be 60% or less; and that Government structural deficits must be 0.5% or less. The structural deficit may be up to 1% if debt to GDP is significantly below 60%, and requires a 1/20th reduction in debt per year if a country has a debt to GDP ratio above 60%. The requirements of the Fiscal Compact have been given effect in Irish law in the Fiscal Responsibility Act 2012.

Ireland is currently in the Excessive Deficit Procedure (EDP) which requires the reduction of the General Government Deficit to under 3% of GDP by 2015. The 1/20th rule applying to the path of debt reduction will begin to fully apply in 2019. Between 2015 and 2019 Ecofin and the European Commission will determine whether the pace of debt reduction is adequate (Department of Finance, 2013a: 5). Following 2015, Ireland must attempt to attain its medium-term budget objective (MTO), a medium-term budgetary position which must be achieved with reference to structural measures (that is, taking account of the difference between potential and actual GDP). Ireland's current MTO is balanced budget in structural terms (Department of Finance, 2013b: 48).

Public spending is governed by an 'Expenditure benchmark', which limits growth in government expenditure. When a member-state has not achieved its MTO, a reference rate for growth in government expenditure is calculated based on potential growth estimates and a convergence rate of expenditure is provided which must be followed to achieve the MTO. In Ireland's case, the reference rate is 0.6% of GDP and the convergence rate is 1.4%, leading to rounded figure of -0.7% of GDP for real expenditure growth - in practice a reduction - between 2014 and 2016 (European Commission, 2013: 30).

We opposed the Compact and wider EU fiscal rules on a number of bases: that it does not address what is essentially a balance of payments crisis created by persistent and excessive private credit creation; that there is considerable debate and confusion about the measure of 'potential' output severely affects the view of structural output; and that it is undemocratic, removing decisions about resource allocation and tax and spending from parliaments. However, it is likely that these rules will remain in place and will have to be adhered to. Given the operation of the 'Expenditure benchmark', any increase in expenditure above the benchmark will require discretionary revenue increases. Given this, there should be a serious debate about the level of revenue required to finance public expenditure over the coming years.

The ESM was accompanied by the Fiscal Compact, which requires the writing of fiscal rules into the law of member-states, a price extracted by Germany for the creation of the ESM. Additionally, the Directorate-General for Economic and Financial Affairs, the most hawkish element of the European Commission, has been given additional powers to monitor both countries fiscal and wider macro-economic policies, including excessive current account surpluses through the 'six-pack' and 'two-pack'. The latter is a belated recognition within the Commission that Germany should engage in a more expansionary fiscal policy.

In June 2012 the Euro Area Group and European Council agreed to recapitalise banks directly through the ESM. They also agreed that the link between bank debt and national debt should be broken, raising the possibility of relief for Spain and Ireland. However, this was seemingly quashed by the finance ministers of Germany, the Netherlands and Finland months later.

The ECB has become increasingly interventionist, willing to play the role of lender of last resort to the banking sector and perhaps even governments through extending liquidity,. From May 2010 the ECB had carried out a Securities Market Programme (SMP), purchasing government debt in the secondary market in an attempt to stabilise yields. Of more significance was the ECB announcement in August 2012 of plans for unlimited purchases in secondary bond markets of selected short-term government bonds in the event of yields rising above a certain level through the Outright Monetary Transactions (OMT) mechanism. This announcement has produced a reduction in the bond yields of both programme and non-programme peripheral countries. However, the ECBs commitment to purchasing government debt on secondary markets through the OMT has yet to be tested.

Chart 2.11 Comparison of 10-year Government Bond yields (Maastricht Criteria), 2005-2011

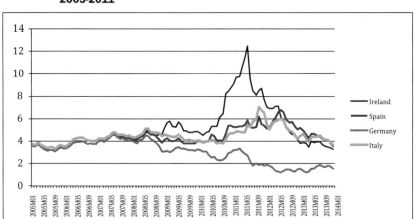

Source: Eurostat (2013).

The current European strategy involves a series of measures:

- reducing deficits throughout the EU through fiscal consolidation;
- lending to distressed countries and requiring they undertake structural adjustment programmes in return;
- promoting 're-balancing' through 'internal devaluation' in those countries with current account deficits to increase 'competitiveness';
- creating a banking union to centralise regulation of European banks and provide a banking resolution scheme;
- creating supervisory structures for the European Commission and other member- states to monitor member-state's budgets and macroeconomic indicators; and the writing of a fiscal rule into the law of each member state.

Between 2010 and 2012 there were proposals by member-states, and even the Commission, for the creation of a genuine 'economic union' with common debt issuance, and eventually, a common fiscal policy. However, the current approach, agreed in December 2013, is to effectively suspend the June 2012 agreement until the creation of a common banking union with shared supervision by the ECB, a common resolution scheme and a deposit insurance scheme. A mutualised funding scheme to resolve – or wind down – bankrupt financial institutions won't be in place for ten years, though under French pressure this could be introduced faster. The focus on the banking union has been used to avoid Europe's and the Eurozone's real social and economic challenges; the erosion of European social security systems, often under the pressure of the European Commission and Troika, the contraction in growth occasioned by the turn to austerity, the growth in European unemployment, growing income inequality and the need to adapt to climate change.

Box 2.3: Democratic Legitimacy

Decisions made during the economic crisis have raised serious questions as to democratic legitimacy of the processes by which these decisions are made, both in Ireland and in Europe. In Ireland, decisions allocating vast resources to the financial sector were made by a few senior politicians and officials, sometimes without a meeting of the full Cabinet, and without a full debate. The establishment of NAMA is a prime example; NAMA was established rapidly, and its operations were initially extremely opaque. In its disposals of assets, NAMA makes decisions affecting communities throughout Ireland, but those communities have little power to influence NAMA.

At the European level, the structural adjustment programmes have been overseen by the IMF, European Commission and the European Central Bank, none of which have a directly elected component. The Troika are involved in making major decisions about resources and economic policy areas which were traditionally the preserve of democratically accountable national governments. Often represented as mere technocrats, Troika members actually have differing and very political views on the role of government in society, the functioning of the labour market, and appropriate level of the social security. For example, the President of the ECB, Mario Draghi, informed the Wall Street Journal in February 2012 that 'The European social model has already gone'.

The stricter European fiscal rules were adopted with relatively little national public debate, and their implications – particularly the increased supervisory powers of the Commission - have not been fully absorbed, except perhaps when the German Bundestag sees elements of the Irish budget before the Dáil does. Streek (2011) has noted that these increased powers may lead to citizens in the EU – particularly in the Programme countries – viewing their governments as nothing but the agents of the Commission, ECB or the IMF.

The current strategy of placing the burden of economic adjustment on prices, wages and government spending throughout the EU is leading to rapid reduction in inflation, and even raising the possibility of deflation. Deflation would raise the real debt burden facing both private and public debtors in Europe, potentially extending a 'balance-sheet' recession. A set of policies – structural adjustment and austerity – intended to reduce debt burdens will actually perpetuate them. This approach is clearly unsustainable. It is also unsustainable that such decisions are taken without consulting European citizens. Ireland needs a public debate about the trajectory of the European Union, and such a debate must reach beyond even the immediate and pressing concerns surrounding the link between Ireland's private bank debt and national debt and instead focus on what type of European Union Irish citizens seek for the future.

When challenged about the role of the ECB and the dangers of monetary union in the early 1990s, Jacques Delors used to reply that 'social Europe is coming'. Unfortunately, the response to the crisis has ignored 'social Europe'; indeed, the European response has been to dismantle many of the social protections that Delors considered, and considers, as constituting the pinnacle of European achievement. The role of a 'social Europe' in the coming debate on Ireland's place in Europe must be central. This will require Irish politicians to take a hard look at their own role in promoting or dismantling 'social Europe' in the last twenty years.

The Irish Response
The dangers of attempting an austerity policy in the face of a 'balance-sheet' recession – characterised by private firms and households holding debts larger than the value of the underlying assets – have been highlighted by many economic commentators, and the effects of Irish austerity have borne them out. Output has contracted rapidly, partly under the pressure of austerity, reducing government's tax revenue, while the severity of unemployment has led to increases in the social protection budget, even as most rates of social protection payments have fallen. This has led to remarkably little reduction in Ireland's deficit to GDP figures, due to a combination of successive bank bailouts, leading to a potentially onerous future interest schedule, and the contraction of GDP, partly due to austerity measures.

Between 2008 and 2010 the policy of austerity failed to increase market and investor confidence and the continuing insolvency of Ireland's banks – despite extensive recapitalisations (see Table 2.2) - led to increasing doubts about the future solvency of the Irish state, as reflected by steadily rising bond yields on Irish government debt. In late 2009, the government sought to achieve a back-door recapitalisation by establishing the National Asset Management Agency (NAMA), which was designed to purchase loans related to commercial property developments at a price above their market value (but below their face value of €74bn) and hold the assets until such return as was possible could be made on the loans. However, the market value (ultimately €32bn) of the loans NAMA sought to acquire was far lower than policymakers initially assumed, requiring extensive recapitalisation of the banking sector in 2010. Attempts were made to enforce some kind of burden sharing on those who held bonds issued by Irish private banks. However, the European Central Bank insisted that there could be no write-downs on any Euro area bank debt, even as unemployment rose rapidly in Ireland and the country came under severe pressure on international debt markets.

Table 2.2 – Total Cost of Irish Banking Rescue by Source of Funding and Year (€bn)

	2009	2010	2011	2012	Total
NPRF	7	3.7	10		20.7
Promissory Notes		30.7			30.7
Exchequer	4	0.9	6.5	1.3	12.7
Total	11	35.3	16.5	1.3	64

Source: http://debates.oireachtas.ie/dail/2012/04/18/00157.asp; Healy (2013).

Though the Irish state had raised significant cash reserves, in September and November 2010 European leaders placed considerable pressure on Irish leaders to be placed in an IMF/EU programme. European policymakers feared that high bond yields on Irish government debt would have a contagion effect on other vulnerable Euro area economies. Ireland's IMF/EU programme required fiscal consolidation to bring the general government deficit (GGD) to GDP ratio below the 3% prescribed in the Growth and Stability Pact by 2015, and a considerable recapitalisation and downsizing of the Irish banking sector. This has brought the total adjustment between 2008 and 2015 to €32.3bn, equivalent to 18% of 2015 forecasted GDP (see Table 2.3). In addition, a structural adjustment programme comprising reforms to social security and the labour market, and privatisation of public utilities, was agreed as part of the programme.

Table 2.3 - Budgetary Adjustments 2008-2015 (€m)

Adjustment Description	Taxation ↑	Expenditure ↓	Total	Running Total
Adjustment July 2008		€1,000	€1,000	€1,000
Budget 2009	€1,215	€747	€1,962	€2,962
Adjustments Feb/March 2009	€2,090	€2,090	€5,052	
Supplementary Budget 2009	€3,621	€1,941	€5,562	€10,614
Budget 2010	€23	€4,051	€4,074	€14,688
Budget 2011	€1,409	€4,590	€5,999	€20,687
Budget 2012	€1,600	€2,200	€3,800	€24,487
Budget 2013	€1,432	€1,940	€3,372	€27,859
Budget 2014	€880	€2,000	€2,480	€30,339
Budget 2015*	€700	€1,300	€2,000	€32,339
Total of Adjustments	€10,880	€21,459		
% Division of Adjustments	33.6%	66.4%		

Notes: *Projected

2.1.3 The Troika Programme, 2010-2013

The Troika Programme – a financing package of €85bn, of which €67.5bn was provided by the EU, IMF, Sweden, Denmark, Britain and €22.5bn by the Irish National Pension Reserve Fund (NPRF) and Irish Exchequer cash balances - was designed to return Ireland to market funding by December 2013, through a radical reorganisation and downsizing of the Irish banking sector – correctly viewed as the source of Ireland's crisis – and a reduction of Ireland's deficit to below 3% of GDP by 2015. Though the IMF and Irish authorities belatedly recognised the damage caused by the policy of austerity, the dominant belief was that a rapid fiscal consolidation would increase confidence in Irish government debt, facilitating Ireland's ability to return to self-financing. Relatively short shrift was given to the idea of pushing out the period of adjustment, which would have reduced the impact on the Irish economy and society. Indeed, the former IMF mission chief to Ireland has argued that a less sharp fiscal contraction combined with a write-down of banking debt was not just possible, but desirable (The Irish Times, 2013).

Table 2.4 – Components of changes in Real GDP, 2008-2014

	2008	2009	2010	2011	2012	2013	2014
Real GDP	-2.2	-6.4	-1.1	2.2	0.2	0.6	1.8
Final Domestic Demand	-2.2	-9.7	5	-3	-1.1	0	0.3
-Private Consumption	0.1	-5.1	0.9	-1.6	-0.3	-0.3	0.5
-Public Consumption	0.6	-3.4	-6.9	-2.8	-3.7	-0.6	-2.8
-Gross fixed investment	-9.6	-26.9	-22.6	-9.5	-0.1	2	4
Net Exports	1.5	4.6	3	5.7	1.6	0.6	1.5
-Exports	-1.1	-3.8	6.4	5.4	1.6	1.1	2.9
-Imports	-3	-9.8	3.6	-0.4	0	0.6	1.9

Source: International Monetary Fund (2013: 34)

The initial assumptions of Ireland's economic performance under the EU/Programme were extremely optimistic – even in the IMF's programme assumptions - particularly in relation to domestic demand (see Table 2.5). This was reflected in the greater confidence in the policy of austerity, particularly in the European institutions. However, as a result of weaker growth the nominal amount of cuts required to achieve the deficit targets under the Programme were correspondingly higher. As with other EU/IMF programmes, the Troika did not adopt a uniform perspective on Ireland's economy. The IMF were more worried about the impact of the rapid pace of fiscal consolidation on Ireland's economy than other members of the Troika, and were supportive of Ireland's efforts to gain relief on legacy banking debt, particularly given the IMF's general fear that IMF financing was being used to delay reforms to the Euro area's banking system.

Table 2.5 – Comparison of IMF Programme Assumptions in 2010 and 2013

	December 2010 IMF			December 2013 IMF			Deficit Target/Deficit Out-turn
	Real GDP	*Real GNP*	*Fiscal Consolidation (€bn)***	*Real GDP*	*Real GNP*	*Fiscal Consolidation (€bn)*	
2011	0.9	-1.5	6	2.2	-1.6	6	-13.1%
2012	1.9	0.8	3.6	0.2	1.8	3.8	-8.2%
2013	2.4	1.4	3.1	0.3	0.2	3.4	-7.3%
2014	3	2.3	n/a	1.7	1.3	2.5*	-4.8%
2015	3.4	3.4	n/a	2.5	2.1	2***	-2.9%

Source: Department of Finance (2010; 2013a); International Monetary Fund (2010; 2013).
Notes: *Budget 2014 was composed of €2.5bn in permanent measures and €0.6bn in once-off measures.
**Budgetary adjustments agreed in second review.
***IMF Staff assume €2.4bn adjustment is required to reach deficit target (IMF, 2013: 15).

Despite considerable latitude in the division of cuts to tax increases, successive governments pursued a fiscal consolidation consisting of two-thirds expenditure cuts to one-third tax increases. Some Troika officials, citing the ESRI, have stated that the overall fiscal adjustment in budgets between 2009 and 2014 has been progressive (Szélsky & Florián, 2013). However, the progressivity is affected by the €9.6bn of measures – included public sector pay cuts - announced in 2009, 50% of which were tax cuts. The ESRI has shown that budgets introduced between 2010 and 2014, including the three budgets introduced under the ministrations of the Troika, were in fact regressive, taking more as a percentage of income from those on lower incomes (Callan et. al., 2013; Callan, 2013). Moreover, measures of the distributional impact of successive budgets do not capture the effects of reductions in expenditures on service provision – such as, for example, health, education or services for the homeless - upon which those on lower incomes, or in vulnerable positions, are more likely to rely.

Table 2.6 – Poverty and Deprivation Rates, 2008-2011

	2008	2009	2010	2011
At risk of poverty rate (%)	14.4	14.1	14.7	16
Deprivation Rate (%)	13.8	17.1	22.6	24.5
Consistent poverty rate (%)	4.2	5.5	6.3	6.9

Source: CSO (2013: 1).

Leading up to the crisis, the percentage of the population at risk of poverty, in consistent poverty and the deprivation rate all declined following a sustained commitment of government to increase social security payments to the most vulnerable during the period between 2004 and 2008. This progress has been partially reversed during the recession, as wages and social welfare payments have fallen (see Table 2.5). This has particularly affected extremely vulnerable groups; in 2011 56% of children in lone parent households suffered two or more types of enforced deprivation, up from 44.1% in 2009. The quintile share ratio – measuring the difference between the average equivalised income of the top 20% of households from the bottom 20% - in 2011 was 4.9, up from 4.3 in 2009. Given the regressive nature of budgets since 2010, it is likely that both relative and absolute poverty have increased since 2011.

The exit from the EU/IMF Programme occurred at the end of 2013. Though hailed as a success, the return to market financing has been largely underpinned – as have bond yields throughout the European periphery – by the ECB's commitment to OMT, a commitment that has yet to be tested. 'Success' in certain areas is the result of wider failures: reductions in expenditure growth in social protection have been partly a result of mass emigration since 2009. The IMF (2012: 5) estimated in December 2012 that without the shrinking labour force – a shrinkage fuelled by emigration - since 2009, unemployment would stand at 20%. However, there have been some positive signs since the middle of 2013, with the decline in numbers in employment finally turning around, and a reduction in unemployment to 12.1%, following a high of 15.1% in the third quarter of 2011 (CSO, 2014).

Additionally, the government has identified the need to raise the investment rate, and has transferred the remainder of the NPRF, some €6.4bn, to the Ireland Strategic Investment Fund (ISIF). The NPRF has already been used to provide the bulk of capital for funds that will supply investment to small and medium sized enterprises (SMEs). The ISIF has been established to focus on commercial and strategic investments. This is too narrow a remit, and before the ISIF is established on a statutory basis government should take a broader view of economic activity, and commit to invest some of the ISIF in the broader social economy. This would involve more investment than currently envisaged in the period immediately ahead in areas such as social housing, primary care facilities, energy efficiency and school facilities.

2.2 The Choices Ahead

Even within the confines of the EU/IMF programme there were real choices; these choices have become even more important as government can no longer attribute its choices to the Troika. We now face stark choices about the amount of resources that our health service and our welfare state should receive, about the distribution of wealth and power in our society, and about the level of taxation required to furnish the resources necessary for a compassionate and civilised society. It is time to have a real debate about our economic and social priorities in the years ahead; whether, for example, it is time to reduce taxes for higher-rate taxpayers, or whether it is time to invest in our social services and infrastructure and strengthen our social security system; whether we want to return to a privately-financed system of housing provision that leads to vacant homes, broken banks and record numbers on the social housing list, or whether we wish to create a society that guarantees quality accommodation for all; whether we wish the standard of healthcare to depend on the contents of our wallets, or the common demands of our humanity. Whether, in a word, we wish to collectively pursue the public purpose, or return to the petty politics of private greed. We had hoped these issues would be addressed in the Government's Medium Term Economic Strategy (MTES) published in December 2013. That document, however, contains very little substantial information and goes into very little detail on the future that Government wishes to build.

Social Justice Ireland has long advocated a new guiding vision for Irish society; one based on the values of human dignity, equality, human rights, solidarity, sustainability and the pursuit of the common good. These values are at the core of the vision for a nation in which all men, women and children have what they require to live life with dignity and to fulfil their potential: including sufficient income; access to the services they need; and active inclusion in a genuinely participatory society. These are not minority views as is sometimes stated, but reflect the aspirations of the majority of Irish citizens. Indeed, in February 2014, 85% of the members of the Convention on the Constitution convened by the government voted to afford greater constitutional protection to Economic, Social and Cultural (ESC) rights. This included a recommendation to include explicit mention of rights to housing, social security, essential healthcare, the rights of people with disabilities, and linguistic and cultural rights, in the Irish Constitution.

Policy will be heavily constrained in future years, not least by the requirement under the 'six-pack' that additional discretionary expenditure must be funded by additional discretionary revenue. The current trajectory of government policy is for a reduction in total expenditure (including interest rates) and a reduction in total revenue (of which tax revenue is by far the largest component) to 2015. The Department of Finance's *April 2013 Stability Programme Update* contained an indicative projection of revenue and expenditure to 2019, assuming expenditure growth of 1% per annum and a growth in total revenue equal to potential growth in GDP.[6] Though these figures are purely indicative they do show one possible scenario, where total revenue falls to 33.9% of GDP and total expenditure falls to 33.1% of GDP, which would take place if additional taxation was not levied. For comparison, the EU-27 is estimated to have a total revenue of 45.2% of GDP and total expenditure of 47.9% of GDP in 2015 (AMECO, 2014).

Graph 2.12 – Total Revenue and Total Expenditure as a % of GDP, 2005-2019[7]

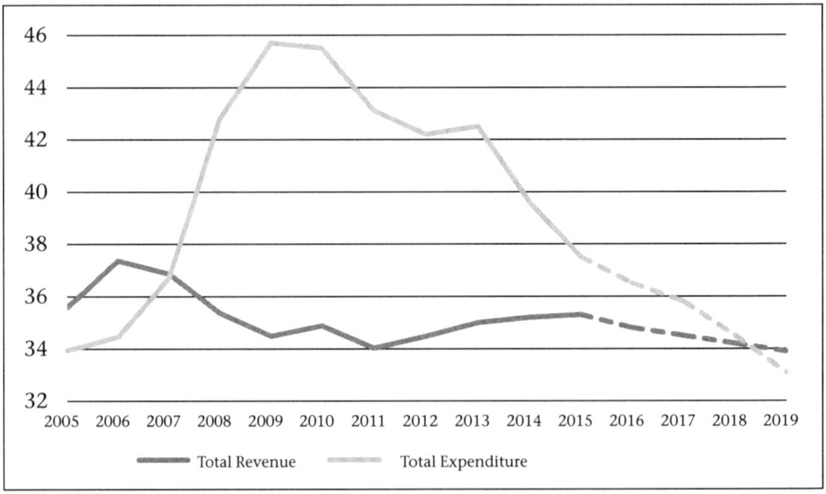

Source: AMECO (2014), Department of Finance (2013a; 2013b).
Notes: *Figures to 2012 are taken from the AMECO database.
**The cost of recapitalisation of banking institutions has been removed.

---

[6] Given the more optimistic outlook for the interest costs published by the Department and possibility of the Commission changing its understanding of Ireland's output gap the 2016 and 2019 figures could change.

[7] Total expenditure takes account of all government expenditure, including interest payments, which in the April 2013 Stability Programme Update account for some 4.8% of GDP per annum between 2016 and 2018 and 4.7% of GDP annum in 2019. It is likely that these figures will be more optimistic upon completion of the April 2014 Stability Programme Update.

***Figures from 2013 to 2015 are taken from Budget 2014 figures and outlined projections.

Can we provide high-quality public services to all while allowing total expenditure to fall as a percentage of GDP? And if there is an improvement in various indicators should any additional revenue be used to reduce taxes or increase expenditure. We believe a new policy framework is required; one that recognises the need to increase taxes towards the European average in order to fund the public services that we need, while implementing new criteria for policy evaluation.

2.3 A Policy Framework for a New Ireland

To achieve our vision we have established a policy framework that identifies five key policy areas for reform.[8]

- The first is macroeconomic stability, which requires a stabilisation of Ireland's debt levels, fiscal and financial stability and sustainable economic growth, and an immediate boost to investment, which has collapsed during the crisis. (Dealt with here and in chapter 4)

- The second is the need for a just taxation system, which would require an increase in the overall tax-take to the European average; such an increase must be implemented equitably and in a way that reduces income inequality. (These issues are dealt with in much greater detail in chapter 4).

- The third area is social protection, the strengthening of social services and social infrastructure, the prioritisation of employment, and a commitment to quantitative targets to reduce poverty. (Chapters 3, 4, 5, 6, 7, 8 and 9).

- The fourth area is that of the governance of our country, which requires new criteria in policy evaluation, the development of a rights-based approach, and the promotion of deliberative democracy. (Chapter 10).

- Fifth, policies must be adopted that create a sustainable future, through the introduction of measures to slow down climate change and protect the environment, the promotion of balanced regional development, and promotion of new economic and social indicators to measure performance, alongside traditional national accounting measures such as GNP, GDP and GNI. (Chapters 11, 12 and 13).

---

8   The authors have presented an earlier version of this framework in Healy et al. (2013).

Table 2.7 – A policy framework for a New Ireland

Ensuring macroeconomic stability	Towards a just taxation system	Enhancing social protection	Reforming governance	Creating a sustainable Future
Debt sustainability	Bring Taxes to European average	Protect services and the social infrastructure	Reform policy evaluation	Combat climate change and protect the environment
Fiscal and financial stability and sustainable economic growth	Increase taxes equitably	Combat unemployment	A Rights-based approach	Balanced regional development
Investment programme	Reduce income inequality	Reduce Poverty	Deliberative democracy	New indicators

i) Ensuring macroeconomic stability

Ensuring macroeconomic stability requires a reduction in Ireland's debt burden, the launching of an investment programme and a restoration of fiscal and financial stability. All of these measures are connected. An investment programme will contribute to growth which would in turn lower Ireland's deficit and real debt burden. A reduction of, or commitment to reduce, Ireland's debt burden will increase confidence in the capacity of Ireland's economy to expand and for the country to fully exit the EU/IMF programme without the requirement of additional credit facilities or the activation of the Outright Monetary Transactions (OMT) programme, thus reducing yields on Irish government debt.

As we have noted, Ireland's macroeconomic policy will be severely constrained. Since Economic and Monetary Union (EMU), monetary policy has rested with the European Central Bank, and the single currency has prevented the kind of currency devaluation engaged in by Ireland during the late 1980s (Kinsella, 2013). Following the introduction of the fiscal rules, Ireland's fiscal policy will also be constrained as noted in Box 2.2.

a) Debt Sustainability

In October 2013, the Department of Finance has estimated that the debt-to-GDP ratio will peak in 2014 at 124.1%, somewhat higher than the 121.4% estimated in 2012 and the 123% estimated in April 2013 (Department of Finance, 2013a: C19). The estimated peak of the debt-to-GDP ratio has tended to rise due to overly optimistic expectations of economic growth. By 2016, the Department expects that 14.3% of general government revenues will be devoted to servicing Ireland's debt (Department of Finance, 2013a: C20). Some improvements to the debt sustainability position have been made in 2013 with the extension of the maturities of the €22.4bn of European Financial Stabilisation Mechanism (EFSM) loans agreed by the European Council in June 2013 (see Chart 2.13). The Department of Finance estimates that Ireland will turn a primary surplus – the budget deficit less interest payments - in 2014. However, a return to debt sustainability is dependent on economic growth, and the ability to issue debt in private capital markets at sustainable rates. In terms of the former, the government and Troika have tended to over-estimate Ireland's capacity to expand through an austerity induced recession. In terms of the latter, the continuing weakness of the Irish banking sector, and doubts about the separation of sovereign and banking debt could pose significant challenges to debt sustainability.

There has yet to be a full recognition by European partners that a large proportion of Ireland's debt was accumulated in the course of rescuing the Irish banking sector, and ensuring that there was relatively lower burden-sharing than would have been expected in any other enterprise. In addition, the loss of confidence in Ireland during 2009-2010 was a direct result of fixed-asset analysts and other observers of the government bond market viewing Ireland's assumption of banking debt as unsustainable with a corresponding change in the pricing of Irish government debt. The total cost of the banking rescue has been €64bn, of which €12.6bn has come directly from the Exchequer, €30.7bn through promissory notes and €20.7bn from the National Pension Reserve Fund (NPRF).[9] Of the €192bn in gross government debt in 2012, over 20% was accounted for directly by the bank recapitalisation alone.

This part of Ireland's debt represents a direct subsidy by the Irish public of international bondholders and the European banking system. In June 2012 the Eurogroup appeared to recognise this, holding out the possibility that the European Stability Mechanism (ESM) would retroactively recapitalise the Irish banking sector by purchasing the Irish government's bank equities. However, differences have since emerged between the leading nation-states in the Eurozone, with considerable uncertainty now surrounding the question of additional bank recapitalisations, let alone retroactive recapitalisations. This has re-opened the question of the connection between sovereign and banking debt. Given the upcoming capital adequacy tests, Irish banks may be judged to require additional capital to account for losses on their mortgage and commercial loan books. It is recognised by Irish policymakers that the Irish banking sector is, and has been, unprepared for recognising widespread losses on distressed mortgages (e.g Honohan, 2013).

---

[9] Parliamentary Question 18719/12.

Chart 2.13 – Maturity Dates of Irish Government Debt, 2014-2053

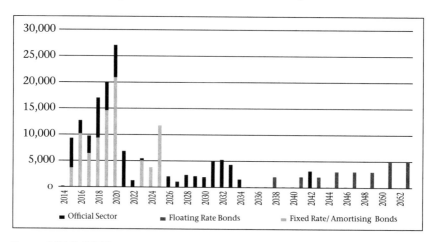

Source: NTMA (2014).

Notes: *Official Sector Includes Bilateral, IMF, EFSF, and EFSM.

**Floating Rate Bonds were issued as part of the restructuring of the IRBC promissory notes.

If there are no additional liabilities arising from the banking sector and no further economic shocks, Ireland's debt may be sustainable, assuming continuing low government debt yields and economic growth. However, deflation in the Eurozone and in Ireland could increase Ireland's real debt burden if it continues. To increase debt sustainability, European authorities should also consider further changes to the status of the government bonds which were issued to replace the promissory notes including further extending the maturity and considering a lower interest rate. Such measures could also be further applied to the loans received under the EU/IMF Programme, in a similar manner to the EFSF loans.

b) Fiscal and financial stability and sustainable economic growth

The connection between fiscal policy, output and employment has been at the heart of the austerity debate in Ireland and Europe. Reducing government expenditure and/or increasing tax revenues are not the same thing as reducing the deficit, and meeting deficit reduction targets requires rapid underlying growth. Ireland should make the case for a European-wide approach to growth, one that takes account of the spill-over effects of combined fiscal consolidation. Unfortunately the fiscal rules introduced mitigate against a European-wide fiscal expansion, though breaching the rules is allowed in 'extraordinary circumstances'.

Sustainable employment growth can be underpinned by an investment programme that invests in both economic and social infrastructure. Kelly and McQuinn (2013) have noted that, given the relationship between government's fiscal accounts and the balance sheets of the banking sector, austerity could have a deeper impact than thought by policymakers given the concomitant increase in mortgage arrears and business loan defaults on banking balance sheets, which necessitate greater levels of recapitalisation. This was not appreciated by policymakers during the crisis as austerity led to bank bailouts which led to further austerity.

Financial stability is also a pre-requisite for a stable supply of credit to households and firms. The Programme for Government promised the creation of a Strategic Investment Bank to carry out lending to SMEs; this seems unlikely to be implemented. A pre-requisite for financial stability is a regulated financial system with a plurality of ownership. For that reason we argue that consideration should be given to the proposal that Permanent TSB be re-mutualised, while government should continue holding a stake in both of the two pillar banks, which should continue to provide universal banking services. The case for a Strategic Investment Bank – similar to the German state-owned KfW remains strong.

c) An Investment Programme
Ireland's GNP, measured at constant market prices, remains 10% under its peak in 2007. GDP remains over 7% under its peak, and domestic demand remains 18% under its 2008 level (CSO, 2013). Investment as % of GDP in Ireland in 2013 was 10%, the lowest in the European Union (Eurostat 2013). Both the Troika and Department of Finance have acknowledged that consumption and domestic demand have remained stagnant, and they have previously relied on growing exports to boost growth in their projections. There is some disagreement about the growth in investment in 2013 and 2014 (see Table 2.8).

Table 2.8 – Projected Growth in Investment, 2013-2014*

	Department of Finance	ESRI	IMF	European Commission
2013	4.9	2.1	2.9	2.9
2014	6.8	4.5	4.4	4.4

Source: Department of Finance (2013), Duffy et. al. (2013), IMF (2013), European Commission (2013).
Notes: *The Department of Finance projections were published in October 2013; December 2013 for all others.

These figures are from an extremely low base. Domestic economic investment is sorely needed to provide employment and provide much-needed infrastructure; this would reduce short-term unemployment and increase the long-run productivity of the Irish economy. The government has created a new investment fund – the Ireland Strategic Investment Fund (ISIF) - using the NPRF's €6.4bn discretionary investment portfolio. However, the fund is orientated towards commercial investment opportunities such as energy, broadband and water.

The authors believe that there must be an off-balance sheet investment programme between 2014 and 2016 of €7bn, as we proposed in our briefing document, *Investing for Growth, Jobs & Recovery* (*Social Justice Ireland*, 2013). This would directly create employment and also enhance growth, which would contribute to reducing the deficit by reducing unemployment and increasing tax returns. We propose that the investment programme target both economic *and* social infrastructure, including the construction of social housing units, investment in water infrastructure, and investment in primary care facilities.

ii) Towards a Just Taxation System
The American jurist Oliver Wendell Holmes once said that 'taxes are the price we pay for a civilized society'. We have long argued that Ireland's total tax-take is simply too low to pay for the services and social welfare provision that is necessary to ensure human dignity for all. We believe that the incidence of taxation falls too much on the shoulders of those on middle and low incomes. Therefore, the overall tax take must rise in such a way that the burden falls of those most able to bear it.

a) Bring Taxes towards the European average
Ireland's tax-take in 2010 was 28.2% of GDP, some 7.4% below the European average. The Department of Finance believes that the total tax-take as a% of GDP will rise to 31.5% of GDP by 2016. Table 2.9 indicates the difference in the projected additional tax yield if Ireland's tax burden moved closer to the European average than that indicated by the Department of Finance in the April 2013 Stability Programme Update. There has been some debate on the appropriate measures of Ireland's fiscal capacity in recent years, given the difference between Ireland's GNP and GDP. The Irish Fiscal Advisory Council (IFAC) has suggested a hybrid measure in the form: [H = GNP+0.4 (GDP-GNP)] (IFAC, 2012: 53). *Social Justice Ireland* has argued that the tax-take should be increased to 34.9% of GDP, below the Eurostat threshold defining a low-tax country. An equivalent figure under the IFAC would be to increase taxes to a level that fluctuates around 39.5% of H.

Table 2.9 – Potential Irish Total Tax Revenues, 2011-2016 (€bn)

Year	Tax as % GDP	Tax as % of H	Total Tax Receipts	The Tax Gap (GDP)
2012	30.3%	34.2%	49,569	7,525
2013	31.0%	35.1%	52,049	6,548
2014	31.7%	36.0%	55,245	5,577
2015	31.9%	36.3%	57,914	5,446
2016	31.5%	36.0%	59,574	6,430

Source: Department of Finance (2013: 49-50).
Notes: *The Tax Gap is calculated as the difference between the projected tax take and that which would be collected if total tax receipts were equal to 34.9% of GDP.

As we noted before, the reliance on relatively low level of taxation to fund vital public services certainly contributed to the scale of the crisis in the public finances. Ireland can never hope to address its longer-term deficits in infrastructure and social provision if we continue to collect substantially less tax income than that required by other European countries (cf chapter 4 for a more detailed discussion of this issue). There should also be a public debate on the appropriate level of taxation required over the next twenty years to fund our public services and social security system. Future policy development will likely involve increasing public spending and tax levels as well as changes in how services are delivered. These questions should be openly debated instead of avoided by policymakers.

b) Increase Taxes equitably
If Ireland is to increase its total tax-take, it must do so in a fair and equitable manner. *Social Justice Ireland* believes that the necessary tax reforms should be partly attained by increasing income taxes for those on highest incomes, and by reforming the tax code and broadening the tax base. This will involve shifting taxation towards wealth, ensuring those who benefit the most from Ireland's economic system contribute the most, in the most efficient manner.

In its Policy Briefing on Budget Choices, *Social Justice Ireland* proposed that the Universal Social Charge apply at a rate of 10% for all those earning over €100,000, rather than the current rate of 7 per cent. We also advocate a minimum effective tax rate of 6 per cent for corporation tax, reform of reliefs accruing to those paying the marginal tax rate, and the introduction of a Financial Transactions Tax (FTT) in line with proposals outlined by the European Commission and accepted by leading member-states.

A key part of Ireland's industrial strategy has been to attract foreign domestic investment through the use of a low headline corporation tax rate. However, this has recently caused reputational damage due to the utilisation of the Irish tax regime by multinational corporations to avoid taxes on their corporate profits. In practice, this policy has delivered some short-term gains in terms of foreign direct investment. In the medium-term, the main beneficiaries of Ireland's tax regime may well be multinational corporations and Irish professional services companies providing tax and legal services.

A key medium-term priority must be the reconceptualization of the role of the Irish corporation tax regime. Under international pressure from the G20 and OECD, controversial loopholes have been closed but a serious discussion must take place about the role of corporation tax in Ireland's industrial strategy, and the role of 'brass-plate' companies headquartered in Dublin for tax purposes.[10] We advocate Ireland change its stance towards the corporation tax debate in Europe and negotiate a Europe-wide minimum headline corporation tax of 17.5%.

c) Reduce income inequality
Income inequality, gender inequality and inequality of opportunity, are problems in Irish society. They produce a range of negative outcomes for those who are poor and/or excluded. Growing inequality exacerbates the negative effects on people who are poor and/or excluded. Pickett and Wilkinson (2011) have pointed to the negative consequences of inequality for all sections of society, pointing to better outcomes in everything from subjective well-being to lower crime in more equal societies. Stigliz (2013) has warned of the wider effects of inequality on the political economy of a nation, as wealthier citizens gain an outsize influence in policy formulation, reducing opportunities for the majority through their choices of policy. In Ireland, increases in social protection payments, particularly between 2004 and 2007, played an important role in reducing inequality. This has reversed since 2010, as successive government prioritised cuts in expenditure over increases in taxation, raising serious questions for Irish society.

While budgets in 2008 were progressive, changes in taxation and expenditure since 2010 have been regressive, with the increase in VAT impacting particularly significantly on those with the lowest incomes (Callan et. al., 2012, 2013). This does not take into account cuts to public services, which have a greater impact on those who rely on services; the sick, poor and vulnerable. The Gini coefficient, a measure of income inequality, has risen from a low in 2009 of 29.3 to 31.1 in 2011 (CSO, 2013). Reducing inequality must be a core objective of Government policy. Though the

---

[10] See Department of Finance (2013) for recent adjustments to Ireland's corporation tax policy.

promotion of pre-distribution income equality is important, redistribution through tax and spending decisions should be used to achieve greater equality in Ireland.

iii) Enhancing social protection

There have been significant cuts to social services and payments since 2008. *Social Justice Ireland* believes many of these cuts have been socially destructive and counter-productive. Many cuts have been capricious and were implemented without an adequate examination of their impact. Moreover, in reducing the deficit the balance between expenditure reductions and taxes has been weighted too much towards cuts. Investment in social infrastructure is required now to ensure that it is not eroded further which could potentially have significant future costs. Gross capital expenditure has fallen from €9bn in 2008 to €3.3bn in 2013, and a social infrastructure deficit will inevitably emerge in a climate of underinvestment as the population continues to grow. Finally, the goal of universal provision for all must remain, particularly in the area of health, where inequalities persist between the insured and uninsured population, as well as within the uninsured population. These inequalities will grow as user charges are introduced, and medical cards removed. As we have noted before, given the widespread aspiration in Irish society for these services, the issue of taxation must be addressed.

a) Protect services and the social infrastructure

Since 2008 the government has cut spending by €20,159m while increasing taxes by €10,180m: a ratio of €2 in spending cuts for €1 in tax rates. By the projected end of the EU/IMF programme in 2015 taxation will have contributed €10,880m and spending cuts €21,459m to the total budgetary adjustments: the ratio of tax cuts to spending cuts will remain unaltered (Department of Finance, 2013b). Measures were, and are, required to reduce the deficit, but they should not fall disproportionately upon the most vulnerable in society.

Cuts to services and social protection payments ensure that they do. *Social Justice Ireland* believes that the ratio of spending cuts to tax increases should have been reversed. Future tax and spending policy should prioritise the building of Ireland's social infrastructure, including as a priority social housing, primary and mental health facilities, and early education facilities. Adequate social infrastructure and services are necessary to achieve sufficient dignity and equality for all citizens, from children to older people, particularly in the context of an increased total fertility rate and gradually ageing population.

b) Combat Unemployment

Unemployment has risen rapidly since 2008 but has recently begun to fall, and by the fourth quarter of 2013 stood at 253,200 or 12.1% of the labour force (CSO, 2014).

Employment has finally begun to rise, with an increase of 61,100 in employment between the fourth quarter of 2012 and fourth quarter of 2013. Long-term unemployment was at 7.2% of the labour force as of the second quarter of 2013, accounting for 61.4% of those who are unemployed. The International Monetary Fund (2013: 12) estimates that unemployment will still be 11.7% in 2015, while the department of Finance believes it will stand at 11.8% in 2015 and 11.4% in 2016 (Department of Finance, 2013a). The Government's *Medium-Term Economic Strategy* estimates unemployment will fall to 8.1% by 2020 (2013).

Government currently operates a number of schemes such as the Community Employment Programme, Tús, and Rural Social Scheme which support part-time work. However, government has also introduced schemes such as JobBridge, an unpaid internship programme which provides an additional €50 a week for working between 30 and 40 hours, and the proposed Local Government Social Employment Scheme, which provides an additional €20 a week for working 19.5 hours a week for a local authority, with the potential for sanctions if the person refuses. There are dangers in the latter schemes, such as labour market displacement, exploitation, demoralisation, and the erosion of the principle of a 'fair day's wage for a fair day's work'. They can also ignore the underlying lack of employment opportunities in the economy.

The Nevin Economic Research Institute (2013: 33) has pointed to the fact that there is currently 1 vacancy for every 32.3 jobseekers. Combining the rate of underemployment – those involuntarily working part-time and seeking full-time work – with the rate of unemployment shows that some 396,500 people, or 18.3% of the labour force, are seeking more work. Without a restoration of domestic demand and investment, it is simply not conceivable that employment will grow in the non-traded sector. Policy discussions on 'labour market activation' often do not take this reality into account, and political rhetoric can verge on the demonization of the unemployed.

With regard to increasing demand and investment in the economy to increase employment, our proposal for an investment programme would have an impact in reducing unemployment.

c) Reduce Poverty
There is a real danger that Irish society will permit those on the lowest incomes, and in particular those dependent on social welfare, to fall behind once again, as it did in the late 1990s. From 2006, Ireland's poverty levels had been slowly falling, driven by increases in social welfare payments delivered in the Budgets of 2005-2007. These increases compensated only partly for the extent to which social welfare rates had fallen behind other incomes in society over the preceding two decades. However,

these advances have been reversed since 2009 with the at risk-of-poverty-rate rising from a low of 14.1% in 2009 to 16% in 2011, consistent poverty has risen from a low of 4.2% in 2008 to 6.9% in 2011 while the deprivation rate has risen from a low of 11.8% in 2007 to 24.5% in 2011 (CSO, 2013c:1). In 2011, the single largest demographic group at-risk-of-poverty was children; nearly one in five was at risk of poverty (CSO, 2013).

It would be a great mistake for Ireland, and Irish policy makers, to repeat the experience of the late 1990s. At that time, economic growth benefited only those who were employed while others, such as those dependent on pensions and other social welfare payments slipped further and further behind. We believe that policy in the future should provide equity in social welfare rates across genders, adequate payments for children, and higher payments for those with disabilities.

iv) Reforming Governance
It has been widely recognised that Ireland's governance was poor in certain areas prior to the economic crisis, particularly in relation to financial regulation. Moreover, the economic crisis has led to government making rash and hasty decisions without consultation, whether in relation to financial or budgetary policy, which have been recognised as damaging or – in the case of the bank guarantee – catastrophic. Reforming governance and widening participation are a necessity; below are three immediate priorities required to achieve this.

a) Reform Policy Evaluation
Policy evaluation has been extremely poor in some cases throughout the crisis. *Social Justice Ireland* welcomes the steps taken by Government to increase their research and evaluative capacity. However, we believe that Government should also take steps to increase the transparency of budgetary and other important decisions, which are often opaque. Government should publish their analysis of the distributional impact of budgetary measures, and engage in public debate in light of that analysis. The government previously published Poverty Impact Assessment Guidelines provided by the Office of Social Inclusion (2008) in the budgetary documentation using the ESRI's SWITCH tax-benefit model which captures the distributional impact of changes in most taxes and benefits, but this practice was discontinued from Budget 2010. Government should begin this practice again and also adopt a gender inequality analysis and apply it to each budgetary measure. This should be a statutory responsibility for Government.

b) A Rights-based approach
Social Justice Ireland believes strongly in the importance of developing a rights-based approach to social, economic and cultural issues. The need to develop these rights

is becoming ever more urgent for Ireland in the context of achieving recovery. Such an approach would go a long way towards addressing the growing inequality Ireland has been experiencing. Social, economic and cultural rights should be acknowledged and recognised, just as civil and political rights have been. We believe seven basic rights that are of fundamental concern to people who are socially excluded and/or living in poverty should be acknowledged and recognised. These are the rights to sufficient income to live life with dignity: meaningful work; appropriate accommodation; relevant education; essential healthcare; cultural respect; and real participation in society. To be vindicated, these rights will require greater public expenditure and provision of services.

c) Democratic Deliberation
Decisions taken by government must be openly debated both inside and outside the Oireachtas. Since 2008, austerity measures have been implemented in a haphazard manner, with little public debate and often a lack of explanation and justification for the measures by Government. Instead of reasoned debate with citizen and civil society participation, decisions have been taken at an elite level. For example, Government has provided a high-level forum called the IFSC Clearing House Group for the financial industry, and 23 changes in the Finance Act 2012 were made to accommodate this group (McGee, 2012). We have already examined the lack of democratic accountability and legitimacy in many of the actions taken during the crisis.

Social Justice Ireland believes that a new social model for Ireland must be founded on the idea of deliberative democracy, in which decisions about what kind of society and economy Ireland needs are founded upon reasoned and enlightened debate, and in which decisions taken by government are justified and accessible to the general public.[11] A deliberative decision making process is one where all stakeholders are involved, but the power differentials are removed (Healy and Reynolds, 2011). In such a process stakeholders are involved in the framing, implementing and evaluating of policies and measures that impact on them. Each citizen should have a role and voice in how our society is governed. This should not be confined to five-yearly general elections, particularly when election debates do not provide substantive discussions on our country's future. The proposed Public Participation Networks to be introduced in Local Authorities as part of the reform of local government will provide an opportunity for real engagement between local people and the local authorities across the country (for further information on this cf. chapter 10).

---

[11] See Gutmann & Thompson (2004) and Healy and Reynolds (2011) for more on the concept of deliberative democracy.

v) Creating a Sustainable Future

Sustainable development is development which meets the needs of the present while not compromising the needs of the future. In this regard financial, environmental, economic and social sustainability are all key objectives. In light of this, new indicators must be compiled measuring both well-being and sustainability in society, and used as an objective beside the traditional measures of GDP and GNP.

a) Combat climate change and protect the environment

Climate change remains the largest long-term challenge facing Ireland today. The challenge of reducing Ireland's fossil fuel emissions should not be postponed in the face of the current recession. We believe that Ireland should adopt ambitious statutory targets regarding the limitation of fossil fuel emissions, and introduce taxation measures necessary to compensate for the full costs of resource extraction and pollution. While the publication of the *General Scheme of a Climate Action and Low Carbon Development Bill 2013* was welcome, it only committed to already existing EU2020 and Kyoto Protocol targets. Additionally, there are not adequate sectoral targets or quantitative measures against which individual stakeholders can measure their progress.

The economic crisis has, for obvious reasons, focused attention on economic growth and financial stability. This should not come at the expense of the physical environment, as the failure to tackle climate change now will have significant impacts into the future, including on food production, regional and global ecosystems, and on flood-prone countries.

b) Balanced Regional Development

A sustained recovery requires balanced regional development. The boom years saw an attempt to redress growing regional imbalances in socio-economic development through National Spatial Strategy (2002-2020), though it failed to do so, partly because of Government's own initiatives such as the decentralisation programme for public servants (Meredith and van Egeraat, 2013).

During the recession, particular regions of Ireland have suffered more than others. The unemployment rate in Dublin is the lowest in the country at 12% while the South-East remains the hardest hit with an unemployment rate of 18.3% (CSO, 2013: 22). Rural areas have been severely impacted by cuts in services. The authors believe that policy must ensure balanced regional development through the provision of public services – including cultural, economic and social services - and through capital spending projects, and the adoption of a new National Spatial Strategy, which could be formulated through a deliberative national debate.

c) New Indicators
Creating a sustainable Ireland requires the adoption of new indicators to measure progress. GDP alone as a measure of progress is unsatisfactory, as it only describes the monetary value of gross output, income and expenditure in an economy. The *Report by the Commission on the Measurement of Economic Performance and Social Progress*, led by Nobel prize winning economists Amartya Sen and Joseph Stiglitz and established by President Sarkozy, argued that new indicators measuring environmental, financial sustainability, well-being, and happiness are required.

The National Economic and Social Council (2009) has published the *Well-Being Matters* report, which suggested that measures of well-being could be constructed that capture data on six domains of people's lives that contribute to well-being including: economic resources; work and participation; relationships and care; community and environment; health; and democracy and values. We believe that a new social model should deploy such indicators alongside national accounting measures. The OECD Global Project on Measuring the Progress of Society has recommended a use of such indicators to inform evidence-based policies (Marrone, 2009: 23). They would serve as an alternate benchmark for success.

2.4 Conclusion

So, having set out our understanding of the economic crisis and the context within which it developed, reflected on the responses to the crisis and its human and economic cost, set out a policy framework for a new Ireland and provided some details of the policy initiatives required under each of its five pillars we now move on to look in much greater detail at key aspects of these five pillars.

We provide a fuller analysis of both the first pillar, **macroeconomic stability**, and the second pillar, a **just taxation** system, in chapter 4 where we also set out a more detailed set of policy proposals.

We address the third pillar, **social protection**, in chapters 3 – on income distribution; 4 – taxation; 5 - work, unemployment and job creation; 6 - public services; 7 - housing and accommodation; 8 – healthcare; and 9 - education and educational disadvantage). On each of these we provide an analysis and critique of the present situation, set out a vision for a fairer future and make a detailed set of policy proposals aimed at moving in that direction.

The fourth pillar, **governance** is addressed in chapter 10, where we again provide analysis and critique together with concrete policy proposals.

The fifth pillar, **sustainability**, is addressed in chapters 11 – sustainability; 12 - rural development; and 13 - the global south following the same approach.

3.

INCOME DISTRIBUTION

CORE POLICY OBJECTIVE: INCOME DISTRIBUTION
To provide all with sufficient income to live life with dignity. This would require enough income to provide a minimum floor of social and economic resources in such a way as to ensure that no person in Ireland falls below the threshold of social provision necessary to enable him or her to participate in activities that are considered the norm for society generally.

The persistence of high rates of poverty and income inequality in Ireland requires greater attention than they currently receive. Tackling these problems effectively is a multifaceted task. It requires action on many fronts, ranging from healthcare and education to accommodation and employment. However, the most important requirement in tackling poverty is the provision of sufficient income to enable people to live life with dignity. No anti-poverty strategy can possibly be successful without an effective approach to addressing low incomes.

This chapter addresses the issue of income in four parts. The first (section 3.1) examines the extent and nature of poverty in Ireland today while the second (section 3.2) profiles our income distribution. The final two sections address potential remedies to these problems by outlining the issues and arguments surrounding achieving and maintaining an adequate social welfare income (section 3.3) and the introduction of a basic income (section 3.4). All address issues related to the achievement of one pillar of *Social Justice Ireland's* Core Policy Framework (see Chapter 2), 'Enhancing Social Protection'.

3.1 Poverty

While there is still considerable poverty in Ireland, there has been much progress on this issue over recent years. Driven by increases in social welfare payments, particularly payments to the unemployed, the elderly and people with disabilities, the rate of poverty significantly declined between 2001 and 2009. However, the most recent data, analysed in this section, indicates that poverty has once again begun to increase. It climbed from a record low level in 2009 to a higher level in 2010 and 2011, driven by recent budgetary policy which reversed earlier social welfare increases.[12]

Data on Ireland's income and poverty levels are now provided by the annual *SILC* survey *(Survey on Income and Living Conditions)*. This survey replaced the *European Household Panel Survey* and the *Living in Ireland Survey* which had run throughout the 1990s. Since 2003 the *SILC / EU-SILC* survey has collected detailed information on income and living conditions from up to 120 households in Ireland each week; giving a total sample of between 4,000 and 6,000 households each year.

Social Justice Ireland welcomes this survey and in particular the accessibility of the data produced.[13] Because this survey is conducted simultaneously across all of the EU states, the results are an important contribution to the ongoing discussion on relative income and poverty levels across the EU. It also provides the basis for informed analysis of the relative position of the citizens of member states. In particular, this analysis is informed by a set of agreed indicators of social exclusion which the EU Heads of Government adopted at Laeken in 2001. These indicators (known as the updated-Laeken indicators) are calculated from the survey results and cover four dimensions of social exclusion: financial poverty, employment, health and education. They form the basis of the EU Open Method of Co-ordination for social protection and social inclusion and the Europe 2020 poverty and social exclusion targets.[14]

What is poverty?

The National Anti-Poverty Strategy (NAPS) published by government in 1997 adopted the following definition of poverty:

> *People are living in poverty if their income and resources (material, cultural and social) are so inadequate as to preclude them from having a standard of living that is regarded as acceptable by Irish society generally. As a result of inadequate income and resources people may be excluded and marginalised from participating in activities that are considered the norm for other people in society.*

---

[12]   Irish household income data has been collected since 1973 and all surveys up to the period 2008-2010 recorded poverty levels above 15 per cent.

[13]   However, we note the delay in publishing the 2012 results, the second such delay in recent years. At a time when income and living standards data are central to much public policy analysis and formation, it is crucial that the SILC data, from the 2013 survey onwards, returns to being published in a timely way.

[14]   For more information on these indicators see Nolan (2006:171-190).

This definition was reiterated in the 2007 *National Action Plan for Social Inclusion 2007-2016 (NAPinclusion)*.

Where is the poverty line?

How many people are poor? On what basis are they classified as poor? These and related questions are constantly asked when poverty is discussed or analysed.

In trying to measure the extent of poverty, the most common approach has been to identify a poverty line (or lines) based on people's disposable income (earned income after taxes and including all benefits). The European Commission and the UN, among others, use a poverty line located at 60 per cent of median income. The median disposable income is the income of the middle person in society's income distribution. This poverty line is the one adopted in the *SILC* survey. While the 60 per cent median income line has been adopted as the primary poverty line, alternatives set at 50 per cent and 70 per cent of median income are also used to clarify and lend robustness to assessments of poverty.

The most up-to-date data available on poverty in Ireland comes from the 2011 *SILC* survey, conducted by the CSO.[15] In that year the CSO gathered data from a statistically representative sample of more than 4,300 households containing 11,005 individuals. The data gathered by the CSO is very detailed. It incorporates income from work, welfare, pensions, rental income, dividends, capital gains and other regular transfers. This data was subsequently verified anonymously using PPS numbers.

According to the CSO, the median disposable income per adult in Ireland during 2011 was €18,148 per annum or €348.05 per week. Consequently, the income poverty lines for a single adult derived from this are:

50 per cent line	€174.03 a week
60 per cent line	€208.84 a week
70 per cent line	€243.65 a week

Updating the 60 per cent median income poverty line to 2014 levels, using published CSO data on the growth in average earnings in 2012 (+0.5 per cent) and ESRI projections for 2013 (+1.0 per cent) and 2014 (+1.4 per cent) produces a relative income poverty line of €214.95 for a single person. In 2014, any adult below this

---

[15] The CSO has delayed the release of the 2012 data (originally scheduled for late 2013). This is due to be published before the end of April 2014 and once available will form the basis of a *Social Justice Ireland* Policy Briefing on this topic.

weekly income level will be counted as being at risk of poverty (CSO, 2013:6; Duffy, FitzGerald, Timoney and Byrne, 2013:iii).

Table 3.1 shows what income corresponds to the poverty line for a number of household types. The figure of €214.95 is an income per adult equivalent figure. It is the minimum weekly disposable income (after taxes and including all benefits) that one adult needs to be above the poverty line. For each additional adult in the household this minimum income figure is increased by €141.87 (66 per cent of the poverty line figure) and for each child in the household the minimum income figure is increased by €70.93 (33 per cent of the poverty line).[16] These adjustments reflect the fact that as households increase in size they require more income to meet the basic standard of living implied by the poverty line. In all cases a household below the corresponding weekly disposable income figure is classified as living at risk of poverty. For clarity, corresponding annual figures are also included.

Table 3.1: The Minimum Weekly Disposable Income Required to Avoid Poverty in 2014, by Household Types

Household containing:	Weekly poverty line	Annual poverty line
1 adult	€214.95	€11,208
1 adult + 1 child	€285.89	€14,907
1 adult + 2 children	€356.82	€18,606
1 adult + 3 children	€427.76	€22,304
2 adults	€356.82	€18,606
2 adults + 1 child	€427.76	€22,304
2 adults + 2 children	€498.69	€26,003
2 adults + 3 children	€569.62	€29,702
3 adults	€498.69	€26,003

One immediate implication of this analysis is that most weekly social assistance rates paid to single people are almost €27 below the poverty line.

---

[16] For example the poverty line for a household with 2 adults and 1 child would be calculated as €214.95 + €141.87 + €70.93 = €427.76.

How many have incomes below the poverty line?

Table 3.2 outlines the findings of various poverty studies since detailed poverty studies commenced in 1994. Using the EU poverty line set at 60 per cent of median income, the findings reveal that 16 out of every 100 people in Ireland were living in poverty in 2011. The table shows that the rates of poverty decreased significantly after 2001, reaching a record low in 2009. These decreases in poverty levels were welcome. They were directly related to the increases in social welfare payments delivered over the Budgets spanning these years.[17] However poverty increased again in 2010 and 2011 as the effect of budgetary changes to welfare and taxes, as well as wage reductions and unemployment, drove more low income households into poverty.

Table 3.2: Percentage of population below various relative income poverty lines, 1994-2011

	1994	1998	2001	2005	2007	2009	2010	2011
50% line	6.0	9.9	12.9	10.8	8.6	6.9	7.6	8.5
60% line	15.6	19.8	21.9	18.5	16.5	14.1	14.7	16.0
70% line	26.7	26.9	29.3	28.2	26.8	24.5	24.7	24.1

Source: CSO (2013:12) and Whelan et al (2003:12), using national equivalence scale.
Note: All poverty lines calculated as a percentage of median income.

Because it is sometimes easy to overlook the scale of Ireland's poverty problem, it is useful to translate the poverty percentages into numbers of people. Using the percentages for the 60 per cent median income poverty line and population statistics from CSO population estimates, we can calculate the numbers of people in Ireland who have been in poverty for a number of years between 1994 and 2011. These calculations are presented in table 3.3. The results give a better picture of just how significant this problem really is in Ireland today.

---

[17] See table 3.8 below for further analysis of this point.

Table 3.3: The numbers of people below relative income poverty lines in Ireland, 1994-2011

	% of persons in poverty	Population of Ireland	Numbers in poverty
1994	15.6	3,585,900	559,400
1998	19.8	3,703,100	733,214
2001	21.9	3,847,200	842,537
2003	19.7	3,978,900	783,843
2004	19.4	4,045,200	784,769
2005	18.5	4,133,800	764,753
2006	17.0	4,232,900	719,593
2007	16.5	4,375,800	722,007
2008	14.4	4,485,100	645,854
2009	14.1	4,533,400	639,209
2010	14.7	4,554,800	669,556
2011	16.0	4,574,900	731,984

Source: Calculated using CSO on-line database population estimates, Whelan et al (2003:12) and CSO SILC results for various years.
Note: Population estimates are for April of each year.

The table's figures are telling. Compared to 10 years ago, 2004, there are over 50,000 less people in poverty; even accounting for the recent increases. Notably, over the period from 2004-2008, the period corresponding with consistent Budget increases in social welfare payments, almost 140,000 people left poverty. Despite this, since the onset of the recession and its associated implications for incomes (earnings and welfare), the number in poverty has increased once again, rising by 90,000 since 2009.

Furthermore, the fact that there are more than 730,000 people in Ireland living life on a level of income that is this low remains a major concern. As shown above (see table 3.1) these levels of income are low and those below them clearly face difficulties in achieving what the NAPS described as *"a standard of living that is regarded as acceptable by Irish society generally"*.

Annex 3 provides a more detailed profile of those groups in Ireland than are living in poverty.

The incidence of poverty

Figures detailing the incidence of poverty reveal the proportion of all those in poverty that belong to particular groups in Irish society. Tables 3.4 and 3.5 report all those below the 60 per cent of median income poverty line, classifying them by their principal economic status. The first table examines the population as a whole, including children, while the second table focuses exclusively on adults (using the ILO definition of an adult as a person aged 16 years and above).

Table 3.4 shows that in 2011, the largest group of the population who are poor, accounting for 25.8 per cent of the total, were children. The second largest group were those working in the home (17.5 per cent). Of all those who are poor, 30.8 per cent were in the labour force and the remainder (64.4 per cent) were outside the labour market.[18]

Table 3.4: Incidence of persons below 60% of median income by principal economic status, 2003-2011

	2003	2005	2006	2007*	2010	2011
At work	16.0	15.7	16.1	16.8	13.5	14.2
Unemployed	7.6	7.5	8.3	9.2	15.1	16.6
Students/school	8.6	13.4	15.0	14.1	12.3	14.7
On home duties	22.5	19.7	18.4	18.7	17.3	17.5
Retired	9.0	7.5	5.8	7.1	4.4	4.3
Ill/disabled	9.1	7.9	8.0	7.4	5.4	4.8
Children (under 16 years)	25.4	26.8	26.6	25.9	29.2	25.8
Other	1.9	1.6	1.8	0.8	2.8	2.1
Total	100.0	100.0	100.0	100.0	100.0	100.0

Source: Collins (2006:141), CSO SILC Reports (2007:19; 2009:48; 2013:15).
Note: * Data for 2007 not excluding SSIA effect as not published by CSO.

---

[18] This does not include the ill and people with a disability, some of whom will be active in the labour force. The SILC data does not distinguish between those temporally unable to work due to illness and those permanently outside the labour market due to illness or disability.

Table 3.5 looks at adults only and provides a more informed assessment of the nature of poverty. This is an important perspective as children depend on adults for their upbringing and support. Irrespective of how policy interventions are structured, it is through adults that any attempts to reduce the number of children in poverty must be directed. The table shows that in 2011 almost one-fifth of Ireland's adults with an income below the poverty line were employed. Overall, 41.5 per cent of adults at risk of poverty in Ireland were associated with the labour market.

The incidence of being at risk of poverty amongst those in employment is particularly alarming. Many people in this group do not benefit from Budget changes in welfare or tax. They would be the main beneficiaries of any move to make tax credits refundable, a topic addressed in Chapter 4.

Table 3.5: Incidence of adults (16yrs+) below 60% of median income by principal economic status, 2003-2010

	2003	2005	2006	2007*	2010	2011
At work	21.4	21.4	21.9	22.7	19.1	19.1
Unemployed	10.2	10.2	11.3	12.4	21.3	22.4
Students/school	11.5	18.3	20.4	19.0	17.4	19.8
On home duties	30.1	26.9	25.1	25.2	24.4	23.6
Retired	12.0	10.2	7.9	9.6	6.2	5.8
Ill/disability	12.2	10.8	10.9	10.0	7.6	6.5
Other	2.5	2.2	2.5	1.1	4.0	2.8
Total	**100.0**	**100.0**	**100.0**	**100.0**	**100.0**	**100.0**

Source: Calculated from Collins (2006:141), CSO SILC Reports (2007:19; 2009:48; 2013:15).
Note: * Data for 2007 not excluding SSIA effect as not published by CSO.

Finally, table 3.6 examines the composition of poverty by household type. Given that households are taken to be the 'income receiving units' (income flows into households who then collectively live off that income) there is a value in assessing poverty by household type. *Social Justice Ireland* welcomes the fact that the CSO has, at our suggestion, begun to publish the *SILC* poverty data broken down by household category, even though this data has yet to be released for the 2010 and 2011 SILC. From a policy making perspective this information is crucial as anti-poverty policy is generally focused on households (households with children, pensioner households, single person households etc.). The 2009 data shows that

22.8 per cent of households which were at risk of poverty were headed by somebody who was employed. Almost 44 per cent of households at risk of poverty were found to be headed by a person outside the labour force.[19]

Table 3.6: Households below 60% of median income classified by principal economic status of head of household, 2004-2009

	2004	2006	2007*	2008*	2009
At work	29.8	29.5	31.3	39.6	22.8
Unemployed	12.0	14.7	12.3	11.5	26.0
Students/school	2.8	4.6	5.1	4.1	5.4
On home duties	28.0	30.7	28.7	25.7	26.7
Retired	13.5	8.5	10.9	7.9	6.6
Ill/disabled	12.0	11.5	11.2	10.1	10.9
Other	1.9	0.7	0.4	1.1	1.6
Total	100.0	100.0	100.0	100.0	100.0

Source: CSO SILC Reports (2007:39; 2008:36; 2009:49; 2010:49)
Note: * Data for 2007 and 2008 not excluding SSIA effect as not published by CSO.

The Scale of Poverty - Numbers of People

As the three tables in the last section deal only in percentages it is useful to transform these proportions into numbers of people. Table 3.3 revealed that 731,984 people were living below the 60 per cent of median income poverty line in 2011. Using this figure, table 3.7 presents the number of people in poverty in that year within various categories. Comparable figures are also presented for 2005, 2009 and 2010.

The data in table 3.7 is particularly useful in the context of framing anti-poverty policy. Groups such as the retired and the ill/disabled, although carrying a high risk of poverty, involve much smaller numbers of people than groups such as adults who are employed (the working poor), people on home duties and children/students. The primary drivers of the 2005-09 poverty reductions were increasing incomes among those who are on home duties, those who are classified as ill/disabled, the retired and children. Between 2005 and 2009 the numbers of workers in poverty declined while the numbers of unemployed people in poverty notably increased.

---

[19] Those on home duties, students and school attendees, retired plus a proportion of the ill and disabled.

This reflected the rise in unemployment in the labour market as a whole during those years. As the table shows, the increase in poverty between 2009 and 2011 can be principally explained by the increase in poverty among people with jobs, people who are unemployed and children.

Table 3.7: Poverty Levels Expressed in Numbers of People, 2005-2011

	2005	2009	2010	2011
Overall	764,753	639,209	669,556	731,984
Adults				
On home duties	150,656	115,058	115,833	128,097
Unemployed	57,356	82,458	101,103	121,509
Students/school	102,477	93,325	82,355	107,602
At work	120,066	91,407	90,390	103,942
Ill/disabled	60,415	40,909	36,156	35,135
Retired	57,356	30,043	29,460	31,475
Other	12,236	9,588	18,748	15,372
Children				
Children (under 16 yrs)	204,954	176,422	195,510	188,852
Children (under 18 yrs)	n/a	223,084	226,979	232,039

Source: Calculated using CSO SILC Reports (2013:15; 2006:13) and data from table 3.3.

Poverty and social welfare recipients

Social Justice Ireland believes in the very important role that social welfare plays in addressing poverty. As part of the *SILC* results the CSO has provided an interesting insight into the role that social welfare payments play in tackling Ireland's poverty levels. It has calculated the levels of poverty before and after the payment of social welfare benefits.

Table 3.8 shows that without the social welfare system almost 51 per cent of the Irish population would have been living in poverty in 2011. Such an underlying poverty rate suggests a deeply unequal distribution of direct income – an issue we address further in the income distribution section of this chapter. In 2011, the actual poverty figure of 16 per cent reflects the fact that social welfare payments reduced poverty by almost 35 percentage points.

Looking at the impact of these payments on poverty over time, it is clear that the increases in social welfare over the period 2005-2007 yielded noticeable reductions in poverty levels. The small increases in social welfare payments in 2001 are reflected in the smaller effects achieved in that year. Conversely, the larger increases, and therefore higher levels of social welfare payments, in subsequent years delivered greater reductions. This has occurred even as poverty levels before social welfare increased. A recent report by Watson and Maitre (2013) examined these effects in greater detail and noted the effectiveness of social welfare payments, with child benefit and the growth in the value of social welfare payments, playing a key role in reducing poverty levels up until 2009.

Table 3.8: The role of social welfare (SW) payments in addressing poverty

	2001	2005	2007	2009	2010	2011
Poverty pre SW	35.6	40.1	41.0	46.2	50.2	50.7
Poverty post SW	21.9	18.5	16.5	14.1	14.7	16.0
The role of SW	-13.7	-21.6	-24.5	-32.1	-35.5	-34.7

Source: CSO SILC Reports (2006:7; 2013:12) using national equivalence scale.

As social welfare payments do not flow to everybody in the population, it is interesting to examine the impact they have on alleviating poverty among certain groups, such as older people, for example. Using data from SILC 2009, the CSO found that without any social welfare payments 88 per cent of all those aged over 65 years would have been living in poverty. Benefit entitlements reduce the poverty level among this group to 9.6 per cent in 2009. Similarly, social welfare payments (including child benefit) reduce poverty among those under 18 years of age from 47.3 per cent to 18.6 per cent – a 60 per cent reduction in poverty risk (CSO, 2010:47).[20] These findings, combined with the social welfare impact data in table 3.8, underscore the importance of social transfer payments in addressing poverty; a point that needs to be borne in mind as Government continues to address Ireland's ongoing crisis.

Analysis in Annex 3 (see table A3.1 and the subsequent analysis) shows that many of the groups in Irish society which experienced increases in poverty levels over the last decade have been dependent on social welfare payments. These include pensioners, the unemployed, lone parents and those who are ill or have a disability. Table 3.9 presents the results of an analysis of five key welfare recipient groups performed by the ESRI using poverty data for five of the years between 1994 and

---

[20] This data has not been updated in the SILC publication for 2011 or the CSO revision of SILC for 2010.

2001. These are the years that the Irish economy grew fastest and the core years of the famed 'Celtic Tiger' boom. Between 1994 and 2001 all categories experienced large growth in their poverty risk. For example, in 1994 only five out of every 100 old age pension recipients were in poverty. In 2001 this had increased ten-fold to almost 50 out of every 100. The experience of widow's pension recipients is similar.

Table 3.9: Percentage of persons in receipt of welfare benefits/assistance who were below the 60 per cent median income poverty line, 1994/1997/1998/2000/2001

	1994	1997	1998	2000	2001
Old age pension	5.3	19.2	30.7	42.9	49.0
Unemployment benefit/assistance	23.9	30.6	44.8	40.5	43.1
Illness/disability	10.4	25.4	38.5	48.4	49.4
Lone Parents allowance	25.8	38.4	36.9	42.7	39.7
Widow's pension	5.5	38.0	49.4	42.4	42.1

Source: Whelan et al (2003: 31)

Table 3.9 highlights the importance of adequate social welfare payments to prevent people becoming at risk of poverty. Over the period covered by these studies, groups similar to *Social Justice Ireland* repeatedly pointed out that these payments had failed to rise in proportion to earnings elsewhere in society. The primary consequence of this was that recipients slipped further and further back and as a consequence more and more fell into poverty. It is clear that adequate levels of social welfare need to be maintained to ensure that the mistakes of the past are not repeated. We outline our proposals for this later in this chapter.

The poverty gap

As part of the 2001 Laeken indicators, the EU asked all member countries to begin measuring their relative "at risk of poverty gap". This indicator assesses how far below the poverty line the income of the median (middle) person in poverty is. The size of that difference is calculated as a percentage of the poverty line and therefore represents the gap between the income of the middle person in poverty and the poverty line. The higher the percentage figure, the greater the poverty gap and the further people are falling beneath the poverty line. As there is a considerable difference between being 2 per cent and 20 per cent below the poverty line this approach is significant

Table 3.10: The Poverty Gap, 2003-2011

	2003	2004	2005	2006	2007*	2009	2011
Poverty gap size	21.5	19.8	20.6	17.5	17.4	16.2	19.6

Source: CSO SILC reports (2008:16; 2013:12)
Note: * Data for 2007 not excluding SSIA effect as not published by CSO.

The *SILC* results for 2011 show that the poverty gap was 19.6 per cent, compared to 17.7 per cent in 2010 (not in table) and 16.2 per cent in 2009. Over time, the gap had decreased from a figure of 21.5 per cent in 2003. The 2011 poverty gap figure implies that 50 per cent of those in poverty had an equivalised income below 80.4 per cent of the poverty line. Watson and Maitre (2013:39) compared the size of the market income poverty gap over the years 2004, 2007 and 2011. Adjusting for changes in prices, they found that in 2011 terms the gap was €261 for households below the poverty line, an increase from a figure of €214 in 2004. They also found that after social transfers, those remaining below the poverty line were further from that threshold in 2011 than in 2004.

As the depth of poverty is an important issue, we will monitor closely the movement of this indicator in future editions of the *SILC*. It is crucial that, as part of Ireland's approach to addressing poverty, this figure declines in the future. It is of concern that recent figures once again record increases.

Poverty and deprivation

Income alone does not tell the whole story concerning living standards and command over resources. As we have seen in the NAPS definition of poverty, it is necessary to look more broadly at exclusion from society because of a lack of resources. This requires looking at other areas where 'as a result of inadequate income and resources people may be excluded and marginalised from participating in activities that are considered the norm for other people in society' (NAPS, 1997). Although income is the principal indicator used to assess wellbeing and ability to participate in society, there are other measures. In particular, these measures assess the standards of living people achieve by assessing deprivation through use of different indicators. To date, assessments of deprivation in Ireland have been limited and confined to a small number of items. While this is regrettable, the information gathered is worth considering.

Table 3.11: Levels of deprivation for eleven items among the population and those in poverty, 2011 (%)

	Total Pop	Those in Poverty*
Without heating at some stage in the past year	12.2	21.7
Unable to afford a morning, afternoon or evening out in the last fortnight	21.1	35.8
Unable to afford two pairs of strong shoes	3.1	5.2
Unable to afford a roast once a week	6.7	9.3
Unable to afford a meal with meat, chicken or fish every second day	2.8	5.8
Unable to afford new (not second-hand) clothes	7.3	16.3
Unable to afford a warm waterproof coat	2.2	4.6
Unable to afford to keep the home adequately warm	6.8	11.9
Unable to replace any worn out furniture	21.7	34.3
Unable to afford to have family or friends for a drink or meal once a month	14.8	26.5
Unable to afford to buy presents for family or friends at least once a year	5.8	13.3

Source: CSO (2013:14)

Note: * Poverty as measured using the 60 per cent median income poverty line.

Deprivation in the SILC survey

Since 2007 the CSO has presented 11 measures of deprivation in the *SILC* survey, compared to just eight before that. While this increase is welcome, *Social Justice Ireland* and others have expressed serious reservations about the overall range of measures employed. We believe that a whole new approach to measuring deprivation should be developed. Continuing to collect information on a limited number of static indicators is problematic in itself and does not present a true picture of the dynamic nature of Irish society.

The details presented in table 3.11, therefore, should be seen in the context of the above reservation. The table shows that in 2011 the rates of deprivation recorded across the set of 11 items varied between 2 and 21 per cent of the Irish population. Overall 59.8 per cent of the population were not deprived of any item, while 15.7 per cent were deprived of one item, 9.2 per cent were without two items and 15.4 per cent were without three or more items. It is of interest that from 2007 onwards, as the economic crisis unfolded, the proportion of the population which experienced no deprivation has fallen steadily from 75.6 per cent in 2007 to 63.9

per cent in 2010 and 59.8 per cent in 2011. Simultaneously, the proportion of the population experiencing deprivation of two or more items has more than doubled, increasing from 11.8 per cent in 2007 to 24.5 per cent in 2011 (CSO, 2013:13).

Deprivation and poverty combined: consistent poverty

'Consistent poverty' combines deprivation and poverty into a single indicator. It does this by calculating the proportion of the population simultaneously experiencing poverty and registering as deprived of two or more of the items in table 3.11. As such, it captures a sub-group of the poor.

The 2007 *SILC* data marked an important change for this indicator. Coupled with the expanded list of deprivation items, the definition of consistent poverty was changed. From 2007 onwards, to be counted as experiencing consistent poverty individuals must be both below the poverty line and experiencing deprivation of at least two items. Up to 2007 the criteria was below the poverty line and deprivation of at least one item. The *National Action Plan for Social Inclusion 2007-2016* (*NAPinclusion*) published in early 2007 set its overall poverty goal using this earlier consistent poverty measure. One of its aims was to reduce the number of people experiencing consistent poverty to between 2 per cent and 4 per cent of the total population by 2012, with a further aim of totally eliminating consistent poverty by 2016. A revision to this target was published as part of the Government's *National Reform Programme 2012 Update for Ireland* (2012). The revised poverty target is to reduce the numbers experiencing consistent poverty to 4 per cent by 2016 and to 2 per cent or less by 2020. *Social Justice Ireland* participated in the consultation process on the revision of this and other poverty targets. While we agree with the revised 2020 consistent poverty target (it is not possible to measure below this 2 per cent level using survey data) we have proposed that this target should be accompanied by other targets focused on the overall population and vulnerable groups.[21] These are outlined at the end of this chapter.

Using these new indicators and definition, the 2011 *SILC* data indicates that 6.9 per cent of the population experience consistent poverty, an increase from 4.2 per cent in 2008 and 5.5 per cent in 2009 (CSO, 2013:12). In terms of the population, the 2011 figures indicate that just over 315,000 people live in consistent poverty. Over time, the reality of the current recession and its austerity measures are pushing Ireland further away from these targets.

Annex 3 also examines the experience of people who are in food poverty, fuel poverty alongside an assessment of the research on minimum incomes standards in Ireland.

---

[21] See also Leahy et al (2012:61).

Moving to Persistent Poverty

Social Justice Ireland is committed to using the best and most up-to-date data in its ongoing socio-economic analysis of Ireland. We believe that to do so is crucial to the emergence of accurate evidence-based policy formation. It also assists in establishing appropriate and justifiable targeting of state resources.

Among the EU Laeken indicators mentioned earlier is an indicator of persistent poverty. This indicator measures the proportion of those living below the 60 per cent of median income poverty line in the current year and for two of the three preceding years. Persistent poverty, therefore, identifies those who have experienced sustained exposure to poverty which is seen to harm their quality of life seriously and to increase their levels of deprivation. To date the Irish *SILC* survey has not produced any detailed results and breakdowns for this measure. We regret the unavailability of this data and note that there remain some sampling and technical issues impeding its annual publication. *Social Justice Ireland* believes that this data should be used as the primary basis for setting poverty targets and monitoring changes in poverty status. Existing measures of relative and consistent poverty should be maintained as secondary indicators. As the persistent poverty indicator will identify the long-term poor, we believe that the CSO should produce comprehensive breakdowns of those in persistent poverty, similar to the approach it currently takes with relative income poverty. Presently, if there are impediments to the annual production of this indicator, they should be addressed and the SILC sample augmented if required. A measure of persistent poverty is long overdue and a crucial missing piece in societies knowledge of households and individuals on low income.

Poverty: a European perspective
It is helpful to compare Irish measures of poverty with those elsewhere in Europe. Eurostat, the European Statistics Agency, produces comparable 'at risk of poverty' figures (proportions of the population living below the poverty line) for each EU member state. The data is calculated using the 60 per cent of median income poverty line in each country. Comparable EU-wide definitions of income and equivalence scale are used.[22] The latest data available is for the year 2012 for all member states except Ireland.

As table 3.12 shows, Irish people experience a below average risk of poverty when compared to all other EU member states. Eurostat's 2008 figures marked the first time Ireland's poverty levels fell below average EU levels. This phenomenon was driven, as outlined earlier in this review, by sustained increases in welfare payments

---

[22] Differences in definitions of income and equivalence scales result in slight differences in the poverty rates reported for Ireland when compared to those reported earlier which have been calculated by the CSO using national definitions of income and the Irish equivalence scale.

in the years prior to 2008. Ireland's poverty levels remained below average EU levels since then to 2011, although over that time poverty rates increased. In 2012, across the EU, the highest poverty levels were found in the recent accession countries of Bulgaria and Romania and the two countries caught up in the EU-wide economic crash - Spain and Greece. The lowest levels were in Denmark, the Netherlands and the Czech Republic.

Table 3.12: The risk of poverty in the European Union in 2012

Country	Poverty Risk	Country	Poverty Risk
Greece	23.1	Luxembourg	15.1
Romania	22.6	Belgium	14.8
Spain	22.2	Cyprus	14.7
Bulgaria	21.2	Austria	14.4
Croatia	20.5	Sweden	14.1
Italy	19.4	France	14.1
Latvia	19.2	Hungary	14.0
Lithuania	18.6	Slovenia	13.5
Portugal	17.9	Slovakia	13.2
Estonia	17.5	Finland	13.2
Poland	17.1	Denmark	13.1
UK	16.2	Netherlands	10.1
Germany	16.1	Czech Rep	9.6
IRELAND	**15.2**	**EU-27 average**	**16.9**
Malta	15.1	**EU-28 average**	**16.9**

Source: Eurostat online database
Note: Table uses the most up-to-date comparable data available for countries and corresponds to the year 2012 for all countries except Ireland where the value is for 2011.

The average risk of poverty in the EU-28 for 2012 was 16.9 per cent. Chart 3.1 further develops the findings of table 3.12 and shows the difference between national poverty risk levels and the EU-28 average.

While there have been some reductions in poverty in recent years across the EU, the data does suggest that poverty remains a large and ongoing EU-wide problem. In 2012 the average EU-28 level implied that 84.9 million people are in poverty across the EU.

Chart 3.1: Percentage difference in National Poverty risk from EU-28 average

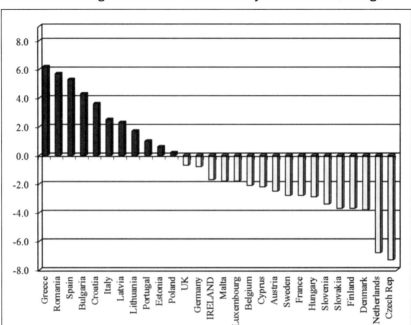

Source: Eurostat online database

Note: Chart uses the most up-to-date comparable data available for countries and corresponds to the year 2012 for all countries except Ireland where the value is for 2011.

Europe 2020 Strategy – Risk of Poverty or Social Exclusion

As part of the Europe 2020 Strategy, European governments have begun to adopt policies to target these poverty levels and are using as their main benchmark the proportion of the population at risk of poverty or social exclusion. This indicator has been defined by the European Council on the basis of three indicators: the aforementioned 'at risk of poverty' rate after social transfers; an index of material deprivation;[23] and the percentage of people living in households with very low work intensity.[24] It is calculated as the sum of persons relative to the national population who are at risk of poverty or severely materially deprived or living in households with very low work intensity, where a person is only counted once even if recorded in more than one indicator. [25]

Table 3.13: People at risk of poverty or social exclusion, Ireland and the EU 2007-2012

	2007	2009	2011	2012
Ireland % Population	23.1	25.7	29.4	n/a
Ireland 000s people	1,005	1,150	1,319	n/a
EU % Population*	24.4	23.2	24.3	24.8
EU 000s people*	119,360	114,328	121,543	124,229

Source: Eurostat online database
Notes: 2012 data for Ireland has yet to be submitted by the CSO to Eurostat.
EU data for 2007 and 2009 is for the EU-27, 2011 and 2012 data are for the EU-28 (including Croatia)

Table 3.13 summarises the latest data on this indicator for Europe and chart 3.2 summarises the latest Irish data (which is for 2011). While *Social Justice Ireland* regrets that the Europe 2020 process shifted its indicator focus away from an exclusive concentration on the 'at risk of poverty' rate, we welcome the added attention at a European level to issues regarding poverty, deprivation and joblessness. Together with Caritas Europa, we have initiated a process to monitor progress on this strategy over

---

[23] Material deprivation covers indicators relating to economic strain and durables. Severely materially deprived persons have living conditions severely constrained by a lack of resources. They experience at least 4 out of 9 listed deprivations items. (Eurostat, 2012)

[24] People living in households with very low work intensity are those aged 0-59 living in households where the adults (aged 18-59) work less than 20% of their total work potential during the past year (Eurostat, 2012)

[25] See European Commission (2011) for a more detailed explanation of this indicator.

the years to come (Mallon and Healy, 2012 and Leahy et al, 2012). However, it is clear already that the austerity measures which are being pursued in many EU countries will result in the erosion of social services and lead to the further exclusion of people who already find themselves on the margins of society. This is in direct contradiction to the inclusive growth focus of the Europe 2020 Strategy. It is reflected in the figures in table 3.13 which show an increase in risk levels in 2011 and 2012.

Chart 3.2: Population at risk of poverty or social exclusion, Ireland 2011

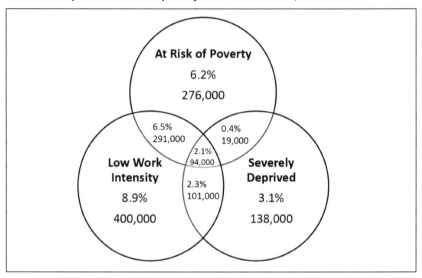

Source: Compiled from Eurostat online database
Note: 2012 data for Ireland has yet to be submitted by the CSO to Eurostat.

3.2 Income Distribution

As previously outlined, despite some improvements poverty remains a significant problem. The purpose of economic development should be to improve the living standards of all of the population. A further loss of social cohesion will mean that large numbers of people continue to experience deprivation and the gap between them and the better-off will widen. This has implications for all of society, not just those who are poor, a reality that has begun to receive welcome attention recently.

Analysis of the annual income and expenditure accounts yields information on trends in the distribution of national income. However, the limitations of this accounting system need to be acknowledged. Measures of income are far from perfect gauges of a society. They ignore many relevant non-market features, such as volunteerism, caring and environmental protection. Many environmental factors, such as the depletion of natural resources, are registered as income but not seen as a cost. Pollution is not registered as a cost but cleaning up after pollution is seen as income. Increased spending on prisons and security, which are a response to crime, are seen as increasing national income but not registered as reducing human well-being.

The point is that national accounts do not include items that cannot easily be assigned a monetary value. But progress cannot be measured by economic growth alone. Many other factors are required, as we highlight elsewhere in this review.[26] However, when judging economic performance and making judgements about how well Ireland is really doing, it is important to look at the distribution of national income as well as its absolute amount.[27]

Ireland's income distribution: latest data

The most recent data on Ireland's income distribution, from the 2011 SILC survey, is summarised in chart 3.3. It examines the income distribution by household deciles, starting with the 10 per cent of households with the lowest income (the bottom decile) up to the 10 per cent of households with the highest income (the top decile). The data presented is for disposable income. This is the amount of money households have in their pocket to spend after they have received any employment/pension income, paid all their income taxes and received any welfare entitlements.

---

[26] We return to critique National Income statistics in chapter 11. There, we also propose some alternatives.

[27] We examine the issue of the world's income and wealth distribution in chapter 13.

Chart 3.3: Ireland's Income Distribution by 10% (decile) group, 2011

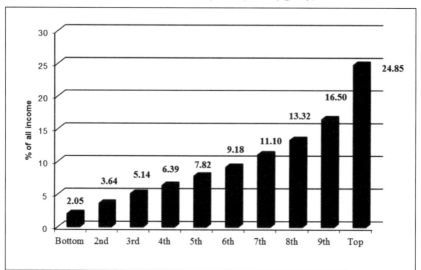

Source: Collins (2013)

In 2011, the top 10 per cent of Irish households received 24.85 per cent of the total disposable income while the bottom decile received 2.05 per cent. Collectively, the poorest 50 per cent of households received a very similar share (25.04 per cent) to the top 10 per cent. Overall the share of the top 10 per cent is more than 12 times the share of the bottom 10 per cent. Table 3.14 outlines the cash values of these income shares in 2011. It shows that the top 10 per cent of households receive an average weekly disposable income (after all taxes and having received all benefits) of just under €2,000 while the bottom decile receives €165 per week. In 2011, the average household disposable income was €801 a week / €41,798 per annum (CSO, 2012: 10). While the nominal value of these shares has declined in recent years, the spread of income reflected in the table has become more unequal according to the CSOs 2011 SILC report. An examination of income distribution over the period 1987-2011 is provided in annex 3.

Table 3.14: Amounts of disposable income, by decile in 2011

Decile	Weekly disposable income	Annual disposable income
Bottom	€164.70	€8,588
2nd	€292.15	€15,234
3rd	€412.27	€21,497
4th	€512.24	€26,710
5th	€626.51	€32,668
6th	€735.99	€38,377
7th	€889.89	€46,401
8th	€1,067.94	€55,685
9th	€1,322.30	€68,949
Top	€1,992.14	€103,876

Source: Calculated from Collins (2013:4).
Note: Annual figures are rounded to the nearest Euro to ease interpretation.

Direct income distribution

It is noteworthy that Ireland's disposable income distribution (after redistribution through taxes and transfers) has been largely static despite improvements in welfare payments which reduced poverty, as highlighted in table 3.8. The implication of this is that simultaneous with improvements in welfare payments and redistributive taxes, the underlying distribution of direct or market income has become more unequal. Collins and Kavanagh (2006: 155, 162) highlighted the 'marked increase in the level of direct income inequality' over the period from 1973 to 2004.

Table 3.15 suggests that the level of direct income inequality has continued to widen. Over the period from 1987 to 2011 the direct income shares of all deciles except the top two have declined. Compared to the situation in 1987, the gap between the bottom and top deciles has dramatically widened. By 2011 the share of the top 10 per cent was more than four and a half times that of the bottom 50 per cent. While the role of the redistribution system is to intervene and address this inequality via taxation and welfare payments, the fact that the underlying income inequality continues to worsen suggests that the challenges faced by the redistribution system have become much greater over time.

Table 3.15: The distribution of household direct income, 1987-2011 (%)

Decile	1987	2004	2011
Bottom	0.38	0.19	0.33
2nd	1.00	0.48	0.46
3rd	1.40	1.05	1.13
4th	3.30	2.64	2.33
5th	6.10	5.70	3.83
6th	8.70	8.65	6.66
7th	11.60	11.49	10.23
8th	15.09	14.96	15.00
9th	20.08	19.54	21.84
Top	32.46	35.31	38.17
Total	100.00	100.00	100.00
Bottom 20%	1.38	0.67	0.79
Bottom 50%	12.08	10.06	8.05
Top 10:Bot 10	85 times	185 times	116 times

Source: Collins and Kavanagh (2006:155) and Collins (2013:2)
Note: Data for 1987 is from the Household Budget Survey, 2004 and 2011 data from SILC.

Income distribution: a European perspective

Another of the indicators adopted by the EU at Laeken assesses the income distribution of member states by comparing the ratio of equivalised disposable income received by the bottom quintile (20 per cent) to that of the top quintile. This indicator reveals how far away from each other the shares of these two groups are – the higher the ratio, the greater the income difference. Table 3.16 presents the most up-to-date results of this indicator for the 28 EU states. The data indicate that the Irish figure increased to 4.6 from a ratio of 4.2 in 2009, reflecting the already noted increase in income inequality in 2011. Ireland now has a ratio just below the EU average and, given recent economic and budgetary policy, this looks likely to persist and may even worsen. Overall, the greatest differences in the shares of those at the top and bottom of income distribution are found in many of the newer and poorer member states. However, some EU-15 members, including the Spain, Greece, Portugal, Italy and the UK also record large differences.

Table 3.16: Ratio of Disposable Income received by bottom quintile to that of the top quintile in the EU-28

Country	Ratio	Country	Ratio
Spain	7.2	France	4.5
Greece	6.6	Germany	4.3
Latvia	6.5	Austria	4.2
Romania	6.3	Luxembourg	4.1
Bulgaria	6.1	Hungary	4.0
Portugal	5.8	Belgium	3.9
Italy	5.5	Malta	3.9
Estonia	5.4	Slovakia	3.7
Croatia	5.4	Finland	3.7
United Kingdom	5.4	Sweden	3.7
Lithuania	5.3	Netherlands	3.6
Poland	4.9	Czech Republic	3.5
Cyprus	4.7	Slovenia	3.4
IRELAND	4.6	**EU-27 average**	**5.1**
Denmark	4.5	**EU-28 average**	**5.1**

Source: Eurostat online database

Note: Chart uses the most up-to-date comparable data available for countries and corresponds to the year 2012 for all countries except Ireland where the value is for 2011.

A further measure of income inequality is the Gini coefficient, which ranges from 0 to 100 and summarises the degree of inequality across the entire income distribution (rather than just at the top and bottom).[28] The higher the Gini coefficient score the greater the degree of income inequality in a society. As table 3.17 shows, over time income inequality has been reasonably static in the EU as a whole, although within the EU there are notable differences. Countries such as Ireland cluster around or just above the average EU score and differ from other high-income EU member states which record lower levels of inequality. As the table shows, the degree of inequality is at a notably lower scale in countries like Finland, Sweden and the Netherlands. For Ireland, the key point is that despite the aforementioned role of the social transfer system, the underlying degree of direct income inequality dictates that our income distribution remains much more unequal than in many of the EU countries we wish to emulate in term of economic and social development.

---

[28] See Collins and Kavanagh (2006: 159-160) who provide a more detailed explanation of this measure.

Table 3.17: Gini coefficient measure of income inequality for selected EU states, 2005-2011

	2005	2007	2008	2009	2011	2012
EU-27/28	30.6	30.6	30.9	30.5	30.8	30.6
IRELAND	31.9	31.3	29.9	28.8	29.8	n/a
UK	34.6	32.6	33.9	32.4	33.0	32.8
France	27.7	26.6	29.8	29.9	30.8	30.5
Germany	26.1	30.4	30.2	29.1	29.0	28.3
Sweden	23.4	23.4	24.0	24.8	24.4	24.8
Finland	26.0	26.2	26.3	25.9	25.8	25.9
Netherlands	26.9	27.6	27.6	27.2	25.8	25.4

Source: Eurostat online database
Notes: The Gini coefficient ranges from 0-100 with a higher score indicating a higher level of inequality.

The table uses the most up-to-date comparable data available for countries and corresponds to the year 2012 for all countries except Ireland, where the value is for 2011.

EU data for 2005-2009 is for the EU-27, 2011 and 2012 data are for the EU-28 (including Croatia)

3.3 Maintaining an Adequate Level of Social Welfare

From 2005 onwards, there was major progress on benchmarking social welfare payments. Budget 2007 benchmarked the minimum social welfare rate at 30 per cent of Gross Average Industrial Earnings (GAIE). This was a key achievement and one that we correctly predicted would lead to reductions in poverty rates, complementing those already achieved and detailed earlier. Annex 3 outlines how this significant development occurred.

Setting a Benchmark: 2011 onwards

In late 2007 the CSO discontinued its *Industrial Earnings and Hours Worked* dataset and replaced it with a more comprehensive set of income statistics for a broader set of Irish employment sectors. The end of that dataset also saw the demise of the GAIE figure from Irish official statistics. It has been replaced with a series of measures, including a new indicator measuring average earnings across all the employment sectors now covered. While the improvement to data sources is welcome, the end of the GAIE figure poses problems for continuing to calculate the social welfare benchmark. To this end, *Social Justice Ireland* commissioned a report in late 2010 to establish an appropriate way of continuing to calculate this benchmark.

A report entitled *'Establishing a Benchmark for Ireland's Social Welfare Payments'* (Collins, 2011) is available on *Social Justice Ireland*'s website. It established that 30 per cent of GAIE is equivalent to 27.5 per cent of the new average earnings data being collected by the CSO. A figure of 27.5 per cent of average earnings is therefore the appropriate benchmark for minimum social welfare payments and reflects a continuation of the previous benchmark using the new CSO earnings dataset.

Table 3.18 applies this benchmark using CSO data for the third quarter of 2013 (published February 2014). The data is updated using ESRI projections for wage growth in 2014 (1.4 per cent); an update for 2015 won't be available until later in 2014 when the ESRI publish wage growth projections for 2015. Between 2012 and 2013 average earnings declined, from €691.93 to €677.13, driven by public sector pay reductions (Haddington Road Agreement).

In 2014 27.5 per cent of average weekly earnings equals €188.82, marginally more than the current minimum social welfare rate of €188. The figure is likely to increase further for 2015 implying that the appropriate budgetary policy in Budget 2015 (October 2014) would be to increase minimum social welfare rates to ensure equivalence with 27.5 per cent of average weekly earnings. This would address some of the losses in buying power over recent years and maintain the benchmark. We will develop this proposal further in our pre-Budget submission in mid-2014.

Table 3.18: Benchmarking Social Welfare Payments for 2014 (€) Year

	Average Weekly Earnings	27.5% of Average Weekly Earnings
2012*	691.93	190.28
2013*	677.13	186.21
2014**	686.61	188.82

Notes: * actual data from CSO average earnings Q3 of each year
      ** simulated value based on CSO data and ESRI QEC wage growth projections

Individualising social welfare payments

The issue of individualising payments so that all recipients receive their own social welfare payments has been on the policy agenda in Ireland and across the EU for several years. *Social Justice Ireland* welcomed the report of the Working Group, *Examining the Treatment of Married, Cohabiting and One-Parent Families under the Tax and Social Welfare Codes*, which addressed some of these individualisation issues.

At present the welfare system provides a basic payment for a claimant, whether that be, for example, for a pension, a disability payment or a job-seeker's payment. It then adds an additional payment of about two-thirds of the basic payment for the second person. For example, following Budget 2014, a couple on the lowest social welfare rate receives a payment of €312.80 per week. This amount is approximately 1.66 times the payment for a single person (€188). Were these two people living separately they would receive €188 each; giving a total of €376. Thus by living as a household unit such a couple receive a lower income than they would were they to live apart.

Social Justice Ireland believes that this system is unfair and inequitable. We also believe that the system as currently structured is not compatible with the Equal Status Acts. People, more often than not, women, are disadvantaged by living as part of a household unit because they receive a lower income. We believe that where a couple is in receipt of welfare payments, the payment to the second person should be increased to equal that of the first. Such a change would remove the current inequity and bring the current social welfare system in line with the terms of the Equal Status Acts (2000-2004). An effective way of doing this would be to introduce a basic income system which is far more appropriate for the world of the 21st century.

3.4 Basic Income

Over the past 12 years major progress has been achieved in building the case for the introduction of a basic income in Ireland. This includes the publication of a *Green Paper on Basic Income* by the Government in September 2002 and the publication of a book by Clark entitled *The Basic Income Guarantee* (2002). A major international conference on basic income was held in Dublin during Summer 2008 at which more than 70 papers from 30 countries were presented. These are available on *Social Justice Ireland*'s website. More recently, Healy et al (2012) have provided an initial set of costing for a basic income and new European and Irish Basic Income networks have emerged.[29]

---

[19] These networks are the European Citizens' Initiative for Unconditional Basic Income and Basic Income Ireland.

The case for a basic income

Social Justice Ireland has consistently argued that the present tax and social welfare systems should be integrated and reformed to make them more appropriate to the changing world of the 21st century. To this end we have sought the introduction of a basic income system. This proposal is especially relevant at the present moment of economic upheaval.

A basic income is an income that is unconditionally granted to every person on an individual basis, without any means test or work requirement. In a basic income system every person receives a weekly tax-free payment from the Exchequer while all other personal income is taxed, usually at a single rate. The basic-income payment would replace income from social welfare for a person who is unemployed and replace tax credits for a person who is employed.

- Basic income is a form of minimum income guarantee that avoids many of the negative side-effects inherent in social welfare payments. A basic income differs from other forms of income support in that:
- It is paid to individuals rather than households;
- It is paid irrespective of any income from other sources;
- It is paid without conditions; it does not require the performance of any work or the willingness to accept a job if offered one; and
- It is always tax free.

There is real danger that the plight of large numbers of people excluded from the benefits of the modern economy will be ignored. Images of rising tides lifting all boats are often offered as government's policy makers and commentators assure society that prosperity for all is just around the corner. Likewise, the claim is often made that a job is the best poverty fighter and consequently priority must be given to securing a paid job for everyone. These images and claims are no substitute for concrete policies to ensure that all members of society are included. Twenty-first century society needs a radical approach to ensure the inclusion of all people in the benefits of present economic growth and development. Basic income is such an approach.

As we are proposing it, a basic income system would replace social welfare and income tax credits. It would guarantee an income above the poverty line for everyone. It would not be means tested. There would be no 'signing on' and no restrictions or conditions. In practice, a basic income recognises the right of every person to a share of the resources of society.

The Basic Income system ensures that looking for a paid job and earning an income, or increasing one's income while in employment, is always worth pursuing, because for every euro earned the person will retain a large part. It thus removes poverty traps and unemployment traps in the present system. Furthermore, women and men would receive equal payments in a basic income system. Consequently the basic income system promotes gender equality because it treats every person equally.

It is a system that is altogether more guaranteed, rewarding, simple and transparent than the present tax and welfare systems. It is far more employment friendly than the present system. It also respects other forms of work besides paid employment. This is crucial in a world where these benefits need to be recognised and respected. It is also very important in a world where paid employment cannot be permanently guaranteed for everyone seeking it. There is growing pressure and need in Irish society to ensure recognition and monetary reward for such work. Basic income is a transparent, efficient and affordable mechanism for ensuring such recognition and reward.

Basic income also lifts people out of poverty and the dependency mode of survival. In doing this, it also restores self-esteem and broadens horizons. Poor people, however, are not the only ones who should welcome a basic income system. Employers, for example, should welcome it because its introduction would mean they would not be in competition with the social welfare system. Since employees would not lose their basic income when taking a job, there would always be an incentive to take up employment.

Costing a basic income

During 2012 Healy et al presented an estimate for the cost of a basic income for Ireland. Using administrative data from the Census, social protection system and taxation system, the paper estimated a cost where payments were aligned to the existing social welfare payments (children = €32.30 per week; adults of working age = €188.00 per week; older people aged 66-80 = €230.30 per week; and older people aged 80+ = €240.30 per week). The paper estimated a total cost of €39.2 billion per annum for a basic income and outlined a requirement to collect a total of €41 billion in revenue to fund this. It is proposed that the revenue should be raised via a flat 45 per cent personal income tax and the continuance of the existing employers PRSI system (renamed a 'social solidarity fund'). It is important to remember that nobody would have an effective tax rate of 45 per cent in this system as they would always receive their full basic income and it would always be tax-free. Healy et al also outlined further directions for research in this area in the future and are likely to contribute future inputs into the evolving Irish and European basic income networks.

Ten reasons to introduce basic income

- It is work and employment friendly.
- It eliminates poverty traps and unemployment traps.
- It promotes equity and ensures that everyone receives at least the poverty threshold level of income.
- It spreads the burden of taxation more equitably.
- It treats men and women equally.
- It is simple and transparent.
- It is efficient in labour-market terms.
- It rewards types of work in the social economy that the market economy often ignores, e.g. home duties, caring, etc.
- It facilitates further education and training in the labour force.
- It faces up to the changes in the global economy.

Key policy priorities on income distribution

- If poverty rates are to fall in the years ahead, *Social Justice Ireland* believes that the following are required:
  - benchmarking of social welfare payments.
  - equity of social welfare rates.
  - adequate payments for children.
  - refundable tax credits.
  - a universal state pension.
  - a cost of disability payment.

Social Justice Ireland believes that in the period ahead Government and policy-makers generally should:

- Acknowledge that Ireland has an on-going poverty problem.
- Adopt targets aimed at reducing poverty among particular vulnerable groups such as children, lone parents, jobless households and those in social rented housing.
- Examine and support viable, alternative policy options aimed at giving priority to protecting vulnerable sectors of society.
- Carry out in-depth social impact assessments prior to implementing proposed policy initiatives that impact on the income and public services that many low income households depend on. This should include the poverty-proofing of all public policy initiatives.

- Provide substantial new measures to address long-term unemployment. This should include programmes aimed at re-training and re-skilling those at highest risk.
- Recognise the problem of the 'working poor'. Make tax credits refundable to address the situation of households in poverty which are headed by a person with a job.
- Introduce a cost of disability allowance to address poverty and social exclusion of people with a disability.
- Recognise the reality of poverty among migrants and adopt policies to assist this group. In addressing this issue also reform and increase the 'direct provision' allowances paid to asylum seekers.
- Accept that persistent poverty should be used as the primary indicator of poverty measurement and assist the CSO in allocating sufficient resources to collect this data.
- Move towards introducing a basic income system. No other approach has the capacity to ensure all members of society have sufficient income to live life with dignity.

4.

TAXATION

CORE POLICY OBJECTIVE: TAXATION

To collect sufficient taxes to ensure full participation in society for all, through a fair tax system in which those who have more, pay more, while those who have less, pay less.

The fiscal adjustments of recent years highlight the centrality of taxation in budget deliberations and to policy development at both macro and micro level. Taxation plays a key role in shaping Irish society through funding public services, supporting economic activity and redistributing resources to enhance the fairness of society. Consequently, it is crucial that clarity exist with regard to both the objectives and instruments aimed at achieving these goals. To ensure the creation of a fairer and more equitable tax system, policy development in this area should adhere to our core policy objective outlined above. In that regard, *Social Justice Ireland* is committed to increasing the level of detailed analysis and debate addressing this area.[30]

This chapter first considers Ireland's present taxation position and outlines the anticipated future taxation needs of the country. Given this, we outline approaches to reforming and broadening the tax base and proposals for building a fairer tax system. The issues addressed in this chapter include a number of the elements of *Social Justice Ireland's* Core Policy Framework (see Chapter 2) including: 'Ensure Macroeconomic Stability', 'Move Towards Just Taxation' and 'Enhance Social Protection'.

---

[30] We present our analysis in this chapter and in the accompanying annex 4.

Table 4.1: The changing nature of Ireland's tax revenue (€m)

	2007	2008	2009	2011	2012
Taxes on income and wealth					
Income tax	13563	13148	11801	14009	15201
Corporation tax	6393	5071	3889	3751	4216
Motor tax - households*	526	583	582	556	580
Other taxes	5	6	201	184	189
Fees - Petroleum & Minerals	5	10	2	4	4
Various Levies on income	411	414	373	317	300
Social Insurance	9053	9259	8924	7532	6786
Total taxes on income and wealth	**29957**	**28491**	**25771**	**26353**	**27276**
Taxes on capital					
Capital gains tax	3097	1424	545	416	414
Capital acquisitions tax	391	343	256	244	283
Pension Fund Levy	0	0	0	463	475
Total taxes on capital	**3488**	**1767**	**801**	**1123**	**1172**
Taxes on expenditure					
Custom duties	30	21	11	18	35
Excise duties including VRT	5993	5547	4909	4904	4809
Value added tax	14057	12842	10175	9588	10029
Rates	1267	1353	1471	1499	1435
Motor tax- businesses**	431	477	476	455	475
Stamps (excluding fee stamps)	3244	1763	1003	936	954
Other fees and levies	194	242	231	282	296
Total taxes on expenditure	**25216**	**22246**	**18275**	**17682**	**18032**
EU Taxes	**519**	**484**	**359**	**416**	**417**
Total Taxation***	**59180**	**52988**	**45207**	**45574**	**46897**
Total Taxation as % GDP#	**31.2**	**29.4**	**27.9**	**28.0**	**28.6**

Source: CSO on-line database tables N1222:T22 and N1202: T02.

Notes: *Motor tax is an estimate of the portion paid by households.

**Motor tax is an estimate of the portion paid by business.

*** Total taxation is the sum of the rows in bold.

Total taxation expressed as a% of published CSO GDP at current prices values.

Ireland's total tax-take: current and future needs

The need for a wider tax base is a lesson painfully learnt by Ireland during the past number of years. A disastrous combination of a naïve housing policy, a failed regulatory system and foolish fiscal policy and economic planning caused a collapse in exchequer revenues. It is only through a determined effort to reform Ireland's taxation system that these mistakes can be addressed and avoided in the future. The narrowness of the Irish tax base resulted in almost 25 per cent of tax revenues disappearing, plunging the exchequer and the country into a series of fiscal policy crises. As shown in table 4.1, tax revenues collapsed from over €59 billion in 2007 to €45 billion in 2009; it has since increased to almost €47 billion in 2011.

While a proportion of this decline in overall taxation revenue is related to the recession, a large part is structural and requires policy reform. As detailed in chapter 2, *Social Justice Ireland* believes that over the next few years policy should focus on increasing Ireland's tax-take to 34.9 per cent of GDP, a figure defined by Eurostat as 'low-tax' (Eurostat, 2008:5). Such increases are certainly feasible and are unlikely to have any significant negative impact on the economy in the long term. As a policy objective, Ireland should remain a low-tax economy, but not one incapable of adequately supporting the economic, social and infrastructural requirements necessary to support our society and complete our convergence with the rest of Europe.

Table 4.2: Projected current tax revenues, 2013-2016

	2013 €m	2014 €m	2015 €m	2016 €m
Customs	250	255		
Excise Duties*	4,720	4,815		
Capital Gains Tax	390	400		
Capital Acquis. Tax	405	380		
Stamp Duties	1,310	1,475		
Income Tax **	15,730	17,045		
Corporation Tax	4,355	4,380		
Value Added Tax	10,365	10,740		
Property / Local Tax	300	550		
Total#	37,825	40,040	42,285	43,985

Source: Department of Finance, Budget 2014: C15, C18.
Notes: * Excise duties include carbon tax and motor tax revenues.
　　　 **Including USC.
　　　 #These figures do not incorporate other tax sources including revenues to the social insurance fund and local government charges. These are incorporated into the totals reported in table 4.3 below.

Looking to the years immediately ahead, Budget 2014 provided some insight into the expected future shape of Ireland's current taxation revenues and this is shown in table 4.2. The Budget provided a detailed breakdown of current taxes for 2013 and 2014 and overall projections for 2015-2016. Over the next three years, assuming these policies are followed, overall current revenue will climb to almost €44 billion.

The Governments April 2013 *Stability Programme Update* also set out projections for the overall scale of the national tax-take (as a proportion of GDP).The document initially looked out to 2016 and then modelled a 'medium-term budgetary objective' out to 2019. These figures are reproduced in table 4.3 and have been used to calculate the cash value of the overall levels of tax revenue expected to be collected. While the estimates in the table are based on the tax-take figures from the *Stability Programme Update* and the national income projections in it, the documents provided limited details on the nature and composition of these figures.

It should be borne in mind that over recent years the Department's projections for the overall taxation burden have continually undershot the end-of-year outcomes. However, even taking the Department's projections as the likely outcome, Chart 4.1 highlights just how far below average EU levels (assuming these remain at a near record low of 35.7 per cent of GDP) and the *Social Justice Ireland* target (34.9 per cent of GDP) these taxation revenue figures are. Table 4.3's Tax Gap, the difference between the 34.9% benchmark and Government's planned level of taxation, stands at €5.5 billion in 2014 and averages at €6.7 billion per annum over the next six years.

Table 4.3: Ireland's projected total tax take and the tax gap, 2012-2019

Year	Tax as% GDP	Total Tax Receipts	The Tax Gap
2012	30.3%	49,569 7	,525
2013	31.0%	52,049	6,548
2014	31.7%	55,245	5,577
2015	31.9%	57,914	5,446
2016	31.5%	59,574	6,430
2017	31.3%	61,442	7,067
2018	31.2%	63,882	7,576
2019	30.9%	66,304	8,583

Source: Calculated from Department of Finance SPU (2013: 49, 50, 53).
Notes: * Total tax take = current taxes (see table 4.1 and 4.2) + Social Insurance Fund income + charges by local government.
  **The Tax Gap is calculated as the difference between the projected tax take and that which would be collected if total tax receipts were equal to 34.9% of GDP.

Chart 4.1: Ireland's Projected Taxation Levels to 2015 and comparisons with EU-27 averages and Social Justice Ireland target

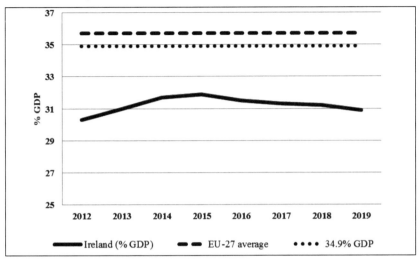

Source: Calculated from Eurostat (2013: 172) and Department of Finance SPU (2013: 49, 50, 53).
Note: The EU-27 average was 35.7% of GDP in 2011 and this value is used for all years.

Future taxation needs

Government decisions to raise or reduce overall taxation revenue needs to be linked to the demands on its resources. These demands depend on what Government is required to address or decides to pursue. The effects of the current economic crisis, and the way it has been handled, carry significant implications for our future taxation needs. The rapid increase in our national debt, driven by the need to borrow both to replace disappearing taxation revenues and to fund emergency 'investments' in the failing commercial banks, has increased the on-going annual costs associated with servicing the national debt.

National debt has increased from a level of 25 per cent of GDP in 2007 - low by international standards - to 124 per cent of GDP in 2013, a figure which the Department of Finance expects will represent it peak (2013: C19). Despite favourable lending rates and payback terms, there remains a recurring cost to service this large national debt – costs which have to be financed by current taxation revenues. Furthermore, the erosion of the National Pension Reserve Fund (NPRF) through using it to fund various bank rescues (over €20 billion) has transferred the liability for future public sector pensions onto future exchequer expenditure. Although there may be some return from a number of the rescued banks, it will be small relative to the funds committed and therefore will require additional taxation resources.

These new future taxation needs are in addition to those that already exist for funding local government, repairing and modernising our water infrastructure, paying for the health and pension needs of an ageing population, paying EU contributions and funding any pollution reducing environmental initiatives that are required by European and International agreements. Collectively, they mean that Ireland's overall level of taxation will have to rise significantly in the years to come – a reality Irish society and the political system need to begin to seriously address.

As an organisation that has highlighted the obvious implications of these long-terms trends for some time, *Social Justice Ireland* welcomes the development over the past year where the Government published a section of the April 2013 SPU focused on the 'long-term sustainability of public finances'.

Research by Bennett et al (2003), the OECD (2008) and the ESRI (2010) have all provided some insight into future exchequer demands associated with healthcare and pensions in Ireland in the decades to come. The Department of Finance drew on the recent European Commission publication entitled '*The 2012 Ageing Report: Economic and budgetary projections for the EU27 Member States (2010-2060)*'. Table 4.4 summarises some of its baseline projections for Ireland. Over that period the report anticipates an increase in the elderly population (65 years +) from 11.5 per cent of the population in 2010 to 21.9 per cent in 2060. Over the same period, the proportion of those of working age will decline as a percentage of the population and the old-age dependency ratio will increase from approximately six people of working age for every elderly person today to three for every elderly person in 2060 (EU Commission, 2012: 399-401; Department of Finance, 2013:42).

While these increases imply a range of necessary policy initiatives in the decades to come, there is an inevitability that an overall higher level of taxation will have to be collected.

Table 4.4: Projected Age Related Expenditure, as % GDP 2010-2060

Expenditure areas	2010	2020	2030	2040	2050	2060
Total pensions	9.3	11.5	11.4	12.5	14.3	15.0
of which:						
Social security pensions	*7.5*	*9.0*	*9.0*	*10.0*	*11.4*	*11.7*
Old-age /early pensions	*5.6*	*7.0*	*7.0*	*7.9*	*9.4*	*9.7*
Other pensions	*1.9*	*1.9*	*1.9*	*2.0*	*2.0*	*2.0*
Public Service pensions	*1.8*	*2.5*	*2.4*	*2.5*	*2.9*	*3.3*
Health care	7.3	7.2	7.7	8.1	8.2	8.3
Long-term care	1.1	1.3	1.5	1.9	2.3	2.6
Education	6.3	7.1	6.5	6.0	6.5	6.4
Other age-related (JA etc)	2.6	3.1	2.0	1.5	1.4	1.3
Total age-related spending	26.6	30.2	29.1	30.0	32.7	33.6

Source: Department of Finance (2013:43) and European Commission (2012:400)

Is a higher tax-take problematic?

Suggesting that any country's tax take should increase normally produces negative responses. People think first of their incomes and increases in income tax, rather than more broadly of reforms to the tax base. Furthermore, proposals that taxation should increase are often rejected with suggestions that they would undermine economic growth. However, a review of the performance of a number of economies over recent years sheds a different light on this issue. For example, in the years prior to the current international economic crisis, Britain achieved low unemployment and higher levels of growth compared to other EU countries (OECD, 2004). These were achieved simultaneously with increases in its tax/GDP ratio. In 1994 this stood at 33.7 per cent and by 2004 it had increased 2.3 percentage points to 36.0 per cent of GDP (it stands at 36.1 per cent in the latest figure, see Annex 4). Furthermore, in his March 2004 Budget the then British Chancellor Gordon Brown indicated that this ratio would reach 38.3 per cent of GDP in 2008-09 (2004:262); it subsequently reached 37.6 per cent in 2008 before the economic crisis took hold. His announcement of these increases was not met with predictions of economic ruin or doom for Britain and its economic growth remained high compared to other EU countries (IMF, 2004 & 2008).

Taxation and competitiveness

Another argument made against increases in Ireland's overall taxation levels is that it will undermine competitiveness. However, the suggestion that higher levels of taxation would damage our position relative to other countries is not supported by international studies of competitiveness. Annually the World Economic Forum publishes a *Global Competitiveness Report* ranking the most competitive economies across the world.[31]

Table 4.5 outlines the top fifteen economies in this index for 2013-14 as well as the ranking for Ireland (which comes 28th). It also presents the difference between the size of the tax-take in these, the most competitive, economies in the world, and Ireland, for 2012.[32]

Only two of the top fifteen countries, for which there is data available, report a lower taxation level than Ireland: Switzerland and the US. All the other leading competitive economies collect a greater proportion of national income in taxation. Over time Ireland's position on this index has varied, most recently rising from 31st to 28th, although in previous years Ireland had been in 22nd position. When Ireland has slipped back the reasons stated for Ireland's loss of competitiveness included decreases in economic growth and fiscal stability, poor performances by public institutions and a decline in the technological competitiveness of the economy (WEF, 2003: xv; 2008:193; 2011: 25-26; 210-211). Interestingly, a major factor in that decline is related to underinvestment in state funded areas: education; research; infrastructure; and broadband connectivity. Each of these areas is dependent on taxation revenue and they have been highlighted by the report as necessary areas of investment to achieve enhanced competitiveness.[33] As such, lower taxes do not feature as a significant priority; rather it is increased and targeted efficient government spending.

A similar point was expressed by the Nobel Prize winning economist Professor Joseph Stiglitz while visiting Ireland in June 2004. Commenting on Ireland's long-term development prospects, he stated that "all the evidence is that the low tax, low service strategy for attracting investment is short-sighted" and that "far more

---

[31] Competitiveness is measured across 12 pillars including: institutions, infrastructure, macroeconomic environment, health and primary education, higher education and training, goods markets efficiency, labour market efficiency, financial market development, technological readiness, market size, business sophistication and innovation. See WEF (2013: 541-545) for further details on how these are measured.

[32] This analysis updates that first produced by Collins (2004: 15-18).

[33] A similar conclusion was reached in another international competitiveness study by the International Institute for Management Development (2007).

important in terms of attracting good businesses is the quality of education, infrastructure and services." Professor Stiglitz, who chaired President Clinton's Council of Economic Advisors, added that "low tax was not the critical factor in the Republic's economic development and it is now becoming an impediment".[34]

Table 4.5: Differences in taxation levels between the world's 15 most competitive economies and Ireland.

Competitiveness Rank	Country	Taxation level versus Ireland
1	Switzerland	-0.1
2	Singapore	*not available*
3	Finland	+15.8
4	Germany	+9.3
5	United States	-4.0
6	Sweden	+16.0
7	Hong Kong SAR	*not available*
8	Netherlands	+10.3
9	Japan	+0.3
10	United Kingdom	+6.9
11	Norway	+13.9
12	Taiwan, China	*not available*
13	Qatar	*not available*
14	Canada	+2.4
15	Denmark	+19.7
28	**IRELAND**	-

Source: World Economic Forum (2013:16)
Notes: a) Taxation data from OECD (2013) for the year 2012 except for the Netherlands and Japan where the taxation data is for 2011.
 b) For some countries comparable data is *not available*.
 c) The OECD's estimate for Ireland in 2010 = 28.283 per cent of GDP

---

[34] In an interview with John McManus, Irish Times, June 2nd 2004.

Reforming and broadening the tax base

Social Justice Ireland believes that there is merit in developing a tax package which places less emphasis on taxing people and organisations on what they earn by their own useful work and enterprise, or on the value they add or on what they contribute to the common good. Rather, the tax that people and organisations should be required to pay should be based more on the value they subtract by their use of common resources. Whatever changes are made should also be guided by the need to build a fairer taxation system, one which adheres to our already stated core policy objective.

There are a number of approaches available to Government in reforming the tax base. Recent Budgets have made some progress in addressing some of these issues while the 2009 Commission on Taxation Report highlighted many areas that require further reform. A short review of the areas we consider a priority are presented below across the following subsections:

> *Tax Expenditures / Tax Reliefs*
> *Minimum Effective Tax Rates for Higher Earners*
> *Corporation Taxes*
> *Site Value Tax*
> *Second Homes*
> *Taxing Windfall Gains*
> *Financial Transactions Tax*
> *Carbon Taxes*

Tax Expenditures / Tax Reliefs

A significant outcome from the Commission on Taxation is contained in part eight of its Report which details all the tax breaks (or "tax expenditures" as they are referred to officially). Subsequently, two members of the Commission produced a detailed report for the Trinity College Policy Institute which offered further insight into this issue (Collins and Walsh, 2010). Since then, the annual reporting of the costs of tax expenditures has improved considerably with much more details than in the past being published in the annual Revenue Commissioners Statistical Report.

The most recent tax expenditure data was published in 2012 by the Revenue Commissioners and covers the tax year 2010 (2012:17-24). In summarising this data, Collins (2013:15-19) noted that the top 30 tax breaks involve revenue forgone of €17 billion. Added to this were the tax break costs of legacy property tax reliefs (€386 million in 2010) and a series of smaller tax expenditures for which the Revenue do not have any data estimates. In their 2010 review, Collins and Walsh (2010) found that 32 per cent of the total number of tax breaks were lacking cost estimates.

Some progress has been made in addressing and reforming these tax breaks in recent Budgets, and we welcome this progress. However, despite this, recent Budgets and Finance Bills have introduced new tax breaks targeted at high earning multinational executives and research and development schemes and extended tax breaks for film production and the refurbishment of older building in urban areas. For the most part, there has been no or limited accompanying documentation evaluating the cost, distributive impacts or appropriateness of these proposals.

Both the Commission on Taxation (2009:230) and Collins and Walsh (2010:20-21) have also highlighted and detailed the need for new methods for evaluation/introducing tax reliefs. We strongly welcome these proposals, which are similar to the proposals the directors of *Social Justice Ireland* made to the Commission in written and oral submissions. The proposals focus on prior evaluation of the costs and benefits of any proposed expenditure, the need to collect detailed information on each expenditure, the introduction of time limits for expenditures, the creation of an annual tax expenditures report as part of the Budget process and the regular scrutiny of this area by an Oireachtas committee. We believe that these proposals should be adopted as part of the necessary reform of this area.

There is further potential to reduce the cost in this area. Recipients of these tax expenditures use them to reduce their tax bills, so it needs to be clearly understood that this is tax which is being forgone. *Social Justice Ireland* has highlighted a number of these reforms in our pre-Budget Policy Briefings, *Budget Choices*, and will further address this issue in advance of Budget 2015. During the past year we have highlighted the need to reform the most expensive tax break, which is associated with pensions. In a report commissioned by *Social Justice Ireland*, Larragy showed that standard rating the pension tax break, combined with a small number of other adjustments, would provide sufficient revenue to fund the introduction of a universal pension for all aged over 65 years (Larragy, 2013).

Social Justice Ireland believes that reforming the tax break system would make the tax system fairer. It would also provide substantial additional resources which would contribute to raising the overall tax take towards the modest and realistic target we have outlined earlier.

Minimum Effective Tax Rates for Higher Earners

The suggestion that it is the better-off who principally gain from the provision of tax exemption schemes is underscored by a series of reports published by the Revenue Commissioners entitled *Effective Tax Rates for High Earning Individuals* and

Analysis of High Income Individuals' Restriction. These reports provided details of the Revenue's assessment of the top earners in Ireland and the rates of effective taxation they incur.[35] The reports led to the introduction of a minimum 20 per cent effective tax rate as part of the 2006 and 2007 Finance Acts for all those with incomes in excess of €500,000. Subsequently, Budgets have revised up the minimum effective rate and revised down the income threshold from where it applies – reforms we have welcomed as necessary and long-overdue. Most recently, the 2010 Finance Bill introduced a requirement that all earners above €400,000 pay a minimum effective rate of tax of 30 per cent. It also reduced from €250,000 to €125,000 the income threshold where restrictions on the use of tax expenditures to decrease income tax liabilities commence.

The documentation accompanying Budget 2014 included the latest Revenue Commissioners analysis of the operation of these new rules using data for 2011 (Revenue Commissioners, 2013). Table 4.6 gives the findings of that analysis for 286 individuals with income in excess of €400,000. The report also includes information on the distribution of effective income tax rates among the 857 earners with incomes between €125,000 and €400,000.

Table 4.6: The Distribution of Effective Income Tax Rates among those earning in excess of €125,000 in 2011 (% of total)

Effective Income Tax Rate	Individuals with incomes of €400,000+	Individuals with incomes of €125,000 - €400,000
0%-5%	0%	1.63%
5% < 10%	0%	10.74%
10% < 15%	0%	17.62%
15% < 20%	0%	19.72%
20% < 25%	0%	26.02%
25% < 30%	20.63%	23.45%
30% < 35%	79.02%	0.70%
35%< 40%	0%	0.12%
> 40%	0.35%	0%
Total Cases	**286**	**857**

Source: Revenue Commissioners (2013).
Notes: Effective rates are for income taxation only as the reliefs are off-set against these liabilities. They do not include tax paid under the USC and PRSI.

---

[35] The effective taxation rate is calculated as the percentage of the individual's total pre-tax income that is liable to income tax and that is paid in taxation.

Social Justice Ireland welcomed the introduction of this scheme which marked a major improvement in the fairness of the tax system. The published data indicate that is seems to be working well for those above an income of €400,000. However, between €125,000 and €400,000 there are still surprisingly low effective income taxation rates being reported; half of these individuals pay less than 20 per cent of their income in income taxes. Such an outcome may be better than in the past, but it still has some way to go to reflect a situation where a fair contribution is being paid.

The report also includes average effective taxation rates paid by these individuals where both income taxes and USC are included. It states that the average effective tax rate faced by earners above €400,000 in 2011 was 39.7 per cent, equivalent to the amount of income tax and USC paid by a single PAYE worker with a gross income of €130,000 in that year. Similarly, the average income tax and USC effective tax rate faced by people earning between €125,000 - €400,000 in 2011 (28.8 per cent) was equivalent to the amount of income tax paid by a single PAYE worker with a gross income of approximately €55,000 in that year. The contrast in these income levels for the same overall rate of income taxation brings into question the fairness of the taxation system as a whole.

Social Justice Ireland believes that it is important that Government continues to raise the minimum effective tax rate so that it is in-line with that faced by PAYE earners on equivalent high-income levels. Following Budget 2014 a single individual on an income of €125,000 gross will pay an income tax and USC effective tax rate of 39.3 per cent; a figure which suggests that the minimum threshold for high earners has potential to adjust upwards over the next few years. We also believe that Government should reform the High Income Individuals' Restriction so that all tax expenditures are included within it. The restriction currently does not apply to all tax breaks individuals avail of, including pension contributions. This should change in Budget 2015.

Corporation Taxes

In Budget 2003 the standard rate of corporation tax was reduced from 16 per cent to 12.5 per cent, at a full year cost of €305m. This followed another reduction in 2002, which had brought the rate down from 20 per cent to 16 per cent. At the time the total cost in lost revenue to the exchequer of these two reductions was estimated at over €650m per annum. Serious questions remain concerning the advisability of pursuing this policy approach. Ireland's corporation tax rate is now considerably below the corresponding rates in most of Europe. Windfall profits are flowing to a sector that is already extremely profitable. Furthermore, Ireland's low rate of corporation tax is being abused by multi-national companies which channel profits through units, often very small units, in Ireland to avail of the lower Irish rate of tax. In many cases this is happening at a cost to fellow EU members' exchequers and with little benefit in terms of jobs and additional real economic activity in Ireland. Understandably, Ireland is coming under increasing pressure to reform this system.

There is no substantive evidence in any of the relevant literature to support the contention that corporations would leave if the corporate tax rate was higher – at 17.5 per cent for example. Furthermore, the logic of having a uniform rate of corporation tax for all sectors is questionable. David Begg of ICTU has stated, "there is no advantage in having a uniform rate of 12.5 per cent corporation tax applicable to hotels and banks as well as to manufacturing industry" (2003:12). In the last few years there has been some improvement in this situation with special, and higher, tax rates being charged on natural resource industries and non-trading income. *Social Justice Ireland* welcomes this as an overdue step in the right direction.

As the European Union expands corporation tax competition is likely to intensify. Already Bulgaria has set its rate at 10 per cent and others continue to reduce their headline rates and provide incentives targeted at reducing the effective corporate tax rate. Over the next decade Ireland will be forced to either ignore tax rates as a significant attraction/retention policy for foreign investors, which would be a major change in industrial policy, or to follow suit, despite the exchequer costs, and compete by further cutting corporation tax. Sweeney has warned of a dangerous situation in which Ireland could end up "leading the race to the bottom" (2004:59). The costs of such a move, in lost exchequer income, would be enormous.

An alternative direction could be to agree a minimum effective rate for all EU countries. Given the international nature of company investment, these taxes are fundamentally different from internal taxes and the benefits of a European agreement which would set a minimum effective rate are obvious. They include protecting Ireland's already low rate from being driven down even lower, protecting the jobs in industries which might move to lower taxing countries and protecting the revenue generated for the exchequer by corporate taxes. *Social Justice Ireland* believes that an EU wide agreement on a minimum effective rate of corporation tax should be negotiated and this could evolve from the current discussions around a Common Consolidated Corporate Tax Base (CCCTB). *Social Justice Ireland* believes that the minimum rate should be set well below the 2012 EU-27 average headline rate of 23.2 per cent but above the existing low Irish level.[36] A headline rate of 17.5 per cent and a minimum effective rate of 10 per cent seem appropriate. This reform would simultaneously maintain Ireland's low corporate tax position and provide additional revenues to the exchequer. Were such a rate in place in Ireland in 2013, corporate tax income would have been between €1.2 billion and €1.7 billion higher – a significant sum given the current economic challenges.

---

[36] Data from Eurostat (2013:38).

The recent attention given to the abuses of the international corporate tax system, whereby some highly profitable multinational are paying very small amounts of profit taxes and in some cases none, further strengthens the need to address effective corporate tax rates. *Social Justice Ireland* welcomes the attention the OECD is now giving this issue via its Base Erosion and Profit Shifting (BEPS) project (OECD, 2013). It is important that this work leads to the emergence of a transparent international corporate finance and corporate taxation system where multinational firms pay a reasonable and credible effective corporate tax rate.

Site Value Tax

Taxes on wealth are minimal in Ireland. Revenue is negligible from capital acquisitions tax (CAT) because it has a very high threshold in respect of bequests and gifts within families and the rates of tax on transfers of family farms and firms are very generous (see tax revenue tables at the start of this chapter). While recent increases in the rate of CAT are welcome, the likely future revenue from this area remains limited given the tax's current structure. The requirement, as part of the EU/IMF/ECB bailout agreement, to introduce a recurring property tax led Government in Budget 2012 to introduce an unfairly structured flat €100 per annum household charge and a value based Local Property Tax in Budget 2013. While we welcome the overdue need to extend the tax base to include a recurring revenue source from property, we believe that a Site Value Tax, also known as a Land Rent Tax, would be a more appropriate and fairer approach.

In previous editions of this publication we have reviewed this proposal in greater detail.[37] There has also been a number of research papers published on this issue over the past decade.[38] Overall they point towards a recurring site value tax that is fairer and more efficient than other alternatives. *Social Justice Ireland* believes that the introduction of a site value tax would be a better alternative than the current Government value based local property tax. A site value tax would lead to more efficient land use within the structure of social, environmental and economic goals embodied in planning and other legislation.

Second Homes

A feature of the housing boom of the last decade was the rapid increase in ownership of holiday homes and second homes. For the most part these homes remain empty for at least nine months of the year. It is a paradox that many were built at the same time as the rapid increases in housing waiting lists (see chapter 7).

---

[37] See for example the 2013 edition of the Socio-Economic Review pages 132-134.
[38] These include O'Siochru (2004:23-57), Dunne (2004:93-122), Chambers of Commerce of Ireland (2004), Collins and Larragy (2011), and O'Siochru (2012).

Results from Census 2011 indicated that since 2006 there had been a 19 per cent increase in the number of holiday homes, with numbers rising from 49,789 in 2006 to 59,395 in 2011. The Census also found that overall, the number of vacant houses on Census night was 168,427 (April 2011) – some of which are also likely to be second homes.

What is often overlooked when the second home issue is being discussed is that the infrastructure to support these houses is substantially subsidised by the taxpayer. Roads, water, sewage and electricity infrastructure are just part of this subsidy which goes, by definition, to those who are already better off as they can afford these second homes in the first place. *Social Justice Ireland* supports the views of the ESRI (2003) and the Indecon report (2005:183-186; 189-190) on this issue. We believe that people purchasing second houses should have to pay these full infrastructural costs, much of which is currently borne by society through the Exchequer and local authorities. There is something perverse in the fact that the taxpayer should be providing substantial subsidies to the owners of these unoccupied houses at a time when so many people do not have basic adequate accommodation.

The introduction of the Non Principal Private Residence (NPPR) charge in 2009 was a welcome step forward. However, notwithstanding subsequent increases, the charge was very low relative to the previous and on-going benefits that are derived from these properties. It stood at €200 in 2013 and was abolished under the 2014 Local Government Reform Act.

While second homes are liable for the local property tax, as are all homes, *Social Justice Ireland* believes that second homes should be required to make a further annual contribution in respect of the additional benefits these investment properties receive. We believe that Government should re-introduce this charge and that it should be further increased and retained as a separate substantial second homes payment. An annual charge of €500 would seem reasonable and would provide additional revenue to local government of approximately €170 million per annum.

Taxing Windfall Gains

The vast profits made by property speculators on the rezoning of land by local authorities was a particularly undesirable feature of the recent economic boom. For some time *Social Justice Ireland* has called for a substantial tax to be imposed on the profits earned from such decisions. While this may not be an issue in Ireland at this time of austerity, it is best to make the system fairer before any further unearned gains are reaped by speculators. Re-zonings are made by elected representatives supposedly in the interest of society generally. It therefore seems appropriate that a sizeable proportion of the windfall gains they generate should be made available to local authorities and used to address the ongoing housing problems they face (see chapter 7). In this regard, *Social Justice Ireland* welcomes the decision to put such a tax in place. The windfall tax level of 80 per cent is appropriate and, as table 4.7 illustrates, this still leaves speculators and land owners with substantial profits from these rezoning decisions. The profit from this process should be used to fund local authorities. We fear that when the property market recovers in years to come there will be lobbying for this tax to be reduced or removed. Government should anticipate and resist this.

Table 4.7: Illustrative examples of the Operation of an 80% Windfall Gain Tax on Rezoned Land

Agricultural Land Value	Rezoned Value	Profit	Tax @ 80%	Post-Tax Profit	Profit as % Original Value
€50,000	€400,000	€350,000	€280,000	€70,000	140%
€100,000	€800,000	€700,000	€560,000	€140,000	140%
€200,000	€1,600,000	€1,400,000	€1,120,000	€280,000	140%
€500,000	€4,000,000	€3,500,000	€2,800,000	€700,000	140%
€1,000,000	€8,000,000	€7,000,000	€5,600,000	€1,400,000	140%

Note: Calculations assume an eight-fold increase on the agricultural land value upon rezoning.

Financial Transactions Tax

As the international economic chaos of the past few years has shown, the world is now increasingly linked via millions of legitimate, speculative and opportunistic financial transactions. Similarly, global currency trading increased sharply throughout recent decades. It is estimated that a very high proportion of all financial transactions traded are speculative currency transactions which are completely free of taxation.

An insight into the scale of these transactions is provided by the Bank for International Settlements (BIS) Triennial Central Bank Survey of Foreign Exchange and Derivatives Market Activity (December 2013). The key findings from that report were:

* In April 2013 the average daily turnover in global foreign exchange markets was US$5.3 trillion; an increase of almost 35 per cent since 2010 and 331 per cent since 2001.

- The major components of these activities were: $2.046 trillion in spot transactions, $680 billion in outright forwards, $2.228 trillion in foreign exchange swaps, $54 billion currency swaps, and $337 billion in foreign exchange options and other products.
- 58 per cent of trades were cross-border and 42 per cent local.
- The vast majority of trades involved four currencies: US Dollar, Euro, Japanese Yen and Pound Sterling.
- Most of this activity (60 per cent) occurred in the US and UK.
- The estimated daily foreign exchange turnover for Ireland was US$11 billion.

The Tobin tax, first proposed by the Nobel Prize winner James Tobin, is a progressive tax, designed to target only those profiting from speculation. It is levied at a very small rate on all transactions but given the scale of these transactions globally, it has the ability to raise significant funds.

Social Justice Ireland regrets that to date Government has not committed to supporting recent European moves to introduce a Financial Transactions Tax (FTT) or Tobin Tax. In September 2011 the EU Commission proposed an FTT and subsequently updated this proposal in February 2013. It suggested that an FTT would be levied on transactions between financial institutions when at least one party to the transaction is located in the EU. The exchange of shares and bonds would be taxed at a rate of 0.1% and derivative contracts, at an even lower rate of 0.01%. The rates are minimums as countries with the EU retain the right to set individual tax rates and could choose higher levels if desired. Overall the Commission projects that the FTT would raise €30-35 billion per annum.

To date 11 of the 27 EU member states have signed up to this tax and *Social Justice Ireland* believes that Ireland should also join this group. In our opinion, the tax offers the dual benefit of dampening needless and often reckless financial speculation and generating significant funds. We believe that the revenue generated by this tax should be used for national economic and social development and international development co-operation purposes, in particular assisting Ireland and other developed countries to fund overseas aid and reach the UN ODA target (see chapter 13). According to the United Nations, the amount of annual income raised from a Tobin tax would be enough to guarantee to every citizen of the world basic access to water, food, shelter, health and education. Therefore, this tax has the potential to wipe out the worst forms of material poverty throughout the world.

Social Justice Ireland believes that the time has come for Ireland to support the introduction of a financial transactions tax.

Carbon Taxes

Budget 2010 announced the long-overdue introduction of a carbon tax. This had been promised in Budget 2003 and committed to in the *National Climate Change Strategy* (2007). The tax has been structured along the lines of the proposal from the Commission on Taxation (2009: 325-372) and is linked to the price of carbon credits which was set at an initial rate of €15 per tonne of CO_2 and subsequently increased in Budget 2012 to €20 per tonne. Budget 2013 extended the tax to cover solid fuels on a phased basis from May 2013 with the full tax applying from May 2014. Products are taxed based on the level of the emissions they create.

While *Social Justice Ireland* welcomed the introduction of this tax, it regrets the lack of accompanying measures to protect those most affected by it, in particular low income households and rural dwellers. *Social Justice Ireland* believes that as the tax increases the Government should be more specific in defining how it will assist these households. Furthermore, there is a danger that given the difficult fiscal circumstances Ireland now finds itself in, any increases in the carbon tax over the next few years may divert from the original intention of encouraging behavioural change, towards a focus on raising revenue.

Building a fairer taxation system

The need for fairness in the tax system was clearly recognised in the first report of the Commission on Taxation more than 25 years ago. It stated:

"...in our recommendations the spirit of equity is the first and most important consideration. Departures from equity must be clearly justified by reference to the needs of economic development or to avoid imposing unreasonable compliance costs on individuals or high administrative costs on the Revenue Commissioners." (1982:29)

The need for fairness is just as obvious today and *Social Justice Ireland* believes that this should be a central objective of the current reform of the taxation system. While we recognise that many of the reforms below can only occur once the current crisis in the exchequer's finances has been resolved, we include them here because they represent necessary reforms that would greatly enhance the fairness of Ireland's taxation system. This section is structured in six parts:

Standard rating discretionary tax expenditures
Keeping the minimum wage out of the tax net
Favouring changes to tax credits rather than tax rates and tax bands
Introducing Refundable Tax Credits
Reforming individualisation
Making the taxation system simpler

Standard rating discretionary tax expenditures

Making all discretionary tax reliefs/expenditures only available at the standard 20 per cent rate would represent a crucial step towards achieving a fairer tax system. If there is a legitimate case for making a tax relief/expenditure available, then it should be made available in the same way to all. It is inequitable that people on higher incomes should be able to claim certain tax reliefs at their top marginal tax rates while people with less income are restricted to claim benefit for the same relief at the lower standard rate of 20 per cent. The standard rating of tax expenditures, otherwise known as reliefs, offers the potential to simultaneously make the tax system fairer and fund the necessary developments they are designed to stimulate without any significant macroeconomic implications. [39]

Recent Budgets have made substantial progress towards achieving this objective and we welcome these developments. However, there remains considerable potential to introduce further reform. In a recent paper, Collins (2013:17) reported that in 2009 (the latest Revenue data available) there were €2.3 billion of tax breaks made available at the marginal rate and that if these were standardised the estimated saving was just over €1 billion.

Keeping the minimum wage out of the tax net

The decision by the Minister for Finance to remove those on the minimum wage from the tax net was a major achievement of Budget 2005. This had an important impact on the growing numbers of working-poor and addressed an issue with which *Social Justice Ireland* is highly concerned.

The fiscal and economic crisis of 2008-13 lead to Government reversing this policy, first via the income levy in second Budget 2009, then via the Universal Social Charge (USC) in Budget 2011 and via a PRSI increase in Budget 2013. Since Budget 2012 the USC is charged on all the income of those who earn more than €10,036 per annum. Using the unadjusted minimum wage of €8.65 per hour, the threshold implies that a low-income worker on the minimum wage and working more than 23 hours per week (earning €199 per week) is subject to the tax. *Social Justice Ireland* believes that this threshold is far too low and unnecessarily depresses the income and living standards of the working poor. Budget 2012 raised the entry point for the USC from €4,004 per annum to €10,036 per annum, a move welcomed by Social *Justice Ireland.* However, the imposition of the USC at such low income levels raises a very small amount of funds for the exchequer. Forthcoming Budgets should continue to raise the point at which the USC commences and in the years to come, as more resources become available to the Exchequer, *Social Justice Ireland* will urge Government to restore the policy of keeping the minimum wage fully outside the tax net.

---

[39] See O'Toole and Cahill (2006:215) who also reach this conclusion.

Favouring changes to tax credits rather than tax rates and tax bands

Social Justice Ireland believes that any future income tax changes should be focused on changes to tax credits rather than tax bands and tax rates. This is more desirable in the context of achieving fairness in the taxation system.

To emphasise this point, table 4.8 presents a comparison of reforms to tax rates, tax credits and tax bands. In all cases the policy examined would carry a full year cost of approximately €205 million.[40] The reforms examined are for changes to the 2014 income taxation system and are:

- a decrease in the top tax rate from 41% to 40% (full year cost €205 million)
- an increase in the personal tax credit of €108 with commensurate increases in couple, widowed parents and lone parents credit (full year cost €205 million)
- an increase in the standard rate band (20% tax band) of €1,350 (full year cost €202.5 million)

Table 4.8: Comparing gains under three possible income tax reforms:
tax rates, tax credits and tax bands (€)

Gross Income	€15,000	€25,000	€50,000	€75,000	€100,000	€125,000
Decrease in the top tax rate from 41% to 40% (full year cost €205 million)						
Single earner	0	0	172	422	672	922
Couple 1 earner	0	0	82	332	582	832
Couple 2 earners	0	0	0	94	344	594
Increase in the personal tax credit of €108 (full year cost €205 million)						
Single earner	0	108	108	108	108	108
Couple 1 earner	0	50	216	216	216	216
Couple 2 earners	0	0	216	216	216	216
Increase in the standard rate band of €1,350 (full year cost €202.5 million)						
Single earner	0	0	283.50	283.50	283.50	283.50
Couple 1 earner	0	0	283.50	283.50	283.50	283.50
Couple 2 earners	0	0	0	567.00	567.00	567.00

Notes: All workers are assumed to be PAYE workers. For couples with 2 earners the income is assumed to be split 65%/35%. Cost estimates are based on the latest available Department of Finance income taxation ready reckoner and are applied to the structure of the 2014 income taxation system. The increase in the personal tax credit assumes a commensurate increase in the couple, widowed parents and lone parent's credit.

---

[40] The cost estimates are based on the most recent income tax ready reckoner available from the Department of Finance (Budget 2012). The cost estimates are unlikely to be significantly different currently.

Although all of the income taxation options cost the same, they each carry different effects on the income distribution. The fairest outcome is achieved by increasing tax credits. It provides the same value to all taxpayers across the income distribution provided they are earning sufficient to pay more than €108 in income taxes. Therefore, the increased income received by a single earner on €25,000 and on €125,000 is the same – an extra €108.

However, a decrease in the top tax rate only benefits those paying tax at that rate. Therefore, the single earner on €25,000 gains nothing from this change while those on €50,000 gain €172 per annum and those on €100,000 gain €672 per annum. The higher the income, the greater the gain. This is the least fair outcome of the three examined.

Changing the entry point to the top tax rate (i.e. increasing the standard rate band) also provides gains which are skewed towards higher incomes. A single earner on €25,000 gains nothing from this reform and it is only from individual incomes of €34,150 plus, and couples with 2 earners with gross income above €68,300, that gains are experienced. Above these thresholds the gains are the same for all single earners and couples.

In terms of fairness, changing tax credits is the best option. Government should always take this option when it has money available to reduce income taxes.

Introducing refundable tax credits

The move from tax allowances to tax credits was completed in Budget 2001. This was a very welcome change because it put in place a system that had been advocated for a long time by a range of groups. One problem persists however. If a low income worker does not earn enough to use up his or her full tax credit then he or she will not benefit from any tax reductions introduced by government in its annual budget.

Making tax credits refundable would be a simple solution to this problem. It would mean that the part of the tax credit that an employee did not benefit from would be "refunded" to him/her by the state.

The major advantage of making tax credits refundable lies in addressing the disincentives currently associated with low-paid employment. The main beneficiaries of refundable tax credits would be low-paid employees (full-time and part-time). Chart 4.2 displays the impacts of the introduction of this policy across various gross income levels. It clearly shows that all of the benefits from introducing this policy would go directly to those on the lowest incomes.

Chart 4.2: How much better off would people be if tax credits were made refundable?

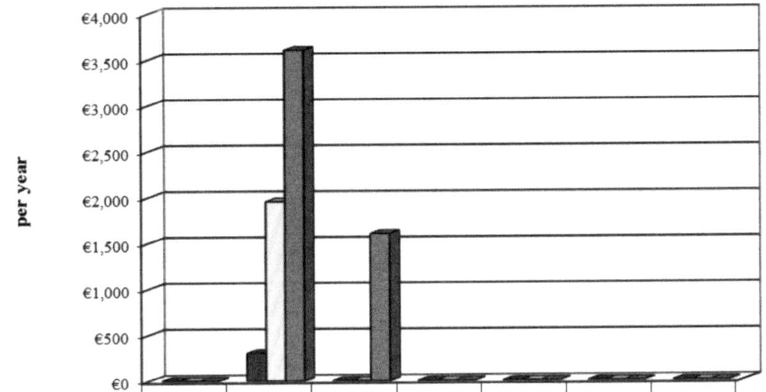

	Unemp	€15,000	€25,000	€50,000	€75,000	€100,000	€125,000
■Single	-	300	-	-	-	-	-
□Couple 1 Earner*	-	1,950	-	-	-	-	-
■Couple 2 Earners*	-	3,600	1,600	-	-	-	-

Note: * Except where unemployed as there is no earner

With regard to administering this reform, the central idea recognises that most people with regular incomes and jobs would not receive a cash refund of their tax credit because their incomes are too high. They would simply benefit from the tax credit as a reduction in their tax bill. Therefore, as chart 4.2 shows, no change is proposed for these people and they would continue to pay tax via their employers, based on their net liability after deduction of tax credits by their employers on behalf of the Revenue Commissioners. For other people on low or irregular incomes, the refundable tax credit could be paid via a refund by the Revenue at the end of the tax year. Following the introduction of refundable tax credits, all subsequent increases in the level of the tax credit would be of equal value to all employees.

To illustrate the benefits of this approach, charts 4.3 and 4.4 compare the effects of a €100 increase in the personal tax credit before and after the introduction of refundable tax credits. Chart 4.3 shows the effect as the system is currently structured – an increase of €100 in credits, but these are not refundable. It shows that the gains are allocated equally to all categories of earners above €50,000. However, there is no benefit for those workers whose earnings are not in the tax net.

Chart 4.4 shows how the benefits of a €100 a year increase in personal tax credits would be distributed under a system of refundable tax credits. This simulation demonstrates the equity attached to using the tax-credit instrument to distribute budgetary taxation changes. The benefit to all categories of income earners (single/couple, one-earner/couple, dual-earners) is the same. Consequently, in relative terms, those earners at the bottom of the distribution do best.

Chart 4.3: How much better off would people be if tax credits were increased by €100 per person?

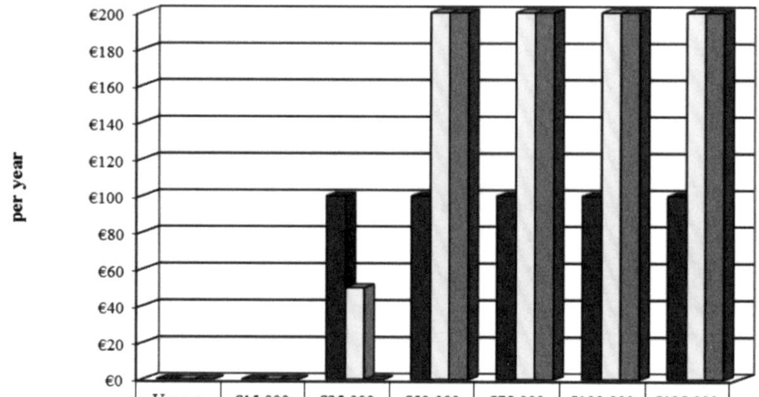

	Unemp	€15,000	€25,000	€50,000	€75,000	€100,000	€125,000
■Single	-	-	100	100	100	100	100
□Couple 1 Earner*	-	-	50	200	200	200	200
■Couple 2 Earners*	-	-	-	200	200	200	200

Note: * Except where unemployed, as there is no earner

Overall the merits of adopting this approach are: that every beneficiary of tax credits would receive the full value of the tax credit; that the system would improve the net income of the workers whose incomes are lowest, at modest cost; and that there would be no additional administrative burden placed on employers.

Outside Ireland, the refundable tax credits approach has gained more and more attention, including a detailed Brooking Policy Briefing on the issue published in the United States in late 2006 (see Goldberg et al, 2006). In reviewing this issue in the Irish context Colm Rapple stated that "the change is long overdue" (2004:140).

Chart 4.4: How much better off would people be if tax credits were increased by €100 per person and this was refundable?

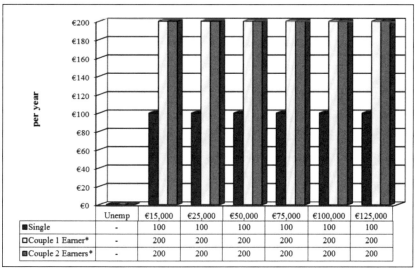

	Unemp	€15,000	€25,000	€50,000	€75,000	€100,000	€125,000
■ Single	-	100	100	100	100	100	100
□ Couple 1 Earner*	-	200	200	200	200	200	200
■ Couple 2 Earners*	-	200	200	200	200	200	200

Note: * Except where unemployed, as there is no earner

During late 2010 *Social Justice Ireland* published a detailed study on the subject of refundable tax credits. Entitled '*Building a Fairer Tax System: The Working Poor and the Cost of Refundable Tax Credits*', the study identified that the proposed system would benefit 113,000 low-income individuals in an efficient and cost-effective manner.[41] When children and other adults in the household are taken into account the total number of beneficiaries would be 240,000. The cost of making this change would be €140m. The *Social Justice Ireland* proposal to make tax credits refundable would make Ireland's tax system fairer, address part of the working poor problem and improve the living standards of a substantial number of people in Ireland. The following is a summary of that proposal:

Making tax credits refundable: the benefits

- Would address the problem identified already in a straightforward and cost-effective manner.
- No administrative cost to the employer.

---

[41] The study is available from our website: www.socialjustice.ie

- Would incentivise employment over welfare as it would widen the gap between pay and welfare rates.
- Would be more appropriate for a 21st century system of tax and welfare.

Details of Social Justice Ireland proposal

- Unused portion of the Personal and PAYE tax credit (and only these) would be refunded.
- Eligibility criteria in the relevant year.
- Individuals must have unused personal and/or PAYE tax credits (by definition).
- Individuals must have been in paid employment.
- Individuals must be at least 23 years of age.
- Individuals must have earned a minimum annual income from employment of €4,000.
- Individuals must have accrued a minimum of 40 PRSI weeks.
- Individuals must not have earned an annual total income greater than €15,600.
- Married couples must not have earned a combined annual total income greater than €31,200.
- Payments would be made at the end of the tax year.

Cost of implementing the proposal

- The total cost of refunding unused tax credits to individuals satisfying all of the criteria mentioned in this proposal is estimated at €140.1m.

Major findings

- Almost 113,300 low income individuals would receive a refund and would see their disposable income increase as a result of the proposal.
- The majority of the refunds are valued at under €2,400 per annum, or €46 per week, with the most common value being individuals receiving a refund of between €800 to €1,000 per annum, or €15 to €19 per week.
- Considering that the individuals receiving these payments have incomes of less than €15,600 (or €299 per week), such payments are significant to them.
- Almost 40 per cent of refunds flow to people in low-income working poor households who live below the poverty line.
- A total of 91,056 men, women and children below the poverty threshold benefit either directly through a payment to themselves or indirectly through a payment to their household from a refundable tax credit.
- Of the 91,056 individuals living below the poverty line that benefit from

refunds, most, over 71 per cent receive refunds of more than €10 per week with 32 per cent receiving in excess of €20 per week.

- A total of 148,863 men, women and children above the poverty line benefit from refundable tax credits either directly through a payment to themselves or indirectly (through a payment to their household. Most of these beneficiaries have income less than €120 per week above the poverty line.
- Overall, some 240,000 individuals (91,056 + 148,863) living in low-income households would experience an increase in income as a result of the introduction of refundable tax credits, either directly through a refund to themselves or indirectly through a payment to their household.

Once adopted, a system of refundable tax credits as proposed in this study would result in all future changes in tax credits being equally experienced by all employees in Irish society. Such a reform would mark a significant step in the direction of building a fairer taxation system and represent a fairer way for Irish society to allocate its resources.

Reforming individualisation

Social Justice Ireland supports individualisation of the tax system. However, the process of individualisation followed to date has been deeply flawed and unfair. The cost to the exchequer of this transition has been in excess of €0.75 billion, and almost all of this money has gone to the richest 30 per cent of the population. A significantly fairer process would have been to introduce a basic income system that would have treated all people fairly and ensured that a windfall of this nature did not accrue to the best off in this society (see chapter 3).

Given the current form of individualisation, couples with one partner losing his/her job end up even worse off than they would have been had the current form of individualisation not been introduced. Before individualisation was introduced, the standard-rate income-tax band was €35,553 for all couples. Above that, they would start paying the higher rate of tax. Now, the standard-rate income-tax band for single-income couples is €41,800 while the band for dual-income couples covers a maximum of a further €23,800 (up to €65,600). If one spouse (of a couple previously earning two salaries) leaves a job voluntarily or through redundancy, the couple loses the value of the second tax band.

Making the taxation system simpler

Ireland's tax system is not simple. Bristow (2004) argued that "some features of it, notably VAT, are among the most complex in the world". The reasons given to justify this complexity vary but they are focused principally around the need to reward particular kinds of behaviour which is seen as desirable by legislators. This, in effect, is discrimination either in favour of one kind of activity or against another. There are many arguments against the present complexity and in favour of a simpler system.

Discriminatory tax concessions in favour of particular positions are often very inequitable, contributing far less to equity than might appear to be the case. In many circumstances they also fail to produce the economic or social outcomes which were being sought and sometimes they even generate very undesirable effects. At other times they may be a complete waste of money, since the outcomes they seek would have occurred without the introduction of a tax incentive. Having a complex system has other down-sides. It can, for example, have high compliance costs both for taxpayers and for the Revenue Commissioners.

For the most part, society at large gains little or nothing from the discrimination contained in the tax system. Mortgage interest relief, for example, and the absence of any residential or land-rent tax contributed to the rise in house prices up to 2007. Complexity makes taxes easier to evade, invites consultants to devise avoidance schemes and greatly increases the cost of collection. It is also inequitable because those who can afford professional advice are in a far better position to take advantage of that complexity than those who cannot. A simpler taxation system would better serve Irish society and all individuals within it, irrespective of their means.

Key Policy Priorities on Taxation

Social Justice Ireland believes that Government should:

- increase the overall tax take
- adopt policies to broaden the tax base
- develop a fairer taxation system

Policy priorities under each of these headings are listed below.

Increase the overall tax take

- Move towards increasing the total tax take to 34.9 per cent of GDP (i.e. a level below the low tax threshold identified by Eurostat).

Broaden the tax base

- Continue to reform the area of tax expenditures and put in place procedures within the Department of Finance and the Revenue Commissioners to monitor on an on-going basis the cost and benefits of all current and new tax expenditures.

- Continue to increase the minimum effective tax rates on very high earners (those with incomes in excess of €125,000) so that these rates are consistent with the levels faced by PAYE workers.
- Move to negotiate an EU wide agreement on minimum corporate taxation rates (a rate of 17.5 per cent would seem fair in this situation).
- Adopt policies to ensure that corporations based in Ireland pay a minimum effective corporate tax rate of 10 per cent.
- Impose charges so that those who construct or purchase second homes pay the full infrastructural costs of these dwellings.
- Retain the 80 per cent windfall tax on the profits generated from all land re-zonings.
- Join with other EU member states to adopt a financial transactions tax (FTT).
- Adopt policies which further shift the burden of taxation from income tax to eco-taxes on the consumption of fuel and fertilisers, waste taxes and a land rent tax. In doing this, government should avoid any negative impact on people with low incomes.

Develop a fairer taxation system

- Apply only the standard rate of tax to all discretionary tax expenditures.
- Adjust tax credits and the USC so that the minimum wage returns to falling outside the tax net.
- Make tax credits refundable.
- Recognise that in terms of fairness, changing tax credits is the best option. Government should always take this option when it has money available to reduce income taxes.
- Ensure that individualisation in the income tax system is done in a fair and equitable manner.
- Integrate the taxation and social welfare systems.
- Begin to monitor and report tax levels (personal and corporate) in terms of effective tax rates.
- Develop policies which allow taxation on wealth to be increased.
- Ensure that the distribution of all changes in indirect taxes discriminate positively in favour of those with lower incomes.
- Adopt policies to simplify the taxation system.
- Poverty-proof all budget tax packages to ensure that tax changes do not further widen the gap between those with low income and the better off.

5.

WORK, UNEMPLOYMENT AND JOB CREATION

CORE POLICY OBJECTIVE: WORK, UNEMPLOYMENT AND JOB CREATION
To ensure that all people have access to meaningful work

The scale and severity of the 2008-2010 economic collapse saw Ireland revert to the phenomenon of widespread unemployment. Since then, despite the attention given to the banking and fiscal collapse, the transition from near full-employment to high unemployment has been the most telling characteristic of this recession. The implications for individuals, families, social cohesion and the exchequer's finances have been serious and the effects are likely to be felt for many years to come. CSO data and economic forecasts for the remainder of 2014 indicate that unemployment will reach an annual rate of between 11.5 and 12 per cent of the labour force in 2014, having been 4.7 per cent before the recession in 2007. Significant improvements have been achieved over the past two years, but there can be little doubt but that we are in a very challenging period in which a high level of long-term unemployment has once again become a characteristic of Irish society.

This chapter reviews the evolution of this situation and considers the implications and challenges which arise for Government and society.[42] It also looks at the impact on various sectors of the working-age population and, given this, it outlines a series of proposals for responding to this unemployment crisis. To date, *Social Justice Ireland* considers that the response has been slow and limited. As the chapter shows, the scale and nature of our unemployment crisis deserves greater attention, in particular given the scale of long-term unemployment. The chapter concludes with some thoughts on the narrowness of how we consider and measure the concept of 'work'.

---

[42] The analysis complements information on the measurement of the labour market and long-term trends in employment and unemployment detailed in annex 5.

The issues addressed in this chapter principally focus on one pillar of *Social Justice Ireland's* Core Policy Framework (see Chapter 2), 'Enhance Social Protection'.

Recent trends in employment and unemployment

The nature and scale of the recent transformation in Ireland's labour market is highlighted by the data in table 5.1. Over the seven years from 2007-2013 the labour force decreased by just over 4 per cent, participation rates dropped, full-time employment fell by almost 18 per cent, representing some 312,000 jobs, while part-time employment increased by almost 17 per cent. By the end of 2013 the number of underemployed people, defined as those employed part-time but wishing to work additional hours, had increased to 143,300 people – almost 7 per cent of the labour force. Over this period unemployment increased by over 150,000 people, bringing the unemployment rate up from 4.6 per cent to 11.7 per cent.

Table 5.1: Labour Force Data, 2007 – 2013

	2007	2010	2013	Change 07-13
Labour Force	2,260,600	2,168,200	2,163,100	-4.3%
LFPR%	63.8	60.2	60.1	-3.7%
Employment%	68.8	59.0	61.4	-7.4%
Employment	2,156,000	1,857,300	1,909,800	-11.4%
Full-time	1,765,300	1,422,800	1,453,000	-17.7%
Part-time	390,700	434,400	456,800	+16.9%
Underemployed	n/a	116,800	143,300	-
Unemployed%	4.6	14.3	11.7	+7.1%
Unemployed	104,600	310,900	253,200	+142.1%
LT Unemployed%	1.4%	7.9%	7.2%	+5.8%
LT Unemployed	31,700	172,100	155,500	+390.5%

Source: CSO, QNHS on-line database.
Notes: All data is for Quarter 4 of the reference year.
LFPR = Labour force participation rate and measures the percentage of the adult population who are in the labour market.
Underemployment measures part-time workers who indicate that they wish to work additional hours which are not currently available.
Comparable underemployment data is not available for 2007.
LT = Long Term (12 months or more).

This transformation in the labour market has significantly altered the nature of employment in Ireland when compared to the pre-recession picture in 2007. Overall, employment fell 11.4 per cent between 2007-2013 and table 5.2 traces the impact of this fall across various sectors, groups and regions. Within the CSO's broadly defined employment sectors, industrial employment has seen the biggest fall of over 37 per cent while there has been a small fall in services employment. Agricultural employment records an increase over the period and a significant increase between 2010 and 2013. However, it is likely that the low figure recorded for 2010 was as a result of sampling problems in the CSO Quarterly National Household Survey (QNHS) and that agricultural employment did not fall to such a low level. A consequence of the correction to this sampling problem over the most recent set of QNHS reports (Q4 2012 to Q4 2013) has been a perceived increased in agricultural employment (and overall employment).[43] A large part of this increase is a sampling correction so that a significant proportion of the 26,600 jobs reported to have been created in agriculture between Q4 2012 and Q4 2013 are statistical corrections rather than new jobs. However, overall employment has been growing, representing a welcome recovery.

Overall, job losses have had a greater impact on males than females with male employment down 15 per cent since 2007 while female employment decreased by 6.7 per cent. The proportional impact of the crisis has hit employment levels for employees and self-employed in much the same way; although there are many more of the former and the actual job losses among employees is significantly higher.

The consequence of all these job losses has been the sharp increase in unemployment and emigration. Dealing with unemployment, table 5.3 shows how it has changed between 2007 and 2013, a period when the numbers unemployed increased by over 140 per cent. As the table shows, male unemployment increased by 92,000 and female unemployment by 56,000. Most of the unemployed, who had been employed in 2007 and before it, are seeking to return to a full-time job with approximately 11 per cent of those unemployed in 2013 indicating that they were seeking part-time employment. The impact of the unemployment crisis was felt right across the age groups and it is only over the past year that there has been a decrease in numbers aged above 34 years that are unemployed. Younger age groups have seen their numbers unemployed consistently fall since 2011 – a phenomenon not unrelated to the return of high emigration figures over recent years.[44]

---

[43] See CSO QNHS (2014) for more details.
[44] See chapter 10 for more information on recent migration trends.

Table 5.2: Employment in Ireland, 2007 – 2013

	2007	2010	2013	Change 07-13
Employment	2,156,000	1,857,300	1,909,800	-11.4%
Sector				
Agriculture	114,300	85,400	116,800	+2.2%
Industry	551,600	355,300	347,200	-37.1%
Services	1,482,900	1,409,900	1,444,600	-2.6%
Gender				
Male	1,221,800	994,100	1,038,200	-15.0%
Female	934,200	863,200	871,600	-6.7%
Employment Status				
Employees*	1,775,900	1,548,900	1,571,400	-11.5%
Self Employed	364,300	298,000	324,500	-10.9%
Assisting relative	15,800	10,300	13,900	-12.0%
Region				
Border	221,100	187,400	185,800	-16.0%
Midlands	126,100	103,400	111,100	-11.9%
West	206,400	181,500	185,900	-9.9%
Dublin	640,000	552,600	572,100	-10.6%
Mid-East	251,900	226,300	225,900	-10.3%
Mid-West	173,200	151,000	151,300	-12.6%
South-East	226,600	185,800	197,100	-13.0%
South-West	310,600	269,300	280,600	-9.7%

Source: CSO, QNHS on-line database.
Notes: * Numbers recorded as employed include those on various active labour market policy schemes. See also notes to table 5.1.

Table 5.3: Unemployment in Ireland, 2007 - 2013

	2007	2010	2013	Change 07-13
Unemployment	104,600	310,900	253,200	+142.1%
Gender				
Male	66,700	211,100	158,900	+138.2%
Female	37,900	99,800	94,300	+148.8%
Employment sought				
Seeking FT work	85,900	272,600	216,600	+152.2%
Seeking PT work	16,200	23,700	27,800	+71.6%
Age group				
15-19 years	9,400	18,300	12,300	+30.9%
20-24 years	21,700	54,200	36,400	+67.7%
25-34 years	33,000	96,800	73,300	+122.1%
35-64 years	40,400	140,700	130,500	+223.0%
Region				
Border	14,000	29,200	29,000	+107.1%
Midlands	6,500	20,300	17,600	+170.8%
West	8,400	33,000	25,000	+197.6%
Dublin	30,200	82,400	63,200	+109.3%
Mid-East	9,400	33,100	32,200	+242.6%
Mid-West	9,500	31,100	18,200	+91.6%
South-East	12,100	41,700	36,200	+199.2%
South-West	14,400	40,200	31,800	+120.8%
Duration				
Unemp. less than 1 yr	72,000	136,700	95,200	+32.2%
Unemp. more than 1 yr	31,700	172,100	155,500	+390.5%
LT Unemp. as % Unemp	30.3%	55.4%	61.4%	

Source: CSO, QNHS on-line database
Note: See also notes to table 5.1.

The rapid growth in the number and rates of long-term unemployment are also highlighted in table 5.3 and in chart 5.1. The number of long-term unemployed was less than 32,000 in 2007 and has increased since, reaching 155,500 at the end of 2013. For the first time on record, the QNHS data for late 2010 indicated that long-term unemployment accounted for more than 50 per cent of the unemployed and by the end of 2013 the long-term unemployed represented just over 60 per cent of the unemployed. The transition to these high levels since 2007 has been rapid – see chart 5.1. The experience of the 1980s showed the dangers and long-lasting implications of an unemployment crisis characterised by high long-term unemployment rates. It remains a major policy failure that Ireland's level of long-term unemployment has been allowed to increase so rapidly in recent years. Furthermore, it is of serious concern that to date Government policy has given limited attention to the issue.

Addressing a crisis such as this is a major challenge and we outline our suggestions for immediate policy action later in the chapter. However, it is clear that reskilling many of the unemployed, in particular those with low education levels, will be a key component of the response. Using the latest data, for 2011, almost 60 per cent of the unemployed had no more than second level education with 30 per cent not having completed more than lower secondary (equivalent to the junior certificate). At the other extreme, the scale and severity of the recession has resulted in high levels of third-level graduates becoming unemployed.[45] While Government should not ignore any group in its overdue attempts to address the unemployment crisis, major emphasis should be placed on those who are most likely to become trapped in long term unemployment – in particular those with the lowest education levels.

Chart 5.1: The Increased Presence of Long-Term Unemployed in Ireland, 2007-2013

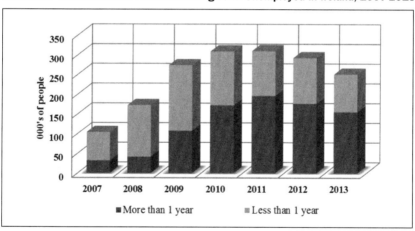

Source: CSO, QNHS on-line database
Note: Data is for Q4 of each year

---

[45]   The CSO has not updated its profile of unemployment by completed education level since this data.

Previous experiences, in Ireland and elsewhere, have shown that many of those under 25 and many of those over 55 find it challenging to return to employment after a period of unemployment. This highlights the danger of the aforementioned large increases in long-term unemployment and suggests a major commitment to retraining and re-skilling will be required. In the long-run Irish society can ill afford a return to the long-term unemployment problems of the 1980s. In the short-run the new-unemployed are adding to the numbers living on low-income in Ireland and this, in turn, will continue to have a negative impact on future poverty figures (see chapter 3).

Two further themes arise from the employment and unemployment data and we address these over the next two subsections: youth unemployment and the increase in precarious work. We then conclude this section by examining trends on the live register.

Youth unemployment

While the increase in unemployment has been spread across all ages and sectors (see table 5.3), chart 5.2 highlights the very rapid increase in the numbers unemployed under 25 years-of-age. The numbers in this group more than doubled between 2007 and 2009 peaking at 83,100 in quarter 2 2009. Since then decreases have occurred, reaching 50,000 in late 2013. Although we have limited empirical knowledge of the reasons for these decreases, a large part of the decrease is probably due to emigration.

Chart 5.2: Youth Unemployment in Ireland, by gender 2007-2013

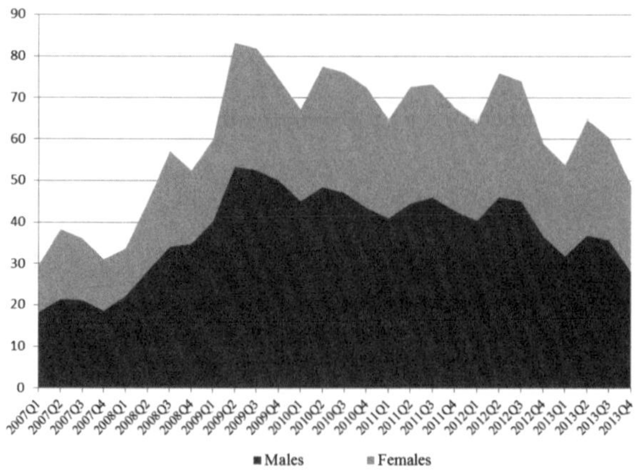

Source: CSO, QNHS on-line database.

Socio-Economic Review 2014

Although youth unemployment represents about one-fifth of the total population that are unemployed, there is merit in giving it particular attention. Experiences of unemployment, and in particular long-term unemployment, alongside an inability to access any work, training or education, tends to leave a 'scaring effect' on young people. It increases the challenges associated with getting them active in the labour market at any stage in the future. The latest data on the number of young people aged 18-24 years in Ireland who are not in education, employment or training (NEETs) is 23.8 per cent in 2012 (NERI, 2013: 36).

In the short-term it makes sense for Government to invest in the 'youth unemployed' and *Social Justice Ireland* considers this to be a central priority of any programme to seriously address the unemployment crisis. At a European level, this issue has been receiving welcome attention over the past year; driven by high levels of youth unemployment in other crisis countries.

Under-employment, Part-time employment and Precarious Work

The figures in table 5.1 also point towards the growth of various forms of precarious work over recent years. Since 2007 employment has fallen by 11 per cent; but this figure masks a bigger decline in full-time employment (18 per cent) and a growth in part-time employment (+ 17 per cent). Within those part-time employed there has also been an increase in the numbers of people who are underemployed, that is working part-time but at less hours than individuals are willing to work. By the end of 2013 the numbers underemployed stood at 143,300 people, about seven per cent of the total labour force and almost one-third of all part-time workers.

While an element of these figures can be explained by the recession, and the suppressed levels of activity in some sectors, they also suggest the emergence of a greater number of workers in precarious employment situations. The growth in the number of individuals with less work hours than ideal, as well as those with persistent uncertainties on the number and times of hours required for work, is a major labour market challenge. Aside from the impact this has on the well-being of individuals and their families, it also impacts on their financial situation and adds to the working-poor challenges we outlined in chapter 3. There are also impacts on the state given that Family Income Supplement (FIS) and the structure of jobseeker payments tends to lead to Government subsidising these families incomes; and indirectly subsidising some employers who create persistent precarious work patterns for their workers.

As the labour market improves, *Social Justice Ireland* believes that now is the time to adopt measures to address and eliminate these problems.

The Live Register

While the live register is not an accurate measure of unemployment, it is a useful barometer of the nature and pace of change in employment and unemployment. Increases suggest a combination of more people unemployed, more people on reduced employment weeks and consequently reductions in the availability of employment hours to the labour force. Table 5.4 shows that the number of people signing on the live register increased rapidly since the onset of the economic crisis in 2007. The numbers peaked in July 2011 and by January 2014 the numbers signing-on the live register had increased more than 240,000 compared to seven years earlier.

Table 5.4: Numbers on the Live Register (unadjusted), Jan 2007 - 2014

Year	Month	Males	Females	Total
2007	January	95,824	62,928	158,752
2008	January	116,160	65,289	181,449
2009	January	220,412	105,860	326,272
2010	January	291,648	145,288	436,936
2011	January	292,003	150,674	442,677
2011	July (peak)	297,770	172,514	470,284
2012	January	283,893	155,696	439,589
2013	January	273,627	155,769	429,396
2014	January	248,723	150,907	399,630

Source: CSO Live Register on-line database.

The live register data offers a useful insight into the skills and experience of those signing on. Table 5.5 presents a breakdown of the January 2014 live register number by people's last occupation and also examines the differences between those over and under 25 years. The figures once again highlight the need for targeted reskilling of people who hold skills in sectors of the economy that are unlikely to ever return to the employment levels of the early part of the last decade.

Table 5.5: Persons on Live Register by last occupation – January 2014

Occupational group	Overall	Under 25 yrs	Over 25 yrs
Managers and administrators	16,795	531	16,264
Professional	22,036	1,789	20,247
Associate prof.& technical	11,284	1,369	9,915
Clerical and secretarial	37,202	2,816	34,386
Craft and related	84,437	7,502	76,935
Personal and protective service	50,508	8,177	42,331
Sales	43,713	10,898	32,815
Plant and machine operatives	66,781	8,630	58,151
Other occupation	46,276	9,678	36,598
Never worked / not stated	20,598	9,147	11,451
Total	399,630	60,537	339,093

Source: CSO Live Register on-line database.

Responding to the unemployment crisis

The scale of these increases is enormous and it is crucial that Government, commentators and society in general remember that each of these numbers represent people who are experiencing dramatic and, in many cases, unexpected turmoil in their lives and their families' lives. As Irish society comes to terms with the enormity of this issue, we believe that this perspective should remain central.

To date, the policy response to this crisis has been limited, comprising announcements of apprenticeship schemes, 'Job Initiative' (2011) reforms, annual Action Plans and the 'Pathways to Work' programme. Each of these has targeted small reforms and had limited success given the scale of the unemployment crisis – for the most part the long-term unemployment, skill deficits, under-employment and precarious work issues have been given limited attention.

In responding to this situation *Social Justice Ireland* believes that Government a clear and integrated set of policy priorities. We set these out in detail in the final section of this chapter.

Even the most optimistic economic and labour market projections for the years to come suggest that unemployment will remain a major factor. The Department of Finance's estimates in Budget 2014 point towards a rate 11.7 per cent in 2016; we anticipate this figure will be revised during 2014 to a figure of approximately 10 per cent in 2016. As recovery emerges, it is important that policy focuses on those furthest from being able to rejoin the numbers employed and assist those within employment but struggling as the working poor.

Work and people with disabilities

Results from Census 2011 have provided new data on the scale and nature of disability in Ireland. In a report published in November 2012, the CSO reported that a total of 595,335 people had a disability in Ireland; equivalent to 13 per cent of the population. The most common disability overall was a difficulty with pain, breathing or other chronic illness or condition which was experienced by 46.2 per cent of all people with a disability; this was followed by a difficulty with basic physical activities, experienced by 41.1 per cent. The report found that both of these disabilities were strongly age-related. It also showed that 1.1 per cent of the population were blind or had a sight related disability (51,718 people); 1.3 per cent of the population suffered from an intellectual disability (57,709 people); 2 per cent of the population were deaf or had a hearing related disability (92,060 people); 2.1 per cent of the population had a psychological or emotional condition (96,004 people); 3 per cent of the population had a difficulty with learning, remembering or concentrating (137,070 people); 5.3 per cent of the population had a difficulty with basic physical activities (244,739 people); and 6 per cent of the population had a disability connected with pain, breathing or another chronic illness or condition (274,762 people) (CSO, 2012: 45, 51-53).[46]

The Census 2011 data also revealed that there was 162,681 persons with a disability in the labour force representing a participation rate of 30 per cent, less than half that for the population in general. These findings reflect earlier results from the 2006 National Disability Survey (CSO, 2008 and 2010) and a 2004 QNHS special module on disability (CSO, 2004). This low rate of employment among people with a disability is of concern. Apart from restricting their participation in society it also ties them into state dependent low-income situations. Therefore, it is not surprising that Ireland's poverty figures reveal that people who are ill or have a disability are part of a group at high risk of poverty (see chapter 3).

---

[46] Note, some individuals will experience more than one disability and feature in more than one of these categories.

Social Justice Ireland believes that further efforts should be made to reduce the impediments faced by people with a disability to obtain employment. In particular, consideration should be given to reforming the current situation in which many such people face losing their benefits, in particular their medical card, when they take up employment. This situation ignores the additional costs faced by people with a disability in pursuing their day-to-day lives. For many people with disabilities the opportunity to take up employment is denied to them and they are trapped in unemployment, poverty or both.

Some progress was made in Budget 2005 to increase supports intended to help people with disabilities access employment. However, sufficient progress has not been made and recent Budgets have begun to reduce these services. New policies, including that outlined above, need to be adopted if this issue is to be addressed successfully. It is even more relevant today, given the growing employment challenges of the past few years.

Asylum seekers and work

Social Justice Ireland is very disappointed that the government continues to reject any proposal that the right to work of asylum seekers should be recognised. Along with others, we have consistently advocated that where government fails to meet its own stated objective of processing asylum applications in six months, the right to work should be automatically granted to asylum seekers. Detaining people for an unnecessarily prolonged period in such an excluded state is completely unacceptable. Recognising asylum seekers' right to work would assist in alleviating poverty and social exclusion in one of Ireland's most vulnerable groups.[47]

The need to recognise all work

A major question raised by the current labour-market situation concerns assumptions underpinning culture and policy making in this area. The priority given to paid employment over other forms of work is one such assumption. Most people recognise that a person can be working very hard outside a conventionally accepted "job". Much of the work carried out in the community and in the voluntary sector comes under this heading. So too does much of the work done in the home. *Social Justice Ireland*'s support for the introduction of a basic income system comes, in part, because it believes that all work should be recognised and supported (see chapter 3).

---

[47] We examine this issue in further detail in chapter 10.

The need to recognise voluntary work has been acknowledged in the Government White Paper, *Supporting Voluntary Activity* (Department of Social, Community and Family Affairs, 2000). The report was prepared to mark the UN International Year of the Volunteer 2001 by Government and representatives of numerous voluntary organisations in Ireland. The report made a series of recommendations to assist in the future development and recognition of voluntary activity throughout Ireland. A 2005 report presented to the Joint Oireachtas Committee on Arts, Sport, Tourism, Community, Rural and Gaeltacht Affairs also provided an insight into this issue. It established that the cost to the state of replacing the 475,000 volunteers working for charitable organisations would be at least €205 million and could be as high as €485 million per year.

Social Justice Ireland believes that government should recognise in a more formal way all forms of work. We believe that everyone has a right to work, to contribute to his or her own development and that of the community and the wider society. However, we believe that policy making in this area should not be exclusively focused on job creation. Policy should recognise that *work* and a *job* are not always the same thing.

The Work of Carers

The work of Ireland's carers receives minimal recognition despite the essential role their work plays in society. Recent results from the 2011 Census offer a new insight into the scale of these commitments, which save the state large costs that it would otherwise have to bear.

Census 2011 found that 4.1 per cent of the population aged over 15 provided some care for sick or disabled family members or friends on an unpaid basis. This figure equates to 187,112 people. The dominant caring role played by women was highlighted by the fact that 114,113 (61 per cent) of these care providers were female.[48] When assessed by length of time, the census found that a total of 6,287,510 hours of care were provided by carers each week, representing an average of 33.6 hours of unpaid help and assistance each. Two thirds of this volume of care was provided by female carers (CSO, 2012: 71-77). Using the minimum wage as a simple (an unrealistically low) benchmark to establish the benefit which carers provide each year suggests that Ireland's carers provide care valued at more than €2.8bn per annum.

---

[48] A CSO QNHS special module on carers (CSO, 2010) and a 2008 ESRI study entitled '*Gender Inequalities in Time Use*' found similar trends (McGinnity and Russell, 2008:36, 70).

Social Justice Ireland welcomed the long overdue publication of a *National Carers Strategy* in July 2012 (Department of Health, 2012). The document includes a 'roadmap for Implementation' involving a suite of actions, and associated timelines and identifies the Government Department responsible for their implementation. However, these actions were confined to those that could be achieved on a cost neutral basis. The first annual progress report of the strategy was published by Minister Kathleen Lynch in January 2014 (Department of Health, 2014). It points towards some progress on the actions set out, but these are, as a group, limited given the unwillingness of Government to allocate some resources to supporting those in this sector.

Social Justice Ireland believes that further policy reforms should be introduced to reduce the financial and emotional pressures on carers. In particular, these should focus on addressing the poverty experienced by many carers and their families alongside increasing the provision of respite care for carers and for those for whom they care. In this context, the 24 hour responsibilities of carers contrast with the improvements over recent years in employment legislation setting limits on working-hours of people in paid employment.

Key policy priorities on work, unemployment and job creation

- Adopt the following policy positions in responding to the recent rapid increase in unemployment:
  - Launch a major investment programme focused on creating employment and prioritise initiatives that strengthen social infrastructure, such as the school building programme and the social housing programme.
  - Resource the up-skilling of those who are unemployed and at risk of becoming unemployed through integrating training and labour market programmes.
  - Maintain a sufficient number of active labour market programme places available to those who are unemployed.
  - Adopt policies to address the worrying trend of youth unemployment. In particular, these should include education and literacy initiatives as well as retraining schemes.
  - Recognise that many of the unemployed are skilled professionals who require appropriate support other than training.
  - Resource a targeted re-training scheme for those previously unemployed in the construction industry, recognising that this industry is never likely to recover to the level of employment it had prior to 2007.
  - Recognise the scale of the evolving long term unemployment problem and adopt targeted policies to begin to address this.

- Ensure that the social welfare system is administered such that there is minimal delays in paying the newly unemployed the social welfare benefits to which they are entitled.
- Funded programmes supporting the community should be expanded to meet the growing pressures arising from the current economic downturn.
- A new programme should be put in place targeting those who are very long-term unemployed (i.e. 5+ years).
- Policy should seek at all times to ensure that new jobs have reasonable pay rates and adequately resource the labour inspectorate.
- As part of the process of addressing the working poor issue, reform the taxation system to make tax credits refundable.
- Develop employment-friendly income-tax policies which ensure that no unemployment traps exist. Policies should ease the transition from unemployment to employment.
- Adopt policies to address the obstacles facing women when they return to the labour force. These should focus on care initiatives, employment flexibility and the provision of information and training.
- Reduce the impediments faced by people with a disability in achieving employment. In particular, address the current situation in which many face losing their benefits when they take up employment.
- Recognise the right to work of all asylum seekers whose application for asylum is at least six months old and who are not entitled to take up employment.
- Recognise that the term "work" is not synonymous with the concept of "paid employment". Everybody has a right to work, i.e. to contribute to his or her own development and that of the community and the wider society. This, however, should not be confined to job creation. *Work* and a *job* are not the same thing.
- Request the CSO to conduct an annual survey to discover the value of all unpaid work in the country (including community and voluntary work and work in the home). Publish the results of this survey as soon as they become available.
- Give greater recognition to the work carried out by carers in Ireland and introduce policy reforms to reduce the financial and emotional pressures on carers. In particular, these should focus on addressing the poverty experienced by many carers and their families as well as on increasing the provision of respite opportunities to carers and to those for whom they care.

6.

PUBLIC SERVICES

CORE POLICY OBJECTIVE: PUBLIC SERVICES

To ensure the provision of, and access to, a level of public services regarded as acceptable by Irish society generally

Later chapters will analyse a range of public services such as healthcare, education and housing. This chapter, however, looks at public services in a range of areas not addressed elsewhere. These include public transport, library services, financial services, information and communications technology, telecommunications, free legal aid, sports facilities and regulation.

In addressing these issues we analyse key parts of their present situation, clarify the challenges they face and set out possible pathways towards developing a fairer future. All of these chapters address issues related to the achievement of one element of *Social Justice Ireland*'s Core Policy Framework (see Chapter 2) i.e. 'Enhance Social Protection'.

It is important to note that 'public services' is not synonymous with 'public sector'. While the public sector delivers a wide spectrum of public services, such services are also delivered by the community and voluntary sector and by the business sector in a variety of combinations with the public sector.

As noted in chapter 2, public services and infrastructure have been eroded since the crisis of 2008. At both national and local level, social services and related initiatives have been cut just as the demands for these services were increasing. We have also noted that particular budgetary decisions may provide a short-term gain or saving for Government but have huge negative long-term consequences. The need to protect services by adjusting deficit reduction is an aspect of *Social Justice Irelands* Core Policy Framework as outlined in chapter 2. *Social Justice Ireland* is very concerned that many decisions made since 2008 will have negative long-term effects. Government's continuing insistence on prioritising expenditure cuts over increasing taxation in Ireland has serious implications for public services and negative effects on Ireland's low and middle-income individuals and households. (For further information on these issues cf. chapters 2 and 3.)

Many public services provided by community and voluntary organisations have come under huge pressure in recent years as the recession has forced an ever-growing number of people to seek their help. But, at the very moment when the demand for services increased, Government reduced the funding being made available to many such organisations providing these services. Because poorer people rely on public services more than those who are better off, it is they who are most acutely affected by cuts to services.

Public transport

'The provision of adequate and affordable public transport will not only address the needs of those who are isolated from services or employment, it will contribute to reduced traffic and environmental pollution and better public health' (Farrell et al. 2008: 44). Increased car dependency compounds issues relating to social isolation, increasing obesity and health hazards connected to heavy traffic and environmental pollution. Coupled with this, access in terms of transport to jobs, health services, education and other facilities is a major factor in ensuring social inclusion (Lucas, et al, 2001; Wilkinson & Mormot, 2003; Considine & Dukelow, 2009). Consequently, public transport is an important component of any strategy to address issues such as health and to ensure social inclusion.

In Ireland there has been a decline in the use of public transport and passenger numbers; Dublin Bus passenger numbers fell by 22% from 2007 to 2012. The main public transport provider, CIE, suffered a decline in passenger journeys of 21 per cent from 2007-2011. Passenger numbers continued to decline in 2013, although tempering slightly (Department of Transport: 2009, Department of Transport Tourism and Sport, 2011, National Transport Authority: 2013).

The Department of Transport (2009), indicates that creating a sustainable transport system involves ensuring that alternatives to car transport are available. Improving public transport systems, along with investment in cycling and walking, is a central means by which this will be achieved. 'Public transport has to gain a higher share than today in the transport mix, become easily accessible for everyone and fully integrated with non-motorised modes' (European Commission, 2011:24). However, the increase in car dependency and the decline in the use of public transport in Ireland suggests that public transport provision is not adequate or of sufficient quality. In a consultation report for *A Sustainable Transport Future: a New Transport Policy for Ireland 2009 – 2020,* concerns were highlighted in regard to the quality of public transport, lack of integration, lack of capacity, overcrowding, poor availability and design of routes.

Further to this, *The European Green City Index* report carried out in 2009 ranked Dublin last out of 30 cities in the transport category. The length of its public transport network and the extent of its cycle lanes are well below the average. It noted that less than 20 per cent of people take public transport to work; nearly 61 per cent use private cars (Economist Intelligence Unit, 2009). This data does not take cognisance of recent developments such as the 'Dublin Bikes' scheme, cross-city cycle lanes and the rollout of integrated public transport ticketing (the 'Leap' card) (The National Competitiveness Council, 2012). However, even with these improvements, problems persist. In 2011 the Environmental Protection Agency (EPA) highlighted that one of the most significant barriers to achieving sustainable transport in Ireland relates to 'lack of reliable and efficient public transport and cycling facilities' (Browne et al. 2011: vii).

The Department of Transport Tourism and Sport acknowledges the 'need to rebalance transport policy to favour public transport' (2011:33). However, subsidy reductions in 2013 resulting in fare increases across all public transport operators [Dublin Bus, Iarnród Éireann, Bus Éireann and Luas] does little to encourage this. Maintaining affordability should be central to delivery of an accessible public transport system. It is crucial that Government continues to give priority to public transport over private transport in allocating funding in the years ahead.

While the main focus so far in this section has been on the provision of alternatives to car transport, it is also important to note that car transport is often the only option, for example in rural areas. Welcome improvements have been made over recent decades relating to motorways and other central routes in Ireland. However 'Ireland's remaining road network often consists of poorly maintained roads which are not capable of meeting usual demand, certainly not to an international level' (Engineers Ireland, 2012:12). In 2014 a package of €332.9 million was announced for the maintenance of regional and local roads 'The focus on road maintenance and repair comes against a backdrop of ongoing limited resources and an overall cut of 17% this year [2014] on the 2013 funding' (Department of Transport, Tourism and Sport, 2014). The condition of these roads is deteriorating; work to improve and maintain regional and local roads is required.

In light of the discussion relating to the role public transport plays in underpinning social inclusion it is also essential that continued support is provided for the development and maintenance of the rural transport programme.[49] It should also be recognised that public transport in Ireland requires a sustained level of investment to ensure that it is of a sufficient quality.

---

[49] Issues specifically related to the provision of public services in rural areas are addressed in chapter 12.

Library services

Libraries play an important role in Irish society, performing a valuable community and educational service and ensuring access to reading, information and learning. 'They provide a focal point for community and intergenerational contact, and enable access to learning and an ever-expanding range of information for a wide constituency through an increasingly broad and varied range of media' (McGrath et al, 2010: 6). Recent research by the Carnegie Trust (2012) indicated that overall more than three quarters (79 per cent) of those in Ireland said that libraries were 'very important' or 'essential' for communities, this was higher than any other jurisdiction included in this research.

Statistics provided for 2011 further underscore the important function that libraries play in Ireland. In that year registered membership of libraries increased by 11.3per cent from 809,169 to 900,811. Fractionally under one in five of the population (19.6 per cent) are registered as members of the public library service, up from 19.1 per cent in 2010. Children's membership of the library saw a decline of 2.7 per cent in 2011, while adult membership in the same period increased by 2.4 per cent. Visits to full-time branches increased by 11.9 per cent from 14.7 million to 16.45 million and estimated visits to all branches increased by 1.1 million over 2010 (Public Library Authority, 2011). In 2012 it was estimated[50] that overall investment in public libraries would be reduced. Local authorities estimated that they would invest €137 million of their revenue budgets on public library services in 2012. This represented a decrease of 2.6 per cent on the 2011 figure of €140.6 million. Total local authority expenditure on library stock was set to decrease by 12.1 per cent on the 2011 figure. The reduced funding for stock is of particular concern in light of the growing demand for the service and the need to preserve quality (An Comhairle Leabharlanna, 2012).

'Branching Out' (Department of Environment, Heritage and Local Government, 2008) was a major review of library services in Ireland and built on a publication of the same name undertaken in 1998 (Department of Environment, Heritage and Local Government, 1998). Between 1998 and 2008, when this review of policy was published, there were significant improvements in the services provided by libraries. These included improvements in book collections, ICT infrastructure and electronic services and building infrastructure. According to the review, it is imperative that the improvements made in the library service to date are maintained. This is particularly important given the continued growth in demand on library services.

While, great improvements have been made and a vision of a vibrant library service is articulated in the new strategy, *Opportunities for AllP: A Strategy for Public Libraries*

---

[50] The actual report for 2012 was not available at the time of writing.

2013-2017 there have been reductions in regard to funding for libraries over the past number of years. One of its key recommendations in this strategy concerns the need for public libraries to 'explore the potential to secure additional funding through philanthropy, enterprise, public-private partnership and other alternative sources' (Department of Environment, Community and Local Government 2013:35). The securing of additional funding should not be utilised as a means to further reduce funding to public libraries.

The issue of fees is viewed as a barrier to use, with An Chomhairle Leabharlanna's 2010 annual report concluding that the benefits of free access outweigh the value of the money gained. This is a particularly important point in the current economic climate and *Social Justice Ireland* urges local authorities to reconsider this measure; indeed, one of the aims in the new strategy indicates that libraries will attempt to ensure equity of access for all through the provision of free core services by 2017.

Public libraries play a crucial role in Irish society and have the potential to play an even more important role into the future. *Social Justice Ireland* believes that, as part of our commitment to providing a continuum of education provision from early childhood to third level and throughout the life-cycle, Ireland needs to recognise the potential that the library service offers. This requires ready availability and easy access to information. Coupled with this is the need for easy access to modern means of communication. Libraries are obvious centres with potential to support these objectives. To play this potential role, continued support for, and expansion of, the library service is essential.

Financial services and inclusion

Financial exclusion refers to a household's difficulty in accessing and using financial services. This has particular implications as we move towards an increasingly cashless society because groups already financially excluded will become more marginalised. A 2011 study by the ESRI examined four dimensions of financial exclusion: access to a bank current account, access to credit, ability to save and access to housing insurance (Russell et al, 2011). Of these, access to a bank current account was considered the most fundamental because exclusion from basic banking services means households may face difficulties carrying out everyday transactions such as paying bills, receiving earnings or welfare benefits, transferring funds or purchasing goods and services.

This research highlighted serious deficiencies in the ability of Irish households to access these basic financial services. In 2008 it was found that 20 per cent of Irish households did not have a bank current account – a figure that is almost three times higher than the average for the EU15. The proportion without a bank current account rose to 40 per cent among those with low education qualifications, 38 per cent in households in the bottom 20 per cent of the income distribution, 50 per cent among local authority tenants, 52 per cent among those who are ill or living with a disability, and 27 per cent among those aged over 55 years (Russell et al 2011:126-127).

The *Strategy for Financial Inclusion* published in 2011 demonstrated that a binding requirement on banks in other EU countries to address the issues faced by people who are financially excluded yielded positive results. 'As a significant first step in this direction, a binding requirement to support the provision of a BPA (basic payment account) was introduced for Allied Irish Banks and Bank of Ireland in 2009 as part of the recapitalisation of those banks, and this commitment was extended to the remainder of the domestic banking sector in a package of sector-wide commitments, which was agreed with the European Commission in 2010 as part of its Decision on the Bank of Ireland Restructuring Plan' (Steering Group on Financial Inclusion, 2011: 7).

While the provision of a basic payment account does not address all elements of financial exclusion, it is considered to be the most important initial requirement. A pilot project of providing a standard bank account ran for 9 months up to the 31st March 2013 with a total of 205 accounts opened. A particular consideration of note is the need for greater involvement from post offices and credit unions in providing an access points, especially given the geographic reach of bank branches (Report of the Financial Inclusion Working Group on the Standard Bank Account Pilot Project, 2013). Further work in regard to development of the product prior to national rollout is currently being pursued.

Information and communications technology

In 2013 an estimated 84 per cent of households had a home computer. This was an increase of 14 percentage points since 2008. Internet connection has also increased substantially over this period, with an estimated 82 per cent now connected to the internet at home compared with 72 per cent in 2010 and 63 per cent in 2008. There has been strong growth each year in internet connections. 78 per cent of individuals used the internet in the 3 months prior to the survey, with 61 per cent of individuals using the internet every day in the 3 months prior to the survey (CSO, 2013). However, almost one in five Irish adults have never used the internet, with over half of people aged 60 to 74 having never used the internet (Department of Communication, Energy, Natural Resources, 2013).

These figures underscore the progressively important role that ICT plays in modern society and the level of progress being made in regard to access to digital technology in Ireland. 'Digital literacy is increasingly becoming an essential life competence and the inability to access or use ICT has effectively become a barrier to social integration and personal development. Those without sufficient ICT skills are disadvantaged in the labour market and have less access to information to empower themselves as consumers, or as citizens saving time and money in offline activities and using online public services (European Commission, 2008: 4). Digital competence is also one of the competencies highlighted as part of the key competencies required for lifelong learning by the European Commission in 2006. Factors such as disability, age and social disadvantage all have significant roles to play in increasing digital exclusion. Apart from the impact on the individual, there are also losses to the business community and the economy at large (McDaid & Cullen, 2008).

In 2012 the Government published its digital strategy for delivering public services. Covering the period 2012 to 2015, this strategy encourages greater sharing of data between Government public bodies, wider adoption of online payments and the use of smartphone optimised sites and apps. It also identified a number of services which may be particularly suitable for electronic delivery, such as the renewal of adult passports, planning applications and objections and welfare applications. With this increasing focus on digital communication and a move to the delivery of services via electronic formats, Government needs to show sustained commitment to counteract the issue of digital exclusion in particular for the more vulnerable sectors of society. The Government in 2013 committed to getting 288,000 people "on line" over the period to 2016. Delivering a new scheme [BenefIT 4] which targets specific groups most likely to be non-internet users for digital skills training-- funding of €1.4m was provided in 2013 for training 24,000 citizens at multiple locations across Ireland (Department of Communication, Energy, Natural Resources, 2013). Resources will continue to be required in this area if this target is to be met. At an economic level this is essential to promote competitiveness and effectiveness, while at a social services level it is essential to ensure digital exclusion does not become another form of exclusion being experienced by those who are already vulnerable.

Telecommunications

Two issues are of note in this area. Firstly, the Commission for Communications Regulation (ComReg) has put in place a system to ensure that a basic set of telecommunications services is available to all consumers throughout the country. This is known as a Universal Service Obligation (USO). The services to be provided include: meeting reasonable requests for connections at a fixed location to the public communications network and access to publicly available telephone service; provision of directory services and maintenance of the national directory database; public telephone provision; specific services for disabled users; affordability of tariffs and options for consumers to control expenditure (ComReg, 2011: 13). Eircom is the designated Universal Service Provider (USP) and has a number of obligations regarding the supply of these services. *Social Justice Ireland* welcomes the vigilance of ComReg in maintaining the quality of the service provided under this obligation, taking into account any potential negative effects on disadvantaged members of the community were these obligations not to be met. Eircom was re-designated as the Universal Service Provider in June 2012 with the term set to last until 30 June 2014 (ComReg, 2012).

Secondly, as part of the Digital Agenda for Europe, the European Commission has set targets of 30mbps broadband for all citizens and 50 per cent of citizens subscribing to 100mbps by 2020. While there have been substantial increases in the numbers of people connecting to the internet (see section on Information and Communications Technology), Ireland is performing badly in relation to the roll-out and take-up of advanced broadband services. The take-up (subscriptions as a percentage of population) of fixed broadband was 24.6 per cent in January 2013, 0.4 percentage points higher than 2012, but below the European average of 28.8 per cent. The share of high speed connections, at least 30 Mbps, was higher than average, 20.4 per cent compared to 14.8 per cent in the EU. However, ultra-fast connections, at least 100 Mbps, remain low and accounted for only 1.4 per cent of all subscriptions compared to 3.4 per cent in the EU (European Commission, 2013). 'Given the weak telecommunications investment climate in Ireland, our dispersed population patterns and the recession, there is a strong risk, if appropriate action is not taken, that Ireland is likely to fall even further behind as other countries are moving ahead to deploy advanced telecoms networks' (Forfas, 2011:27).

Government has recognised the need to address Ireland's performance in regard to advanced broadband technology, The National Broadband Plan was published in August 2012 committing to the role-out of:

- 70Mbps – 100Mbps to more than half of the population by 2015;
- at least 40Mbps, and in many cases much faster speeds, to at least a further 20 per cent of the population and potentially as much as 35 per cent around smaller towns and villages; and
- a minimum of 30Mbps for every remaining home and business in the country – no matter how rural or remote (Department of Communications, Energy and Natural Resources, 2012:1).

A recent release from Eurostat revealed that while, 82% of Irish households have internet access above the EU average of 79%,, only 67% of Irish households have access to a broadband connection; this is well below the EU average of 76% (Eurostat, 2013). The targets in the NBS are ambitious and will require substantial investment to be achieved. However, there will be many advantages to businesses and individuals. The plan recognises the need to bring faster broadband to rural areas and, where the market fails to deliver, the Government will intervene (Department of Communications, Energy and Natural Resources, 2012). The roll-out and delivery of high quality broadband particularly to rural areas will need to be monitored carefully, in terms of cost and quality; this is vital to ensure access for all.

Free legal aid

Citizens depend on the law and associated institutions to defend their rights and civic entitlements. The free legal aid system is a central part of this system, particularly for those with limited incomes. The Legal Aid Board provides civil legal aid to people of modest means, with recipients contributing a nominal sum. *Social Justice Ireland* believes that free legal aid is an important public service. In the current economic climate, with rising unemployment and decreasing income, the demands on the Legal Aid Board are continuing to grow. Most notably, there has been an increase in demand for services regarding debt issues.

According to the Legal Aid Board Annual Report, while 2012 saw a reduction of 9 per cent in applicants, the cumulative increase in applicants for such services over the six years to 2012 is well over 70 per cent (2012:8).

The Board has indicated that the sustained increase in demand is being primarily driven by two factors. The first, and most significant, is the economic downturn which has resulted in many more people becoming eligible for the legal services provided by the Board. Secondly, there appears to be a greater need for legal services during times of economic crisis, particularly in areas such as family law, debt issues and employment.

There has been a massive increase in demand for this service at a time when resources are being reduced. The budget allocation for general legal services (excluding refugee/asylum related matters) was reduced from €26.988 million in 2008 to €26.31 million in 2009, €24.225 million in 2010, and €24.125 million in 2011 (Legal Aid Board, 2009, 2010 &2011).

Despite an increased throughput by the Legal Aid Board's staff in law centres, those people entitled to access the civil legal aid scheme are having to wait longer. This is seen as an area of particular concern; tighter financial constraints, a moratorium on staffing and an increase in demand for services is having a very significant impact. Waiting times for a first appointment other than those deemed priority were in excess of four months in 16 of the law centres (Legal Aid Board, 2012). It is important to remember that justice delayed is justice denied.

Social Justice Ireland believes that the provision of, and adequate support for, this service is a basic requirement of governance. In light of the increasing pressure on this service, it is vital that it is adequately resourced and supported by the Government.

Sports

A report carried out by Indecon International Economic Consultants (2010) highlighted the contribution provided by sport to the Irish economy. It also showed the important role played by sport in assisting the development of social capital and in contributing to the health and quality of life of the population. Therefore, the considerable rise in participation in sports, from 34 per cent in 2009 to 46 per cent in 2011, with further increases recorded in the initial 6 months of 2013 (preliminary results from The Irish Sports Monitor, 2103) on the same period in 2011, are hugely welcome (Irish Sports Council, 2013).

The Draft *National Sports Facilities Strategy 2012-2015* acknowledges the important role that sport plays in terms of health, economic and social benefits. It outlines three overall objectives (Department of Transport Tourism and Sport, 2012:3):

- participation in sport and physical activity at all levels;
- opportunities for the achievement of excellence at the elite levels of sport, both nationally and internationally; and
- social inclusion.

It must be noted that firstly, income plays a large role when it comes to participation in sports in Ireland, with only 38 per cent of those in the lowest income bracket playing sport compared with 56 per cent of those in the highest income bracket (The Irish Sports Council, 2011). Secondly, people who are socially disadvantaged are less likely to participate in sport and, therefore, less likely to obtain the health benefits of physical activity. With this in mind an aspect of sports policy which is important is the 'need to improve the provision and accessibility of sports facilities in socially disadvantaged areas' (Department of Transport Tourism and Sport, 2012:12). The National Sports Council has developed a creative initiative of local sports partnerships. Some of these are working effectively to address this problem. Continued funding for local sports partnerships would be most worthwhile.

Another aspect of the sporting landscape in Ireland which deserves consideration is the issue of volunteerism. The 2010 Indecon study conservatively estimated that over 270,000 people participate in some form of sport-related voluntary activity; the Irish Sports Council Strategic Plan (2009) estimated that the number was closer to 400,000. The estimated value of volunteering is between €321 million and €582 million per annum (Indecon, 2010). People engaging in volunteering bring numerous social benefits. In 2011 the proportion of people volunteering for sport increased from 7 per cent to 15 per cent. However, preliminary results from the 2013 Sports Monitor suggest that volunteering has decreased (Irish Sports Council, 2013). Government should continue to support policies aimed at encouraging volunteering and enhancing the experience of volunteers.

As sports policy is developed against the background of increasingly scarce public expenditure resources, *Social Justice Ireland* believes that in-depth consideration needs to be given as to how the returns on these investments can be maximised. In many cases simple schemes to encourage participation and use of existing sports facilities are all that is required.

Regulation

Regulatory policy in Ireland has failed in many areas and requires significant reform. This has been clearly demonstrated in the problems that have emerged in the financial services sector. While some of the required reforms have been put in place, a serious re-think is required to ensure that regulation plays a stronger and far more effective role to ensure there is no repetition of the huge failures of the past decade. Central to our opinion on how regulation should develop is the view that all current and future regulation be required to consider the societal impact of any reforms proposed. They should also have the capacity to monitor what is happening and to act effectively and quickly when problems are identified. Regulation should be judged on how it affects social, cultural and sustainability issues in society as well as on the economy. Implementing regulation with this as its central aim would certainly achieve better regulation for all. It would also ensure consistently better outcomes for consumers. Such an approach, for example, would have prevented the failure of the regulatory process in the current banking crisis.

Social Justice Ireland also believes that there should be solid and justifiable reasons for introducing regulation. It should not be introduced just to create choice/competition within the market. For example, to achieve competition in the electricity market the electricity regulator increased the price of electricity. While this may achieve competition, we question the benefit to the public at large.. Furthermore, assessment mechanisms should be established to allow an analysis of regulation pre and post implementation. Examination of societal impacts should be central to such an assessment procedure. We also believe that inputs should be sought from interested parties, including the community and voluntary sector, as part of the assessment procedure.

The impact of regulation within the context of regional policy is another important consideration. Cross-subsidisation issues, in postal or electrical services, are important to retain equity between rural and urban dwellers. A further challenge for regulatory authorities must be to retain this inter-regional equity.

Regulation and regulatory law has profoundly failed Ireland in recent years. It should be framed in ways that ensure it is effective, timely, accessible and interpretable. Currently regulatory law is complex and in many cases requires those being regulated to divert a considerable quantity of resources to keep abreast of developments. Complex regulation also makes it difficult for interested parties to actively participate in the pre and post-regulation assessment mechanisms. *Social Justice Ireland* believes it is important that where regulation has been judged to be a failure, Government should reform it at the earliest opportunity.

Key Policy Priorities for Public Services

- Focus policy on ensuring that there is provision of, and access to, a level of public services regarded as acceptable by Irish society generally.
- Ensure equality of access across all public services.
- Target funding strategies to ensure that far greater priority is given to providing an easy-access, affordable, integrated and high-quality public transport system as well as ensuring the maintenance of roads.
- Ensure adequate support for the Rural Transport Initiative that increases significantly the quality of life of those living in remote rural areas, particularly older people and women.
- Support the further development of library services throughout the country, including provision of open-access information technology.
- Ensure that financial institutions provide people with easily accessed and affordable basic bank accounts and financial facilities, as per the Strategy for Financial Inclusion (2011), to ensure accessibility, explore the possibilities of achieving this through the post office and credit union network in addition to other financial institutions.
- Give more in-depth consideration to how public funds are used to encourage sport and sporting activity. In many cases simple schemes to encourage participation and use of existing sports facilities are required.
- Adopt further information technology programmes to increase the skills of disadvantaged members of society.
- With increased investment in advanced broadband systems, continued monitoring is required in regard to both the quality and cost of its provision to ensure accessibility.
- Take action to address the huge failures identified in regulatory processes. These processes should ensure that all types of regulation take into account potential impact on social, cultural and sustainability issues within society as well as on the economy. Implementing regulation with this balance as its central aim would achieve better regulation for all.

7.

HOUSING AND ACCOMMODATION

CORE POLICY OBJECTIVE: HOUSING & ACCOMMODATION
To ensure that adequate and appropriate accommodation is available for all people and to develop an equitable system for allocating resources within the housing sector

Issues relating to housing and accommodation have featured prominently in policy debates in Ireland over recent years. Most of this has been concerned with the provision and cost of privately owned accommodation. However, more recent developments in the area of housing relate to challenges involving the large surplus housing stock in areas of low demand, and low housing stock in areas of high demand, high levels of mortgage arrears, unfinished developments and increasing social housing need, as well as changes in tenure patterns and the focus of housing policy. All of these issues are discussed in this chapter and they all relate to one element of *Social Justice Ireland*'s core policy framework (see chapter 2) 'Enhance Social Provision'.

During the boom years, Ireland experienced an astonishing growth in property construction and house prices. Initially the increase in housing construction was a response to rising demand, as a result of a sustained growth in the population, low interest rates and increasing income per capita. As noted in chapter 2, this situation changed and construction was promoted and supported as an end in itself because it appeared to generate economic growth. Construction became a major element and driver of the Irish economy. Housing construction increased at a rate which was not supported by demand. The result was a housing bubble which contributed to the economic crisis. According to Kitchin et.al (2010), poor financial and planning regulations, along with tax incentives, served to support this negative phenomenon.

Housing: a New Philosophy

Given the changes which have occurred in the housing landscape in Ireland it is imperative that a new paradigm from which to progress housing policy into the future is identified. Drudy (2006) outlines the basic elements of two approaches to housing – housing as a commodity or housing as a home.

When housing is viewed as a commodity the market is seen to be the ideal provider and state intervention is limited to facilitating and encouraging private provision through, for example, tax incentives. While some state provision of housing would exist, it would be limited to very low income groups. The implications of this standpoint is to develop a housing system which provides speculative profit for those with the resources, excluding people based on their ability to pay and generating a housing system which perpetuates inequality and segregation (Drudy, 2006). The alternative to this is to view 'housing as a home', placing the emphasis on– 'shelter, a place to stay, to feel secure, to build a base, find an identity and participate in a community and society' (Drudy, 2006:244). This view regards housing as a fundamental social requirement, in much the same way as education or health.

Social Justice Ireland strongly endorses the need to view housing as a fundamental social right as per the Core Policy Framework discussed in Chapter 2. Over recent times it is clear that housing in Ireland has been seen as a commodity rather than a home and this has had major implications for Irish society. Had society adopted the approach of viewing housing as a social right over the past decade the Irish economy, and many Irish families, would not be in the precarious financial position they are now in. It is time that we formally incorporated this approach into our national housing policy.

Government Housing Policy Statement 2011

The framework for the current national housing policy is found in the Government's Housing Policy Statement which was released in June 2011. It states 'Our vision for the future of the housing sector in Ireland is based on choice, fairness, equity across tenures and on delivering quality outcomes for the resources invested. The overall strategic objective will be to enable all households to access good quality housing appropriate to household circumstances and in their particular community of choice' (Department of Environment, Community and Local Government, 2011). The statement further specifies that it will not entice people to treat housing as a commodity.

The statement focuses on:

• the removal of incentives to purchase;

- the creation of a viable and well regulated private rental sector containing quality housing provision;
- the standing down of affordable housing programmes;
- Review of Part V of the Planning and Development Act 2000 (currently underway);
- the move to greater provision through options such as the Rental Accommodation Scheme and the long term leasing initiative;
- the remaining capital build programmes to focus, in particular, on regeneration and projects that cater for special needs; and
- bolstering the role of the voluntary and co-operative sector.

This has been accompanied by a massive reduction in capital spending on housing over the past number of years. The allocation for housing in budget 2014 (Department of Finance, Budget 2014) was €576 million (i.e. €304 million in current spending and €273 million in capital expenditure)[51]. The dramatic decline in the allocation for social housing illustrates the Government's approach to housing policy, with a reorientation of funding from construction towards leasing initiatives but no coherent approach to reducing the number of households on waiting lists. New figures indicate that there are almost 90,000 households on waiting lists for social housing, showing housing need in Ireland is at a crisis point [while there was a reduction of approximately 9,000 households on the 2011 figure, differing methodologies used for the collection of data means that numbers are not comparable]. It appears that Government has no credible plan of sufficient scale to address this issue in the foreseeable future.

Housing tenure in Ireland

Ireland's housing policy historically resulted in very high levels of owner occupation to the detriment of other tenure types. Housing policy in the past favoured investment in residential development which, combined with policies of mortgage-interest tax relief and very favourable tenant purchase schemes, has resulted in a high level of home ownership. The abolition of local rates on residential property and the

---

[51] Revised estimates Budget 2014 indicate the following output targets in housing. Secure 1,200 housing units through leasing arrangements. Transfer 4,000 households from rent supplement to rental accommodation scheme & other social housing supports. Deliver 200 units under Social Housing Investment Programme. Deliver an additional 500 units under Social Housing Stimulus Programme. Deliver 175 Special Needs Units under Capital Assistance Scheme. Deliver 40 Traveller Specific Units. Upgrade 14,166 units under retrofitting programme. Meet the housing needs of up to 150 people with disabilities transitioning from institutional care.

subsequent failure to implement a system of residential property tax ensured that owner occupation was additionally subsidised. Further to this, in the social housing sector people had the option of purchasing their own house and many did. In practice this transferred wealth to the purchaser as these houses were available for far less than their real market value. These policies over years produced a housing system that was not tenure neutral and led to the residualisation of the rental sector, both public and private. Using data from various Censuses of Population, table 7.1 shows how Irish tenure patterns have changed. In 2006 77.2 per cent of households were owner-occupiers, a figure which gave Ireland one of the highest rates of owner occupancy in the EU. Irelands traditionally high-level of home ownership is indicative of two factors: it shows the value which Irish people placed on owning their own home and it underscores the level to which Irish housing policy has supported owner occupation, placing little value on other tenure types.

This trend has begun to reverse with a substantial reduction in the level of owner-occupied dwellings in 2011 and a return to levels in renting which have not been seen since 1971 (see table 7.1). In 2011 owner occupied dwellings accounted for 70.8 per cent, down from 77.2 per cent in 2006, a reduction of almost 7 percentage points in this period and just under 10 percentage points since 1991. There has also been a dramatic 47 per cent increase in the number of households in rented accommodation between 2006 and 2011, up from 323,007 to 474,788. The overall percentage of households renting their accommodation rose to 29.2[52] per cent, causing home ownership rates to fall sharply (see table 7.1) (CSO, 2012). People's reluctance to buy property and to continue to rent instead may be due to such factors as the unavailability of mortgage finance and instability in the housing and employment markets.

---

[52] 'Other' refers to the category of people who indicated that they were living in their dwellings rent free. In the CSO publication *The roof over our heads* this category of people is included in the number of households renting, giving a total of 474,788 or 29.2%.

Table 7.1- Nature of Occupancy of Private Households, Ireland 1961-2011

Year	Owner-occupied	Rented	Other
1961	59.8%	35.6%	4.6%
1971	68.8%	28.9%	2.3%
1981	74.7%	22.6%	2.6%
1991	80.0%	17.9%	2.1%
2002	79.8%	18.5%	1.7%
2006	77.2%	21.3%	1.5%
2011[53]	70.8%	27.7%	1.6%

Source: CSO (2012:63)

Total Housing Stock

Census 2011 revealed interesting insights into the total housing stock in Ireland. In April 2011 there were 1,994,845 permanent dwellings or housing units in the State. This is an increase of 225,232 units, or 12.7 per cent, on the level in 2006, representing an annual average growth rate of 2.4 per cent. While this increase is significant it is a notable reduction on the increase in stock which occurred between 2002 and 2006, when the housing stock increased by 309,560 (21 per cent), representing an average annual growth rate of 4.9 per cent, which is the highest on record (CSO, 2012:7). Comparing figures from census 2002, 2006 and 2011, it is clear that a significant slowdown in the housing stock growth has occurred – a slowdown which was inevitable due to the oversupply of housing in many areas of the country which took place over the last 20 years.

Housing Stock and Population Growth

Table 7.2 shows the growth in housing stock compared to the growth in population over a 20 year period. The rise in housing stock was significantly greater than the growth in population (71.9 per cent compared with 30.1 per cent). There were 785 new housing units for every 1,000 persons added to the population between 1991 and 2011 (CSO, 2012:7). This illustrates that the increase in housing which occurred over the 10 year period leading up to census 2011 was unsustainable, with more than one in four of all occupied dwellings in Ireland being built during this decade.

---

[53] The 2011 data cited in this table differs slightly from the publication released by the CSO *The roof over our heads*. This is because in order for the data to be comparable with other years it required that the category of people who 'did not state' the nature of their occupancy be removed from the total number of dwellings prior to calculating the percentage of owner-occupied, rented and other. This is in keeping with other CSO publications, such as *Measuring Irelands Progress 2011*.

Table 7.2- Population and housing stock 1991-2011

Census Year	Population	% Change in Population	Housing Stock	% Change in Housing Stock
1991	3,525,719	-	1,160,249	-
1996	3,626,087	2.8	1,258,948	8.5
2002	3,917,203	8.0	1,460,053	16.0
2006	4,239,848	8.2	1,769,613	21.2
2011	4,588,252	8.2	1,994,845	12.7

Source: CSO (2012:7)

House completions

Table 7.3 outlines the rate of house completions in the various sectors from 2001 up to the third quarter of 2013. The peak was in 2006 when over 93,000 units were completed. Since then the rate of dwelling completion has declined rapidly. The total number of house completions in 2010 was 14,602, with a further fall to 8,488 in 2012, with preliminary data for 2013 showing a continuation of this trend. 2012 figures for total house completions have more than halved when compared with levels in 1993 (21,391 units across all sectors). In 1993, Local Authorities completed 1,200 units, voluntary/non-profit accounted for 890 units with the private sector making up the remaining 19,301 units (cf. annex 7).

In 2009 the vast majority of new houses (80 per cent) were built by the private sector (down from 91 per cent in 2007). In 2012 private sector completions accounted for 88 per cent of total completions. While the private sector still is responsible for the highest number of completions the fall-off has been dramatic, going from over 70,000 in 2007 to almost 7,500 in 2012.

Local authorities completed 3,362 new homes in 2009, this figure dropped substantially to 363 in 2012. The Government has indicated that a return to large scale building of local authority housing is unlikely and has instead decided to focus resources in the area of social leasing initiatives and the Rental Accommodation Scheme (RAS) in order to ensure social housing provision. The figures for 2009 revealed a welcome growth in the levels of voluntary/non-profit and co-op housing. These organisations built 2,011 dwellings during that year. This trend underscored the growing role this sector is playing in Irish housing. Currently according to the Irish Council for Social Housing (2013) the housing association sector manages up to 27,000 homes. However, a reduction in capital funding has a seen a major reduction in completions of housing from this sector, with only 653 completions in 2012 and again preliminary data for 2013 showing a continuation of this trend.

The Government's housing policy statement indicates that the role of the voluntary and cooperative sector will be central in providing social housing into the future. With the elimination of the Capital Loans and Subsidy Scheme, it is essential that this sector is supported.

Table 7.3 - House Completions, 1993–2013 (Q.3)

Year	Local Authority Housing	Voluntary/ Non Profit Housing	Private Housing	Total
2001	3,622	1,253	47,727	52,602
2002	4,403	1,360	51,932	57,695
2003	4,516	1,617	62,686	68,819
2004	3,539	1,607	71,808	76,954
2005	4,209	1,350	75,398	80,957
2006	3,968	1,240	88,211	93,419
2007	4,986	1,685	71,356	78,027
2008	4,905	1,896	44,923	51,724
2009[28]	3,362	2,011	21,076	26,420
2010	1,328	741	12,533	14,602
2011	486	745	9,295	10,480
2012	363	653	7,472	8,488
2013 up to Q3	253	100	5,318	5,671

Source: Department of Environment, Community and Local Government Housing Statistics (2013) Note: Local authority house completions do not include second-hand houses acquired by them. New units acquired under Part V, Planning & Development Acts 2000-2006 for local authority rental purposes are included. Voluntary & co-operative housing consists of housing provided under the capital loan & subsidy and capital assistance schemes.

[54] There is a discrepancy of 29 in total house completions. This is as a result 39 voluntary and co-operative units completed in this year being represented by just 10 ESB connections due to the nature of the units.

Social Justice Ireland believes that the voluntary and co-operative sector has the capacity to make a significant contribution in addressing housing need in Ireland and that Government must provide the assistance needed to ensure its continued growth. With the Government's housing policy statement focusing on the bolstering of this sector, it will be necessary to ensure appropriate regulation, while also ensuring that sufficient funding and pathways to funding are available in order for this sector to contribute towards addressing the level of housing need in Ireland. However this sector cannot be expected to provide for all of Ireland's social housing needs.

Further to the completions the local authorities also acquire a number of units. The downward trend in output is further mirrored in the data relating to acquisitions for social housing from local authorities. Going from 2,002 acquisitions in 2007, to 325 in 2011 and 351 in 2012. The number of new units in social housing output has been declining significantly over the past number of years. The total number of new social housing units (includes completions for both local authority and voluntary and cooperative housing as well as local authority acquisitions) in 2007 was 8,673 falling to 6,100 in 2009 down to 1,391 in 2012. In addition to this there were also a number of new properties acquired on long-term lease under The Rental Accommodation Scheme (RAS) (cf. Annex 7). However, even with the inclusion of the new RAS units and acquisitions, the output of new social housing units has fallen considerably.

Government should ensure it provides sufficient, continued investment in developing and maintaining the stock of some 130,000 local authority houses. Bringing back into use the numerous voids in this stock throughout the country will assist. The major scaling back which is currently occurring in regard to local authority stock will have long term negative consequences for people in housing need.

Vacant housing stock

As the increase in housing stock significantly outstripped the growth in population it became increasingly clear that there would be insufficient demand to sustain this growth, particularly given the uneven geographical distribution. Given the vacancy rate, the trend in house building in Ireland has been counter to what might be expected. Counties with the highest rates of vacant stock in 2006 subsequently enlarged their housing stock by the highest percentage in the ensuing years, and those counties with low vacancy levels increased their stock the least (Kitchin, et.al. 2010), with Cavan, Donegal, Leitrim and Longford recording a more than 18% increase in housing stock over that period (CSO, 2012).Coupled with this, according to Kitchen (2010), the lack of a residential property tax ensured that local authorities adopted a model of funding which pursued income from development levies. This was further supported by central Government through tax incentive schemes and poor regulation of local planning. These factors have resulted in vacant housing stock in areas where there is the least demand as well as unfinished estates and developments across the country.

In 2011 the overall vacancy rate was 14.5 per cent (if holiday homes are excluded the vacancy rate drops to 11.5 per cent). In 2011 the vacant units consisted of 59,395 holiday homes, 168,427 houses and 61,629 apartments. The total vacancy rate in 2011 fell by 0.5 per cent compared to 2006. However, the increase in total housing stock over this period means that the number of vacant units increased by 23,129 (see table 7.4). The vacancy rate for 2011 varies considerably across the country. It is highest in Leitrim, at 30.5 per cent, followed by Donegal (28.6 per cent), Kerry (26.4 per cent) and Mayo (24.7 per cent). The lowest vacancy rate was recorded in South Dublin (5.4 per cent), followed by Fingal (7.0 per cent), Dun Laoghaire Rathdown (7.7 per cent) and Kildare (8.0 per cent). A vacancy rate of 10.2 per cent, or 24,638 units, was recorded for Dublin City (CSO, 2012).

Table 7.4 Vacancy rate and number of vacant units for 1991, 1996, 2002, 2006 & 2011

Year	Vacancy Rate%	% Change on vacancy rate	Number of units vacant	Change in number of units vacant
1991	9.1	———	105,142	——-
1996	8.4	- 0.7%	105,250	+ 108
2002	9.8	+1.4%	143,418	+ 38,168
2006	15	+5.2%	266,322	+122,904
2011	14.5	-.5%	289,451	+ 23,129

Source: CSO (2012)

Unfinished housing estates

The plethora of unfinished housing estates throughout Ireland is largely a result of many local authorities disregarding good planning guidelines. Consideration was not given to 'regional and national objectives, sensible demographic profiling of potential demand and the fact that much of the land zoned lacked essential services such as water and sewage treatment plants, energy supply, public transport or roads' (Kitchin, et.al. 2010: 28). This has obvious social and economic implications for people owning houses, often in negative equity and living in poorly finished estates. In some instances these home owners have few neighbours, no street lighting, paths or green areas and are located a good distance away from amenities or services (Kitchin et.al. 2010).

The Progress Report on Actions to Resolve Unfinished Housing Developments (Department of Environment, Community and Local Government, 2012) indicates that as a result of recommendations from the Advisory Group on Unfinished Housing Developments (2011) the Government's initial priority was to address public safety issues. But it also aimed to bring together the main stakeholders at national, regional and local level to ensure that there was a coordinated response, to put in place stronger legislation with a view to ensuring the engagement of developers in resolving any unfinished estates and to build confidence in the housing sector by engaging in best practice in regard to utilising vacant housing for beneficial use.

The first report assessing the numbers of unfinished housing developments released in 2011 indicated that from a total of 2,876 housing development sites of two or more dwellings, there are 2,066 unfinished housing developments in the country. Of these, 1,822 were predominantly inactive at the time of inspection and only 245 active. The number of developments still considered 'unfinished' in the 2013 survey had fallen to 1,258, of which 992 developments have residents living in them (Department of Environment, Community and Local Government, 2011, 2013). *Social Justice Ireland* believes that Government should continue to meet commitments given to prioritise those estates with people living in them and which remain unfinished; this is vital given the social consequences as outlined above.

It has been indicated that the numbers of vacant homes and the completion of unfinished housing estates are features of the current housing landscape in Ireland which provide some opportunities for the Government to address ongoing housing need. The Irish Council for Social Housing and the National Association of Building Cooperatives have indicated that 'opportunities exist for the voluntary and cooperative sector to have an impact on the issue of unfinished housing developments by working in partnership with Local Authorities to serve local social housing need' (Advisory Group on Unfinished Housing Developments, 2011:12).

Social Justice Ireland considers it imperative that the Government continue to assess the appropriateness of vacant estates/individual sites to be used for social housing and advise local authorities/AHBs on how best to transfer these units to social use. The potential role which could be played by NAMA in addressing social housing need has been indicated but progress has been slow. 'To date demand has been confirmed by the Local Authorities for 1,900 properties that NAMA has made available (This relates to all developments and not just developments identified as 'unfinished'). A further 290 properties are currently being evaluated bringing the total that may be deemed suitable to 2,190 potentially. Contracts have been signed and transactions completed for 466 units. 384 of these units relates to units within Unfinished Housing Developments' (Department of Environment, Community and Local Government, 2013:12).

While these options have the potential to provide a number of housing units for social housing purposes it also must be acknowledged that this flow of houses will be limited in terms of the scale of social housing need. Therefore it is important that Government begin to plan for social housing need into the future, identifying ways in which this can be met.

Mortgage arrears

A further problem relating to housing in Ireland is the ongoing issue of mortgage arrears. Central Bank figures (table 7.5) reveal the scale of this difficulty and also the level to which it has grown over the period from June 2012 to September 2013. The total number of mortgage arrears has been increasing steadily. At end-September 2013, there were 768,136 private residential mortgage accounts for principal dwellings held in the Republic of Ireland. Of these 99,189 or 12.9 per cent, were in arrears of more than 90 days. This compares to 81,035 accounts (10.6 per cent of total) that were in arrears of more than 90 days at end of June 2012 or 91,358 arrears cases[29] (11.5 per cent of total) at end of September 2012. At end of September 2013 there were a further 42,331 mortgages in arrears of less than 90 days, a slight fall off from 50,031 in the previous September. In total there were 141,520 mortgages in arrears of some form at end of September 2013. This amounts to almost 18.5 per cent of the total residential mortgage loans at that time. These figures highlight the scale of this issue and the necessity to implement long term sustainable solutions.

With regard to this, the report of the Inter-Departmental Mortgage Arrears Working Group (2011) (The Keane Report) made a range of recommendations, including, the need for new bankruptcy legislation, non-judicial debt settlement options and further mortgage restructuring solutions. The report also recommended the establishment of mortgage-to-rent schemes. Such schemes would allow certain struggling mortgage holders to remain in the family home as social housing tenants.

---

[55] The figures published are the total stock of mortgage accounts in arrears of more than 90 days, as reported to the Central Bank of Ireland. They include mortgages that have been restructured and are still in arrears of more than 90 days as well as mortgages in arrears of more than 90 days that have not been restructured (Central Bank, 2012) .

Table 7.5 - Mortgage Arrears

	Jun-12	Sep-12	Jun-13	Sep-13
Outstanding: Total residential mortgage loan accounts outstanding	765,267	794,275	770,610	768,136
Total mortgage arrears cases outstanding	128,197	141,389	142,892	141,520
In arrears up to 90 days	47,162	50,031	45,018	42,331
In arrears 91 to 180 days	18,764	19,814	17,612	16,680
In arrears over 180 days	62,271	71,544	80,262	82,509
Total arrears cases over 90 days outstanding	81,035	91,358	97,874	99,189
% of accounts in arrears for more than 90 days	10.6%	11.5%	12.7%	12.9%
Repossessions: Residential properties in possession	944	944	1,001	1,050
Restructured Mortgages: Total outstanding classified as restructured	84,941	81,634	79,357	80,555
of which are not in arrears	40,221	43,600	42,309	43,034

Source: Central Bank (2013)

Since then, several responses to this issue have occurred, among them the revised Code of Conduct on Mortgage Arrears (CCMA), which came into effect from July 2013, setting out the framework which must be utilised by lenders when dealing with borrowers in or at risk of falling into arrears. Under the CCMA the lenders must operate within a revised Mortgage Arrears Resolution Process (MARP), which has four steps, communication, financial information, assessment and resolution.

The Central Bank has also set targets for the main banks whereby they must propose sustainable mortgage solutions for a specific number of mortgages by specific dates; at the last review these targets were being met. However, the Central Bank did indicate that some issues in regard to the long term sustainability of solutions being offered remained to be addressed, for instance, short term loan modifications being offered in instances where there was no tangible evidence of the borrower's circumstances changing (Central Bank, 2013). This needs continued monitoring.

The Personal Insolvency Act 2012 introduced new debt resolution processes and the Insolvency Service of Ireland has been established under this act. This service is only in operation a short time and its effectiveness remains to be analysed.

The Mortgage Arrears Information and Advice Service was established in September 2012. The service is made up of three strands of which two relate to the provision of general mortgage arrears information, an information helpline run within the Citizens Information Board and a website. The third element relates to the provision of independent financial advice at the point where a mortgage lender has presented the borrower with long term forbearance proposals relating to the mortgage. The level of calls made to the helpline is relatively low, at 8,500 calls in the course of over one year; the website seems to be a more successful resource with 177,000 visitors over the same period. The Independent Financial Advice Service had a very small number of users, with figures indicating that from 11,000 borrowers who had been advised of the service, only 200 invoices from accountants for provision of this service were issued (it is possible that there is in excess of this number utilising this services and the invoices have yet to be issued). The low level of people utilising these services is concerning, especially when the scale of the problem is considered (table 7.5) (Department of Social Protection, 2013).

A mortgage to rent scheme and mortgage to lease arrangements were rolled out by the Department of Environment, Community and Local Government in 2012. Under this approach the property is bought by an approved housing body (housing association or co-operative) at current market value and the household becomes a social housing tenant of the housing body. The purchase of the house is partly financed by a loan from the original mortgage lender and partly from the Exchequer. Included in the criteria for qualification is the necessity for the person to qualify for social housing, the net household income must not exceed specific limits, and the individual must have been involved in the MARP with their lender. These schemes are designed to assist the most distressed mortgage holders and should only be viewed as a small component in addressing the overall issue.

The scale of this issue requires action which will bring about long term sustainable solutions for those individuals involved. It is imperative that those facing major adjustments as a result of mortgage arrears are dealt with fairly by banks. This requires that under any repayment schedule they have sufficient income to provide a minimum adequate standard of living.

Housing needs assessment:
Waiting lists – how many and how long?

Social housing support 'is broadly defined as accommodation provided, or arranged, by housing authorities or approved housing bodies for households who are unable to provide for their accommodation needs from their own resources' (Department of Environment, Community and Local Government, 2011, pg.48). A national summary of social housing assessments is carried out on a periodic basis and provides a vital insight into the level of need for social housing support across the country. The most recent assessment of housing needs took place in 2013. The following section provides an overview of the key findings of the Summary of Social Housing Assessments 2013. It must be noted that the approach used in the collection of the data in 2013 differs from that employed in previous years and therefore the figures are not strictly comparable. However, it is clear that large and lengthy waiting lists are becoming a feature of Irish society.

These waiting lists are developed on the basis of a concept called 'net need'. 'Net need' refers to 'the number of households in need of housing support who are not currently receiving social housing support (those already in local authority, voluntary cooperative or RAS accommodation are excluded)' (Housing Agency, 2011:1). The net need figure for 2008 showed that 56,249 households were in need of social housing support at 31 March 2008. This is an increase of 31 per cent on the level of need in 2005. While acknowledging that the data from 2008 and 2011 are not strictly comparable, it is still alarming to see that the increase reported in net need from 2008 to 2011 amounted to 42,069 households. This is a 74.8 per cent increase over the period. Again although numbers are not directly comparable due to changes in methodologies employed, in 2013, **89,872 households were assessed as qualified for housing support,** this is a reduction of 8,446 households or 9 per cent on the 2011 total, but is still 33,623 households more than in 2008 (Housing Agency, 2013) [refer to Annex for further data relating to housing need in Ireland].

Categorisation of main need for social housing support has been revised, therefore it is not possible to present a comparative table [refer to annex 7 for comparative data in regard to net need categories for periods 2005, 2008, 2011]. Table 7.6 displays information in regard to the major categories of need for social housing support in 2013, the largest category accounting for 52 per cent or 46,584 households requiring support relates to those dependent on rent supplement. The next largest section, 20,349 households or 23 per cent, had their main need categorised as 'unsuitable accommodation due to particular household circumstances'. According to the Housing Agency 'It is likely that this category is populated by households not in receipt of rent supplement, but with a difficulty in affording private accommodation' (2013:6).

Table 7.6 - Main Need for social housing support 2013

Main need for social housing support	Number of households	%
Dependent on Rent Supplement	46,584	52
Unsuitable accommodation due to particular household circumstances	20,349	23
Reasonable requirement for separate accommodation	9,587	11
In an institution, emergency accommodation or hostel	2,808	3
Household member has a physical disability	1,392	2
Household member has a sensory disability	190	—
Household member has a mental health disability	1,034	1
Household member has an intellectual disability	1,078	1
Household member has another form of disability	244	—
Unsuitable accommodation due to exceptional medical or compassionate grounds	2,909	3
Overcrowded Accommodation	2,896	3
Unfit Accommodation	647	1
Unsustainable mortgage*	154	—
Total	**89,872**	**100**

Source: Housing Agency, (2013:10)
*Where mortgage deemed unsustainable under the Mortgage Arrears Resolution Process (MARP)

Further to this, 11 per cent of households were found to have specific accommodation requirements, 4 per cent due to a disability, 3 per cent due to homelessness and 2 per cent requiring traveller specific accommodation, with the final 2 per cent in need of age specific accommodation.

The household structure of those who were on the waiting list in 2011 shows that 48,748 households, or 49.6 per cent, were single adult households. This was the highest category again in 2013, accounting for 44 per cent or 39,803 households. In 2013, single persons with children represented over 27,005 households or 30 per cent of the total. Two or more adults (with or without children) accounted for 22,174

(25 per cent) of households, with the remaining 1 per cent (890 households) being multi adult households.

The majority of people in need of housing support in 2011 were under 40 years of age at 69 per cent. This is again the case in 2013 with this cohort accounting for 64 per cent. In 2011 the largest category, 30.5 per cent, occurred within the age range of 31 – 40 years. In 2013 the largest category, 29,353 households or 33 per cent, were those categorised in the age range of 30 but less than 40, with 5 per cent aged 60 years or over; 71 per cent of households in need of housing support in 2013 had Irish citizenship, while 21 per cent were EU citizens and the balance of 8 per cent were categorised as having refugee status, permission to remain in the state or subsidiary protection status.

There is a clear association between being in housing need and low income. According to the OECD (2011) people with low incomes are more likely to face poorer basic housing conditions and are also less likely to be satisfied with their housing arrangements. Breakdown of net income data for the 2013 needs assessment is not currently available. However, it is interesting to note that the majority of households qualifying for social housing support were found to be dependent on social welfare as their only source of income. Social welfare was the only source of income for 72 per cent of households, 6 per cent had income from employment and social welfare, with 11 per cent of households having income from employment only.

The length of time spent by households on waiting lists once they have applied for social housing support is another area which deserves attention. Table 7.7 has the details. While 24 per cent of households had qualified in the previous 12 months, it is extremely concerning that 32 per cent of those assessed as being in need of social housing support were waiting in excess of four years.

Table 7.7- Length of time on record of qualified households

Length of time	Number of Households	%
Less than 6 months	11,696	13
Between 6 and 12 months	9,645	11
Between 1 and 2 years	14,436	16
Between 2 and 3 years	13,841	15
Between 3 and 4 years	11,986	13
Between 4 and 5 years	10,449	12
Between 6 and 7 years	9,765	11
More than 7 years	8,004	9
Total	89,872	100

Source: Housing Agency (2013:11)

The need for housing in Ireland is currently at an intolerable level. These numbers represent the most vulnerable people in Irish society. *Social Justice Ireland* has repeatedly highlighted the unacceptable level of progress being made in regard to counteracting this issue; it is imperative that swift and significant action is taken to address this current state of affairs.

The private rented sector

Traditionally, the private rented sector has been the residual sector of the Irish housing system, characterised by poor-quality accommodation and non-secure tenure at the lower end of the housing market. Today, this sector is highly differentiated, with high-quality housing and relatively secure tenure at the upper end of the market and low-quality housing and insecurity of tenure at the lower end. Reliance on this sector as a housing option fell to its lowest point of 7 per cent in 1991. Since then, however, it has risen substantially. The census of 2011 showed that almost 19 per cent of all households were renting from a private landlord (table 7.8). The private rental sector is increasingly becoming the tenure of choice for a substantial number of households (see table 7.8) as well as being viewed as means by which to address social housing provision.

Table 7.8 Percentage distribution of housing units by occupancy status, 1961-2011

Occupancy Status	1961	1971	1981	1991	2002	2006	2011
LA Rented	18.4	15.9	12.7	9.7	6.9	7.5	7.9
Private Rented	17.2	10.9	8.1	7.0	11.1	10.3	18.8
Owner Occupied	53.6	60.7	67.9	80.2	77.4	77.2	70.8
Other	10.8	12.5	11.2	3.0	4.6	5.0	2.5[56]
Total	100	100	100	100	100	100	100

Source: CSO (2003, 2007 & 2012)

As noted above, Irish Government policy did not prioritise the private rental sector; which was viewed as secondary to owner-occupation. Reflecting this approach, legislation and regulation of this sector was often lacking. In an attempt to address this, the Private Residential Tenancy Board was established in 2004. The role of the PRTB includes the establishment and maintenance of a register of all private rental residential accommodation, the provision of a cheap and efficient resolution service to handle tenant and landlord disputes and the undertaking of research into the private rental market (PRTB, 2010).

However, despite legal requirements and the linking of tax deductions to registration, a number of privately rented residences in the country are not registered with the PRTB. The total number of tenancies registered with the Board at the end of 2010 was 231,818 (PRTB, 2010). This compares with findings in census 2011, in which 305,377 households indicated that they were renting from a private landlord, a discrepancy of over 31 per cent. At end of 2012 there were 264,434 tenancies registered with the PRTB. While this is a significant increase, it is still lower than the findings in census 2011 (PRTB, 2012).

The task of ensuring that the standard of accommodation offered by this sector is at an appropriate level falls to the Private Residential Tenancy Board (PRTB) and Local Authorities. The level and geographical distribution of inspections carried out by the Local Authorities of the registered properties indicates that in some areas inspections are common while in others they are far lower. Overall there has been a notable increase in the number of inspections being carried out. In 2007, 14,008 inspections were carried out. This rose to 17,186 in 2008 and 19,801 in 2009. 2010

---

[56] Other refers to households who indicated that they were living rent free or renting from a voluntary body. Those who did not state the nature of their occupancy have not been included.

saw another increase with 21,614 inspections being carried out. However this fell by almost 1000 in 2012 to 19,616. This should be monitored closely to ensure the momentum of enforcing regulatory standards is not lost. In 2012 of the 16,055 dwellings inspected, 7,348 were found to be failing to meet regulatory standards. This is a serious issue and needs to be tackled appropriately especially given the increasingly important role that this sector is playing in the housing scene in Ireland.

The Government's housing policy statement recognises the need to deliver a well regulated rental sector, ensuring that rental is a real housing option for everyone. Considering the growth in the private rental sector in Ireland, and bearing in mind the figures relating to the registration and inspection of these tenancies, further development of the work of the Private Residential Tenancy Board (PRTB) in regard to ensuring official registration of all private rented properties is necessary. While there have been huge improvements in regard to the regulation of this sector, given the increasing demand for private rented accommodation, the risk of an increase is substandard accommodation is a real concern. *Social Justice Ireland* believes that the Government must take the necessary steps to ensure that all local authorities carry out a reasonable number of inspections and enforce minimum standards. This will assist in ensuring the quality of accommodation offered by this sector is of appropriate standard.

Beyond this, it appears that pressures are building in the private rental market in certain regions. Increasing demand for private rented accommodation, as illustrated (table 7.8), a decrease in availability, [Daft, 2013 indicating that the stock of rental properties on the market in Q3 2013 was at its lowest since the same period in 2007], added to increasing rents, the PRTB Rent Index Q3 2013, showed that rents increased nationally by 1.9 per cent on the same quarter in 2012. While, this rise is primarily driven by substantial increases in the Dublin market of 6.4 per cent on an annual basis, there has been an annual increase 0.5 per cent in rents for houses outside of Dublin. These trends underscore the questionable nature of pursuing the delivery of social housing through the private rental sector. In light of the changes relating to affordability and stock availability in certain areas, the ability to meet housing need through this tenure is unclear. These developments need to be monitored closely in order to establish whether recent developments are persistent.

Rent supplement

When rent supplement was introduced it was only intended as a short-term housing support for those who suffered a sudden drop in income. While there has been a fall of almost 10, 000 recipients over the period from 2010 to 2012, over time this programme has seen a massive increase in participants and costs as outlined in table 7.9. Rising form 59,726 recipients in 2007 to 87,684 in 2012, an increase of over 27,958, resulting in this mechanism becoming a housing support for many. In addition, a large cohort of recipients are in receipt for prolonged periods of time. In December 2011 there were approximately 53,000 recipients of rent supplement for a period of 18 months or more. In December 2012 this cohort accounted for almost half the rent supplement recipients or 41, 670. These are the target group for the Rental Accommodation Scheme (RAS) (Department of Social Protection 2011&2012). It is clear that people are in receipt of rent supplement for long periods of time as progression to other social housing provision such as RAS has not occurred.

Table 7.9 Rent Supplement Cost and number of Recipients for 2002, 2007, 2009, 2010, 2011, 2012

Year	Expenditure €000	Recipients
2007	391,466	59,726
2008	440,548	74,038
2009	510,751	93,030
2010	516,538	97,260
2011	502,748	96,803
2012	422,536	87,684

Source: Department of Social Protection (2012)

Rent supplement operates under maximum rent limits. These should reflect local conditions and family composition. The review in 2013 established new maximum rent limits regionally which are in line with the most up-to-date market data available. The 2013 review increased these limits for a number of areas. Even though these limits have been increased, voluntary agencies [Focus, Threshold] expressed concern in the past that increases in minimum contributions towards rent supplement over a number of years has increased difficulty for some recipients to source good quality accommodation appropriate to their needs, forcing them into substandard accommodation. This is an issue of great concern which needs to be monitored closely.

Plans are in place to move the operation of rent supplement from the Department of Social Protection to the Department of Environment, Community and Local Government developing a Housing Assistance Payment (HAP), this is due to be piloted in 2014. The Department states: 'The housing policy framework contains the announcement of the transfer of responsibility in providing housing needs for long-term rent supplement recipients to housing authorities on a phased basis. A multi-agency steering group has been established by the Department of

Environment, Community and Local Government to give effect to the Housing Policy Initiative and this group is currently developing proposals and operational protocols for the transfer of tenants' (Department of Social Protection, 2011:23). This is a welcome move and will hopefully result in increased efficiency as well as ensuring better quality and more secure accommodation for tenants. It is also considered likely that this move will eliminate the poverty trap associated with rent supplement as people will pay differential rents to allow them to proceed to work while retaining some of their housing support benefit.

Rental Accommodation Scheme (RAS) and Social Housing Leasing

As previously discussed the Government has ruled out a return to large capital funded construction programmes by local authorities, instead focusing on the enhanced role that the Rental Accommodation Scheme (RAS) and the Social Housing Leasing Initiative will play in the delivery of social housing.

RAS was designed to address the needs of people on rent supplement for periods of over 18 months. It provides a longer term contract and more security of tenure than is associated with people who have their accommodation needs met under rent supplement. The local authority rents the unit from the landlord at reduced market rent for periods of between one and four years. Unlike rent supplement, which involves the tenant dealing with the landlord, under the RAS the local authority deals directly with the landlord. At the end of 2012, since its inception in 2005, 25,463 households had been transferred from rent supplement directly to RAS, with a further 17,747 transferred to other social housing options. This gives a total of 43,210, 5,451 of these transfers occurred in 2012 (Department of Environment, Community and Local Government, 2013).

With the longer term leasing option, units are leased to either local authorities or approved housing bodies (AHB) for a period of 10 – 20 years [properties have been sourced within the private sector, from NAMA and also the unsold affordable properties]. Unlike RAS, where the landlord retains responsibility for the upkeep and maintenance of the property, under this initiative the local Authority or the AHB take on this responsibility. In both instances people have increased security of tenure and improved quality of accommodation as the property must comply with standards for rented houses. The Long Term Leasing Initiative has resulted in approximately, 3,700 units over the period from 2010 to 2012 (Department of Environment, Community and Local Government, 2010, 2011, 2012). The growing role of Approved Housing Bodies can be seen from the number of units acquired under this initiative; this sector had acquired a total of 2449 units by Q1 2013. The majority of these units have come through the unsold affordable units. By Q1 of

2013 nearly 2000 units were leased by housing association via this stream (ICSH, 2013:6).

With almost 90,000 households on local authority waiting lists in 2013, it is clear that the scale at which property is being provided under these schemes is insufficient to meet demand. It is now necessary for alternative options in regard to supply of social housing to be developed and implemented. If this does not occur there will be no progress made in regard to addressing the huge level of social housing need. *Social Justice Ireland* recognises that the means by which social housing provision on the scale required is to be financed is of central concern and requires exploration. For example consideration could be given to the establishment of a National Housing Authority which would be answerable to the Minister for the Environment, Community and Local Government and would assume charge of the current stock of local authority houses and a range of other issues related to social housing. Such a body could have responsibility for the delivery of social housing and could also take on the role of providing finance to voluntary and cooperative housing agencies as well as assisting in addressing the issue of mortgage arrears.

Homelessness

People experiencing homelessness are not a homogenous group and there are many reasons why people become homeless. 'Structural explanations locate the reasons for homelessness in social and economic structures and cite poverty, negative labour market forces, cuts and restrictions in social welfare payments and reductions or shortfalls in the supply of affordable housing as the leading causes. Individual accounts, on the other hand, focus on the personal characteristics and behaviours of homeless people and suggest that homelessness is the consequence of personal problems, such as mental illness and addiction' (O'Sullivan, 2008:21).

Census 2011 revealed that 3,808 persons were either sleeping rough or in accommodation designated for the homeless on the night of the count. Of these, 2,539 were male and 1,269 were female. Of the 64 persons found sleeping rough, all but six were males. Dublin accounted for 59 of the 64 rough sleepers. The Dublin rough sleeper count in November 2013 shows that rough sleepers are on the increase with 139 indicated in this count a worrying trend which will need to be monitored and addressed. Further to this, the proportion of persons with disabilities among the homeless population was significantly higher, at 42 per cent, than for the general population, at 13 per cent. 49 per cent reported that they did not have an educational qualification beyond lower secondary level compared to 25 per cent of the general population. Almost one third reported that their health was 'fair, 'bad' or 'very bad' compared to 10 per cent of the general population (CSO, 2012). These statistics show the myriad of difficulties surrounding the phenomenon of homelessness. Furthermore, even though comparisons between data is limited, a recent report by the Homelessness Oversight Group (2013) suggests that there has been little improvement in the numbers of people experiencing long term homelessness.

In addressing homelessness, policy needs to focus on both the structural and individualistic causes. Decreases in funding for homeless services places severe pressure on services dealing with the many complexities of this issue at a time when service providers are reporting a significant increase in demand. The need to support service delivery in regard to preventative strategies is clear, however it is also important to note that people who experience homelessness require ongoing support after being housed to ensure the sustainability of the tenancy. It is therefore imperative that the Government make available an adequate level of funding for organisations providing such supports.

Another issue associated with homelessness relates to gaining an accurate measure of the numbers of people experiencing this difficulty. Clearly complications arise due to the complexity of matters surrounding homelessness and the level to which, by its very nature, is a hidden problem. There has traditionally been a gap between the administrative data (local authority Needs Assessment) held and the numbers of people accessing homeless services. There have, however, been major welcome developments in regard to the collection and collation of data in regard to homelessness, with the introduction and rollout of PASS [Pathway Accommodation and Support System]. *Social Justice Ireland* believes that it is important that resources continue to be put in place to ensure that comparable accurate data in regard to persons experiencing homelessness is available. Accurate data will allow for timelier and more appropriate responses to homelessness.

In February 2013 Government published a Homelessness Policy Statement which commits it to prioritising the provision of long-term housing as early as possible, rather than putting homeless people through a process of short and medium-term housing 'steps', This would amount to a housing led approach, ultimately achieving the goal of ending long-term homelessness and the incidence of rough sleeping by 2016. The Homelessness Oversight Group (2013) indicate that this high level goal is attainable by 2016 if certain recommendations are in place. Among these are; The need to establish a co-ordinating body to oversee that actions are put in place to achieve the 2016 target; the need for broader policy in relation to social housing to fully integrate the 2016 objective; the development of a structured plan in order to assist in the move from a shelter led approach to a sustainable housing led response coupled with more preventative measures in regard to homelessness; also the social housing leasing scheme should be made more efficient, along with a requirement to ensure that AHBs, Local Authorities and NAMA identify a certain proportion of housing for homeless people; as well as the development of lending products by the Housing Finance Agency which would support the provision of housing for the homeless.

Social Justice Ireland has also previously indicated that it should be possible to end long term homelessness and incidence of rough sleeping by 2016 if sufficient resources are targeted at the goal without delay. To demonstrate that its commitment to addressing the issue of homelessness in Ireland is real and not just rhetorical *Social Justice Ireland* believes that Government should immediately allocate the resources required to end long term homelessness in Ireland by 2016.

Traveller accommodation

The number of people enumerated as Irish Travellers in Census 2011 increased by 32 per cent from 22,435 to 29,573, with all counties apart from Limerick and Waterford showing increases larger than the increase in the general population. Further findings in Census 2011 indicate that only 12 per cent of Irish Travellers lived in caravans and mobile homes, with almost 84 per cent of the Traveller population living in permanent housing. This is a significant fall from 2006, when one in four Irish Travellers lived in temporary accommodation (CSO, 2012).

The All-Ireland Traveller Health Study (2010) showed that while the majority of Traveller families have basic household amenities [flush toilet, running water, waste disposal], there are still a disproportionately greater amount of Traveller families without these amenities than in the general population. Significant numbers of families in group housing or sites reported lack of footpaths, public lighting, fire hydrants and safe play areas. A quarter (24.4 per cent) of Traveller families in the Republic considered where they lived to be 'unhealthy' or 'very unhealthy' and significant numbers (26.4 per cent) considered their place of residence unsafe. 'Traveller accommodation is inextricably linked to almost all other aspects of Travellers' lives – their traditions, health, education, employment prospects and any number of other issues' (Coates et.al. 2008:81). Despite many legislative and policy changes and increased support for Traveller specific accommodation, there is widespread consensus that in practice Traveller accommodation is a challenging area to address. According to Coates et al (2008), politicians, policy makers and local authorities as well as Traveller organisations and members of both the Traveller and settled community, are dissatisfied with the existing situation in regard to Traveller accommodation in Ireland.

Capital funding for Traveller accommodation has been significantly reduced. Concerns have also been raised regarding the failure on the part of the Local Authorities to draw down funding ring-fenced for traveller specific accommodation [refer to written Dail Answers #43692/13]. Given the link between housing and quality of life, there is a need for the Government to ensure that local authorities fulfil their obligations in relation to Traveller accommodation.

Housing and people with disabilities

'The housing options available to people with disabilities generally fall far short of those available to the general population. Limited understanding of disability and the needs and aspirations of people with disabilities on the part of society generally may result in inadequate policy responses to the housing needs of people with disabilities' (Browne, 2007: iv).

Additional housing costs are a feature of having a disability. Primarily these costs are for adjustments to residences to ensure access and continued use and there are several housing adaptation grants available for this purpose. The Government indicates in the *National Housing Strategy for People with a Disability 2011-2016*, that promotion of independent living for people with disabilities and the elderly is supported by the availability of such grants. According to the Housing Agency (2013), while a substantial number of grants have been awarded since 2007, data in 2013 indicated that Authorities were approving far fewer grants. Funding for these grants has been substantially reduced over recent years. Coupled with this, a review of the qualifying criteria took place with many organisations [Disability Federation of Ireland, Age Action] expressing serious concern regarding new criteria and the consequent reduction in the level of grants available to individuals. *Social Justice Ireland* believes that given social and economic benefits of people remaining in their own homes, it is imperative that adequate funding should be made available to ensure that they can do so; this would also be in keeping with the recent *National Housing Strategy for People with a Disability 2011-2016*.

The national strategy represents a very welcome policy outline aimed at ensuring that the rights of people with disability are upheld. It sets out a framework for delivering housing to people with disabilities through mainstream housing policy. The vision underpinning this strategy is: 'To facilitate access for people with disabilities to the appropriate range of housing and related support services, delivered in an integrated and sustainable manner, which promotes equality of opportunity, individual choice and independent living' (Department of the Environment, Community and Local Government, 2011: 34). The National Implementation Framework to support this strategy was released in 2012. This framework identifies the manner in which the Government and other stakeholders will ensure the continued implementation of the objectives established in the strategy. It focuses on several aspects of housing in regard to people with disabilities. Among them are ensuring people with disabilities within the community are provided with the requisite supports to access and maintain housing which meets their needs, and addressing the manner in which the transitioning of people from institutional care to more independent living is to be achieved. The Government should make available the appropriate level of funding to ensure the ongoing implementation of this framework.

Housing and children

Factors which impact on child wellbeing and development are varied and interconnected. The OECD (2011), highlighted that housing conditions and child development outcomes are strongly linked because children spend the largest proportion of their time indoors. Poor housing affects children at different stages of their life. For example, lack of affordable housing may have an impact during early childhood as it weakens the family's ability to meet basic needs, while neighbourhood effects are more likely to have negative impacts on adolescents. Furthermore, associations between poor housing conditions and child development are more often than not irreversible and transfer to adulthood. One of the objectives of the National Children's Strategy is to ensure that 'Children will have access to accommodation appropriate to their needs' (Department of Health and Children, 2000, pg. 65). One of the ways in which this was to be achieved was through the prioritisation of families with children for accommodation under the new streams of housing to become available under the local authority and Voluntary Housing Programmes.

In 2008, 27,704 households with children were identified as being in need of social housing. In 2005 this figure was 22,335 (Office of Minister for Children and Youth Affairs, 2010). Figures from 2008 and 2011 are not strictly comparable and it is difficult, therefore to assess the extent to which this trend has continued. Nonetheless, in 2011 a total of 43,578 households which were in need of social housing support included children. The 2013 assessment of housing need does not provide sufficient breakdown of data in order to allow analyses of the numbers of households with children. However, single persons with children accounted for 27,005 (30 per cent) households on the waiting list, with a further 22,174 households in the category of two or more adults with or without children. Therefore, it is possible to conclude that well in excess of 30 per cent of households on the waiting list were households which included children. The special report relating to homeless people in Census 2011 revealed a further disturbing finding that there were 457 children aged 14 and under in the homeless count, representing 12 per cent of the total number of homeless people in Ireland (CSO, 2012). As already highlighted, low income and low accommodation standards are associated with poor health levels and poor future educational and life opportunities. Given Ireland's already deplorable record in regard to child poverty, *Social Justice Ireland* believes that the area of children and housing requires urgent action.

In reviewing the current context relating to housing and accommodation in Ireland it is apparent that a new approach is required. Growing affordability problems in the private rental sector in some regions combined with vast social housing need and very limited private construction, indicate a housing and accommodation system which is in disarray. The existing approach to housing is disjointed and does not tackle the situation in a comprehensive manner.

The development of a national housing strategy is long overdue. A national housing strategy should seek to address the myriad of problems relating to housing in Ireland, across the spectrum from private rented accommodation through to social housing provision. The development of a national housing strategy would ensure overall policy coherence in a complex system. This policy should take cognisance of projections of need based on accurate regional and demographic analysis, allowing for the identification of appropriate provision both in the private and social housing spheres. Finally it must be noted that a prerequisite for the efficacy of any housing policy is suitable policies for planning, transport and infrastructure, ensuring sustainable development into the future. Fundamentally there is a need for a considered approach to addressing the complex range of concerns relating to housing and accommodation; if not there will be limited progress made in resolving housing issues. Policy to date has failed to balance the advancement of home ownership, the development of a stable rental sector, both public and private, and the use of property for private determination. This balance still needs to be achieved.

Policy Priorities on Housing and Accommodation in Ireland

- Develop an Integrated Housing Strategy for Ireland
- Take the required action to ensure the supply of social housing, including co-op and voluntary/non-profit housing, is on the scale required to eliminate local authority housing waiting lists.
- Explore the potential for a National Housing Agency, answerable to the Minister for Environment, which would assume charge of the current stock of local authority houses and a range of other issues related to social housing. Such a body could have responsibility for the delivery of social housing and could also take on the role of providing finance to voluntary and cooperative housing agencies as well as assisting in addressing the issue of mortgage arrears.
- Ensure continued investment in developing social housing in order to maintain an adequate stock of social housing units including bringing back into use any vacant social housing units.
- Ensure prompt delivery and adequate resources to support Long Term Leasing initiatives and the Rental Accommodation Scheme (RAS).
- Ensure that adequate resources are made available for the national roll out of the Housing Assistance Payment.
- Make adequate funding available to resolve effectively, ongoing issues regarding unfinished housing estates so that suitable units can be brought into beneficial use. *Social Justice Ireland* considers it imperative that the Government continue to assist and advise local authorities/AHBs on how best to transfer these units to social use.

- Government should also meet commitments given, in regard to prioritising those unfinished estates which are currently occupied by residents.
- Take the necessary steps to ensure that all local authorities carry out a reasonable number of inspections annually of private rented accommodation and that further efforts are made to ensure official registration of all such properties.
- Allocate the resources required to end long term homelessness in Ireland by 2016.
- Ensure that those facing major adjustments as a result of mortgage arrears are dealt with fairly by banks. This requires that under any repayment schedule they have sufficient income to provide a minimum adequate standard of living.[57] Provide sufficient funding for the ongoing implementation and monitoring of the *National Housing Strategy for People with Disability 2011-2016*.
- Ensure the adequate resourcing of housing adaptation grants for people in need of such assistance.
- Provide continued investment in the Traveller accommodation programme and ensure local authorities are fulfilling their obligations in this area.

---

[57] Details of what these income levels should be are provided by the *Vincentian Partnership for Social Justice* in its studies – 2006 and 2010 – on this issue.

8.

HEALTHCARE

CORE POLICY OBJECTIVE: HEALTHCARE

To provide an adequate healthcare service focused on enabling people to attain the World Health Organisation's definition of health as a state of complete physical, mental and social wellbeing and not merely the absence of disease or infirmity.

Healthcare is a social right that every person should enjoy. People should be assured that care is guaranteed in their times of illness or vulnerability. Being so fundamental to wellbeing, healthcare services are important in themselves and they are also important as a factor in economic success in a range of ways, including improving work participation and productivity. Protection of services is one of the key policy areas that must be addressed urgently as part of the Core Policy Framework we set out in Chapter 2 under the heading of Enhancing Social Protection. This is amongst five priority areas identified by *Social Justice Ireland* which must be addressed in order to realise the vision for Ireland articulated there.

The standard of care is dependent to a great degree on the resources made available, which in turn are dependent on the expectations of society. The obligation to provide healthcare as a social right rests on all people. In a democratic society this obligation is transferred through the taxation and insurance systems to government and other bodies that assume or contract this responsibility. Health services need to be available as a right as envisaged in our Core Policy Areas, Enhance Social Provision and Reform Governance set out in Chapter 2. These are very important considerations in Ireland today as fundamental changes are underway in Ireland's healthcare system. This chapter outlines some of the major considerations *Social Justice Ireland* believes Government should bring to bear on such decision-making.

Poverty and Health

Health is not just about healthcare. The link between poverty and ill-health has been well established by international and national research. A World Health Organization Commission that reported in 2008 on the social determinants of health found that health is influenced by factors such as poverty, food security, social exclusion and discrimination, poor housing, unhealthy early childhood conditions, poor educational status and low occupational status. A more recent report by the World Health Organization into 53 European countries highlights how people have not shared equally in Europe's social, economic and health development and that in fact health inequalities are not diminishing but are increasing in many countries (WHO, Regional Office for Europe, 2013). In Ireland, studies conducted by the Irish Public Health Alliance (IPHA) detail striking differences in life expectancy and premature death between people in different socio-economic groups. The Pfizer Health Index published in 2012 showed that those from a lower socio-economic background are more likely to be affected by a wide range of medical conditions (including heart disease, cancer, depression and arthritis) than middle class people (ABC1) (Pfizer, 2012).

Analysis of Census 2011 data by the CSO confirms the relationship between social class and health. While 95 per cent of people in the top social class enjoyed good or very good health, this proportion fell across the social groups to below 75 per cent in social class 7 (CSO, 2012a). In summary, poor people get sick more often and die younger than those in the higher socio-economic groups. Poverty directly affects the incidence of ill-health, it limits access to affordable healthcare and reduces the opportunity for those living in poverty to adopt healthy lifestyles. A recent study by Eurofound reveals that the health status of Europeans has deteriorated during the economic crisis in respect of the prevalence of chronic diseases and that the gap between the self-reported health of low-income earners and that of the highest income earners is increasing (Eurofound, 2012). In Ireland a survey conducted by the CSO during 2012 measuring the response of households to the economic downturn (CSO 2013), shows that a large majority have reduced their spending with more than half having cut back spending on groceries. This is of particular concern. The latest report from a study that has tracked a large cohort of Irish children from birth highlights a widening health and social gap by the time they are just 5 years old. Children from the highest social class (professional/managerial) are more likely than those from the lowest socio-economic group to report that their children are very healthy and have no problems. The socio-economic background of the child is also shown to be associated with being overweight or obese (Growing Up in Ireland, 2013). Appendix 8 discusses the social determinants of health and health inequality in Ireland in more detail.

Table 8.1 - Life Expectancy at Birth by sex, 2011

Country	Males	Females	Difference
Italy	80.1	85.3	-5.2
Sweden	79.9	83.8	-3.9
Spain	79.5	85.6	-6.1
Netherlands	79.4	83.1	-3.7
Cyprus	79.3	83.1	-3.8
United Kingdom	79.0	83.0	-4.0
France	78.7	85.7	-7.0
Ireland	**78.6**	**83.0**	**-4.4**
Malta	78.6	83.0	-4.4
Luxembourg	78.5	83.6	-5.1
Germany	78.4	83.2	-4.8
Austria	78.3	83.8	-5.5
Belgium	78.0	83.3	-5.3
Greece	78.0	83.6	-5.6
Denmark	77.8	81.9	-4.1
Portugal	77.3	83.8	-6.5
Finland	77.3	83.8	-6.5
Slovenia	76.8	83.3	-6.5
EU	**76.7**	**82.6**	**-5.9**
Czech Republic	74.8	81.1	-6.3
Poland	72.6	81.1	-8.5
Slovakia	72.3	79.8	-7.5
Estonia	71.4	81.3	-9.9
Hungary	71.2	78.7	-7.5
Romania	71.1	78.2	-7.1
Bulgaria	70.7	77.8	-7.1
Latvia	68.6	78.8	-10.2
Lithuania	68.1	79.3	-11.2

CSO, 2013. Note: 2009 data used for EU

Life expectancy

According to Eurostat's figures for 2011, Irish males had life expectancies of 78.6 years while Irish females were expected to live 4.4 years longer, reaching 83 years (CSO, 2013), figures which have gradually improved over the past decade. Based on these figures, Ireland's life expectancy performance is slightly above the European average. The EU average, however, is pulled down by low life expectancies, especially among men, in such countries as Bulgaria, Latvia and Lithuania (see Table 8.1). Relative to the older member states of the EU, the Irish figures are somewhat less impressive. Furthermore, life expectancy at birth for both men and women in Ireland is lower in the most deprived geographical areas than in the most affluent (CSO, 2010). For example, life expectancy at birth of men living in the most deprived areas was 73.7 years (in 2006/07) compared with 78 years for those living in the most affluent areas. For women the corresponding figures were 80 and 82.7 years (CSO, 2010).

Ireland's life expectancy figures should be considered in the context of many of the findings of the PHAI reports referred to above and in Appendix 8 and the poverty figures discussed earlier (see Chapter 3). Ireland's poverty problem has serious implications for health, because of the link between poverty and ill health. Thus, those in lower socio-economic groups have a higher percentage of both acute and chronic illnesses.

Access to Healthcare: Medical Cards and Health Insurance

In a report from 2012, international experts noted that Ireland is the only EU health system that does not offer universal coverage of primary care. People without medical or GP visit cards (approximately 60 per cent of the population) must pay the full cost of almost all primary care services and outpatient prescriptions. These experts also noted that gaps in population and cost coverage distinguish Ireland from other EU countries, as does an element of discretion and lack of clarity about the scope of some services, especially community care services, in which there are service and regional differences (World Health Organisation & European Observatory on Health Systems and Policies, 2012). In 2011 Ireland's public spending on healthcare was 67% down from 75.9% in 2007 (OECD, 2013).

An increasing share of payments being transferred to households due to the results of the economic crisis has been observed by the OECD in a number of countries (2013). According to the OECD, in Ireland, the share of public financing of health spending decreased by nearly 6 percentage points between 2008 and 2010, while the share of out-of-pocket payments by households increased (OECD, 2012). The share of private spending as a proportion of all health spending in Ireland increased by 2 percentage points between 2009 and 2011 (OECD, 2013). Out-of-pocket expenses in healthcare tend to operate as a much bigger barrier for poorer people who defer visits or treatment as a result and this trend is being continued through measures contained in Budget 2014, such as increases in prescription charges.

In 2010, 47 per cent of adults over 18 years had private health insurance, a percentage that had decreased since 2007 (CSO, 2011). Figures released by the Health Insurance Authority suggest that those people with private health insurance continues to decline, and that an estimated 44.6 per cent of the population had inpatient health insurance plans at end September 2013 (HIA, 2013). Department of Health figures suggest that in 2012, 40.4 per cent of the population (1,853,877 people) had a medical card and 2.9 per cent (131,102 people) had a GP visit card (Department of Health, 2013).

The length of waiting lists remains a cause of major concern in the Irish healthcare system. According to monthly trends published by the Department of Health, there have been very significant increases during 2013 in the numbers waiting for elective procedures (in-patient and day-case) both for adults (waiting more than 8 months) and children (waiting more than 20 weeks) (2013, Figure 3.3). For example, in October 2012 the number of adults waiting more than 8 months was under 3,000; in September 2013 it was approaching 6,000 and it had exceeded 6,000 in July and August.

Budget 2014 provided for a cut of €666million to healthcare. The amount allocated for the health services was €13,660 billion (including €397 million in capital expenditure) (Department of Health, 2013). This level of cut comes at a time when there is already an underlying deficit of €419billion with the HSE and follows successive government budgets that have cut spending in the health service by 22% between 2008 and 2013 (HSE, 2013). This has occurred while simultaneously a major system transformation is being pursued (including major organizational change such as the abolition of the HSE, the establishment of separate Directorates and a reconfiguration toward a universal primary care system). One commentator has noted that the two things happening at once – cutbacks and fundamental transformation - 'has exposed faultlines in the ability of the health service to ensure acceptable levels of safe patient care' (Houston, 2013). International evidence from the World Health Organization and others suggests that significant year-on-year variations in the level of statutory funding available for health services is disruptive to the sustained delivery of services of a given quality and desired level of access (World Health Organization & European Observatory on Health Systems and Policies, 2012). These international experts who reviewed the Irish healthcare system in 2012 concluded that continuing budgetary cuts and consequent adjustments raises 'serious concerns whether this can be achieved without damaging access to necessary services for certain groups' (World Health Organization & European Observatory on Health Systems and Policies, 2012, p.47). The Chief Executive of the HSE has acknowledged to the Oireachtas Committee on

Health stating that it will not be possible to meet fully in 2014 all of the growing demands being placed on the health service (Wall, 2014).

Social Justice Ireland believes that the cuts of over €600 million imposed by Budget 2014 are not consistent with Ireland having a decent healthcare service characterized by safety and high quality outcomes and we do not believe that the Budget targets will be met. Furthermore, this places an impossible requirement on the health services, particularly at a time of population growth and population ageing.

Budget 2014 envisaged the equivalent of a cut of a further 2,400 full-time jobs in healthcare by end of 2014[58], and this will inevitably affect frontline services that are already struggling to deliver services on a day-to-day basis. According to the HSE, there has already been a loss of the equivalent of 12,505 full-time jobs since September 2007 (-11 per cent) (HSE, 2013). Between 2011 and 2012 alone, there was a reduction of 1.7 per cent in nursing staff (Department of Health, 2013).

In addition, the very significant increase in prescription charges introduced in Budget 2014 (from €1.50 to €2.50 per item) will present a significant additional cost to many people, especially those whose medical conditions require several different medicines such as older people.[59] This, along with a further increase in the threshold in the Drug Repayment Scheme, will cause some people to avoid accessing the medicines they need. The introduction of a GP visit card on return to work for unemployed people (instead of retention of a full medical card) will exacerbate an existing poverty trap, as some parents are afraid to take up a job and consequently lose their medical card even though their income remains low. The 'doctor visit only' cards can create problems because many people are in the unenviable situation of knowing what is wrong with them but not having the resources to purchase the medicines they need.

Social Justice Ireland believes these measures will most adversely affect people on low-incomes. This is not compatible with a health-service characterised by quality and equity. An international study of the Irish health system has noted the existence of financial barriers to access to healthcare, especially among those just above the threshold for a medical or GP visit card (World Health Organisation & European Observatory on Health Systems and Policies, 2012).

---

[58] And for reasons explained in the HSE Service Plan for 2014 such as recruitment already in train for new services, this involves a gross reduction of 3,500 full-time equivalent jobs in 2014.

[59] For example, evidence from TILDA, the Irish Longitudinal Study on Ageing shows that 20per cent of people over 50 take five or more medications; nearly 50 per cent of those over 75 take five or more medications (WHO and the European Observatory on Health Systems and Policies, 2012).

Full medical card coverage is necessary for all people in Ireland who are vulnerable. The number of people benefitting from Discretionary Medical Cards fell by 15 per cent between 2011 and 2012, from 74,281 people to 63,126 (HSE, 2012). During 2013, examples of arbitrary cancellation of medical cards for people dealing with serious health conditions such as families with children with serious congenital illnesses, were highlighted in the media. Despite this, Budget 2014 envisaged a cut of €113 from medical cards by way of 'probity' measures. Although it is welcome that the HSE Service Plan for 2014 has since acknowledged that this level of savings are not feasible from 'probity' measures (the cutback has been reduced to €23million), nonetheless reduction of €87 million (3.5%) in Community (demand-led) primary care schemes is also provided for in the 2014 Service Plan. This does not represent a commitment to moving more toward primary care, which is government policy (under the *Future Health* strategy).

One aspect of Budget 2014 measures that has been welcomed by *Social Justice Ireland* is the introduction of free GP care for children under five, as a first step toward providing free GP care for all.

However, one would have to conclude that overall the thrust of policy is disjointed, lacks coherence and involves a level of expenditure reduction that is not compatible with a well-managed system.

Health expenditure

Healthcare is a social right for everyone and a move to a rights based approach is a key action under the heading of Governance Reform in the Core Policy Framework set out in Chapter 2 - one of five priority areas identified by *Social Justice Ireland* which must be addressed in order to realise its vision for Ireland. For this right to be upheld governments must provide the funding needed to ensure that the relevant services and care are available when required. While cutbacks during the recent recession initially led to a big rise in the health spending share of GDP in Ireland, since 2010 there has been a decrease in health spending relative to GDP (OECD, 2013). Comparative statistics are available for total expenditure on health (i.e. public plus private) across the EU. Table 8.2 shows that Ireland spent 9.2 per cent of GDP on healthcare, slightly below the EU-27 average of 9.9 per cent in 2010 (the latest comparable data available from the CSO). In Gross National Income (GNI) terms this expenditure translates into a figure of 11 per cent.[60] More recent comparable figures available from the OECD reflect reductions in health expenditure in recent years, indicating that the health expenditure as a percentage of GDP had fallen to 8.9 per cent in 2011, below the OECD average of 9.3 per cent (amongst 34 OECD countries) (OECD, 2013).

---

[60] GNI is similar to the concept of GNP and has a similar value. GDP includes profit exports not available for domestic consumption

Table 8.2 - EU 27 Expenditure on Health as a percentage of GDP, 2009 and 2010

Country	2009	2010
Netherlands	12.0	11.9
France	11.9	11.9
Germany	11.7	11.6
Denmark	11.5	11.4
Portugal	10.7	11.0
Austria	11.0	11.0
Ireland (% of GNI)	**11.3**	**11.0**
Belgium	10.8	10.7
Greece	10.6	10.3
EU	**9.9**	**9.9**
Sweden	10.0	9.6
United Kingdom	9.8	9.6
Italy	9.4	9.5
Spain	9.6	9.5
Slovenia	9.3	9.4
Ireland (% of GDP)	**9.4**	**9.2**
Finland	9.1	9.0
Slovakia	9.1	8.8
Malta	8.5	8.7
Czech Republic	8.0	7.9
Luxembourg	7.9	7.8
Poland	7.4	7.5
Hungary	7.6	7.3
Lithuania	7.5	7.0
Bulgaria	7.2	6.9
Latvia	6.6	6.7
Estonia	6.7	6.0
Cyprus	6.1	6.0
Romania	5.6	5.6

CSO, 2013 from the WHO Health for all database; Includes public and private spending

Healthcare costs tend to be higher in countries which have a higher old age dependency ratios. This is not yet a significant issue for Ireland as the old age dependency ratio is low compared to the much higher EU average (11.6 per cent of the population is aged 65 years and over according to the 2011 Census and the old-age dependency rate is 17.4 per cent (CSO, 2012c)).

However, Ireland's public spending on healthcare has reduced in recent years as Table 8.3 shows. The decline between 2008 and 2012, 10.4 per cent, has been particularly rapid in the opinion of international experts (WHO & European Observatory on Health Systems and Policies, 2012).

Table 8.3 Ireland: Current public expenditure on health care, 2002-2011

Year	Total (€m)	% of GNI	% of GDP	Per capita at constant 2012 prices (€)
2002	7,933	7.3	6.1	2,645
2003	8,853	7.4	6.3	2,755
2004	9,653	7.5	6.4	2,773
2005b	11,160	7.9	6.9	3,026
2006	12,248	7.9	6.9	3,091
2007	13,736	8.4	7.2	3,223
2008	14,588	9.3	8.1	3,193
2009	15,073	11.1	9.3	3,269
2010	14,452	10.9	9.1	3,249
2011	13,728	10.4	8.4	3,044

CSO, 2013. b: break in the series.

The public share of health spending in Ireland (67%) had dropped to below the OECD average (72 per cent from general govt revenue and social security) by 2011, as Figure 8.1 shows (OECD, 2013a). The reduction in the public share of health funding in Ireland can be explained by a series of measures introduced to make people pay more out of their pockets such as increases in the share of direct payments for prescribed medicines and appliances (OECD, 2013). As already noted, out-of-pocket expenses in healthcare tend to operate as a much bigger barrier for poorer people who defer visits or treatment as a result.

Figure 8.1 - Expenditure on health by type of financing, 2011 (or nearest year)

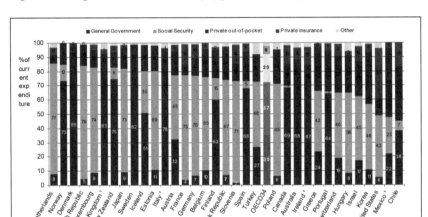

OECD, 2013: OECD Health Statistics 2013, http://dx.doi.org/10.1787/health-data-en
1. Data refer to total health expenditure

An open and transparent debate on funding of healthcare services is needed. Ireland must decide what services are expected and how these should be funded. Despite expenditure of 9.2 per cent of GDP going to fund healthcare (in 2010) there are still recurring problems in such areas as waiting lists, bed closures, staff shortages, long-term care and community care. However, this debate must acknowledge the enormous financial expenditure on healthcare. Public healthcare expenditure grew rapidly over the decade 2000 to 2010, from €5.334bn to €14.165bn. This was an increase of 160 per cent over a period in which inflation increased by 33 per cent. The difference is attributed in part to improved and expanded services, as well as to organisational changes such as home-helps, for example, becoming salaried members of staff within the HSE. However, the issue of medical inflation also needs to be addressed. International experts have noted that, despite increased investment during the previous decade, when the financial crisis occurred in 2008 Ireland still had poorly developed primary and community care services (WHO & European Observatory on Health Systems and Policies, 2012).

The Minister for Health has announced that €13.660bn (including €397 million in capital expenditure) has been allocated for 2014 on current and capital spending (Department of Health, 2013). In 2013, the budget allocation for gross public expenditure on healthcare was €14.023bn. In terms of government's overall expenditure, healthcare accounted for 27 per cent in 2011, the second largest area of expenditure (after social protection) (Department of Expenditure & Reform, 2011).

Clearly there are significant efficiencies to be gained in restructuring the healthcare system. Obtaining value for money is essential. However, these efforts should be targeted at areas in which efficiencies can be delivered without compromising the quality of the service. *Social Justice Ireland* continues to argue that there is a need to be specific about the efficiencies that are needed and how they are to be delivered.

As well as a debate on the overall budget for healthcare, there should be discussion and transparency on the allocation to each of the services. Currently about 60% per cent of the budget is allocated to Primary, Community and Continuing Care, which includes the medical card services schemes (Department of Health, Key Trends 2013, figure 6.2). *Social Justice Ireland* recommends an increase in this percentage and greater clarity about the budget lines.

The model of healthcare

Community-based health and social services require a model of care that:

- is accessible and acceptable to the communities they serve;
- is responsive to the particular needs and requirements of local communities;
- is supportive of local communities in their efforts to build social cohesion; and
- accepts primary care as the key component of the model of care, affording it priority over acute services as the place where health and social care options are accessed by the community.

Action is required in four key areas if the basic model of care that is to underpin the health services is not to be undermined. There areas are:

Older people's services
Primary care, primary care teams and primary care networks
Children and family services
Disability and mental health

Older people's services

Although Ireland's population is young in comparison to those of other European countries, it is still ageing. Those over 65 years of age increased by 14.4 per cent between 2006 and 2011 and those aged over 85 years increased by 22 per cent (CSO, 2012). By 2025 the number over 85 years will have doubled (Department of Health, 2012, p.2).

The HSE Service Plan for 2014 envisages making no new places available under the Nursing Home Support Scheme (NHSS or 'Fair Deal' scheme) and acknowledges that 'will require careful management of NHSS applications as places become vacant' (HSE, 2014). In fact, the expected outturn for December 2014 shows almost 1,000 fewer people in receipt of the scheme than at end 2013. This approach risks leading to more older people remaining in inappropriate care facilities such as acute hospitals, an outcome in the best interests of neither the individual nor the hospital. The HSE National Service Plan for 2014 commits to a strong emphasis on home care and other community support services but it also envisages that the absence of a significant capital investment to improve standards within long-term care facilities, to bring them into line with HIQA standards, means a reduction in residential care capacity; this will result in increases in hospital and community waiting times. The Plan commits no extra resourcing notwithstanding population ageing. This is not an appropriate response when the number of people aged over 85 is increasing rapidly as many of them are dependent on public services to continue to live with dignity.

The HSE service plan does envisage shifting €23million from budget for the NHSS to provide care in the community. Support for people to remain in their own homes is a key and appropriate policy objective and coincides with the wish of most older people. But increased demand for long-term care is also a predicted outcome of population ageing (CARDI, 2012). There were over 500 people on waiting lists for the NHSS (Fair Deal scheme) at end September 2013 (HSE, 2013a). Furthermore, a commitment to a comprehensive system of care in the community, as announced in January 2014, is not supported by making no further funding available, nor by further cutbacks in housing grants intended to help older and disabled people to continue living at home. Neither is it evidenced by the significant decrease in the provision of home help hours since in recent years [61]. As Table 8.4 shows, there were more than 10,000 fewer people in receipt of home help support in 2012 than there had been in 2007 (a decrease of 18 per cent) and there was a decrease of some 2.5million in the hours delivered (a decrease of 21 per cent). During the same period there was an increase in the numbers in receipt of Home Care Packages (by 2,491 people) representing an increase of nearly 24 per cent. However, the numbers in receipt of Home Care Packages had decreased slightly between 2011 and 2012. See Table 8.4.

---

[61] HSE reports make it clear that older people are the main beneficiaries of Home Help services and Home Care Packages.

Table 8.4 – HSE Support to Older People in the Community, 2007 - 2012

	2007	2008	2009	2010	2011	2012
Home Help:						
People in receipt	54,736	>53,000	53,971	54,000	50,986	44,387
Hours delivered	12.35m	12.64m	11.97m	11.68m	11.09m	9.8m
Home Care Packages						
People in receipt	8,035	8,990	8,959	9,941	10,968	10,526

December Performance Reports, 2008, 2009, 2011, 2012; November Performance Report, 2010 and HSE Annual Report 2010.

Other Budget 2014 measures, such as the increase in prescription charges and the abolition of the Telephone Allowance (part of the Household Benefits Package), will have negative effects on many older people and their families, falling most heavily on poorer groups. Over the past six years, cuts in public services such as home help and community nursing units, reductions in the Fuel Allowance, cuts in the Household Benefits Package and the abolition of the Christmas bonus, have all adversely affected older people. Between 2011 and 2012 alone, there was a reduction of 4.7 per cent in expenditure on care of older people (Department of Health, 2013). Furthermore, the level of overall cut to the health budget for 2014 and the reduction in staffing makes it inevitable that all front-line services will affected, including those for older people. International experts have identified that the drop in Ireland's public health spending on over 65s will have fallen by approximately 32 per cent per head between 2009 and 2016 (World Health Organization & European Observatory on Health Systems and Policies, 2012). However, this was based on government estimates to 2014 and assumed that funding levels would remain static for 2015 and 2016.

Supports that enable people to live at home need to be part of a broader integrated approach that ensures appropriate access to acute services when required. To achieve this, the specific deficits in infrastructure that exist across the country need to be addressed urgently. There should be an emphasis on replacement and/or refurbishment of facilities. If this is not done the inappropriate admission of older people to acute care facilities will continue, along with the consequent negative effects on acute services and unnecessary stress on older people and their families.

It is crucial that funding be released in a timely manner when a person is deemed in need of a 'Fair Deal' bed and that sufficient capital investment is provided to ensure that enough residential care beds are available to meet the growing demand for them. The focus on the development of community based services to support older people in their own homes/communities for as long as possible is welcome. But a commitment to supporting people at home is only aspirational if funding is not provided for home help services, day care centres and home care packages – areas that have received serious and unwelcome cuts in recent Budgets.

Social Justice Ireland believes that a total investment of €500 million over five years, (i.e. €100 million each year), is required to meet this growing need. This would enable some 12 to 15 community nursing facilities with about 50 beds each to be replaced or refurbished each year. In addition to supporting the needs of older people, this proposal would also stimulate economic activity and increase employment in many local communities during the construction periods.

Primary care

Primary care is one of the cornerstones of the health system and was acknowledged as such in the strategy document *Primary Care – A New Direction* (2001). It has also been identified as an essential pre-requisite in the new health services reform strategy, *Future Health* (2012) and its importance to health promotion and the prevention of illness is recognised in *Healthy Ireland* (2013). Between 90 and 95 per cent of the population is treated by the primary care system. The model of a primary care adopted must be flexible so that it can respond to the local needs assessment. Paying attention to local people's own perspective on their health and understanding the impact of the conditions of their lives on their health is essential to community development and to community orientated approaches to primary care. A community development approach is needed to ensure that the community can define its own health needs, work out collectively how these needs can best be met, and decide on a course of action to achieve this in partnership with service providers. This will ensure greater control over the social, political, economic and environmental factors that determine the health status of any community.

The principle underlining this model should be a social model of health, in-keeping with the World Health Organization's definition of health as a 'state of complete physical, mental and social well-being and not merely the absence of disease or infirmity'. Ireland's Healthy Ireland strategy describes health as 'a personal, social and economic good' (Department of Health, 2013). Universal access is needed to ensure that a social model of health can become a reality and Government commitment to achieving this, which is contained in the *Future Health* reform strategy, is to be welcomed in principle. However, the strategy lacks detail on how its aims will be achieved. There are also areas in which the approaches outlined may well face serious challenges. Amongst them is how to deliver a truly integrated system of care, especially for people with complex or chronic conditions, within a system in which primary and hospital care is to be funded through the proposed Universal Health Insurance system, but social care services, including long-term care, are not. Will access to social care services, for example, be universal as well as access to GP services? For the strategies outlined to be implemented there is a clear need for an increase in the proportion of the total healthcare budget being allocated to primary care and a more comprehensive and integrated approach to social care services to support people living at home. Instead, a net reduction of €87 million (3.5%) in Community (demand-led) primary care schemes is provided for in the HSE Service Plan, 2014.

Primary care teams and primary care networks

Ireland's healthcare system has struggled to provide an effective and efficient response to the health needs of its population. Despite a huge increase in investment in recent years great problems persist. The development of primary care teams (PCTs) across the country could have a substantial positive impact on reducing these problems.

Developing PCTs and primary care networks is intended as the basic building block of local public health care provision. The Primary Care Team (PCT) is intended to be a team of health professionals that includes GPs and Practice Nurses, community nurses (i.e. public health nurses and community RGNs), physiotherapists, occupational therapists and home-care staff. PCTs are expected to link in with other community-based disciplines to ensure that health and social needs are addressed. These include speech and language therapists, dieticians, area medical officers, community welfare officers, addiction counsellors, community mental health nurses, consultant psychiatrists and others.

It was envisaged that 530 Primary Care Teams supported by 134 Health and Social Care Networks would cover the country by 2011. According to the HSE, there were 486 PCTs in place by the end of 2012 (Department of Health, 2012). The work done on existing teams is very welcome but much more is needed to ensure they command the confidence and trust of local communities and there is a need for greater transparency in relation to their roll-out.

The Government's introduction of a new system of seven Directorates to run the health system is of concern because this approach is likely to obstruct the delivery of an integrated healthcare system for service users at local level. There are real concerns that the new approach will increase rather than reduce costs and bureaucracy. Instead of an integrated system based on primary care teams at local level, seven 'silos' could emerge, competing for resources and producing a splintered system that is not effective, sustainable or viable in the long term.

Social Justice Ireland believes that reform of the healthcare system is necessary but is seriously concerned that the proposed new structure will see each Directorate establish its own bureaucracy at national, regional and local levels.

Children and family services

There is a need to focus on health and social care provision for children and families in tandem with the development of primary care team services. The 2006 Concluding Observations of the UN Committee on the Rights of the Child noted the lack of a comprehensive legal framework and the absence of statutory guidelines safeguarding the quality of, and access to, health care services, particularly for children in vulnerable situations (Children's Rights Alliance, 2013). The Committee also raised concerns about the practice of treating children with mental health issues in adult in-patient facilities. *Social Justice Ireland* welcomed the announcement of free GP care for under-fives announced as part of Budget 2014. However, its implementation is awaited and it will require negotiation with providers and legislative changes.

Many community and voluntary services are being provided in facilities badly in need of refurbishment or rebuilding. Despite poor infrastructure, these services are the heart of local communities, providing vital services that are locally 'owned'. There is a great need to support this activity and, in particular, to meet its infrastructural requirements. *A Vision for Change* (revised as per Census 2011 data) (Department of Health, 2012) recommended the establishment of 107 specialist Child and Adolescent Mental Health teams, but by the end of 2012 there were 63 teams operating and staffing was at just 38 per cent of what had been recommended (Children's Rights Alliance, 2013).

Social Justice Ireland believes that a total of €250 million is required over a five year period to address the infrastructural deficit in Children and Family Services. This amounts to €27 million per area for each of the nine Children Services Committee areas and a national investment of €7 million in Residential and Special Care.

As well as the issue of Child Safeguarding, we believe current key issues are the second National Children's Strategy, policy on early childhood care and education, child poverty, youth homelessness, disability among young people and the issue of young carers.

Disability

Disability policy remains largely as set out in the National Disability Strategy from 2004. A long-awaited implementation plan for the strategy was published in 2013. There are many areas within the disability sector in need of further development and core funding and an ambitious implementation process needs now to be pursued.[62]

---

[62] Other disability related issues are addressed throughout this review.

People with disabilities have been cumulatively affected by a range of policies introduced as part of successive Budgets in recent years. These include cuts to disability allowance, changes in medical card eligibility criteria and increased prescription charges, cuts in respite services, cuts to home help and personal assistant hours and other community-based supports as well as the non-replacement of front-line staff providing services to people with disabilities. The overall cut in health spending in Budget 2014 as well as specific measures (such as the increase in prescription charges) will affect many people with disabilities and families. Changes announced in January 2014 to the Housing Adaptation Grants Scheme may make it more difficult for some people to continue to live in their communities. Furthermore, people with disabilities experience higher everyday costs of living because of their disabilities and, as Chapter 3 discusses, they are one of the groups in Irish society at greatest risk of poverty.

Mental health

The National Health Strategy entitled *Quality and Fairness* (2001) identified mental health as an area needing development. The Expert Group on Mental Health Policy published a report entitled *A Vision for Change – Report of the Expert Group on Mental Health Policy* (2006). This report offered many worthwhile pathways to adequately address mental health issues in Irish society. Unfortunately, to date little has been implemented to achieve this vision. In 2009, the Mental Health Commission noted with concern that the slow pace of implementation of *A Vision for Change* impacts directly on the quality of mental health services available to those who need them (2009).

There is an urgent need to address this whole area in the light of the World Health Report (2001) *Mental Health: New Understanding, New Hope.* This estimated that in 1990 mental and neurological disorders accounted for 10 per cent of the total Disability-Adjusted Life Years (DALYs) lost due to all diseases and injuries. This estimate increased to 12 per cent in 2000. By 2020, it is projected that these disorders will have increased to 15 per cent. This has serious implications for services in all countries in coming years.

In June 2011 the Institute for Public Health published a study on the impact of the recession on men's health, especially mental health. Entitled *Facing the Challenge: The Impact of Recession and Unemployment on Men's Health in Ireland,* the study showed that employment status was the most important predicator of psychological distress, with 30.4 per cent of those unemployed reporting mental health problems.

Social Justice Ireland has welcomed the allocation of €20 million in Budget 2014 for the development of community mental health teams, but has expressed the view that a minimum of €35million was needed to support the development of extended catchment areas and community mental health teams. According to the HSE's divisional plan for mental health, published in January 2014, staffing levels are still at approximately 75% of what was recommended in *A Vision for Change* and have reduced by 11 per cent on 2006 levels (2014). The mental health services are going through a significant change process at a time when demands on services are growing, as the HSE has noted, in line with population increases and the effects of the prolonged recession (2014). It is vital that ongoing reductions in inpatient beds are matched by adequate and effective alternative provision in the community.

Areas of concern in mental health

There is a need for effective outreach and follow-up programmes for people who have been in-patients in institutions upon their discharge into the wider community. These should provide:

- sheltered housing (high, medium and low supported housing);
- monitoring of medication;
- retraining and rehabilitation; and
- assistance with integration into community.

In the development of mental health teams there should be a particular focus on people with an intellectual disability and other vulnerable groups, including children, the homeless, prisoners, Travellers, asylum seekers, refugees and other minority groups. People in these and related categories have a right to a specialist service to provide for their often complex needs. A great deal remains to be done before this right could be acknowledged as having been recognised and honoured in the healthcare system.

The connection between disadvantage and ill health when the social determinants of health (housing, income, childcare support, education etc.) are not met is well documented. This is also true in respect of mental health issues.

Suicide – a mental health issue

Suicide is a problem related to mental health issues. For many years the topic was rarely discussed in Irish society and, as a consequence, the healthcare and policy implications of its existence were limited. Over time Ireland's suicide rate has risen significantly, from 6.4 suicides per 100,000 people in 1980 to a peak of 13.9 in 1998, and to 11.7 suicides per 100,000 people in 2008 (National Office of Suicide Prevention, 2011).

There was a downward trend in the rate from 2003, which stopped in 2007, something partly attributed to the change in the economy by the National Office of Suicide Prevention (2011). According to the latest figures available from the National Suicide Research Foundation, which are still provisional, there were 507 recorded suicides in 2012, of which 413 were males and 94 were females. According to the HSE, international studies indicate that for every 1 per cent increase in unemployment, there is a 0.9 per cent increase in suicides (2014).

Table 8.5 shows that suicide is predominantly a male phenomenon, accounting for approximately 80 per cent of such deaths. Young males in particular, are the group most at risk, although the rate for men remains consistently high at all ages up to mid-sixties. At every age the rate is higher for men than for women (National Office for Suicide Prevention, 2013). The highest rate is among 20-24 year old males at 31.9 per 100,000 population. Some 42% of those who died by suicide in 2010 were men less than 40 years of age (National Office for Suicide Prevention, 2013).

Identification of overall trends in suicide rates is a complex process particularly using international comparisons. World Health Organization statistics suggest that where overall rates of suicide are concerned, Ireland ranked 6th lowest in the EU. However, where younger age-groups are concerned (5-24 year olds), Ireland ranks fourth highest for deaths by suicide at 13.9 per 100,000 population (National Office of Suicide Prevention, 2013).

Table 8.5 – Suicides in Ireland 2003-2012

	Overall		Males		Females	
Year	No.	Rate	No.	Rate	No.	Rate
2003	497	12.5	386	19.5	111	5.5
2004	493	12.2	406	20.2	87	4.3
2005	481	11.6	382	18.5	99	4.8
2006	460	10.9	379	17.9	81	3.8
2007	458	10.6	362	16.7	96	4.4
2008	506	11.4	386	17.5	120	5.4
2009	552	12.4	443	20.0	109	4.9
2010	490	11	405	18.3	90	4.0
2011	554	12.2	458	20.2	96	4.1
2012*	507	11.1	413	18.2	94	4.1

Notes: * Provisional figures
Rate is rate per 100,000 of the population.
National Suicide Research Foundation (2013)

The sustained high level of suicides in Ireland is a significant healthcare and societal problem. Of course, the statistics only tell one part of the story. Behind each of these victims are families and communities devastated by these tragedies. Likewise, behind each of the figures is a personal story which leads to victims taking their own lives. *Social Justice Ireland* believes that further attention and resources need to be devoted to researching and addressing Ireland's suicide problem.

Older people and Mental Health

Mental health issues affect all groups in society. Some 41,700 people in Ireland are estimated to be affected by dementia or Alzheimer's disease (Cahill, O'Shea and Pierce, 2012). Most are over 65 but this figure includes people of all ages and some 3,600 of them are likely to be under 65. The projections for those likely to be affected by 2041 are between 141,000 and 147,000. Older people with dementia are a particularly vulnerable group because they often 'fall between two stools' (i.e. between mental health services and general medical care). A co-ordinated service needs to be provided for this group. It is important that this be needs-based and service-user led and should be in keeping with the principles set out in the World Health Organisation's 2001 annual report. A national dementia strategy is in development and its publication is awaited.

Research and development in all areas of mental health are needed to ensure a quality service is delivered. Providing good mental health services should not be viewed as a cost but rather as an investment in the future. Public awareness needs to be raised to ensure a clearer understanding of mental illness so that the rights of those with mental illness are recognised.

Future healthcare needs

A number of the factors highlighted elsewhere in this review will have implications for the future of our healthcare system. The projected increases in population forecast by the CSO imply that there will be more people living in Ireland in 10 to 15 years time. One clear implication of this will be additional demand for healthcare services and facilities. In the context of our past mistakes it is important that Ireland begins to plan for this additional demand and begins to train staff and construct the needed facilities.

The new health reform strategy, 2012-2015, *Future Health,* envisages major changes in the way that health services are organised and delivered. Legislation passed in 2013 provided for the replacement of the HSE Board with a new governing body and the establishment of seven separate Service Directorates. Ultimately, the strategy aims to introduce a system of Universal Health Insurance intended to facilitate access to healthcare based on need not income. This aim is an important one, but, as previously mentioned, full details of the approach are not yet available and a proposed White Paper has yet to be published. The time-frame for the introduction of the new system (2016) is also relatively short, given the very complex health system that currently operates and the degree of budgetary cuts and consequent disruption that has occurred in recent years and is set to continue. It has not been established that the proposed system of a number of competing insurers will succeed in achieving the necessary improvements in equity, quality and efficiency.

We share the concerns of the Council for Justice and Peace of the Irish Episcopal Conference (2012) about a lack of focus on outcomes. We agree with it that the: 'public health strategy should ... not only spell out goals for public health but also set out the role that each major field of intervention is expected to perform in achieving those goals, the implications for resource allocation that arise from such roles, and the mechanisms that will be used to ensure that spending actually goes to the areas where it will achieve greatest benefit'.

Key policy priorities on healthcare

- Recognise the considerable health inequalities present within the Irish healthcare system, develop strategies and provide sufficient resources to tackle them.
- Give far greater priority to community care and restructure the healthcare budget accordingly. Care should be taken to ensure that the increased allocation does not go to the GMS or the drug subsidy scheme.
- Resource and complete the roll out of primary care teams.
- Increase the proportion of the health budget allocated to health promotion and education in partnership with all relevant stakeholders.
- Focus on obtaining better value for money in the health budget.
- Provide the childcare services with the additional resources necessary to effectively implement the Child Care Act.
- Provide additional respite care and long stay care for older people and people with disabilities and proceed to develop and implement a coherent dementia strategy.
- Promote equality of access and outcomes to services within the Irish healthcare system.
- Develop and resource mental health services, recognising that they will be a key factor in determining the health status of the population.

- Continue to facilitate and fund a campaign to give greater attention to the issue of suicide in Irish society. In particular, focus resources on educating young people about suicide.

- Enhance the process of planning and investment so that the healthcare system can cope with the increase and diversity in population and the ageing of the population projected for the next few decades.

- Ensure that structural and systematic reform of the health system reflects the key principles of the Health Strategy aimed at achieving high performance, person-centred quality of care and value for money in the health service.

- Ensure the new healthcare structure is fit for purpose and publish detailed evidence of how the decisions taken will meet healthcare goals.

9.

EDUCATION AND EDUCATIONAL DISADVANTAGE

CORE POLICY OBJECTIVE: EDUCATION AND EDUCATIONAL DISADVANTAGE

To provide relevant education for all people throughout their lives, so that they can participate fully and meaningfully in developing themselves, their community and the wider society.

Education can be an agent for social transformation. *Social Justice Ireland* believes that education can be a powerful force in counteracting inequality and poverty while recognising that, in many ways, the present education system has quite the opposite effect. The primary focus of education is to prepare students for life enabling them to participate in and to contribute to society. Education allows people to live a full life. Living a full life requires both knowledge and skills appropriate to age, environment, and social and economic roles, as well as the ability to function in a world of increasing complexity and to adapt to continuously changing circumstances without sacrificing personal integrity (Department of Education and Skills, 1995). Education makes a fundamentally important contribution to the quality and well-being of our society. It is a right for each individual and a means to enhancing well-being and quality of life for the whole of society (ibid). Investment in education at all levels can deliver a more equal society and prepare citizens to participate in a democracy. Education is one of the key policy areas that must be addressed urgently as part of the Core Policy Framework we set out in Chapter 2 under the heading of Enhancing Social Protection. Education must also be available as a right as envisaged in our Core Policy Area, Reform Governance, set out in the same chapter.

Education in Ireland – the numbers

There are just over one million full-time students in the formal Irish education system. Of these, 520,444 are at primary level, 360,567 at second level and 166,088 at third level. The numbers at primary level have been increasing since 2001 and this will have knock on implications for provision at second and third level. (CSO 2012:100). This demographic growth and the knock-on pressure on the education system and the need to develop long-term policies to cater for increased demand have been acknowledged by the Minister for Education and Skills.[63] By 2017 there will be an extra 105,000 extra students in education in Ireland; 64,000 at primary level, 25,000 at second level and 16,000 at third-level.[64]

Ireland's expenditure on education equalled 6.5 per cent of GDP in 2010, an increase of almost two percentage points since 2008. This is due mainly to the decrease of GDP in Ireland over this period (CSO 2014). However, education accounts for only 9.7 per cent of total public expenditure in Ireland compared with an OECD average of 13 per cent. Over much of the last decade, as national income has increased, the share allocated to education has slowly increased; a development we strongly welcome. Table 9.1 (CSO 2014) details a real expenditure increase per student of 16.4 per cent at first level and 11.6 per cent at second level over the period 2003-2012. During the same period real expenditure per student at third level declined by one fifth (20.1 per cent). Real expenditure per student in 2012 at primary level was three quarters that at third level. Between 2003 and 2012 the numbers of students in Ireland grew by 17 per cent at first level and by 6.5 per cent at second level. Over the same period, the number of full-time third level students increased by 24.1 per cent (CSO 2014). The number of part-time third-level students increased by just 0.3 per cent in the same period. It should also be noted, however, that Ireland's young population as a proportion of total population is large by EU standards and, consequently, a higher than average spend on education would be expected.

Investment and planning for future education needs

Education is now regarded as a central plank in the economic, social and cultural development of Irish society (Department of Education and Skills, 2004). Education and training are also crucial to achieving the objective of an inclusive society where all citizens have the opportunity to participate fully and meaningfully in social and economic life. The development of the education and skills of people is as important a source of wealth as the accumulation of more traditional forms of capital.

---

[63] See address by Minister Quinn at Nordic Education Seminar 12/09/2012 http://www.education.ie/en/Press-Events/Speeches/2012-Speeches/SP2012-09-17.html

[64] ibid

Table 9.1: Ireland: Real current public expenditure on education, 2003-2013

Year	First Level* €	Second Level* €	Third Level* €	Real Current Public Expenditure** €m
2003	5,390	7,825	10,539	6,687
2004	5,794	7,914	10,332	6,893
2005	5,898	8,262	10,689	7,133
2006	6,103	8,625	11,206	7,498
2007	6,246	9,085	11,078	7,822
2008	6,361	9,207	10,866	8,061
2009	6,605	9,307	10,314	8,343
2010	6,493	9,010	9,898	8,293
2011	6,455	8,911	9,161	8,326
2012	6,272	8,735	8,417	8,005

*€ per student at 2012 prices   **€m at 2012 prices
Source: Department of Education and Skills, CSO (2014)

The fundamental aim of education is to serve individual, social and economic well-being and to enhance quality of life. Policy formulation in education should value and promote all dimensions of human development and seek to prepare people for full participation in cultural, social and economic life. This requires investment in education at all levels, from early childhood right up to lifelong learning.

Social Justice Ireland welcomes the fact that the Department of Education has begun to use the population projections by the CSO based on the census results to plan for future education needs, timing and spatial distribution. Using these figures, the Department of Education now projects the following possible increases in enrolment across the system:

- an additional 32,500 places will be needed at primary level between now and 2014 and an increase in enrolments to 601,820 by 2020;[65]
- an additional 17,000 places will be needed at second level between now and 2014

---

[65] http://www.education.ie/en/Publications/Statistics/Projections-of-full-time-enrolment-Primary-and-Second-Level-2012-2030.pdf

with significant increases projected in the years after 2014, to peak at an enrolment of 413,118 in 2026;[66]

• at third level, the number of students is expected to rise by 15,000 by 2015; between 205,000 and 210,000 students are expected by 2026/27.[67]

The Department of Education has published a capital works programme amounting to €2.2 billion between now and 2016 to address this issue and increase the number of places available through a School Building Programme. *Social Justice Ireland* believes it is critically important that Government, and in particular the Department of Education and Skills, pays attention to the population projection by the CSO for the years to come in order to adequately plan and provide for the increased places needed within the education system in the coming decades. Budget 2012 introduced an increase in the number of pupils required to gain and retain a classroom teaching post in small primary schools. The reasoning given for this change was that small schools benefitted disproportionately from the staffing schedule and that it acted as a disincentive to consider amalgamation. To date 79 schools have lost a classroom post and 42 schools have not gained a classroom post as a result of this decision. A further 75 posts are to be removed from rural schools in 2014. This policy, which has had a significant impact on rural schools and education in rural areas seems to be based on a philosophy that rural schools should be forced to amalgamate. Such a philosophy ignores the economic and social impact of the closure of a school on rural communities.

Education is widely recognised as crucial to the achievement of our national objectives of economic competitiveness, social inclusion and active citizenship. However, the overall levels of public funding for education in Ireland are out of step with these aspirations. This under-funding is most severe in early childhood education and in the areas of lifelong learning and second chance education – the very areas that are most vital in terms of the promotion of greater equity and fairness. The projected increased demand outlined above in all areas of our education system must be matched by a policy of investment at all levels that is focussed on protecting and promoting quality services for those in the education system.

Early Childhood Education

It is widely acknowledged that early childhood (pre-primary) education helps to build a strong foundation for lifelong learning and ensure equity in education. It

---

[66] ibid
[67] http://www.education.ie/en/Publications/Statistics/Projections-of-demand-for-Full-Time-Third-Level-Education-2011-2026.pdf

also improves children's cognitive abilities, reduces poverty and can mitigate social inequalities (OECD 2012: 338). It is seen as the essential foundation for successful lifelong learning, social integration, personal development and later employability (European Commission, 2011). It is important that adequate resources are invested in this area because early childhood education plays a crucial role in providing young people with the opportunity to develop to their fullest potential.

The most striking feature of investment in education in Ireland relative to other OECD countries is our under-investment in early childhood education relative to international norms. Ireland spends 0.1 per cent of GDP on pre-primary education compared with the OECD average of 0.5 per cent (OECD 2012: 339). The introduction of the Early Childhood Care and Education Scheme (ECCE) has been a positive move in addressing this under investment. The ECCE Scheme entitles every child between the ages of 3 years and 3 months and 4 years and 6 months to three hours of pre-school care for thirty-eight weeks in one year free of charge. The ECCE scheme is availed of by over 68,000 children and is administered by the Department of Children and Youth Affairs at a cost of approximately €175 million.[68] In 2011, 95 per cent of 4 year olds in Ireland were enrolled in early childhood education as a result of this initiative. However only 47 per cent of 3 years olds were enrolled in early childhood education compared with an OECD average of 67 per cent. Clearly Ireland still has quite a way to go to catch up with the OECD average.

Early childhood is also the stage where education can most effectively influence the development of children and help reverse disadvantage (European Commission, 2011). It has the potential to both reduce the incidence of early school leaving and to increase the equity of educational outcomes. Early childhood education is also associated with better performance later on in school. A recent OECD study found that 15-year-old pupils who attended pre-primary education perform better on PISA testing (Programme for International Student Assessment) than those who did not, even allowing for differences in their socio-economic backgrounds (OECD, 2012:338). This is mirrored in the PISA 2012 results for Ireland which show that Irish students who attended pre-school scored significantly better than those who did not (Department of Education and Skills, 2013).

Chart 9.1 below illustrates that the highest return from investment in education is between the ages of 0 to 5. This is the point in the developmental curve where differences in early health, cognitive and non-cognitive skills, which are costly sources of inequality, can be addressed most effectively. The evidence shows that early childhood education has the greatest potential to provide more equal educational opportunity to those students from lower socio-economic backgrounds. The importance of investment in education is widely acknowledged and the rewards

---

[68] Budget 2014 estimate

for both individuals and the state are clear. The Oireachtas Spotlight on Early Childhood Education and Care details that the return on investment can be as much as €7 for every €1 invested in a child. Longitudinal studies internationally also show returns of between three and ten times the original investment in children[69]. It is critically important that Ireland invest in this area and provide universal early childhood education services for children. This will provide an economic and social return for many years to come.

Chart 9.1: The Heckman Curve

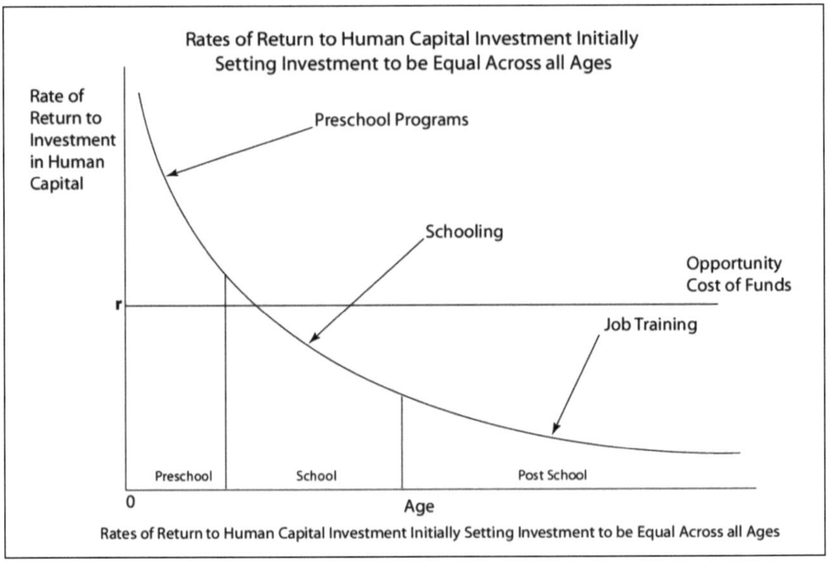

Rates of Return to Human Capital Investment Initially Setting Investment to be Equal Across all Ages

Source: Carneiro and Heckman, 2003

The European Commission believes that Europe's future will be based on smart, sustainable and inclusive growth and that improving the quality and effectiveness of education systems is essential to this (European Commission, 2011). Achieving such growth, and honouring the educational commitments outlined in the Programme for Government and National Recovery in the process, will require significant strategic investment in early childhood education and lifelong learning through a policy making process that has long-term planning at its core. Our success in educating future generations of pre-school children will be a major determinant of our future sustainability.

---

[69] http://www.dcya.gov.ie/viewdoc.asp?DocID=1751

Primary and Second Level Education

Ireland has a pupil teacher ratio (PTR) of 15.7 at primary level and 14.4 at second level (CSO, 2014), the eleventh highest in the EU. The average class size in Ireland at primary level is 24.1, the second highest in the EU. Government should address this issue and take action to reduce class sizes at primary level. In 2011 Ireland took part in the Progress in International Reading Literacy Study (PIRLS) and the Trends in International Mathematics and Science Study (TIMSS). These test primary school pupils in the equivalent of fourth class in reading, mathematics and science in over 60 countries. Ireland preformed relatively well, ranking 10th out of 45 participating countries in reading, 17th out of 50 participating countries in mathematics and 22nd out of 50 participating countries in science. A detailed analysis has been published by the Educational Research Centre (Eivers and Clerkin eds., 2013).

Some of the most interesting findings are in the differences in results for children in Northern Ireland and the Republic. Northern Irish primary school pupils performed better in reading and numeracy than any other English speaking country, coming 5th out of 45 participating countries in reading and 6th out of 50 participating countries in mathematics. A revised primary school curriculum and targeted literacy and numeracy programmes were introduced in Northern Ireland in 2007. The new curriculum is based on the skills that children should attain rather than on content to be covered, with a focus on preparation for learning and child-led learning. The revised curriculum has been a considerable success and provides an excellent example of how to redesign a school curriculum, putting quality programmes and services at the heart of the system. This is particularly relevant at a time when the Minister for Education and Skills claims to be implementing a reform agenda to radically improve teaching and learning in Ireland and the learning experience of students in the Irish education system.

At second level, Irish students performed relatively well in the 2012 PISA tests in reading, literacy, mathematics and science. The performance of Ireland's fifteen-year-olds shows a significant improvement on the 2009 performance. However, when compared with 2003 PISA results, the overall performance showed very little progress. Students from fee paying schools significantly out-performed those from non-fee paying schools, and students who never attended pre-school performed less well than those who attended pre-school (Perkins et al, 2013). The PISA findings suggest that while reading levels among the school-going population are better than the population generally, this difference is much smaller than should be expected. The fact that the proportion of male students unable to read at the most basic level (Level 2 PISA) is almost unchanged since 2000 (Perkins et al., 2013:143) must be a cause of considerable concern for policymakers. It is clear that fundamental reforms are needed to Ireland's education system[70] to address this problem.

Social Justice Ireland welcomes the reforms to the Junior Cycle and the implementation of the national literacy and numeracy strategy *'Literacy and Numeracy for Learning and Life'*. The strategy sets out national targets and a range of significant measures to improve literacy and numeracy in early childhood education and in primary and post-primary schools. These measures include improving the performance of children and young people in PISA literacy and numeracy tests at all levels. The impact of these measures and of Project maths should be seen in the next round of PISA 2015. The strategy also proposes fundamental changes to teacher education and the curriculum in schools and radical improvements in the assessment and reporting of student progress at student, school and national level. Progress on this issue is overdue and budgetary and economic constraints must not be allowed to impede the implementation of the strategy.

The 'reform agenda' currently pursued by the Minister for Education and Skills is being implemented at second level with the phased replacement of the Junior Certificate examination with the new Junior Cycle Student Award incorporating a school-based approach to assessment. This award was developed in response to weaknesses in the current model highlighted by the National Council for Curriculum and Assessment[71] and to address the issue of second level students not achieving their potential and the wake-up call in Irish education of students failing PISA tests.[72] *Social Justice Ireland* welcomes the new student centred approach to the Junior Cycle and the new emphasis on helping students who are not performing well in Irish schools. It is important that such reforms be followed through to the Leaving Certificate to ensure policy coherence and a truly student centred approach in the second level education system. It is equally important that policymakers, whilst implementing a reform agenda, remember that the primary focus of education is to prepare students for life, not just for work.

---

[70] A discussion paper by Áine Hyland for the HEA Summer School 2011 suggested that the emphasis on rote learning at second level might have affected our results as the PISA test is based on the application of prior knowledge.

[71] For more detail see Junior Cycle Briefing Note http://www.education.ie/en/Schools-Colleges/Information/Curriculum-and-Syllabus/A-Framework-for-Junior-Cycle-Briefi ng-Note.pdf

[72] See Speech by Minister Quinn http://www.education.ie/en/Press-Events/ Speeches/2012-Speeches/04-October-2012-Speech-by-Ruair%C3%AD-Quinn-TD-Minister-for-Education-and-Skills-On-the-launch-of-his-Junior-Cycle-Framework.html

Literacy and Adult Literacy

The OECD PIAAC study 2013 provides the most up to date data on adult literacy in Ireland. On literacy, Ireland is placed 17th out of 24 countries with 18 per cent of Irish adults having a literacy level at or below level 1. People at this level of literacy can understand and follow only basic written instructions and read only very short texts (OECD, 2013). On numeracy, Ireland is placed 19th out of 24 countries with 26 per cent of Irish adults scoring at or below level 1. In the final category, problem solving in technology rich environments, 42 per cent of Irish adults scored at or below level 1. In other words, a very significant proportion of Ireland's adult population does not possess the most basic literacy, numeracy and information-processing skills considered necessary to success in the world today. The report also found that there is no statistical difference between average literacy scores of adults in Ireland from IALS in 1994 and PIAAC in 2012. In other words, the adult literacy strategy implemented by successive governments in the intervening years was grossly inadequate in terms of dealing with Ireland's adult literacy problem. A significant proportion of Ireland's labour force is not equipped with the skills required for the modern labour market. Those with low literacy skills are almost twice as likely to be unemployed (OECD, 2013) and are more likely to report poor health outcomes and are less likely to participate in social and civic life.

The Programme for Government and National Recovery states that the government will address the widespread and persistent problem of restricted adult literacy through the integration of literacy in vocational training and through community education. The previous target for adult literacy policy set out in NAPInclusion was that 'the proportion of the population aged 16-64 with restricted literacy will be reduced to between 10 per cent to 15 per cent by 2016 from the level of 25 per cent found in 1997'. This target was completely unacceptable and unambitious at the time and showed a lack of interest in seriously addressing the problem. The recent PIAAC results confirm this analysis. The lack of focus on this issue has been further underscored by successive budget cuts to funding for adult literacy programmes. By 2015, funding for adult literacy will have been reduced by 11 per cent since 2010.[73]

No new target or strategy for adult literacy has yet been outlined, despite the Department of Education and Skills commencing a review of adult literacy provision in late 2012, and publishing the report of the review group in September 2013. The Department accepted the findings of the Report and as an initial step the Adult Literacy Operational Guidelines were revised to incorporate many of the recommendations. These guidelines were published in December 2013. The

---

[73] Department of Public Expenditure and Reform 2011 (Budget 2011reduced capitation grants for adult and further education courses by 5%, a 2% reduction in Budget 2012, 2% in 2013 and 1% in 2014 and 2015).

Department has transferred responsibility for implementation of the adult literacy strategy (including the incorporation of the outstanding review group recommendations) and the setting of targets to SOLAS, the new Further Education and Training Authority. SOLAS is due to present its strategy for approval by the Minister in March 2014. *Social Justice Ireland* recommends that the new targets to be set out in the forthcoming adult literacy strategy be ambitious and realistic in the context of the future social and economic development of Ireland, and that the necessary funding is provided to ensure that this target is met.

Lifelong learning

Equality of status is one of the basic democratic principles that should underpin lifelong learning. Access in adult life to desirable employment and choices is closely linked to level of educational attainment. Equal political rights cannot exist if some people are socially excluded and educationally disadvantaged. The lifelong opportunities of those who are educationally disadvantaged are in sharp contrast to the opportunities for meaningful participation of those who have completed a second or third level education. Unlike the rising earnings premium and earnings rewards enjoyed by those who have completed higher education, the earnings disadvantage for those who have not completed upper secondary education increases with age. Therefore, lifelong education should be seen as a basic need. In this context, second chance education and continuing education are vitally important and require on-going support.

The OECD recommends that lifelong learning opportunities should be accessible to all through systems that combine high-quality initial education with opportunities and incentives for the entire population to continue to develop proficiency in reading and numeracy skills, whether outside work or in the workplace, after initial education and training are completed. It notes that the joint impact of investing in the skills of many individuals may exceed the sum of the individual parts.

There is a strong link between educational attainment and employment. Those aged 25 to 64 with only primary level qualification are three times more likely to be unemployed than those with a third level qualification (24 per cent versus 7 per cent) (CSO 2011:1). This gap has increased 10 percentage points since 2009, demonstrating the difficulties faced by Government in helping those with low levels of educational attainment up-skill and improve their prospects of getting a job. The Programme for Government makes reference to lifelong learning as a high priority for jobseekers. However, labour market activation cannot be the sole factor defining the lifelong learning agenda and education and training curricula. Various reports identify generic skills and competences as a core element of the lifelong learning framework. The Forfás Report *'Sharing our future: Ireland 2025'* (Forfas 2009) highlights the increasing range of generic skills that individuals require to operate within society and the economy. These include basic skills such as literacy, numeracy, use of technology, language skills, people related and conceptual skills. The report of the Expert Group on Future Skills Needs *'Tomorrow's Skills – Towards a National Skills Strategy'* (2007) indicates that there is substantial evidence to show that employers regard generic skills as equal to, if not more important than, technical or job specific skills.

Eight key competences for lifelong learning have been identified by the Council of Europe and the European Parliament (Council of Europe, 2006):

- Communication in the mother tongue (reading, writing, etc.);
- Communication in foreign languages;
- Mathematical and basic competences in science and technology;
- Digital competence;
- Learning to learn;
- Social and civic competences;
- Sense of initiative and entrepreneurship;
- Cultural awareness and expression.

These key competences are all interdependent, with an emphasis in each on critical thinking, creativity, initiative, problem solving, risk assessment and decision taking. They also provide the framework for community education and training programmes within the European Education and Training 2010 work programme and the Strategic Framework for European Cooperation in Education and Training (ET 2020) (European Commission 2011). These key competences should be included as part of the reform of apprenticeship programmes. Many of these key competences are already included in one of the recommendations of the report of the review group of apprenticeship training which recommends that apprenticeship programmes should provide for the appropriate integration of transversal skills, particularly literacy, numeracy, maths, science and ICT. The reform of apprenticeship training in Ireland will be important in terms of providing training and lifelong learning opportunities to those who are low skilled or those who are early school leavers. A reformed system has the opportunity to provide relevant skills and meaningful and clear progression paths to those involved.

Access to educational opportunity and meaningful participation in the system and access to successful outcomes, are central to the democratic delivery of education. Resources should be made available to support people who wish to engage in lifelong learning, in particular those people who completed second level education but who chose not to progress to third level education at that point. *Social Justice Ireland* welcomes the provision in the Technological Universities Act 2014 that a combined minimum of 30 per cent of all enrolments are to be in flexible learning programmes; professional or industry based programmes or mature learners. It is important that enrolment policies for higher education are revised and amended in conjunction with the reforms to further education and training.

Early school leaving

The proportion of persons aged 18-24 who left school with, at most, lower secondary education in Ireland was 9.7% in 2012 (CSO, 2014). The rate has been decreasing steadily since 2002 and there has been positive progress made in this area. However it is still remains a serious issue. Early school leaving not only presents problems for the young people involved but it also has economic and social consequences for society. Education is the most efficient means by which to safeguard against unemployment. The risk of unemployment increases considerably the lower the level of education. Early school leavers are:

- at higher risk of poverty and social exclusion;
- confronted with limited opportunities to develop culturally, personally and socially;
- likely to have poor health status; and
- face a cyclical effect associated with early school leaving, resulting in the children of early school leavers experiencing reduced success in education (European Commission, 2011).

The unemployment rate for early school leavers is 37 per cent, almost twice that for other persons in the same 18 to 24 age cohort. They also had an employment rate that was half that of their peers (21 per cent compared to 42 per cent) (CSO 2011:7). Government has invested heavily in trying to secure a school-based solution to this problem through, for example, the work of the National Educational Welfare Board (NEWB). Seventy nine per cent of early school leavers are either unemployed or classified as economically inactive, a situation that is simply unacceptable and cannot be allowed to continue. Combined with Ireland's very high NEET (young people aged 15-24 not in education, employment or training) rate of 18.4 per cent, early school leaving is a major issue for government that requires a long-term policy response. It may well be time to try alternative approaches aimed at ensuring that people in this cohort attain the skills required to progress in the future and participate in society. With this in mind the review of apprenticeship training should include this cohort of young people as one of its target groups.

Contributing to higher education

There are strong arguments from an equity perspective that those who benefit from higher education and who can afford to contribute to the costs of their higher education should do so. This principle is well established internationally and is an important component of funding strategies for many of the better higher education systems across the world. People with higher education qualifications reap a substantial earnings premium in the labour market which increases with age (OECD, 2012:140). The earnings premium in Ireland for those with higher education has increased by 22 percentage points since 2010. Third-level graduates in employment in Ireland earn on average 64 per cent more that those with a leaving certificate only (OECD, 2011), and 81 per cent of people aged 25 to 64 with a third-level qualification are in employment compared with 35 per cent of those with a primary level qualification only. Ireland is one of the few countries where the relative earnings of 25-64 year olds with qualifications from tertiary type A (largely theory based) and advanced research programmes are more than 100 per cent higher than the earning of people with upper secondary or post-secondary education (OECD, 2013).

Ireland is the highest ranking country in the EU in terms of higher education attainment, with 48 per cent of all 25-34 year olds having a third-level qualification. At present third-level students do not pay fees but do incur a student contribution charge at the beginning of each academic year. Undergraduate students are supported through the provision of maintenance grants under the Student Grant Scheme 2013. As a result of decisions taken in Budget 2012 postgraduate students are no longer eligible for maintenance grant support. Without the introduction of some form of income-contingent loan facility this decision is likely to have a significant impact on entry into postgraduate courses in Ireland over the coming years.

There has been much discussion regarding the future funding for Higher Education Institutions (HEIs) and how they might be configured in the future. In the '*National Strategy for Higher Education to 2030*' the Higher Education Authority (HEA) discusses broadening the base of funding for HEIs and sets out in detail how a student contribution framework might be developed and managed. Various policy options for student contributions are discussed in a report to the Minister (Department of Education, 2009) and the fiscal impact of these options are outlined in detail. Further research concludes that an income contingent student loan rather than a graduate tax system would be the most equitable funding option for Ireland (Flannery & O'Donoghue, 2011). *Social Justice Ireland* believes that Government should introduce a system in which fees are paid by all participants in third-level education with an income-contingent loan facility being put in place to ensure that all participants who need to do so can borrow to pay their fees and cover their living costs, repaying such borrowing when their income rises above a prescribed level. In this system:

- All students would be treated on the same basis insofar as both tuition and living cost loans would be available on a deferred repayment basis;
- All students would be treated on the same basis as repayment is based on their own future income rather than on current parental income; and
- Inclusion of all part-time students would reduce the present disparity between full-time and part-time students.

Were such a scheme introduced, *Social Justice Ireland* calculates that the gain to the Exchequer would be €445 million in a full year (2011 estimates) and proposes that €120 million of this should go towards early childhood education and adult literacy programmes.

Key Priorities on Education and Educational Disadvantage

- Invest in universal, quality early childhood education.
- Set an ambitious adult literacy target and ensure adequate funding is provided for adult literacy programmes.
- Increase resources available to lifelong learning and alternative pathways to education.
- Introduce an income-contingent loan facility for all third-level students and develop a system in which fees are paid by all participants in third-level education.

10.

PEOPLE AND PARTICIPATION

CORE POLICY OBJECTIVE: PEOPLE AND PARTICIPATION

To ensure that all people from different cultures are welcomed in a way that is consistent with our history, our obligations as world citizens and with our economic status. To ensure that every person has a genuine voice in shaping the decisions that affect them and that every person can contribute to the development of society.

People have a right to participate in shaping the decisions that affect them and to participate in developing and shaping the society in which they live. These rights are part of *Social Justice Ireland*'s Core Policy Area, Reform Governance as set out in Chapter 2. In this chapter we set out some of the implications of these rights and how they might be met in Ireland today.

People

Migration issues of various kinds, both inwards and outwards, present important challenges for Government and Irish society. The circumstances that generate involuntary emigration must be addressed in an open, honest and transparent manner. For many migrants immigration is not temporary. They will remain in Ireland and make it their home. Irish society needs to adapt to this reality. Ireland is now a multi-racial and multi-cultural country and Government policies should promote and encourage the creation of an inclusive and integrated society in which respect for and recognition of their culture is an important right for all people.

The key challenge of integration

The rapid internationalisation of the Irish population in recent years presents Ireland with the key challenge of avoiding mistakes made by many other countries. The focus should be on integration rather than on isolating new migrant communities. Census 2011 showed that there were a total of 544,357 non-Irish nationals – representing 199 different nations - living in Ireland in 2011 (CSO, 2012: 8). It also showed that that 268,180, or 15.1%, of the workforce are non-Irish nationals (CSO, 2012: 19). These figures are unlikely to change significantly over the next few years, even when allowance is made for emigration. Spending cuts have had significant impact on strategies on integration. The fourth report (2012) of the European Commission against Racism and Intolerance (ECRI) highlighted:

- the closing of the National Consultative Committee on Racism and Interculturalism (NCCRI) in December 2008, and the subsequent loss of the reporting of racist incidents carried out by the NCCRI;
- the lack of adequate language support in the classroom for the 10% of primary school and 12% of post-primary school children from an immigrant background;
- the withdrawal of funding of the Integrate Ireland Language and Training centres;
- and the non-renewal of the Action Plan Against Racism (2005-2008).

Discrimination against Travellers

In Irish society, Travellers have often faced discrimination and the state has been slow to recognise Traveller's culture to be respected as a right. In the Programme for Government and National Recovery 2011-2016 the Government commits to promoting 'greater coordination and integration of delivery of services to the Traveller communities across Government, using available resources more effectively to deliver on principles of social inclusion particularly in the area of Traveller education' (Government of Ireland 2011: 53). While the structures recommended by the Task Force on the Travelling People have been established, it is very important to ensure that the recommendations of the report are fully implemented. The fourth report of the ECRI highlighted the fact that Travellers still face problems related to adequate accommodation and recommended that Government introduce measures binding on local authorities to support the National Traveller/Roma Integration Strategy and fully implement the 1998 Traveller Accommodation Act. It also called on the Government to reduce health inequalities, particularly in relation to the Travelling Community.

Migrant Workers

The latest figures from the Central Statistics Office for nationality and employment are presented in Table 10.1. They show that after a significant fall between 2008 and 2011 the numbers of non-Irish nationals in employment has begun to increase, though the numbers in employment have yet to recover to the peak level in the fourth quarter of 2007.

Table 10.1: Estimated number of persons aged 15 years and over in employment and classified by nationality Q4 2007-2013, by '000

	2007	2008	2009	2010	2011	2012	2013
Irish	1,804.20	1,736.00	1,632.50	1,603.20	1,584.30	1,579.70	1,626.20
Non-Irish	334.7	316	255.2	220	223.5	269.2	283.6
Including							
UK	51.4	51.8	44.9	34.1	29.4	46.5	49.8
EU15*	34.5	33.7	28.5	22.9	21.1	29.1	27.7
EU15/27**	167.7	150.9	114	107.8	114.3	125.9	130.2
Other	81	79.6	67.9	55.3	58.7	67.7	75.9
Total	2,138.9	2,052.0	1,887.7	1,823.2	1,807.8	1,848.9	1,909.8

Source: CSO QNHS Series (2008-2013). All figures from Q4. *excluding Ireland and UK **EU15 to EU27 states.

There has been criticism of Irish immigration policy and legislation specifically due to the lack of support for the integration of immigrants and a lack of adequate recognition of the permanency of immigration. Three significant areas of concern are:

- Work permits are issued to employers, not to employees, which ties the employee to a specific employer, increasing their vulnerability to exploitation and reducing their labour market mobility.
- The Irish asylum process can take many years and most refugees coming onto the Irish labour market are *de facto* long-term unemployed. A process for training and education of asylum seekers is needed so that they can retain and gain skills (ECRI, 2006 & Employers Diversity Network, 2009).
- The existence of up to 30,000 undocumented migrants in Ireland. Without credentials they are denied access to basic services and vulnerable to exploitation by employers. The Irish Migrant Rights Centre has proposed an Earned Regularisation Scheme to provide a pathway to permanent residency.

Refugees and Asylum Seekers

Until recently, the number of refugees forced to flee from their own countries in order to escape war, persecution and abuses of human rights had been declining worldwide over a number of years. In its most recent reports, however, the United Nations High Commission for Refugees (UNHCR) signalled a sizeable reversal of this trend. In 2012 alone, 7.6 million people were newly displaced due to conflict or persecution (UNHCR, 2013a: 2). At the end of 2012 the total population of concern to UNHCR was estimated at 35.8 million people, including: 10.5 million refugees; 928,226 asylum seekers; 525,941 refugees who had been repatriated in 2012 (almost double the 2010 figure); 17.6 million internally displaced persons; and an estimated number of 3.3 million stateless people worldwide (UNHCR, 2013b: 73). There were 4.9 million Palestinians refugees registered with the United Nations Relief and Works Agency for Palestine Refugees in the Near East.

Irish people have had a long tradition of solidarity with people facing oppression within their own countries, but that tradition is not reflected in our policies towards refugees and asylum-seekers. *Social Justice Ireland* believes that Ireland should use its position in international forums to highlight the causes of displacement of peoples. In particular, Ireland should use these forums to challenge the production, sale and free access to arms and the implements of torture.

Despite this tradition of solidarity with peoples facing oppression, racism is an everyday reality for many migrants in Ireland. Preliminary figures from the Immigrant Council of Ireland show an 85 per cent increase in the number of racist incidences reported in 2013 with the majority of cases occurring in a person's local community or workplace[74]. This increase in reported racism is very worrying and *Social Justice* Ireland urges Government to provide leadership in dealing with the issue. An integrated policy response is needed to address the root causes of racism within communities; political and institutional responses are required to address this problem in order to prevent it deteriorating. The establishment of Citizenship Ceremonies by the Minister for Justice, Equality and Defence and the reforms to the procedure of assessing and processing citizenship applications are welcome and have the potential to promote inclusiveness and integration.

Table 10.2 shows the number of applications for asylum in Ireland between 2000 and 2012. In 2012 Ireland experienced a small reduction in applications, reflecting a consistent decrease in applications. In 2012, there were 319,185 applicants for asylum in the European Union; the top two single largest nation of origin for applicants were Afghanistan and Syria, reflecting the terrible situations in those countries (Eurostat, 2013). Almost 2,250 people were deported from Ireland in 2012, of whom 1,890 were refused entry into the country at ports of entry (Department of Justice and Equality, 2014).

---

[74] http://www.immigrantcouncil.ie/media/press-releases/775-85-in-racist-incidents

Table 10.2 – Applications for Asylum in Ireland, 2000-2012

Year	Number	Year	Number	Year	Number
2000	10,938	2005	4,323	2010	1,939
2001	10,325	2006	4,314	2011	1,290
2002	11,634	2007	3,985	2012	956
2003	7,900	2008	3,866	2013	946
2004	4,766	2009	2,689		

Source: Office of the Refugee Applications Commissioner (2013), Statistical Report December 2013.

The third report of the ECRI identified difficulties in gaining recognition for professional qualifications as a major challenge facing refugees and asylum-seekers when they have been granted leave to stay in Ireland. It means refugees are often unable to find employment commensurate with their qualifications and experience, impeding their full integration into society. It also means their valuable skills, which could contribute to the Irish economy, are unused or underused (ECRI, 2006). *Social Justice Ireland* proposes that asylum-seekers who currently are not entitled to take up employment should be allowed to do so with immediate effect and that structures are established to recognise professional qualifications. The fourth ECRI report has already been highlighted; its recommendations should be implemented in full.

While asylum-seekers are assigned initial accommodation in Dublin, most are subsequently allocated accommodation at locations outside Dublin, pending the completion of the asylum-seeking process. The Reception and Integration Agency (RIA) was established to perform this task. The latest statistics from the RIA show that there are 34 accommodation centres throughout the country accommodating 4,360 people (RIA, 2013). The policy for "direct provision" employed in almost all of these centres results in these asylum-seekers receiving accommodation and board, together with €19.10 direct provision per week per adult and €9.60 per child. Over time this sum has remained unchanged and its value has therefore been eroded by inflation. Between 2001 and 2013 the purchasing power of these payments has been decreased by almost 20 per cent. Furthermore, many asylum-seekers have been placed for long periods of time in these centres, with over 59 per cent residing in the centres for more than three years, 31 per cent for over five years and 9 per cent for over seven years (Joyce, C. & Quinn, E., 2014). This situation, combined with the fact that asylum-seekers are denied access to employment, means that asylum-seekers are among the most excluded and marginalised groups in Ireland.

Social Justice Ireland proposes that asylum-seekers who currently are not entitled to take up employment should be allowed to do so with immediate effect and that the direct provision payments should be increased immediately to at least €65 per week for an adult and €38 per week for a child. Removing employment restrictions and increasing the direct provision allocation would cost €12.5m per annum[75] and provide noticeable improvements in the subsistence life being led by these asylum-seekers. The accommodation centres must also be examined; some of the centres, which include a former leisure centre, are not appropriate places for people to live, and serve to isolate asylum seekers. A recent report by the European Migration Network and the ESRI highlights some of the problems with Ireland's reception system. These are a lack of privacy, overcrowding, limited autonomy, and insufficient homework and play areas for children (Joyce, C. & Quinn, E. 2014). Despite Government acknowledging that the reception system is unsuitable for long-term residence of asylum seekers, progress on developing an alternative procedure has been extremely slow.

Emigration

Emigration has increased dramatically since 2009. It should be noted that in all migration statistics the year end is April of the year in question. Net migration was negative in 2010; the first time since 1995 more people had left Ireland than returned or arrived from elsewhere. Net outmigration was 27,400 in 2011, rose to 34,400 in 2012, and fell slightly to 33,100 in 2013. During 2008 and 2009 the majority of those emigrating were from the new accession countries. However, from 2010 the largest group emigrating were Irish nationals; 42,000 left in 2011, 46,500 left in 2012, while 50,900 left in 2013. Overall, emigration of all nationalities is estimated to have reached 89,000 in 2012. Table 10.3 below outlines the numbers of people leaving the country between 2006 and 2013, both Irish and non-Irish nationals.

The rate of emigration of Irish nationals has more than tripled since 2008. This demonstrates the lack of opportunities available for people in Ireland, especially for those seeking employment in the 15-44 age group. Of those who emigrated in 2013, more than 75,800 were in this age group, while 34,800 were in the 15-24 age cohort. Net migration amongst this age group in 2013 reached a height of 21,800. The austerity programme is contributing to Ireland's loss of young people, the implications of which are stark as this loss will pose significant problems for economic recovery.

---

[75] *Social Justice Ireland* calculation based on 2010 data.

Table 10.3: Estimated Emigration by Nationality, 2006 – 2012, by'000

Year	Irish	UK	EU 13*	EU 10/12**	Rest of World	Total
2013[76]	50.9	3.9	9.9	14.0	10.3	89.1
2012[77]	46.5	3.5	11.2	14.8	11.1	87.1
2011	42	4.6	10.2	13.9	9.9	80.6
2010	28.9	3	9	19	9.3	69.2
2009	19.2	3.9	7.4	30.5	11	72
2008	13.1	3.7	6	17.2	9	49.2
2007	12.9	3.7	8.9	12.6	8.2	46.3
2006	15.3	2.2	5.1	7.2	6.2	36

Source: CSO (2013), Population and Migration Estimates.
*EU 15 excluding UK and Ireland. **EU MS that joined in 2004 and 2007

Chart 10.1 – Immigration, Emigration and Net Migration, 2000-2013

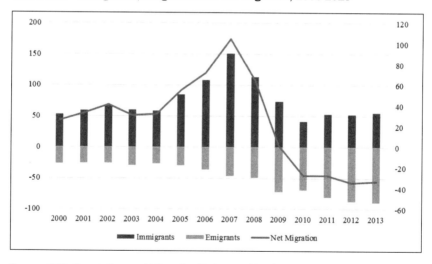

Source: CSO, Population and Migration Estimates (2013).

---

[76] Preliminary.
[77] Preliminary.

This emigration 'brain drain', which in some quarters is perversely being heralded as a 'safety valve', is in fact a serious problem for Ireland. It may well result in a significant skills deficit in the long-term and hamper Ireland's recovery. Sadly, outmigration has been one of the factors keeping the unemployment rate down. In December 2012, the IMF estimates that had all the employees who lost their job at the outset of the crisis remained in the labour force, then unemployment would now by 20 per cent (IMF, 2012: 5). Given the continuing weakness of domestic demand and investment in the economy induced by austerity budgets it is likely that emigration will continue at a very high rate. Unless there are measures in place to increase employment at a faster pace by boosting domestic demand and investment, outmigration will continue. This is particularly a concern in the building and construction sector due to the large section of the workforce employed in construction between 2000 and 2008. The ESRI (2013: 18) has estimated that net out-migration will fall to 26,000 in 2014.

Participation

The changing nature of democracy has raised many questions for policy-makers and others concerned about the issue of participation. Decisions often appear to be made without any real involvement of the many affected by the decisions' outcomes. The most recent in-depth analysis of voter participation was undertaken in 2011 by the CSO. In a quarterly national household survey module on voter participation and abstention, issued in November 2011, the CSO provided an insight into how people regarded the electoral process. It found that just over 62 per cent of those aged 18 to 24 voted in the 2011 general election. This contrasts with participation figures of 92 per cent for older voters aged 55 to 64 years (CSO 2011: 3). The survey also found that over one-third of those who did not vote were not registered to vote, 11 per cent of non-voters said they had 'no interest', 10 per cent were 'disillusioned' with politics and 11 per cent had difficulty getting to the polling station (this was particularly common among non-voters aged 55 and over). (CSO, 2011:4) Those educated to primary level or below were most likely to say they did not vote because they were disillusioned with politics.

These findings suggest that many people, especially young people and those who have lower educational attainment levels, have little confidence in the political process. They have become disillusioned because the political process fails to involve them in any real way, while also failing to address many of their core concerns. Transparency and accountability are demanded but rarely delivered. Many of the developments of recent years will simply have added to the disillusionment of many people. A new approach is clearly needed to address this issue. Although Government is engaging with members of civil society on eight specific issues as part of the Constitutional Convention,[78] it can ill afford to ignore the lack of trust and engagement of civil society in the democratic processes of the state.

---

[78] For more information see https://www.constitution.ie/Convention.aspx

Some of the decision-making structures of our society and of our world, allow people to be represented in the process. However, almost all of these structures fail to provide genuine participation for most people affected by their decisions, resulting in an apathy towards participating in political processes. The decline in participation is exacerbated by the primacy given to the market by many analysts, commentators, policy-makers and politicians. Most people are not involved in the processes that produce plans and decisions which affect their lives. They know that they are being presented with a *fait accompli*. More critically, they realise that they and their families will be forced to live with the consequences of the decisions taken. This is particularly relevant in Ireland in 2014, where people are living with the consequences of the bailout programme and repaying the debts of European banks through a programme of austerity and upward redistribution of resources. Many feel disenfranchised by a process that produced this outcome without any meaningful consultation with citizens.

Many people feel that their views or comments are ignored or patronised, while the views of those who see the market as solving most, if not all, of society's problems are treated with the greatest respect. This situation seems to persist despite the total failure of market mechanisms in recent years and despite the role these very mechanisms played in producing Ireland's range of current crises and the associated EU-level crises that are not currently being recognised by most decision-makers. Markets have a major role to play. But it needs to be honestly acknowledged that they produce very mixed results when left to their own devices. Recent experience has shown clearly that markets are extremely limited in terms of many policy goals. Consequently other mechanisms are required to ensure that some re-balancing, at least, is achieved. The mechanisms proposed here simply aim to be positive in improving participation in a 21st century society. Modern means of communication and information make it relatively easy to involve people in dialogue and decision-making. The big question is whether the groups with power will share it with others?

A forum for dialogue on civil society issues

A new forum and structure for discussion of issues on which people disagree is becoming more obvious as political and mass communication systems develop. A civil society forum and the formulation of a new social contract against exclusion has the potential to reengage people with the democratic process. Democracy means 'rule by the people', which implies that people participate in shaping the decisions that affect them most closely. What we have, in practice, is a highly centralised government in which we are 'represented' by professional politicians. The more powerful a political party becomes, the more distant it seems to become from the electorate. Party policies on a range of major issues are often difficult to discern.

Backbenchers have little control over, or influence on, Government ministers, opposition spokespersons or shadow cabinets. Even within the cabinet some ministers seem to be able to ignore their cabinet colleagues. The democratic process has certainly benefited from the participation of various sectors in different arenas. It would also benefit from taking up the proposals to develop a new social contract against exclusion and a new forum for dialogue on civil society issues.

The failure to discuss openly a range of civil society issues that are of major concern to large numbers of people is contributing to disillusionment with the political process. When discussion or debate does take place, furthermore, many people feel that they are not allowed to participate in any real way. The development of a new forum within which a civil society debate could be conducted on an on-going basis would be a welcome addition to Ireland's political landscape. Such a forum could make a major contribution to improving participation by a wide range of groups in Irish society.

Social Justice Ireland proposes that Government authorises and resources an initiative to identify how a civil society debate could be developed and maintained and to examine how it might connect to the growing debate at European level around civil society issues. There are many issues such a forum could address. Given recent developments in Ireland, the issue of citizenship, its rights, responsibilities, possibilities and limitations in the twenty-first century is one that springs to mind. Another topical issue is the shape of the social model Ireland wishes to develop in the decades ahead. Do we follow a European model or an American one? Or do we want to create an alternative – and, if we do, what shape would it have and how could it be delivered? What future levels of services and taxation will be required and how are resources to be distributed? The issues a civil society forum could address are many and varied and Ireland would benefit immensely from having one.[79]

Deliberative Democracy

To facilitate real participation a process of 'deliberative democracy' is required. Deliberative democratic structures enable discussion and debate to take place without any imposition of power differentials. Issues and positions are argued and discussed on the basis of the available evidence rather than on the basis of assertions by those who are powerful and unwilling to consider the evidence. It produces evidence-based policy and ensures a high level of accountability among stakeholders. Deliberative participation by all is essential if society is to develop and, in practice, to maintain principles guaranteeing satisfaction of basic needs, respect for others as equals, economic equality, and religious, social, sexual and ethnic equality.

---

[79] For a further discussion of this issue see Healy and Reynolds (2003:191-197).

Social Justice Ireland believes a deliberative democracy process, in which all stakeholders would address the evidence, would go some way towards ensuring that local issues are addressed. This process could be implemented under the framework of the Council of Europe's *Charter on Shared Social Responsibilities*. The Charter states that shared social responsibility in terms of local government requires that local government 'frame local policies which acknowledge and take into account the contribution made by everyone to strengthening social protection and social cohesion, the fair allocation of common goods, the formation of the principles of social, environmental and intergenerational justice and which also ensure that all stakeholders have a negotiation and decision-making power' (Council of Europe, 2011). We believe these guidelines can be adapted to the Irish context and would be useful tools for devising a policy to promote greater alignment between local government and the community & voluntary sector in promoting participation at local level. This would involve:

- Local government, the community & voluntary sector and the local community working together to ensure the design and efficient delivery of services for local communities to cater for the specific needs of that particular local community.
- Highlighting the key role of social citizenship in creating vibrant, participative and inclusive communities.
- Direct involvement of local communities, local authorities, state bodies and local entrepreneurs in the policy making and decision making processes.
- Ensuring all voices are heard (especially those of people on the margins of society) in the decision making process.
- Reform of current local government structures to better involve local communities in the governance of and decision making in their local area.
- An increased sense of 'ownership' over local government by the local community, which will only come about with increased participation. The community & voluntary sector has a key role to play in this.

All communities are different and not every community has the capacity or the infrastructure to engage meaningfully with and participate in local government. This is where the community and voluntary sector has a key role to play in informing, engaging with and providing the local communities with the skills to participate in and contribute to local government.

Citizen Engagement

In October 2012 the Department of Environment, Community and Local Government published '*Putting People First: Action Programme for Effective Local Government*'. The document outlines a vision for local government as 'leading economic, social and community development, delivering efficient and good value services, and representing citizens and local communities effectively and accountably' (Department of Environment, Community and Local Government, 2012: iii). One of the stated aims of this process of local government reform is to create more meaningful and responsive local democracy (DECLG 2012:148) with options for citizen engagement and participative democracy outlined in the report. The report also deals with the issues of good governance, strong leadership and democratic accountability and outlines the reforms identified by Government as necessary to ensure that:

- local government is accountable and effective;
- local objectives, national interests and the common good are balanced; and
- community involvement in the policy and decision making process is promoted.

The establishment of a Working Group on Citizen Engagement to report and make recommendations for more diverse and extensive input by citizens into decision making at local level was a positive move by Government.

The objective of the Working Group report was to provide structures and guidance to assist local authorities in consultation with the public and communities to create communities where the well-being of all, and future generations, is protected and promoted. The report proposes a structure for participatory engagement in decision-making on an on-going basis at local level. The proposed new framework for public engagement and participation is called "The Public Participation Network" (PPN). The PPN facilitates input by the public into local government through a structure that ensures public participation and representation and decision-making committees within local government. The role of the PPN[80] is:

1. To contribute to the local authority's development for the County/City a vision for the well-being of this and future generations.

2. to facilitate opportunities for networking, communication and the sharing of information between environmental, community and voluntary groups and between these groups and the local authority.

3. to identify issues of collective concern and work to influence policy locally in relation to these issues.

4. to actively support inclusion of socially excluded groups, communities experiencing high levels of poverty, communities experiencing discrimination, including Travellers, to enable them to participate at local and county level and to clearly demonstrate same.

---

[80] For a detailed outline of the structure of the PPN see section 3 of the Working Group Report.

5. to encourage and enable public participation in local decision-making and planning of services.

6. to facilitate the selection of participants from the environmental, social inclusion and voluntary sectors onto city/county decision making bodies.

7. to support a process that will feed the broad range of ideas, experience, suggestions and proposals of the Network into policies and plans being developed by agencies and decision makers in areas that are of interest and relevant to the Network

8. to work to develop the Environmental, Community and Voluntary sectors so that the work of the sectors is clearly recognised and acknowledged and the sectors have a strong collective voice within the County/City.

9. to support the individual members of the Public Participation Network so that:

    •   They can develop their capacity and do their work more effectively.

    •   They can participate effectively in the Public Participation Network activities.

    •   They are included and their voices and concerns are heard.

The proposed PPN structure outlined in the report is a significant departure in terms of citizen engagement in the decision making and policy making process at local level. It also embeds the need to develop sustainable communities and to consider the well-being of communities at the heart of the local decision making process. It is important that the necessary resources are made available to ensure that the PPNs function effectively and that members are given the training and support required to enable them to represent their communities.

A deliberative democracy structure and framework embedded into the citizen engagement and local government structures would enhance community involvement in decision making and the policy making process at a local level. It would also ensure that governance, participation and policy evaluation are reformed in line with the core policy framework detailed in chapter 2.

Supporting the Community & Voluntary Sector

The issue of governance is of major importance for Government and for society at large. Within this wider reality it is an especially crucial issue for the community & voluntary sector. The community & voluntary sector is playing a major role in responding to both the causes and the consequences of these crises. It should also play a major role in public discussion regarding what type of economic and social vision Ireland wants to pursue in the future. Support for the work of the community and voluntary sector is crucial and it should not be left to the welcome but very limited charity of philanthropists. Funding required by the sector has been provided over many years by Government. In recent years, however, the level of state funding has been reduced, with obvious consequences for those depending on the community & voluntary sector. It is crucial that Government appropriately resource this sector into the future and that it remains committed to the principle of providing multi-annual statutory funding.

Social dialogue is a critically important component of effective decision making in a modern democracy. The Community & Voluntary Pillar provides a mechanism for social dialogue that should be engaged with by Government across the range of policy issues in which the Pillar's members are deeply engaged. All aspects of governance should be characterised by transparency and accountability. Social dialogue contributes to both transparency and accountability. We believe governance along these lines can and should be developed in Ireland.

Key Policy Priorities on People and Participation

- Address involuntary emigration and the long-term policy problems it presents to society by promoting integration and an inclusive society.
- Conduct an immediate audit of "direct provision" accommodation centres, and commit to providing appropriate and humane accommodation for asylum seekers.
- Immediately increase the weekly allowance allocated to asylum-seekers on 'direct provision' to at least €65 per week for an adult and €38 for a child and give priority to recognising the right of all refugees and asylum-seekers to work.
- Introduce an Earned Regularisation Scheme similar to that proposed by the Migrant Rights Centre Ireland to provide a pathway to permanent residency for the 30,000 undocumented migrants in Ireland.

Establish and resource a forum for dialogue on civil society issues. This initiative should identify how a civil society debate could be developed and maintained in Ireland and should examine how it might connect to the growing debate at European level around civil society issues.

- Implement the PPN framework recommendations for citizen engagement at local level and ensure adequate resources are made available for capacity building.
- Ensure that there is real and effective monitoring and impact assessment of policy implementation using an evidence-based approach. Involve a wide range of perspectives in this process, thus ensuring inclusion of the experience of those currently excluded.

11.

SUSTAINABILITY

CORE POLICY OBJECTIVE: SUSTAINABILITY
To ensure that all development is socially, economically and environmentally sustainable

The search for a humane, sustainable model of development has gained momentum in recent times. After years of people believing that markets and market forces would produce a better life for everyone, major problems such as resource depletion and pollution have raised questions and doubts. There is a growing awareness that sustainability must be a constant factor in all development. Sustainability is about ensuring that all development is socially, economically and environmentally sustainable. This understanding underpins all the other chapters in this review. This chapter focuses in more detail on promoting sustainable development and on reviewing environmental issues. These are key policy areas that must be addressed urgently as part of the Core Policy Framework we set out in Chapter 2 under the heading of Creating a Sustainable Future.

Promoting Sustainable Development

Sustainable development is defined as 'development which meets the needs of the present, without compromising the ability of future generations to meet their needs *(World Commission on Environment and Development, 1987)*. It encompasses three pillars; environment, society and economy. These three pillars of sustainability must be addressed in a balanced manner if development is to indeed be sustainable. Maintaining this balance is crucial to the long-term development of a sustainable resource-efficient future for Ireland. While growth and economic competitiveness are important, they are not the only issues to be considered and cannot be given precedence over others. They must be dealt with using a framework for sustainable development which gives equal consideration to the environmental, social and economic pillars. It is also important to note that, although economic growth is seen as the key to resolving many aspects of the current crisis across the EU, it is this very growth that may be damaging the possibility of securing sustainable development in the Global South.

Sustainable development is our only means of creating a long term future for Ireland, with the environment, economic growth and social needs met in a balanced manner with consideration for the needs of future generations. Sustainability and the adoption of a sustainable development model presents a significant policy challenge: how environmental policy decisions with varying distributional consequences are to be made in a timely manner while ensuring that a disproportionate burden is not imposed on certain groups e.g. low income families or rural dwellers. This policy challenge highlights the need for an evidence-based policy process involving all stakeholders. The costs and benefits of all policies must be assessed and considered on the basis of evidence only. This is essential in order to avoid the policy debate being influenced by hearsay or vested interests or the thoughtless exercise of power. Before the current recession began the global economy was five times the size it had been 50 years before and, had it continued on that growth path, it would be 80 times that size by 2100 (SDC, 2009). This raises the fundamental question of how such growth rates can be sustained in a world of finite resources and fragile ecosystems. Continuing along the same path is clearly not sustainable. A successful transition to sustainability requires a vision of a viable future societal model and also the ability to overcome obstacles such as vested economic interests, political power struggles and the lack of open social dialogue (Hämäläinen, 2013).

Promoting a sustainable economy requires that we place a value on our finite natural resources and that the interdependence of the economy, wellbeing and natural capital are recognised (EC 2011). A sustainable economy requires us to acknowledge the limitations of finite natural resources and the duty we have to preserve these for future generations. It requires that natural capital and ecosystems are assigned value in our national accounting systems and that resource productivity is increased. Policy frameworks and business models should give priority to renewable energy, resource efficiency and sustainable land use. A sustainable economy would involve transformative change and policies being implemented similar to those being proposed by Stahel in the 'performance economy' and Wijkman in the 'circular economy'. The 'circular economy' theory is based on the understanding that it is the reuse of vast amounts of material reclaimed from end of life products, rather than the extraction of new resources, that is the foundation of economic growth (Wijkman, 2012:166). This theory involves a shift towards servicing consumer products rather than constantly producing new goods to be consumed. The policy instruments proposed to implement a circular economy are those which are also considered to be at the heart of the sustainable development debate. They are:

- Binding targets for resource efficiency;
- Sustainable innovation and sustainable design being given priority in terms of research; and
- Tax reform: lowering taxes on labour and raising taxes on the use of natural resources.

Alongside the theories of the 'performance economy' and the 'circular economy' is the concept of the 'Economy of the Common Good[81]'. This model, designed by Felber (2010) is based on the idea that economic success should be measured in terms of human needs, quality of life and the fulfilment of fundamental values. This model proposes a new form of social and economic development based on human dignity, solidarity, sustainability, social justice and democratic co-determination and transparency.

It is clear that the current economic path is not sustainable and consideration must be given to how we, as a society, can transform our present system and move to a more sustainable future pathway. Creating a sustainable Ireland is one of the five pillars of *Social Justice Ireland's* core policy framework outlined in more detail in chapter 2.

Beyond 2015 – Towards Sustainable Development Goals

Discussions and negotiations at the RIO+20 summit in June 2012 culminated in the *'Future We Want'* outcome document which outlines UN commitments for a sustainable future and the development of Sustainable Development Goals (SDGs) to replace the Millennium Development Goals[82] (MDGs) after 2015. Work on developing SDGs began in earnest in January 2013 with the establishment of the Open Working Group (OWG) on Sustainable Development Goals.[83] The *'Future We Want'* indicates that the SDGs should address and incorporate in a balanced way all three dimensions of sustainable development and their inter-linkages and should be universally applicable to all countries. All stakeholders should be included in the process of creating the SDGs and the measurable targets and indicators. While the development of SDGs is welcome, it is of concern that there is no mention of the common good in the *'Future We Want'*, even though it does give significant consideration to sustained economic growth. This commitment to sustained economic growth indicates a failure to learn from past mistakes and the current crises by the international community – an issue that is of concern to *Social Justice*

---

[81] http://www.gemeinwohl-oekonomie.org/en/content/downloads
[82] For a more detailed discussion on MDGs see Annex 14 of this socio-economic review
[83] For further information see http://sustainabledevelopment.un.org/index.php?menu=1549

Ireland. The common good must be at the core of sustainable development to ensure that natural resources are protected for future generations.

Civil society organisations engaged with the post-2015 development agenda have given a cautious welcome to the development of the SDGs. They emphasise the need for a meaningful and inclusive framework to engage people who are affected by poverty and experience marginalisation in order to promote ownership of the SDGs. This was one of the failures of the MDG process because those who were to benefit from the MDGs being achieved were not involved in the development of these goals. It is also crucial that the SDG targets are equitable, that priority is given to meeting the challenge faced by the most disadvantaged and that fair allocation of resources is secured for both poor people and poor countries.

The OWG is beginning the second phase of its work and is due to report to the UN General Assembly at its sixty-eighth session. In the first phase of its work the group had input from experts on a variety of issues such as poverty, food security, water, employment and health. This input will now be processed into a report containing a strategic outlook and a proposal for sustainable development goals (UN, 2014). The OWG has also stated that it can build on the convergence of ideas around the need to balance the economic, social and environmental dimensions of sustainable development and integrating more comprehensively economic growth and environmental sustainability (UN, 2014). The OWG state that in order to ensure that progress is measurable and measures quantified, targets will be required. The strategy for SDGs being developed by the UN is in contrast with that adopted recently by the European Commission in the 2030 Framework on Climate and Energy. The European Commission commits to reducing emissions by 40% in Europe, but the document contains no national targets. The incoherence of policy at international level does not bode well for the successful adoption and implementation for SDGs.

When formulating SDG proposals and strategies, the OWG on Sustainable Development Goals must take into account the shortcomings of the MDGs, specifically their failure to address the structural causes of poverty, inequality and exclusion. The set of SDGs which are eventually agreed should be truly universal, integrate sustainable development and the environment and should confront the root causes of our current crises and the reality that the world needs to move towards a sustainable path in order to guarantee a future for generations to come.

The need for shadow national accounts

According to Repetto, Magrath, Wells, Beer and Rossini (1989:3) the 'difference in the treatment of natural resources and other tangible assets [in the existing national accounts] reinforces the false dichotomy between the economy and "the environment" that leads policy makers to ignore or destroy the latter in the name of economic development.' By not assigning value to our natural capital and environmental resources, a major national asset, we are not measuring the cost to our society of the ongoing depletion of these resources.

Acceptance of the need to move away from money-measured growth as the principal economic target and measure of success towards sustainability in terms of real-life, social, environmental and economic variables must be central to any model of development with sustainability at its core. This is at the core of the 'circular economy' and 'Economy for the Common Good' theories and is a key part of our core policy framework. Our present national accounts are based on GNP/GDP as scorecards of wealth and progress and miss fundamentals such as environmental sustainability. These measures completely ignore unpaid work because only money transactions are tracked. Ironically, while environmental depletion is ignored, the environmental costs of dealing with the effects of economic growth, such as cleaning up pollution or coping with the felling of rainforests, are added to, rather than subtracted from, GNP/GDP.

It is widely acknowledged that GDP is 'an inadequate metric to gauge wellbeing over time, particularly in its economic, environmental, and social dimensions, some aspects of which are often referred to as sustainability (Stiglitz Commission 2009: 8). A new scorecard or metric model is needed which measures the effects of policy decisions on people's lives as well as the environmental, social and economic costs and benefits of those policies. The United Nations High Level Panel on Global Sustainability recommends that the international community measure development beyond GDP and that national accounts should measure and cost social exclusion, unemployment and social inequality and the environmental costs of growth and market failures.

Development of 'satellite' or 'shadow' national accounts should be a central initiative in this. Already a number of alternative scorecards exist, such as the United Nations' Human Development Index (HDI), former World Bank economist Herman Daly's Index of Sustainable Economic Welfare (ISEW) and Hazel Henderson's Country Futures Index (CFI). A 2002 study by Wackernagel et al presented the first systematic attempt to calculate how human demands on the environment are matched by its capacity to cope. It found that the world currently uses 120 per cent of what the earth can provide sustainably each year.

In the environmental context it is crucial that dominant economic models are challenged on, among other things, their assumptions that nature's capital (clean air, water and environment) are essentially free and inexhaustible, that scarce resources can always be substituted and that the planet can continue absorbing human and industrial wastes. These are issues that most economists tend to downplay as externalities. Shadow national accounts would help to make sustainability and 'green' procurement mandatory considerations in the decision and policy making process. They would also go some way towards driving a civil society awareness campaign to help decouple economic growth from consumption.

Social Justice Ireland welcomes the publication by the Departments of Environment, Community and Local Government and Public Expenditure and Reform of the Action Plan for Green Public Procurement as a step on the road towards making green procurement mandatory in public sector procurement decisions. However the lack of reference to Green Public Procurement in the current Draft Partnership Agreement for European Social and Structural Funds 2014-2020 prepared by the Department of Public Expenditure and Reform is worrying[84].

Some governments and international agencies have picked up on these issues, especially in the environmental area and have begun to develop 'satellite' or 'shadow' national accounts that include items not traditionally measured. *Social Justice Ireland's* 2009 publication *Beyond GDP: What is prosperity and how should it be measured?* explored many of these new developments. It included contributions from the OECD, the New Economics Foundation, and other informed bodies and proposed a series of policy developments which would assist in achieving similar progress in Ireland.

There has, in fact, been some progress in this area, including commitments to better data collection and broader assessment of well-being and progress by the CSO, ESRI and EPA. The CSO published Sustainable Development Indicators Ireland in 2013 and this is a welcome development. However, much remains to be achieved in terms of communicating these sustainable development indicators to the public and the inclusion of well-being in the monitoring process. *Social Justice Ireland* strongly urges Government to adopt this broader perspective and commit to producing these accounts alongside more comprehensive indicators of progress. Measures of economic performance must reflect their environmental cost and a price must be put on the use of our natural capital.

The OECD Global Project on measuring the progress of society recommends that sets of key environmental, social and economic indicators be developed and that these should be used to inform evidence-based decision making across all sectors (Morrone, 2009: 23).

Social Justice Ireland recommends that government commit to producing shadow national accounts and that these accounts include indicators that measure the following:

---

[84] per.gov.ie/wp-content/uploads/Draft-Partnership-Agreement-Ireland-081113website.docx

- the use of energy and materials to produce goods;
- the generation of pollution and waste;
- the amount of money spent by industry, government and households to protect the environment or manage natural resources;
- natural resource asset accounts measuring the quantity and quality of a country's natural resources;
- sustainability of the growth being generated *vis-a-vis* our social and natural capital;
- natural resource depletion and degradation as a cost to society;
- the output of waste and pollution as a result of commercial activity as a cost within the satellite national accounts; and
- the measures of the GPI (Genuine Progress Indicator) which measure and deduct for income inequality, environmental degradation and cost of crime, amongst other items. By measuring and differentiating between economic activities that diminish natural and social capital and those activities that enhance them, we can ensure that our economic welfare is sustainable (Daly & Cobb, 1987).

Stakeholder involvement

One of the key indicators of sustainability is how a country runs stakeholder involvement. Sustainable Development Councils (SDCs) are a model for multi-stakeholder bodies comprising members of all major groups – public, private, community, civil society and academic – engaged in evidence-based discussion.[85] The EU-wide experience has been that SDCs are crucial to maintaining a medium and long-term vision for a sustainable future whilst concurrently working to ensure that sustainable development policies are embedded into socio-economic strategies and budgetary processes.

Ireland established its sustainable development council (Comhar) in 1999 and disbanded it in 2011, transferring its functions to NESC (National Economic and Social Council). This is unfortunate in the light of the United Nations recommendation that the link between informed scientific evidence and policy making on sustainable development issues be strengthened (United Nations, 2012). While it is admirable that Government wishes to place sustainable development at the core of policy making and has asked NESC to ensure it gives sustainable development major consideration in all it does, it is also important to note that NESC is not in a position to do the detailed work done previously by Comhar.

---

[85] For more information see http://www.eeac.eu/images/doucments/eeac-statement-backgr2011_rio_final_144dpi.pdf

All areas of governance, from international to national to local, along with civil society and the private sector, must fully embrace the requirements of a sustainable development future (United Nations, 2012). In order to facilitate a move towards a sustainable future for all, stakeholders from all arenas must be involved in the process. Sustainable local development should be a key policy issue on the new local government agenda. There is need for a deliberative democracy arena within which all stakeholders can discuss evidence without power differentials impeding outcomes.

Principles to underpin sustainable development

Principles to underpin sustainable development were proposed in a report for the European Commission prepared by James Robertson in May 1997. The report, *The New Economics of Sustainable Development*, argued that these principles should include the following:

- systematic empowerment of people (as opposed to making and keeping them dependent) as the basis for people-centred development;
- systematic conservation of resources and environment as the basis for environmentally sustainable development;
- evolution from a 'wealth of nations' model of economic life to a 'one-world' economic system;
- evolution from today's international economy to an ecologically sustainable, decentralising, multi-level one-world economic system;
- restoration of political and ethical factors to a central place in economic life and thought;
- respect for qualitative values, not just quantitative values; and
- respect for feminine values, not just masculine ones.

At first glance these might not appear to be the type of concrete guidelines that policymakers so often seek. Yet they are principles that are relevant to every area of economic life. They also apply to every level of life, ranging from personal and household to global issues. They influence lifestyle choices and organisational goals. If these principles were applied to every area, level and feature of economic life they would provide a comprehensive checklist for a systematic policy review. Many of these principles underpin the 'Economy for the Common Good' Balance Sheets which rates companies based on areas including ecological sustainability, social justice and transparency[86].

---

[86] http://www.gemeinwohl-oekonomie.org/en/content/creating-common-good-balance-sheet

A key challenge for Ireland is to ensure that the economy and key sectors develop in a sustainable way and that economic growth is decoupled from environmental pressures. This would require environmental considerations being placed at the centre of policy and decision making at national, regional and local levels (EPA, 2012). Protecting our natural resources and ensuring they are not degraded or exhausted is crucial to the economic and social wellbeing of future generations in Ireland.

It is also important that any programme for sustainable development should take a realistic view of human nature, recognising that people can be both altruistic and selfish, both co-operative and competitive. It is important, therefore, to develop the economic system to reward activities that are socially and environmentally benign (and not the reverse, as at present). This, in turn, would make it easier for people and organisations to make choices that are socially and environmentally responsible. Incorporating social and environmental costs in regulating and pricing both goods and services, combined with promoting those goods and services which are sustainable, should also become part of sustainable development policy. In order to transition to an economy based on sustainable development and a 'green growth strategy' a policy framework is needed that is adaptive and supports shifts away from traditional economic models. This would include user charges for environmental resources to reflect environmental costs and environmental taxes to shift the tax base towards environmental pollutants and consumption and away from labour and production (EPA, 2012).

Any programme for sustainable development has implications for public spending. In addressing this issue it needs to be understood that public expenditure programmes and taxes provide a framework which helps to shape market prices, rewards some kinds of activities and penalises others. Within this framework there are other areas which are not supported by public expenditure or are not taxed. This framework should be developed to encourage economic efficiency and enterprise, social equity and environmental sustainability. Systematic reviews should be carried out and published on the sustainability effects of all public subsidies and other relevant public expenditure and tax differentials. Governments should identify and remove those subsidies which cause the greatest detriment to natural, environmental and social resources (United Nations, 2012:14). Systematic reviews should also be carried out and published on the possibilities for re-orientating public spending programmes, with the aim of preventing and reducing social and environmental problems.

Social Justice Ireland welcomed the publication entitled *'Our Sustainable Future – A Framework for a Sustainable Development for Ireland'* (Department of the Environment, Community and Local Government, 2012) which is a late but positive step on the road towards a sustainable development model. One area of concern, however, is the failure by governments to implement earlier sustainability strategies (2000 & 2007) and another is the lack of quantitative and qualitative targets and indicators to accompany the Framework itself. *Social Justice Ireland* welcomes the Framework's emphasis on the need for a whole of government approach to sustainability and the need for all areas of government policy to have regard for sustainable development. Clear leadership from Government and public bodies are needed to ensure that existing and future activities maintain and improve the quality of the environment (EPA, 2012). It will be important that the Cabinet Committee on Climate Change and the Green Economy and the High-Level Inter-Departmental Group on Sustainable Development are given the necessary resources to ensure that the framework is at the heart of policy making in all Government departments and that the recommendations of the report are incorporated right across Government.

Monitoring sustainable development

Many studies have highlighted the lack of socio-economic and environmental data in Ireland required to assess trends in sustainable development. The empirical and methodological gaps which continue to impede the incorporation of sustainable development issues into public policy making and assessment are known (ESRI, 2005). It is only through a sustained commitment to data collection in all of these areas that these deficiencies will be addressed. We welcome recent developments in this area, particularly at the CSO, and look forward to all of these data impediments being removed in the years to come.

Comhar undertook a lot of work developing indicators in order to set targets and quantitative means of measuring the progress of sustainable development. *Social Justice Ireland* does not believe that the full range of the work of Comhar[87] has been satisfactorily adopted by NESC to date and a great deal of work needs to be done in the area of indicators. There should be real consultation between NESC, the CSO, and the Community & Voluntary Pillar (which has done extensive work in this area)[88] to ensure that these issues are addressed, appropriate indicators are immediately put in place and the necessary data collected. These could be used in conjunction with indicators developed by the CSO and data being collected by the EPA and ESRI (through ISus) to measure Ireland's progress towards sustainable development.

---

[87] http://www.comharsustainableindicators.ie/explore-the-indicators/comhar-indicators.aspx

[88] This work involved extensive engagement with a range of government departments on agreeing appropriate indicators to measure progress on the high-level goals contained in the national agreement *'Towards 2016'*. Much of this work remains valid despite the changing context.

In a study of national strategies towards sustainable development in 2005 (Niestroy, 2005: 185) Ireland's sustainability strategy was criticised for:

- having no systematic monitoring system;
- having no general timetable;
- its lack of quantitative national targets.

The lack of quantitative and qualitative targets and indicators to accompany the new sustainability framework means that Ireland remains open to similar criticism for its current strategy. Implementation, targets and monitoring will be crucial to the success of any policy approach that genuinely promotes sustainable development. It is important that these targets and indicators and the mechanisms for monitoring, tracking and reviewing them are developed and clearly explained to ensure that responsibility is taken across all departments and all stakeholders for its implementation.

The publication by the Central Statistics Office of *Sustainable Development Indicators Ireland 2013*, aims to achieve continuous improvement in the quality of life and well-being for present and future generations through linking economic development with protection of the environment and social justice (CSO, 2013). These sustainable development indicators should be discussed and debated in the Dáil alongside shadow national accounts and indicators of well-being as a step towards integrating sustainable development across the entire policy agenda in Ireland.

Environmental Issues

Maintaining a healthy environment remains one of the greatest global challenges. Without concerted and rapid collective action to curb and decouple resource depletion and the generation of pollution from economic growth, human activities may destroy the very environment that supports economies and sustains life (UNEP 2011: II).

Our environment is a priceless asset. It is also finite – a fact that is often ignored in current debates. Protection and conservation of our environment is of major importance as it is not just for our use alone; it is also the natural capital of future generations.

For environmental facts and details for Ireland see Annex 11.

The economic growth of recent decades has been accomplished mainly by drawing down natural resources without allowing stocks to regenerate and causing widespread degradation and loss to our eco-system. Careful stewardship of Ireland's natural resources is required to ensure the long term health and sustainability of our environment. Unsustainable use of natural resources is one of the greatest long-term threats to humankind (European Commission, 2012:3). It is crucial therefore, that Ireland meets the challenges of responding to climate change and protecting our natural resources and biodiversity with policies that are based on scientific evidence and protecting the common good.

Climate change

Climate change is one of the most significant and challenging issues currently facing humanity. Increased levels of greenhouse gases, such as CO2, increase the amount of energy trapped in the atmosphere which leads to global effects such as increased temperatures, melting of snow and ice and raised global average sea-level. If these issues are not addressed with urgency the projected effects of climate change present a serious risk of dangerous and irreversible climate impacts at national and global levels. Food production and ecosystems are particularly vulnerable.

The 2013 report by the Intergovernmental Panel on Climate Change (IPCC) outlines the global challenge of climate change. The report sets out the effect climate change and greenhouse gas emissions have had on the planet and the impact of human influence on the climate system. Some of the main findings are:

- More than 60% of the net energy increase in the climate system is stored in the upper ocean;

- The global ocean will continue to warm during the 21st century and global mean sea level will continue to rise;

- Sea level rise is projected in more than 95% of the ocean area with 70% of coastlines worldwide expected to experience sea level change;

- It is virtually certain that global mean sea level rise will continue beyond 2100, with sea level rise due to thermal expansion to continue for many centuries;

- Carbon dioxide concentrations have increased by 40% since pre-industrial times. The ocean has absorbed 30% of the emitted carbon dioxide, causing ocean acidification;

- Global surface temperature change for the end of the 21st century is likely in the range 1.5C to 4.5C;

- It is very likely that heat waves will occur with a higher frequency and duration;

- The contrast in precipitation between wet and dry regions and between wet and dry seasons will increase, although there may be regional exceptions;

- Cumulative emissions of CO_2 largely determine global mean surface warming by the late 21st century and beyond. Most aspects of climate change will persist for many centuries even if CO_2 emissions are stopped.

The IPCC report serves to highlight the challenges ahead for all countries in dealing with climate change. It is very disappointing therefore that the European Commission Policy Framework for Climate and Energy 2020-2030 published in January 2014 does not contain any binding national targets for member states for reducing energy use or for increasing renewable energies. This is despite the fact that the plan commits the European Commission to reducing gas emissions by 40 per cent. By not setting binding or measurable targets the European Commission is taking the opposite approach to that recommended by the SDG Open Working Group. The European Commission claims that the 2030 climate plan sets in stone a commitment to cap the temperature increase at 2°C. The IPCC data shows that a 40 per cent emissions target for 2030 means in effect there is a 50/50 chance of exceeding the 2°C threshold. This is consistent with the 450 Scenario of the IEA's *World Energy Outlook 2011* which shows that an energy pathway consistent with a 50 per cent chance of limiting global temperature increase to 2°C requires CO_2 emissions to peak at just 1.0 Gt above 2011 levels in 2017. This will be very difficult to achieve.

Climate change and implementation of climate policy have been challenges for Ireland. Despite two National Climate Change Strategies (one in 2000 and one in 2007), there have been significant delays in implementing these policies. In some cases policies have still not been implemented. The mobilisation of vested interests has been a decisive factor in many of these delays and cases of non-implementation (Coughlin (2007). This is very disappointing because if these policies had been implemented on time, and as specified, Ireland's climate policy commitments could have been met from domestic measures. Now Ireland is faced with the prospect of overshooting its EU 2020 emissions targets as early as 2016 (EPA 2012).

Social Justice Ireland welcomes the publication of the *General Scheme of a Climate Action and Low Carbon Development Bill 2013* by the Department of Environment, Community and Local Government. It is crucial that all expert and evidence-based advice should be made available in an accessible manner to increase Irish people's understanding, engagement and participation on climate change policy and also to enhance political accountability and transparency on climate policy. However, there are a number of areas of concern:

1. *Social Justice Ireland* is concerned that the only mention of targets in the Bill are those that Ireland is committed to under European Union law to reach by 2020 and those under the Kyoto Protocol. The only target beyond 2020 is to reach a low carbon, climate resilient and environmentally sustainable economy by 2050. The absence of sectoral targets and quantitative measures and outputs has already impeded climate change policy progress internationally (UNEP 2011: vii). Without sectoral targets and a system whereby they are regularly reviewed, the monitoring of progress on climate change policy will be very difficult. It will also make enforcing responsibility and accountability for implementation of

climate policy across all Government departments and stakeholders in all sectors extremely challenging.

2. A national low carbon roadmap is to be submitted within 12 months of the passing of the Bill. A public consultation process on the roadmap began in November 2013. This means that Government will not adopt a national policy position on climate legislation and the transition to a low carbon future until mid-2014 at the earliest. This will give the Government less than six years to reach the targets set in the EU 2020 strategy (European Commission, 2010). Given that we are on course to overshoot emissions targets by 2016, there is a real danger that short-term planning to limit our liabilities in respect of missed targets will overshadow the requirement for long-term planning and policy goals for a sustainable and low carbon future. The long-term goal of a low carbon economy beyond 2020 must be at the core of climate policy.

3. *Social Justice Ireland* is concerned that the Bill refers to the objective of achieving the national low carbon roadmap at the least cost to the national economy. By failing to take appropriate actions and measures on climate change and carbon emissions now Ireland's economy and society will bear a far greater cost in the future. It is important that the National Expert Advisory Body on Climate Change is not constrained by economic and cost issues and that its recommendations should be based solely on scientific evidence and best practice.

A recent study examining climate change and governance in Ireland points out that local authorities have made little progress on climate change due to barriers related to resources, prioritisation and integration and a lack of public consensus for proactive measures (EPA, 2013). The report concludes that the national government has side-lined the climate change issue by not establishing a separate ministry for climate change; this signals a lack of priority on this issue at national level, resulting in a limited response at regional and local level. An integrated, cross-departmental approach is recommended and the potential of local authorities for innovative solutions is highlighted. Government must support local authorities to coordinate climate change policy and adopt legislation that clearly signals climate change as a priority. Without a shift in attitudes and strong leadership nationally Ireland will remain unprepared for upcoming challenges related to climate change.

Emissions challenge[44]

Ireland has two sets of emissions targets to meet: the Kyoto Protocol and the EU 2020 Targets. Ireland is on track to meet its Kyoto commitments when the effects of the EU Emissions Trading Scheme and forest sinks are taken into account. However, it

---

[89] More detail on emissions and targets is available in Annex 11

is already facing significant challenges in meeting its future EU emissions targets for greenhouse gases under the EU Climate and Energy package for 2020 and further anticipated longer term targets up to 2050. This is despite substantial declines in greenhouse gas emissions in 2009, 2010 and 2011 which the EPA attributes primarily to the economic recession.

Under the *Climate and Energy Package,* as part of the EU 2020 targets Ireland is required to deliver a 20 per cent reduction in non-Emissions Trading Scheme (ETS) greenhouse gas emissions by 2020 (relative to 2005 levels). Ireland also has binding annual emissions limits over the period 2013 to 2020 to ensure movement towards the EU 2020 target. The latest EPA projections indicate that Ireland will exceed its annual binding limit in 2016 and that it will exceed its obligations over the 2013 to 2020 period, cumulatively by 7-24 Mtonnes of CO_2eq.

Ireland's emissions profile is dominated by emissions from the energy supply, transport and agriculture sectors (EPA, 2012). The domestic sector comprises transport, agriculture and residential waste activities and is also responsible for 72 per cent of Ireland's total emissions. The immediate challenge for Irish climate policy is to meet the EU 2020 targets for the domestic sector, which is a reduction of at least 20 per cent on the 2005 emission levels by 2020. If achieved, the projected strong growth in the agriculture sector set out in the Department of Agriculture, Fisheries and Food vision *Food Harvest 2020* will likely result in agricultural emissions increasing by 7 per cent by 2020. There is a significant challenge for Government in achieving the binding EU 2020 targets whilst also pursuing its *Food Harvest* agenda.

Support for sustainable agricultural practice is important to ensure the long-term viability of the sector and consideration must also be given to how the projected increase in agriculture emissions can be offset. It is important that the agriculture sector be at the fore of developing and implementing sustainable farming practices and be innovative in terms of reducing emissions. Consideration should also be given to the European Commission proposals to establish a framework for land use, land use change and forestry (LULUCF) to be included in the emission reduction targets. This is important for Ireland because it is estimated that forest sinks could provide significant relief in reaching emissions targets (see Annex 11).

Transport and agriculture represent the most intractable sectors in terms of carbon offsets and emissions mitigations, with the transport sector recording a 120 per cent increase in emissions between 1990 and 2011.[90] A national sustainable transport network would represent a major step towards a low carbon, resource efficient

---

[90] Transport emissions have decreased for four consecutive years and are now 22% below peak levels in 2007.

economy. Capital investment will be required in sustainable transport infrastructure projects to ensure the reduction of transport emissions. Agriculture, which accounted for 32 per cent of total emissions in 2011, faces major difficulties in limiting emissions and meeting future targets. In the agriculture sector progress towards changing farm practices has been limited and incentives to reduce on-farm greenhouse emissions have not been delivered on a wide scale (Curtin & Hanrahan 2012: 9). The agriculture and food sector must build on its scientific and technical knowledge base to meet the emissions challenge.

The European Network for Rural Development has highlighted a number of opportunities for Ireland to use the development of renewable energy to mitigate the effects of climate change by delivering additional reductions to Ireland's CHG emissions. The opportunity and capability exist to significantly mitigate climate change through growth in afforestation and renewable energy sources. Forestry can play a significant role in combating climate change and the development of the forestry sector and renewable energy lack supported in the Irish CAP Rural Development Programme 2014-2020 (discussed further in chapter 12). It is important, therefore, that Government departments work together to tackle climate change and recognise that action on climate change is not just a challenge but a great opportunity to create jobs and develop a genuine, indigenous, low carbon economy.

Biodiversity

Nature and biodiversity are the basis for almost all ecosystem services and biodiversity loss is the greatest challenge facing humanity (EPA 2011: vii). Biodiversity loss and ecosystem degradation directly affect climate change and undermine the way we use natural resources (EEAC 2011: 114). Pollution, over-exploitation of natural resources and the spread of non-native species are causing a decline in biodiversity in Ireland. The Environmental Protection Agency (EPA) has identified the four main drivers (EPA 2011: 11) of biodiversity loss in Ireland all caused by human activity:

- habitat destruction and fragmentation;
- pollution;
- over-exploitation of natural resources; and
- the spread of non-native species.

Our eco-system is worth €2.6 billion to Ireland annually (EPA 2011) yet our biodiversity capital is decreasing rapidly. Ireland missed the 2010 target to halt biodiversity loss and lacks fundamental information on such issues as the distribution of species and habitats that inform planning and policy in other countries. *Social Justice Ireland* is concerned that responsibility for biodiversity now lies with the Department of Arts, Heritage and the Gaeltacht, whereas responsibility for all environmental issues lies with the Department of Environment, Community and Local Government. Both departments must work together to ensure that the policies they implement are designed to complement each other and will not have any negative consequences on other areas of environmental concern.

Biodiversity underpins our eco-system, which supports our natural capital and in particular the agriculture industry. It is critically important that our biodiversity is preserved and maintained and that the effects of policies and developments on biodiversity are monitored in order to inform environmental policy in the short and long-term. Ireland has less land designated as a Special Protected Area under the EU Habitats Directive than the EU average The majority of Ireland's habitats listed under the Habitats Directive are reported to be in poor or bad conservation status (EPA 2012:76).

The economic value of biodiversity and how it contributes to our well-being needs to be better promoted and understood. The data collected by the National Biodiversity Data Centre on the environment and the eco-system goods and services provided by biodiversity should be included in any proposed shadow national accounting system. This is our greatest national asset yet we do not factor it into our present national accounting system. Without biodiversity and our eco-system the development of a sustainable, low-carbon future for Ireland will not be possible and the value of our natural capital will be lost. Climate change will not go away and initial costs will have to be incurred in order to preserve and conserve our natural resources. Environmental and socio-economic decision making should be integrated with biodiversity and resource management to maximise the benefit to society of our natural resources.

The long-term benefits of these investments, both for the present and future generations, will far outweigh the initial cost. It is important that the economic value of biodiversity be factored into decision making and reflected in national accounting and reporting systems. The EPA notes that the continuing loss of biodiversity is one of the greatest challenges facing us (EPA 2012:82). *Social Justice Ireland* believes that Government should implement the EPA's recommendations regarding evidence-based decision making on biodiversity issues and the integration of the economic value of ecosystems into the national accounting and reporting systems.

Environmental taxation

The extent of Ireland's challenge in terms of climate change and maintaining and preserving our national resources is clear from the information outlined above. One way of tackling this challenge whilst also broadening the tax base is through environmental taxation. Eco-taxes, which put a price on the full costs of resource extraction and pollution, will help move towards a resource efficient, low carbon green economy. Carbon taxation was introduced in Ireland in Budget 2010 and was increased from €15 to €20 per tonne in Budget 2012. *Social Justice Ireland* welcomed the introduction of a carbon tax but is disappointed that Government has not used some of the money raised by this tax to target low income families and rural dwellers who were most affected by it. When considering environmental taxation measures to support sustainable development and the environment and to broaden the tax base, the Government should ensure that such taxes are structured in ways that are equitable and effective and do not place a disproportionate burden on rural communities or lower socio-economic groups.

Key Policy Priorities on Sustainability

- A common understanding of sustainable development must be communicated across all Government departments, policy makers, stakeholders and civil society. This should underpin all public policy decisions.

- The economic value of biodiversity must be accounted for in all environmental policy decisions.

- Shadow national accounts should be developed to move towards a more sustainable, resource efficient model of growth.

- A progressive and equitable environmental taxation system should be developed in a structured way that does not impose a disproportionate burden on certain groups.

- A detailed roadmap towards the development of a low carbon sustainable economy, with targets to be met towards 2020 and beyond, should be adopted and published.

- Investment should be made in sustainable infrastructure projects which will have substantial long-term dividends.

12.

RURAL DEVELOPMENT

CORE POLICY OBJECTIVE: RURAL DEVELOPMENT

To secure the existence of substantial numbers of viable communities in all parts of rural Ireland where every person would have access to meaningful work, adequate income and to social services, and where infrastructures needed for sustainable development would be in place.

Rural Ireland continues to change dramatically. The composition and population patterns of rural Ireland are changing and there is a need to revise and update how we measure rurality in Ireland. No county has shown an increase in the share of rural population since 2006, however the numbers living in small towns (<3,000 population) has doubled since 2002. The Central Statistics definition of rural (places with a population of less than 1,500) shows that the population living in rural areas has declined to 28 per cent. However, examining the next category above rural (towns of 1,500 to 2,999 people) the population living in this category increased by 33 per cent (Walsh & Harvey, 2013). This changing composition shows the need to redefine rural areas and how we measure them. In European discourse the concept of 'rural' is often linked to regional development and includes 'non-urban' and 'non-metropolitan areas'[91]. The need for an integrated transition from an agricultural to a rural and regional development agenda to improve the quality of life for all rural dwellers has never been more pressing. Balanced regional development is one of the key policy areas that must be addressed urgently as part of the Core Policy Framework we set out in Chapter 2 under the heading of Creating a Sustainable Future.

---

[91] See O'Hara, P in Healy & Reynolds (Eds) (2013) for a more detailed discussion on rurality and the regions.

Rural and Regional Development

The Commission for the Economic Development of Rural Areas (CEDRA) adopts a holistic definition of rural areas as those areas being outside the main metropolitan areas and recognises the relational nature of economic and social development and the interconnections between urban and rural areas[92]. Among the objectives of the commission is to ensure that rural areas can benefit from and contribute to economic recovery and to provide research to inform the medium term economic development of rural areas to 2025. The first White Paper on Rural Development (1999) defined rural development policy in Ireland as *"all Government policies and interventions which are directed towards improving the physical, economic and social conditions of people living in the open countryside, in coastal areas, in towns and villages and in smaller urban centres outside of the five major urban areas"*. Given the changing population patterns and composition of rural Ireland it is now an appropriate time to revisit this definition of rural development policy in Ireland. The present model of rural development policy in Ireland has a dominant agricultural focus. There is a need to broaden this model of rural development to encompass coastal areas, towns and small urban centres and to support the diversification of the rural economy.

Rural development is often confused with agricultural development. This approach fails to grasp the fact that many people living in rural Ireland are not engaged in agriculture. This, in turn, leads to misunderstanding when the income from agriculture increases because many people fail to realise that not everyone in rural Ireland benefits from such an increase. Long-term strategies to address the failures of current and previous policies on critical issues, such as infrastructure development, the national spatial imbalance, local access to public services, public transport and local involvement in core decision-making, are urgently required. The 1999 White Paper on rural development provided a vision to guide rural development policy (something *Social Justice Ireland* had advocated for over a decade previously). Rural economies are increasingly designed around towns of various sizes which provide a local labour market area. It is important that rural development is seen in the context of the relationship between a particular rural area and the nearest town or centre of economic activity. The interactions between more rural areas and the small towns and villages with which they connect should provide the framework and foundation for a rural development policy. In order to have successful rural communities, rural development policy must move beyond one dominated by agricultural development and towards policies designed to support the provision of public services, investment in micro businesses and small or medium enterprises, innovation and the sustainable use of natural resources and natural capital.

---

[92] http://www.ruralireland.ie/index.php/objectives-of-the-commission

Rural areas and small villages are connected and networked to the local regions and these local regional economies are dependent on the interaction with the rural areas they connect with for sustainability (Walsh & Harvey, 2013). Given this interconnection, it is important that rural and regional development are integrated in order to support sustainable local economies and to ensure that local services are utilised most effectively to address the specific needs of a particular region and the rural communities within it.

The new Rural Development Programme 2014-2020 will be funded by the European Agricultural Fund for Rural Development and the national Exchequer. A plan for the Rural Development Programme (RDP) 2014-2020 will be submitted to the European Commission by Government by late Spring 2014. The Department of Agriculture, Food and the Marine propose a national co-financing rate of 46 per cent be applied to measures under the RDP via this Department in the period 2014-2020. The allocation for the delivery of LEADER is 7 per cent of Pillar 2 under the new programme. Irish Rural Link has called for this to be increased to 10 per cent in order to ensure real investment in rural areas to support job creation, biodiversity and environmental protection. The new RDP is based on six priority areas for rural development whilst contributing to the Europe 2020 Strategy objectives of smart growth, inclusive growth and sustainable growth.

The six priority areas are:

- Fostering knowledge transfer and innovation,
- Enhancing competitiveness,
- Promoting food chain organisation and risk management in agriculture,
- Restoring, preserving and enhancing ecosystems,
- Promoting resource efficiency and supporting the shift towards a low carbon and climate resilient economy,
- Promoting social inclusion, poverty reduction and economic development in rural areas.

The European Commission has proposed community led local development (CLLD) as one of the cohesion policy tools to help rural communities build capacity, stimulate innovation, increase participation and assist communities to ensure that they can be full actors in the implementation of EU objectives in all areas. The reform of local government and work on citizens engagement could consider the CLLD process as a means of ensuring local communities have a voice in designing, shaping and delivery policy in their local area. The Department of Agriculture, Food and the Marine has published a draft RDP Consultation paper outlining some proposals under each of the six priority areas. The changes to the composition of rural areas and rural economies and the subsequent need to move rural development away from a focus dominated by agriculture has been well documented[93]. Therefore, it is disappointing that the draft proposals for the RDP 2014-2020 are still predominantly focussed on agriculture and supporting the agri-sector and insufficient attention is given to diversifying and developing rural areas and the rural economy. The draft plan is predominantly focussed on complimenting and supporting the Food Harvest 2020 strategy. It points to LEADER measures to address areas of need in rural Ireland including support for enterprise development and job creation, supporting local development of rural areas and initiatives to improve broadband and communications infrastructure. Given the scope of the challenges facing rural Ireland the lack of a broader rural development and diversification focus in the draft plan is disappointing.

Diversification of rural economies

A study on rural areas across Europe (ECORYS, 2012:26) identified the key drivers of and key barriers to growth in rural economies. The key drivers of employment and growth were identified as (i) natural resources and environmental quality, (ii) the sectoral nature of the economy, (iii) quality of life and cultural capital and (iv) infrastructure and accessibility. The key barriers to growth in rural areas were identified as (i) demographic evolutions and migration (loss of young people and ageing), (ii) infrastructure and accessibility and (iii) the sectoral structure of the economy. Across Europe the secondary and tertiary sectors[94] are now the main drivers of economic growth and job creation in rural regions. These sectors support activities such as tourism, niche manufacturing and business services (ECORYS: 2010). For rural areas to become sustainable in the long-term these sectors must form an integral part of any future rural development strategy both in Ireland and in Europe. The *AGRI Vision 2015* report (Department of Agriculture, Food and the Marine, 2004), highlighted the fact that many rural dwellers are not linked to agriculture and that in order to improve the standard of living and quality of life in rural communities opportunities must be created so that the rural economy can develop agriculture in conjunction with much needed alternative enterprises. The report also stated that the primary purpose of rural policy development is to underpin the economic and social wellbeing of rural communities. It is clear that in order to diversify the rural economy, Ireland needs to move from agricultural development to rural development, from maritime development to supporting coastal communities and to support small, local, sustainable and indigenous

---

[93] See O'Hara, P in Healy & Reynolds (Eds) 2013, Shucksmith, M (2012), ECORYS (2010) and Walsh, K. & Harvey, B. (2013)

[94] The EU traditionally splits economic activities into three sectors. Primary sector includes agriculture, forestry and fisheries; secondary sector includes industry and construction, tertiary sector includes all services.

enterprises, farming and fishing. The areas that are highlighted as possible drivers of rural job creation are social enterprise and social services (e.g. child care and elder care), tourism, 'green' products and services and cultural and creative industries. In order to promote development of these drivers of employment and to support local entrepreneurs and local enterprises in rural and coastal areas the economic policies for these areas must take into account specific local needs such as accessible transport and access to childcare.

The economies of rural areas have become increasingly dependent on welfare transfers, with the 'at risk of poverty' rate in rural areas being 4.6 percentage points higher than that of urban areas. In 2011 the 'at risk of poverty' rate in rural areas was 18.8 per cent and 14.2 per cent in urban areas. The economic recession and restructuring of agriculture and subsequent decline in off-farm employment has led to a narrowing of the economic base in rural areas. Small and medium sized towns have seen unemployment increase by 193 per cent during the recession and the share of working age households with no one in work is 20 per cent higher than the national average at 31 per cent[95]. Low-paid, part-time and seasonal work and long-term underemployment are also significant factors in rural poverty and exclusion (Walsh & Harvey (2013). The problem of underemployment is further highlighted by the recent assessment of the Rural Social Scheme (RSS) by the Department of Public Expenditure and Reform. It found that 60 per cent of participants have been on the scheme for more than six years, and 82 per cent for more than three years. The majority of participants are male and over 70 per cent of these are aged fifty and over. The RSS was designed as an income support scheme for people in rural occupations, not as an employment activation scheme. The assessment acknowledges that the RSS was established to support people who were underemployed in their primary activity. However in light of Government's new labour market activation policies whereby income supports must be integrated with activation measures the RSS is under increasing scrutiny. The assessment concludes that the RSS is not having a meaningful impact in terms of moving people into sustainable employment and that the social cohesion objective of the RSS needs to be set against broader high level policy objectives. What this assessment does not consider is the lack of sustainable and appropriate employment in rural areas, nor does it appropriately measure the social value of such a scheme in terms of combating social exclusion and isolation. Government does not have an explicit strategy to generate sustainable employment creation in rural areas and appears to have dropped a commitment on targeting investment outside of Ireland's two major urban areas. The Action Plan for Jobs 2012 contained a target of 50 per cent of Foreign Direct Investment to be outside of the Dublin and Cork regions. This target is not contained in the Action Plan for Jobs 2013. To ensure policy coherence, no changes should be made to the RSS without a corresponding commitment from Government to develop and deliver a strategy to promote sustainable employment creation in rural areas.

---

[95] http://www.teagasc.ie/news/2014/201402-24.asp

Rural development and the challenges facing rural areas in terms of generating sustainable employment are either absent or barely referenced in key national policies such as the Action Plan for Jobs and the National Skills Strategy. As a result there is a mismatch between a Government policy aimed at attracting Foreign Direct Investment and export-led industry and rural areas which are dominated by micro-businesses and small and medium sized enterprises. Employment and enterprise policy should have a rural specific element designed to support local enterprises, rural specific jobs and be cognisant of the need to create full-time, high quality jobs with career progression opportunities. Approximately 90 per cent of enterprises in the regions employ ten people or less and underemployment and flat career structures are particular features of rural areas that require attention (Walsh & Harvey, 2013).

With the on-going challenges facing traditional rural sectors, including agriculture, the future success of the rural economy is inextricably linked with the capacity of rural entrepreneurs to innovate and to develop new business opportunities that create jobs and income in rural areas. Some of the key needs of rural entrepreneurs have been highlighted as:

- Better, more locally-led access to finance;
- Harnessing local knowledge at all stages of policy formulation, delivery and evaluation;
- Developing better communication between national, regional and local actors to ensure the needs of entrepreneurs can be met;
- Acknowledgement that rising costs and Government revenue raising measures can hit rural businesses disproportionately compared to their urban counterparts e.g. fuel is often a bigger cost for rural businesses and entrepreneurs who need to transport produce or goods greater distances. (EU Rural Winter Review 2011)

Lack of quality broadband in rural areas is a considerable barrier to the diversification and growth of the rural economy in Ireland. Case studies show that several large firms have moved out of the South West of Ireland as a result of poor broadband speed and quality (ECORYS, 2010:237:241). The provision of quality broadband to rural areas must be a priority in the future if rural development is to be facilitated in a meaningful manner. The commitment to between 40Mbps and 30Mbps broadband speed in rural areas contained in the National Broadband Plan for Ireland is insufficient to encourage diversification and economic growth in rural areas. A rural broadband strategy should be developed and implemented by Government as a matter of priority to support the development and growth of rural enterprise and the creation of employment in rural areas. State intervention must be prioritised in order to prevent a two-tier digital divide developing between urban and rural areas.

Small rural firms and rural entrepreneurs need to be supported in developing their businesses and in overcoming the spatial disadvantage to benefit from the growth in the 'knowledge economy'. Sustainable, integrated public transport serving rural Ireland and reliable high speed broadband must be given priority in order to support rural businesses and the development of the rural economy through diversification and innovation. The current strategy of relying on 'global demand' and foreign direct investment (FDI) has led to a widening of the development gap between urban and rural areas. One of the major problems faced by the government in trying to develop and promote sustainable rural communities is the restricted opportunities in secondary labour markets in rural areas. Data from the IDA and Forfás highlight the need for a rural and regional employment strategy. In 2012 only 23 per cent of IDA investments were located outside of Dublin and Cork, and just 34 per cent of the jobs approved were located outside of Dublin and Cork (IDA, 2013). Significant regional disparities also show up in the Forfás annual employment survey. In the period 2003-2012 agency supported employment in Dublin increased by 14.8 per cent. In the same period agency supported employment in the Border, Midlands and West (BMW) region fell by 7 per cent and in the Rest of South and East[96] by 6.2% (Forfás, 2012). This shows a trend of falling agency assisted employment in rural areas.

Emigration

A recent Irish study on emigration showed that at least one household in four in rural areas has been directly affected by the emigration of at least one member since 2006 (Mac Éinrí et al, 2013). The same study found that 28 per cent of the households in this cluster expected that another member would emigrate within the next three years. This has profound implications for the future of rural areas. Rural areas in Ireland have already suffered a loss of young people due to out migration to urban areas and an ageing demographic prior to the recession, such an enduring loss of educated young people will have a negative impact on social structures, service provision, cultural capital and levels of poverty and social exclusion.

The impact of sustained high levels of unemployment and subsequent high levels of emigration among young people in rural communities cannot be overestimated. It has led to a loss of young people in rural communities. This in turn means that the development of the rural economy has been hindered and it will continue to struggle in any future upturn due to the lack of skilled workers and the corresponding emergence of an ageing population. By failing to support young people to stay in their communities Government is potentially failing to address a key aspect of sustainability while supporting an emergence of an ageing demographic profile for rural areas which undermines both employment and growth targets (ECORYS, 2010:249).

---

[96] Mid-East, Mid-West, South East, South West

Public services and rural transport

The provision of public services in rural areas in the context of a falling and ageing population is a cause for concern. With increased levels of emigration the population in rural areas has become dominated by those who are more reliant on public services (the elderly, children and people with disabilities). There is a need to develop a new rural strategy to take account of the changes in rural areas since the 1999 White Paper. Decisions need to be made regarding the provision and level of public services in rural areas, investment in childcare and transport and the integration of rural and regional development into a new Spatial Strategy[97]. Some European countries adopt the equivalence principle for the provision of services in rural areas that is public services in rural areas should be equivalent quality to those in urban areas. Walsh and Harvey (2013) propose that this would be a useful guidance for investment in an Irish context. The OECD has also noted the need for investment in rural areas in key sectors of transport, information technologies, quality public services, rural firms, conservation and development of local amenities and rural policy proofing (OECD, 2006). Investment in childcare, transport, progression and outreach are all required as part of a cohesive strategy in order to promote employment and innovation in rural areas.

The design and implementation of a new rural development strategy would provide Government and all stakeholders with the opportunity to consider how public services should be provided and delivered in the regions and rural areas. It would also provide an opportunity for the consideration of social, ecological and cultural benefits to and reasons for investing in rural areas. The benefits of such investment must be considered in terms which can encompass more than just economic measurements. The withdrawal of services or lack of provision of services in rural areas undermines rural development and compromises the needs of those most reliant on these services (Shucksmith, 2012). It is critical that the costs of not investing in rural areas, including social exclusion, continued under-employment, poverty and isolation, are taken into account in any new strategy.

The lack of an accessible, reliable and integrated rural transport system is one of the key challenges facing people living in rural areas. Rural dwellers at present shoulder a disproportionate share of the burden of insufficient public transport, according to a recent report (EPA 2011: 10), 45 per cent of the rural district electoral divisions in Ireland have a minimal level of scheduled public transport services with varying frequency and timing. Among the main identified issues contributing to rural deprivation and depopulation are:

*   access to secure and meaningful employment;

---

[97] Government stated in February 2013 that a new Spatial Strategy would be developed. It has yet to be published.

- availability of public transport in order to access employment and public services;
- access to childcare; and
- access to transport.

(McDonagh, Varley & Shortall 2009: 16)

Government has acknowledged the importance of an integrated and accessible rural transport network and has pledged to maintain and extend the Rural Transport Programme with other local transport services as much as possible (Government of Ireland 2011: 63).

Car dependency and the reliance of rural dwellers on private car access in order to avail of public services, employment opportunities, healthcare and recreational activities is a key challenge for policy makers. Transport policy must be included in planning for services, equity and social inclusion. The social inclusion element of an integrated rural public transport system can no longer be ignored. The links between better participation, better health, access to public services, access to employment opportunities and a public integrated rural transport service have been documented (Fitzpatrick, 2006). Thus far there has been a failure to incorporate this knowledge fully into rural development policy. The Rural Transport Programme (RTP) (formerly the Rural Transport Initiative) has certainly improved access in some areas. However, the lack of a mainstream public transport system means that many rural areas are still not served. People with disabilities, women, older people, low income households and young people are target groups still at a significant disadvantage in rural areas in terms of access to public transport. Policy makers must ensure that local government and the local community are actively involved in developing, implementing and evaluating rural transport policies as national planning has not worked to date. In 2000 there was a call for a national rural transport policy and the prioritisation of government funding in this area (Farrell, Grant Sparks, 2000). Fourteen years later this policy has yet to be delivered. By 2021 it is estimated that the number of people with unmet transport needs could number 450,000 and of this group an estimated 240,000 will be from the target groups of vulnerable rural dwellers outlined above.

The National Transport Authority (NTA) has been given responsibility for the rural Transport Programme and progressing integrated local and rural transport. It published plans for restructuring the rural transport programme in 2013. The previous RTP Groups will be replaced by eighteen Transport Coordination Units with responsibility for delivering rural transport services. The restructuring plan also outlines the relationship between local authority, Socio-Economic Committees and Transport Coordination Units in terms of developing local transport policies and objectives. The National Integrated Rural Transport Committee was established to oversee six pilot programmes to integrate all state transport services in rural areas and provide access for the whole community to health services, education, employment and retail, recreational and community facilities and services. While the integration of rural transport with national transport policy is welcome, it is important that the models of best practice that emerge from the pilot programmes are put into a national rural transport strategy without delay. A mainstreamed rural public transport service is required to service those in need of rural public transport and those who are potential users. Investment in a national sustainable rural transport network is required to support rural development. It is required to ensure access to employment, access to services and to ensure rural economies are supported in terms of economic diversification.

Improved rural public transport and improved accessibility to services also provide Ireland with an opportunity to deliver a key change which would in turn help deliver a significant reduction of climate harming gas (CHG) emissions (Browne 2011: 12). This is all the more pressing in terms of Ireland's EU 2020 emissions target and CHG emissions from private vehicles. By investing in a sustainable national public transport system covering all rural areas, government could significantly reduce CHG emissions in the long run. The long term costs of not investing in rural areas and not providing adequate and quality public services to rural and regional communities should be factored into all Government expenditure decisions. A new rural strategy is required which should incorporate the social infrastructure, governance and sustainability elements of the core policy framework outlined in Chapter 2.

Farm incomes

Preliminary results from the Teagasc Farm Income Survey 2013[98] suggests that agricultural sector income was relatively unchanged in 2013 compared with 2012. There are significant variations between sectors, with milk production doing well in 2013. However, the drystock sector and cereal production had mixed years with increased production costs and a drop in prices respectively. Rural Ireland has high dependency levels, increasing outmigration and many small farmers living on very low incomes. The data from the most recent SILC study (CSO 2011: 10) shows there is a very uneven national distribution of poverty. The risk of poverty in rural Ireland is 4.6 percentage points higher than in urban Ireland – 18.8 per cent and 14.2 per cent respectively.

---

[98] http://www.teagasc.ie/news/2013/201312-10.asp

Key farm statistics:

- Average family farm income was €25,483 in 2012, a fall of 15 per cent on the 2011 figure, but still 10 per cent ahead of the 2010 figure. This income decrease was entirely driven by input expenditure (Teagasc, 2013). Incomes in 2012 are the second highest on record since 2005.

- There is a wide variation of farm incomes with 19 per cent of farms producing a family farm income of less than €5,000 in 2012 compared to 13 per cent in 2011.

- At the opposite end of the spectrum in 2012, 16 per cent of farms produced a farm income of over €50,000 and almost 3 per cent produced an income of over €100,000.

- The Border region has the lowest average farm income and is the most reliant on direct payments, contributing 122 per cent of farm income.

- The number of farm households in which the farmer and/or spouse were engaged in off-farm employment was 49.4 per cent in 2012 (Teagasc, 2013).

- Teagasc classified 33 per cent of Irish farm households (26,000) as being 'economically vulnerable', meaning the farm business is not economically viable and neither the farmer nor the spouse worked outside the farm in 2012.

- Direct payments comprised 81 per cent of farm income in 2012 and averaged €20,534 per farm.

- According to Eurostat, real agricultural income per worker in Ireland in 2012 decreased by 10.1 per cent.[99]

These statistics mask the huge variation in farm income in Ireland as a whole. Only a minority of farmers are at present generating an adequate income from farm activity and even on these farms income lags considerably behind the national average. An important insight into the income of Irish farmers is provided by Teagasc in its National Farm Survey. Table 13.1 below outlines the huge variations in farm income in Ireland in 2012, with 57 per cent of farms in Ireland having an income €20,000 or less.

---

[99] http://ec.europa.eu/ireland/press_office/news_of_the_day/eurostat-estimates-agricultural-income_en.htm

Table 13.1: Distribution of Family Farm Income in Ireland 2012

€	< 5,000	5,000 – 10,000	10,000 - 20,000	20,000 - 50,000	> 50,000
%	19	17	21	27	16
Number	15,030	13,448	16,612	21,358	12,656

Source: IFA, 2014

The majority of farm families rely on income support and payments from the state to supplement their income. The value of *subsidies less taxes on production* decreased by 7.1% from €1,667.1m in 2012 to €1,548.8m in 2013 (CSO, 2014). Table 13.2 shows that by the end of 2013 there were 10,500 families receiving the Farm Assist payment. Off-farm employment and income is extremely important to farming households and the fall in availability of off-farm employment due to the recession will increase the dependence of farms on direct subsidies to avoid rural poverty and social exclusion.

Table 13.2: Farm Assist Expenditure (€m) 2006-2013

Year	Expenditure (€m)	Number Benefiting	Average Payment (€/week)
2006	71	7,650	179
2007	79	7,400	205
2008	85	7,710	213
2009	96	8,845	209
2010	111	10,700	199
2011	114	11,300	190
2012	99	11,200	171
2013	92	10,500	168

Source: IFA 2014

Agriculture and direct employment from agricultural activities have been declining in Ireland. The Department of Agriculture, Food and the Marine has outlined its vision of the future of Irish Agriculture in *Food Harvest 2020* (Department of Agriculture, Food and the Marine, 2011). It envisages that by 2020 the Irish agri-food industry will have developed and grown in a sustainable manner by delivering high quality, natural-based produce. This requires the industry to adopt a 'smart economy' approach by investing in skills, innovation and research. This signals a move away from traditional farming methods and to a method of collaboration across the agricultural, food and fisheries industries. In implementing this policy there needs to be significant investment in sustainable agriculture, rural anti-poverty and social inclusion programmes in order to protect vulnerable farm households in the transition to a rural development agenda.

Future of rural Ireland

Rural Ireland faces significant challenges in terms of job creation, service provision for an ageing population, ensuring the natural capital and biodiversity of rural areas is protected and encouraging young people who have left to return and settle in rural areas.

The cumulative impact of measures introduced in Budgets 2012-2014 are likely to have a negative effect on rural families[100] and on the weakest people in rural Ireland as inflation rises, unemployment persists, employment creation is disproportionately urban-based, and services are either reduced or have their charges increased. The removal of resources from rural areas will make it difficult to maintain viable communities. Small rural schools are under threat, with 121 schools affected by the increase in the pupil threshold for teacher allocations introduced in budget 2012. A value for money review of smaller schools was initiated by the Department of Education and Skills in 2012 but the results have not yet been made public. Concern has already been raised about the significant socio-economic impact of the possible closure of these schools on rural communities. Combined with the closure of 139 rural Garda stations in 2012 and 2013,[101] the quality of life for rural dwellers and the sustainability of our rural communities are facing a significant threat. The removal of resources from rural areas will make it difficult to maintain viable communities. Government is failing to deal with the new challenges an ageing population brings to rural areas in relation to health services, social services and accessibility for older and less mobile people. Employment, diversification of rural economies, adapting to demographic changes and supporting young people to stay in their communities, are areas that need immediate attention from Government.

Social Justice Ireland believes that we are now reaching a crucial juncture that requires key decisions on social infrastructure, governance and sustainability to ensure the necessary structures are put in place so that rural communities can survive and flourish.

---

[100] For further detail c.f. Social Justice Ireland (2013) *Budget 2014 Analysis and Critique* p.11
[101] 39 Garda Stations were closed in 2012 and 100 Garda Stations were closed in 2013.

Key Policy Priorities on Rural Development

- Develop a new national rural strategy. This strategy should be part of a new national spatial strategy.
- Develop a rural and regional employment strategy as part of the Action Plan for Jobs.
- Ensure all policies are based on equity and social justice and take account of rural disadvantage.
- Decisions around services and provision of services must be made in the context of a national spatial strategy.
- Support young people to remain in their communities and implement policies to ensure rural areas can adapt to a changing demographic profile in the longer-term.
- Prioritise rolling out high speed broadband to rural areas.

13.

THE GLOBAL SOUTH

CORE POLICY OBJECTIVE: THE DEVELOPING WORLD

To ensure that Ireland plays an active and effective part in promoting genuine development in the Global South and to ensure that all of Ireland's policies are consistent with such development.

At the end of 2013 and in early 2014 two reports were published within weeks of each other: The UN Human Development Report 2013 and an Oxfam Briefing paper. Both reports give us a current snapshot of human development across the Globe at this time. The Human Development Report entitled *The Rise of the South: Human Progress in a Diverse World*, sounded a note of optimism. It points to the transformation of a large number of developing countries into dynamic major economies and it noted that much of the expansion is being driven by new trade and technology partnerships within the South itself. However it moves quickly to point out that economic growth alone does not automatically translate into human development progress. Significant investment in anti-poverty strategies, education, healthcare, nutrition and employment skills is necessary. The Report finds that 'most regions show declining inequality in health and education but a worrying rise in inequality in income.'(Figure 4 p5)

The reality of income inequality is graphically reported in the Oxfam briefing paper. Entitled *Working For the Few,* the paper shows that the richest 85 people in the world share a combined wealth of €1.22 trillion which is the same as the poorest half of the world's population (3.5 billion people). Winnie Byanyima of Oxfam notes that 'Widening inequality is creating a vicious circle where wealth and power are increasingly concentrated in the hands of a few, leaving the rest of us to fight over the crumbs from the table' and that 'Seven out of ten people live in countries where economic inequality has increased in the last 30 years'. She notes that in the 'US the wealthiest one percent captured 95 percent of the post-financial crisis growth since 2009, while the bottom 90 percent became poorer'. Promoting genuine development in the Global South is one of the key policy areas that must be addressed urgently as part of the Core Policy Framework we set out in Chapter 2 under the heading of Creating a Sustainable Future.

The 2013 UN World Hunger and Poverty Facts and Statistics show that there are 1.35 billion people in the Global South living on $1.25 a day or less. In a world with resources many times what is required to eliminate global poverty this situation is intolerable. There has been some progress in East Asia but the situation has changed little since the 1980s in Sub-Saharan Africa.

The 2013 United Nations Human Development Report gives an outline of the size of underdevelopment and inequality. Table 13.1 shows this outline.

Table13.1: United Nations development indicators by region and worldwide

Region	GNI per capita (US$ PPP)*	Life Expectancy at Birth (yrs)	Adult Literacy%**
Least Developed Countries	1,385	59.5	60.7
Arab States	8,317	71.0	74.5
East Asia + Pacific	6,874	72.7	93.8
Europe + Central Asia	12,243	71.5	98.1
L. America + Caribbean	10,300	74.7	91.3
South Asia	3,343	66.2	62.8
Sub-Saharan Africa	2,010	54.9	63.0
Very High HDI^	33,391	80.1	n/a
Worldwide total	**10,184**	**70.1**	**81.3**

Source: UNDP (2013: 144, 172)
Notes: * Gross National Income (GNI) Data adjusted for differences in purchasing power.
** Adult defined as those aged 15yrs and above.
^47 Countries including the OECD with very high human development indicators.

The comparable rates for Ireland are: GNI per capita: $28,671; Life expectancy: 80.7; adult literacy: not available

Tables 13.1 and 13.2 show the sustained differences in the experiences of various regions in the world. These differences go beyond just income and are reflected in each of the indicators reported in both tables. Today, life expectancies are 17 years higher in the richest countries than in Sub-Saharan Africa. Similarly, the UN reports that more than 1 in 3 Southern Asians and Sub-Saharan Africans are unable to read.

These phenomena are equally reflected in sizeable differences in income levels (GNI per person) and in the various mortality figures in table 13.2. There has been some progress on this front as the deaths of children under five declined in most regions since the last report. While there has been some improvement in the maternal mortality rates, thanks to the many successful health aid programmes, these rates are still very high in developing countries. Table 13.2 shows that there are 394 deaths per 100,000 live births in Least Developed Countries as against 15 in OECD countries

Table 13.2: Maternal and Infant Mortality Rates

Region	Maternal Mortality Ratio#	Under-5yrs mortality rate*
Least Developed Countries	394	108
Arab States	176	48
East Asia + Pacific	73	24
Europe + Central Asia	28	21
L. America + Caribbean	74	23
South Asia	203	65
Sub-Saharan Africa	475	120
Very High HDI^	15	6
Worldwide total	**145**	**55**

Source: UNDP 2013:156, 166
Notes: # ratio of the number of maternal deaths to the number of live births expressed
            per 100,000 live births
      ^47 Countries including the OECD with very high human development indicators.
      *number of deaths per 1,000 live births
The comparable rates for Ireland are: Maternal mortality: 2; Under 5 mortality: 4

UN millennium development goals

In response to these problems the UN Millennium Declaration was adopted in 2000 at the largest-ever gathering of heads of state. It committed countries - both rich and poor - to doing all they can to eradicate poverty, promote human dignity and equality and achieve peace, democracy and environmental sustainability. World leaders promised to work together to meet concrete targets for advancing development and reducing poverty by 2015 or earlier. Emanating from the Millennium Declaration, a set of Millennium Development Goals (MDGs) was agreed. These bind countries to do more in the attack on inadequate incomes, widespread hunger, gender inequality, environmental deterioration and lack of education, healthcare and clean water. They also include actions to reduce debt and increase aid, trade and technology transfers to poor countries. These goals and their related targets are listed in Annex 13.

Progress on the MDGs has been mixed. The 2013 UN Human Development Report notes that the first goal of having the proportion of people living on less than $1.25 a day relative to 1990 has been met three years before the target date. This outcome is primarily because of the success of Brazil, China and India in reducing income poverty (p.13). A recent report shows that in Sub-Saharan Africa this figure was only reduced from 57% to 48% between 1990 and 2008. (CSO 2013:1:3). The research shows that the increase in income inequality slows the pace of poverty reduction. A 2012 UN report claimed the goal to halve the proportion of people living without access to safe drinking water has been reached but with little focus on quality monitoring. In mid-February 2014, concerned about the lack of progress, the UN General Assembly hosted a high level meeting to discuss water, sanitation and sustainable energy. In his address to the Assembly the President, John Ashe noted that 783 million people live without clean water, 2.5 billion have no adequate sanitation and 1.4 billion people are without access to electricity.

The 2013 UN Human Development Report notes that 'The actual progress in the achievement of these goals has been very much at the country level, through national initiatives and ownership' (p 109). It is widely acknowledged now that these goals were dictated by donors, written by donors, and made sense in the Aid Effectiveness agenda and process (Paris 2005 - Accra 2008 – Busan 2011), rather than in the development agenda. As a consequence, there was very little ownership of the MDGs by development actors, very few countries attempted to localise them. In the years ahead a different approach is needed, one that engages the people who are meant to benefit from this process. It is also essential that the focus be on development that is sustainable (environmentally, economically and socially) and focused on all countries and not just the poorest.

Poverty and its associated problems of poor health, low educational attainment, poor infrastructure etc. remain the root cause of regional conflicts and civil wars in many of these poor countries. States and societies that are poor are prone to conflict. It is very difficult for governments to govern adequately when their people cannot afford to pay taxes, and industry and trade are almost non-existent. Poverty is also a major cause of environmental degradation. Large-scale food shortages, migration and conflicts lead to environmental pressures.

Wars, inter-community disputes and the easy availability of arms are increasing vulnerability and instability for many communities. Scarcity of resources especially water, energy and land have become more acute and highlight the need for urgent action. The overwhelming majority of violent conflicts are fought within States, their victims mostly civilians. These conflicts are fought with small arms. The production and trade of these arms is the least transparent of all weapons systems. Stockholm International Peace Research Institute (SIPRI) reports that world military expenditure in 2012 is estimated to have been $1,756 billion or $249 for each person. Nearly three-quarters of the companies in the Top 100 for 2012 are headquartered in North America or Western Europe, and they account for 87 per cent of the total arms sales. Ireland as a neutral country should have a role in researching, challenging and advocating for tight controls in the production and distribution of these weapons.

Climate change has been very obvious in recent years. While we in Ireland have not been insulated from the effects of climate change the consequences are much more acute in developing countries. The effects of climate change have increased the vulnerability of many communities, leading to migration, poverty and hunger. Food production is a huge challenge for communities constantly forced to move. Ireland should be a world leader in combating climate change. In particular, it should lead the EU 2020 Strategy on climate change and sustainability. (A fuller treatment of this issue is to be found in chapter 11)

Human Rights and Governance.

Social Justice Ireland welcomed the Review of Ireland's Foreign Policy and External Relations and we look forward to reading the outcome. In our submission to the Review we noted the importance of articulating a vision that is inspirational, attractive and achievable and how this vision can be promoted at home and abroad. We urged that a major focus of this review be on human rights and governance.

Social Justice Ireland is a signatory of the *Galway Platform on Human Rights in Irish Foreign Policy*. This document reflects the views of many groups and academics and is a comprehensive contribution to development policy. We advocated that the current Review of Ireland's Foreign Policy and External Relations reflect the principles and recommendations made in that document.

Governance is the institutional context within which rights are achieved or denied. It is about how power and authority are exercised in the management of the affairs and resources of a country. Good governance is an issue for both developing countries and the developed world. The review should spell out how the Irish Government intends to promote and support good governance at home and abroad.

In order to ensure good governance, strong independent civil society organisations are necessary to articulate the views of the people, challenge injustices, and highlight social exclusion. The Irish Government should ensure a space and support for a vibrant civil society.

Social Justice Ireland echoes the call in the UNDP Report 2013 for new guiding principles for international organisations which incorporate the experience of the South. 'The emergence of the Group of 20 is an important step in this direction but the countries of the South also need more equitable representation in the Bretton Woods institutions, United Nations and other international bodies'. (p13)

Trade and debt

The fact that the current inequality between rich and poor regions of the world persists is largely attributable to unfair trade practices and to the backlog of unpayable debt owed by the countries of the South to other governments, to the World Bank, the International Monetary Fund (IMF) and to commercial banks.

The effect of trade barriers cannot be overstated; by limiting or eliminating access to potential markets the Western world is denying poor countries substantial income. In 2002 at the UN Conference on Financing and Development Michael Moore, the President of the World Trade Organisation (WTO), stated that the complete abolition of trade barriers could 'boost global income by $2.8 trillion and lift 320 million people out of poverty by 2015'.

Supporting developing countries to develop and implement just taxation systems would give a huge boost to local social and economic activity. *Social Justice Ireland* notes the initiatives outlined in the Irish Aid Report to help developing countries to raise their own revenue. We urge Government to learn from and expand these programmes. Prior to the G20 meeting in September 2013 Oxfam issued a briefing. While calling on the G20 to rewrite the international trade rules Oxfam noted that developing countries lose an estimated $100 - €160 billion annually to tax evasion. *Social Justice Ireland* supports the introduction of a financial transaction tax (FTT) which it sees as progressive since it is designed to target only those profiting from speculation. (for more on FTT see chapter 4) . It is clear that all countries would gain from trade reform. As the UN Human Development Report 2013 notes 'The rise of the South presents new opportunities for providing global public goods more effectively and for unlocking today's many stalemated global issues'.(p 14)

The high levels of debt experienced by Third World countries have disastrous consequences for the populations of these indebted countries. Governments that are obliged to dedicate large percentages of their country's GDP to debt repayments cannot afford to pay for health and educational programmes for their people. Ellmers

& Hulova (2013) estimate that the external debt of countries of the global South has doubled over the past decade to reach $4.5 trillion. Debt and Development Coalition estimate that revenue lost from global South countries through illicit capital flight is at €660 - €870 billion per year. It is not possible for these countries to develop the kind of healthy economies that would facilitate debt repayment when millions of their people are being denied basic healthcare and education and are either unemployed or earn wages so low that they can barely survive.

The debt relief initiatives of the past 10 years have been very welcome. These initiatives need to be further developed as there is growing concern that the debts of the poorest countries are beginning to rise again. It is now important that Ireland campaign on the international stage to reduce the debt burden on poor countries. Given Ireland's current economic circumstances, the Irish population now has a greater appreciation of the implications of these debts and the merit in having them reduced.

International Development post 2015

In planning for the post-2015 development agenda, *Social Justice Ireland* believes that the international community needs to play an active role in developing the proposed Sustainable Development Goals and in assisting less developed countries achieve their potential. *Social Justice Ireland* welcomed the Government's publication of *One World, One Future: Ireland's Policy for International Development* (2013) with its overall vision to work for *"A sustainable and just world where people are empowered to overcome poverty and hunger and fully realise their rights and potential".* The three goals and six priority areas highlighted in this document are a basis for an integrated framework for global development post-2015. In the development of this framework we recommend the following

- Priorities should be shaped by the views of people living in poverty. People living in poverty should be supported in an appropriate manner so they can participate fully in processes that are influencing the post 2015 framework. This principle should also apply to goal setting, targets, monitoring and evaluation processes.
- As spelled out in the *Galway Platform on Human Rights in Irish Foreign Policy,* the framework should affirm the full set of social, economic, cultural, civil and political rights of all people everywhere. Goals and targets (global and national) should be linked to human rights obligations.
- Equality should be mainstreamed across all goals and targets. Groups experiencing discrimination should be enabled to actively participate in identifying appropriate indicators to provide disaggregated data to assess progress.
- Establish effective accountability mechanisms for the implementation of the post-2015 framework. The mechanisms should operate at local, national and global levels. Involve people living in poverty and marginalisation in these evaluations.

- Sustainability should be the core concept around which international development post 2015 is organised. This should include environmental, economic and social sustainability.

Ireland's commitment to ODA

Ireland's Policy for International Development, *One World, One Future,* reiterates the Programme for Government's commitment to achieve the target of 0.7 per cent of Gross National Income allocated to international development cooperation. It goes on to state: 'Recognising the present economic difficulties, the Government will endeavour to maintain aid expenditure at current levels, while moving towards the 0.7 per cent target'. (p3) *Social Justice Ireland* had welcomed this commitment. It is with regret that we heard the announcement that the Government will not meet the target by 2015 (March 2014). The ODA budget has been cut every year for the past six years both in terms of allocation and as a percentage of GNP (Table 13.3). This is an allocation to the poorest people on the planet and should have first priority. We urge Government to halt this slide and begin the process of increasing the allocation to reach the 0.7per cent of GNP target.

As table 13.3 shows, over time Ireland had achieved sizeable increases in our ODA allocation. In 2006 a total of €814m (0.53 per cent of GNP) was allocated to ODA – reaching the interim target set by the Government. Budget 2008 further increased the ODA budget to reach €920.7m (0.6 per cent of GNP). However, since then the ODA budget has been a focus of government cuts and has fallen by €319.1m – more than 34 per cent.

Table 13.3: Ireland's net overseas development assistance, 1905-2014

Year	€m's	% of GNP
2005	578.5	0.42
2006	814.0	0.53
2007	870.9	0.53
2008	920.7	0.60
2009	722.2	0.55
2010	675.8	0.53
2011	657.0	0.50
2012	628.9	0.48
2013	622.0	0.48
2014	601.6	0.43

Source: Irish Aid (2012:73) and various Budget Documents.

The priorities for Irish Aid as outlined in their 2012 Report (p44) were:

Hunger: The Report noted that Irish Aid had reached its target of spending 20 per cent of its budget on fighting hunger by 2012.

Environment: €111m was contributed to a number of initiatives on climate related disasters, science based climate information and water management.

Gender Equality: Irish Aid supported capacity building, women's rights initiatives, agricultural inputs, Education and Health programmes.

Governance: Irish Aid supported NGOs and UN organisations in their work for transparency and accountability. It also supported initiatives to help developing countries to raise their own revenue.

Health: Improving health is a major cornerstone of sustainable development. Irish Aid spent over €100m on health and HIV/AIDS in 2012.

Education: 775 million people in the world today cannot read, nearly two thirds of them are women. Irish Aid worked with education ministries and NGOs to address this issue especially in areas of conflict.

Rebuilding our commitment to ODA and honouring the UN target should be important policy paths for Ireland to pursue in the years to come. Not only would its achievement be a major success for government, and an important element in the delivery of promises made, but it would also be of significance internationally. Ireland's success would not only provide additional assistance to needy countries, but would also provide leadership to those other European countries which do not meet the target. In 2011 Ireland was ranked ninth in the list of Development Assistance Committee donors in terms of their contribution as a percentage of GNI (CSO 2013, 1:5). Despite the challenges, we believe that we should care for those less well-off particularly the world's poorest people.

HIV/AIDS

Target seven of the UN Millennium Development Goals committed the international community to 'have halted by 2015 and begun to reverse the spread of HIV/AIDS'. Published in November 2013 the UN AIDS Global Report evaluated the progress being made. It highlighted the continued progress towards the global vision of zero new HIV infections, zero discrimination and zero AIDS related deaths. (p2) The Report shows that in 2011:

- 35.3 million people globally are living with HIV
- 2.3 million people became infected with HIV, a reduction of 33 per cent since 2001.
- 1.6 million people died from AIDS related illness, a reduction of 30 per cent since 2001.
- New HIV infections among children have been reduced by 52 per cent since 2001.

A region of major concern for the Report is Sub-Saharan Africa. It calls for an intensification of preventive efforts in this region. The following statistics give the reality:

- About 70 per cent of all people living with HIV are in Sub-Saharan Africa.
- Nearly 88 per cent of all children living with HIV are in this region.
- 70 per cent of all new infections are in this region
- 75 per cent of AIDS related deaths are in Sub-Saharan Africa.

However, the overall Report shows very welcome progress in the fight against AIDS. There was a 50 percent reduction in the rate of new HIV infections across 26 low and middle income countries. Half of all reductions in new HIV infections in the past two years has been among new born children.

The Report notes that there is a 20 per cent gap in the resources needed to fully fund the AIDS response by 2015. It is encouraging to note that domestic spending accounted for 53 per cent of all HIV related spending in 2012. Although increases in domestic investment have occurred among countries at all income levels, spending has risen most sharply among upper middle-income countries, with many lower middle-income countries remaining heavily dependent on international assistance. (p7). The international community must take its commitment seriously and act with urgency. Despite our difficulties *Social Justice Ireland* urges Government to meet its commitments in this area – one where Ireland plays a key role internationally in responding to this crisis.

Key Policy Priorities

- Ensure that Ireland delivers on its promise to meet the United Nations target of contributing 0.7 per cent of GNP to Overseas Development Assistance by the EU deadline of 2015.

- Take a far more proactive stance at government level on ensuring that Irish and EU policies towards countries in the South are just.

- Continue to support the international campaign for the liberation of the poorest nations from the burden of the backlog of unpayable debt and take steps to ensure that further progress is made on this issue.

- Ireland should play a prominent role in the development of Sustainable Development Goals for the planet and, within these, maintain the focus on the issues raised earlier in this chapter.

- Engage pro-actively and positively in the Post-Rio+20 process already referred to in chapter 11 on sustainability.

- Work for changes in the existing international trading regimes, to encourage fairer and sustainable forms of trade. In particular, resource the development of Ireland's policies in the WTO to ensure that this goal is pursued.

- Ensure that the government takes a leadership position within the European and international arenas to encourage other states to fund programmes and research aimed at resolving the AIDS/HIV crisis.

14.

VALUES

"Few can doubt that we have been in a period of economic transition. The financial collapse has shown that many aspects of the 'new economy', so widely praised just a few years ago, are unstable and unsustainable. For years we were told that we had entered a brand new world of unlimited financial possibilities, brought about by sophisticated techniques and technologies, starting with the internet and the information technology revolution, spread through the world by "globalisation" and managed by 'financial engineers' who, armed with the tools of financial derivatives, could eliminate risk and uncertainty. Now we can see that the new financial structure was a house of cards built on sand, where speculation replaced enterprise, and the self-interest of many financial speculators came at the expense of the common good."

"While there were many factors that contributed to the financial meltdown of 2008, they start with the exclusion of ethics from economic and business decision making. The designers of the new financial order had complete faith that the 'invisible hand' of market competition would ensure that the self-interested decisions of market participants would promote the common good." (Clark and Alford, 2010).

When the initial shock of the meltdown was absorbed many questions remained. Why did we fail to see the crash coming? "Where did the wealth go?" People want to know who benefitted from the meltdown. The people who are bearing the cost of the economic crash are obvious, the unemployed, emigrants who were forced to leave Ireland, poor, sick and vulnerable people who have had their income and social services cut. We are conscious of much fear, anxiety and anger in our communities. Today, more and more of society are questioning how the policies and decisions of the past decade could have failed Irish society so badly. The critical question now is how do we prevent a recurrence of this type of economic crash? While some people advocate good regulation as the solution, others are sceptical and search for more radical approaches.

Now six years after the economic crash some commentators are urging us to look to the new 'shoots' and new signs of economic recovery. We are being encouraged to accept the current reality and 'move on'. We are discouraged from taking a critical look at what has happened to sections of our society especially people on middle and lower incomes and the socio-economic gap that has opened between them and the better off.

These observations, reflections and questions bring to the fore the issue of values. Our fears are easier to admit than our values. Do we as a people accept a two-tier society in fact, while deriding it in principle? The earlier chapters of this review document many aspects of this divided society. It is obvious that we are becoming an even more unequal world. Scarce resources have been taken from poorer people to offset the debts of bankers and speculators. This shift of resources is made possible by the support of our national value system. This dualism in our values allows us to continue with the status quo, which, in reality, means that it is okay to exclude almost one sixth of the population from the mainstream of life of the society, while substantial resources and opportunities are channelled towards other groups in society. This dualism operates at the levels of individual people, communities and sectors.

To change this reality requires a fundamental change of values. We need a rational debate on the kind of society in which we want to live. If it is to be realistic, this debate should challenge our values, support us in articulating our goals, and formulating the way forward. *Social Justice Ireland* wishes to contribute to this debate. We approach the task from the concerns and values of Christian thinking. While many people are not Christians they support the concerns and values identified here.

Christian Values

Christianity subscribes to the values of both human dignity and the centrality of the community. The person is seen as growing and developing in a context that includes other people and the environment. Justice is understood in terms of relationships. The Christian scriptures understand justice as a harmony that comes from fidelity to right relationships with God, people and the environment. A just society is one that is structured in such a way as to promote these right relationships so that human rights are respected, human dignity is protected, human development is facilitated and the environment is respected and protected (Healy and Reynolds, 2003:188).

As our societies have grown in sophistication, the need for appropriate structures has become more urgent. The aspiration that everyone should enjoy the good life, and the goodwill to make it available to all, are essential ingredients in a just society. But this good life will not happen without the deliberate establishment of structures to facilitate its development. In the past charity, in the sense of alms-giving by some individuals, organisations and Churches on an arbitrary and ad hoc basis, was seen as sufficient to ensure that everyone could cross the threshold of human dignity. Calling on the work of social historians it could be argued that charity in this sense was never an appropriate method for dealing with poverty. Certainly it is not a suitable methodology for dealing with the problems of today. As recent world disasters have graphically shown, charity and the heroic efforts of voluntary agencies cannot solve these problems on a long-term basis. Appropriate structures should be established to ensure that every person has access to the resources needed to live life with dignity.

Few people would disagree that the resources of the planet are for the use of the people - not just the present generation, but also the generations still to come. In Old Testament times these resources were closely tied to land and water. A complex system of laws about the Sabbatical and Jubilee years (Lev 25: 1-22, Deut 15: 1-18) was devised to ensure, on the one hand, that no person could be disinherited, and, on the other, that land and debts could not be accumulated. This system also ensured that the land was protected and allowed to renew itself

These reflections raise questions about ownership. Obviously there was an acceptance of private property, but it was not an exclusive ownership. It carried social responsibilities. We find similar thinking among the leaders of the early Christian community. St John Chrysostom, (4th century) speaking to those who could manipulate the law so as to accumulate wealth to the detriment of others, taught that *"the rich are in the possession of the goods of the poor even if they have acquired them honestly or inherited them legally"* (Homily on Lazarus). These early leaders also established that a person in extreme necessity has the right to take from the riches of others what s/he needs, since private property has a social quality deriving from the law of the communal purpose of earthly goods (*Gaudium et Spes* 69-71).

In more recent times, Pope Paul VI (1967) said *"private property does not constitute for anyone an absolute and unconditional right. No one is justified in keeping for his/her exclusive use what is not needed when others lack necessities.... The right to property must never be exercised to the detriment of the common good"* (*Populorum Progressio* No. 23). Pope John Paul II has further developed the understanding of ownership, especially in regard to the ownership of the means of production.

One of the major contributors to the generation of wealth is technology. The technology we have today is the product of the work of many people through many generations. Through the laws of patenting and exploration a very small group of people has claimed legal rights to a large portion of the world's wealth. Pope John Paul II questioned the morality of these structures. He said *"if it is true that capital as the whole of the means of production is at the same time the product of the work of generations, it is equally true that capital is being unceasingly created through the work done with the help of all these means of production"*. Therefore, no one can claim exclusive rights over the means of production. Rather, that right *"is subordinated to the right to common use, to the fact that goods are meant for everyone"*. (*Laborem Exercens* No.14). Since everyone has a right to a proportion of the goods of the country, society is faced with two responsibilities regarding economic resources: firstly, each person should have sufficient to access the good life; and secondly, since the earth's resources are finite, and since "more" is not necessarily "better", it is time that society faced the question of putting a limit on the wealth that any person or corporation can accumulate. Espousing the value of environmental sustainability requires a commitment to establish systems that ensure the protection of our planet.

In his recent exhortation, *The Joy of the Gospel,* (Evangelii Gaudium) Pope Francis named the trends that are detrimental to the common good, equality and the future of the planet. He says:

> "While the earnings of the minority are growing exponentially, so too is the gap separating the majority from the prosperity enjoyed by those happy few. This imbalance is the result of ideologies which defend the absolute autonomy of the marketplace and financial speculation. Consequently, they reject the right of states, charged with vigilance for the common good, to exercise any form of control. A new tyranny is thus born, invisible and often virtual, which unilaterally and relentlessly imposes its own laws and rules. Debt and the accumulation of interest also make it difficult for countries to realise the potential of their economies and keep citizens from enjoying their real purchasing power. To all this we can add widespread corruption and self-serving tax evasion, which have taken on worldwide dimensions. The thirst for power and possessions knows no limits. In this system, which tends to devour everything which stands in the way of increased profits, whatever is fragile, like the environment, is defenceless before the interests of a deified market, which become the only rule." (par 56)

The concern of Pope Francis to build right relationships extends from the interpersonal to the inter-state to the global.

Interdependence, mutuality, solidarity and connectedness are words that are used loosely today to express a consciousness which resonates with Christian values. All of creation is seen as a unit that is dynamic - each part is related to every other part, depends on it in some way, and can also affect it. When we focus on the human family, this means that each person depends on others initially for life itself, and subsequently for the resources and relationships needed to grow and develop. To ensure that the connectedness of the web of life is maintained, each person depending on their age and ability is expected to reach out to support others in ways that are appropriate for their growth and in harmony with the rest of creation. This thinking respects the integrity of the person, while recognising that the person can achieve his or her potential only in right relationships with others and with the environment.

As a democratic society we elect our leaders regularly. This gives an opportunity to scrutinise the vision politicians have for our society. Because this vision is based on values it is worth evaluating the values being articulated. Check if the plans proposed are compatible with the values articulated and likely to deliver the society we desire.

Most people in Irish society would subscribe to the values articulated here. However these values will only be operative in our society when appropriate structures and infrastructures are put in place. These are the values that *Social Justice Ireland* wishes to promote. We wish to work with others to develop and support appropriate systems, structures and infrastructures which will give practical expression to these values in Irish society.

Annex 3

INCOME DISTRIBUTION

To accompany chapter 3, this annex outlines details of the composition of poverty in Ireland over recent years alongside offering an overview of Ireland's income distribution over the past two decades. It also reviews the process by which the basic social welfare payment became benchmarked to 30 per cent of Gross Average Industrial Earnings. The material underpins the development of many of the policy positions we have outlined in chapter 3.

Poverty - Who are the poor?

Two interchangeable phrases have been used to describe those living on incomes below the poverty line: *'living in poverty'* and *'at risk of poverty'*. The latter term is the most recent, introduced following a European Council meeting in Laeken in 2001 where it was agreed that those with incomes below the poverty line should be termed as being 'at risk of poverty'.

The results of the *SILC* survey provided a breakdown of those below the poverty line. This section reviews those findings and provides a detailed assessment of the different groups in poverty.

Table A3.1 presents figures for the risk of poverty facing people when they are classified by their principal economic status (the main thing that they do). These risk figures represent the proportion of each group that are found to be in receipt of a disposable income below the 60 per cent median income poverty line. In 2011 the groups within the Irish population that were at highest risk of poverty included the unemployed and those not at work due to illness or a disability. Almost one in five classified as being "on home duties", mainly women, have an income below the poverty line. The "student and school attendees" category represents a combination of individuals living in poor families while completing their secondary education and those attending post-secondary education but with low incomes. The latter element of this group are not a major policy concern, given that they are likely to only experience poverty while they gain education and skills which should ensure they live with sufficient income subsequently. Those still in school and experiencing poverty are more aligned to the issue of child poverty, which is examined later in this annex.

Despite the increase in poverty between 2009 and 2011 (see chapter 3), the table also reveals the groups which have driven the overall reduction in poverty over the period (falling from 19.7 per cent to 16 per cent). Comparing 2003 and 2011, the poverty rate has fallen for all groups other than students while there have been pronounced falls among the welfare-dependent groups, i.e. the unemployed, retired and those not at work due to illness or a disability.

Table A3.1 Risk of poverty among all persons aged 16yrs + by principal economic status, 2003-2011

	2003	2006	2011
At work	7.6	6.5	6.5
Unemployed	41.5	44.0	30.6
Students and school attendees	23.1	29.5	31.4
On home duties	31.8	23.8	21.6
Retired	27.7	14.8	8.9
Unable to work as ill/disabled	51.7	40.8	22.8
Total	19.7	17.0	16.0

Source: CSO SILC reports (2005:11, 2007:15, 2013:9), using national equivalence scale

One obvious conclusion from table A3.1 is that any further progress in reducing poverty should be driven by continuing to enhance the adequacy of welfare payments.

The working poor

Having a job is not, of itself, a guarantee that one lives in a poverty-free household. As table A3.1 indicates 6.5 per cent of those who are employed are living at risk of poverty. Despite decreases in poverty among most other groups, poverty figures for the working poor have remained static, reflecting a persistent problem with low earnings. In 2011, almost 105,000 people in employment were still at risk of poverty.[102] This is a remarkable statistic and it is important that policy makers begin to recognise and address this problem.

---

[102] See table 3.7.

Many working families on low earnings struggle to achieve a basic standard of living. Policies which protect the value of the minimum wage and attempt to keep those on that wage out of the tax net are relevant policy initiatives in this area. Similarly, attempts to highlight the concept of a 'living wage' and to increase awareness among low income working families of their entitlement to the Family Income Supplement (FIS) are also welcome; although evidence suggests that FIS is experiencing dramatically low take-up and as such has questionable long-term potential. However, one of the most effective mechanisms available within the present system to address the problem of the working poor would be to make tax credits refundable. We have addressed this proposal in chapter 3 of this review.

Recent data from Eurostat estimates the proportion of the Irish workforce who are low paid, defined as those below 66 per cent of the median hourly wage. Using data for 2010, they found that threshold to be €12.20 for Ireland and that an estimated one in five Irish workers earn below that threshold.

Child poverty

Children are one of the most vulnerable groups in any society. Consequently the issue of child poverty deserves particular attention. Child poverty is measured as the proportion of all children aged 17 years or younger that live in households with an income below the 60 per cent of median income poverty line. The 2011 *SILC* survey indicates that 18.8 per cent were at risk of poverty and, as table A3.2 shows, in recent years the rate of child poverty has begun to increase (2013:9).

Table A3.2 Child Poverty – % Risk of Poverty Among Children in Ireland.

	2006*	2007*	2009	2011
Children, 0-17 yrs	19.0	17.4	18.6	18.8

Source: CSO (various editions of SILC)
Note: * 2006 and 2007 data exclude SSIA effect.

Translating the data in table A3.2 into numbers of children implies that in 2011 almost 190,000 children lived in households that were experiencing poverty.[103] The scale of this statistic is alarming. Given that our children are our future, this situation is not acceptable. Furthermore, the fact that such a large proportion of our children are living below the poverty line has obvious implications for the education system, for the success of these children within it, for their job prospects in the future and for Ireland's economic potential in the long-term.

---

[103] See table 3.7.

Child benefit remains a key route to tackling child poverty and is of particular value to those families on the lowest incomes. Similarly, it is a very effective component in any strategy to improve equality and childcare. It is of concern, therefore, that child payments were cut in recent Budgets. On foot of these policies, it is likely that child poverty will increase further over the next few years. This will represent a major setback in an area in which the state already has a dismal record.

Older people

According to the CSO's 2011 *Census Results* there were 535,393 people aged over 65 years in Ireland in 2011. Of these, more than a quarter live alone comprising over 87,000 women and 49,000 men (CSO, 2012:26, 27). When poverty is analysed by age group the 2011 figures show that 9.7 per cent of those aged above 65 years live in relative income poverty (CSO, 2013:97).

Among all those in poverty, the retired have experienced the greatest volatility in their poverty risk rates. As table A3.3 shows, in 1994 some 5.9 per cent of this group were classified as poor; by 1998 the figure had risen to 32.9 per cent and in 2001 it peaked at 44.1 per cent. The most recent data record a decrease in poverty rates, mainly driven by increases in old age pension payments. While recent decreases are welcome, it remains a concern that so many of this county's senior citizens are living on so little.

Table A3.3 Percentage of older people (65yrs+) below the 60 per cent median income poverty line.

	1994	1998	2001	2003	2004	2005	2009	2011
Aged 65 +	5.9	32.9	44.1	29.8	27.1	20.1	9.6	9.7

Source: Whelan et al (2003: 28) and CSO (various editions of SILC)

The Ill /People with a Disability

As table A3.1 showed, those not employed due to illness or a disability are one of the groups at highest risk of poverty with 22.8 per cent of this group classified in this category. Much like the experience of Ireland's older people, the situation of this group has varied significantly over the last decade and a half. The group's risk of poverty climbed from approximately three out of every ten persons in 1994 (29.5 per cent) to over six out of every ten in 2001 (66.5 per cent) before decreasing to approximately two out of every ten in the period 2008-2011. As with other welfare dependent groups, these fluctuations parallel a period where policy first let the value of payments fall behind wage growth before ultimately increasing them to catch-up.

Overall, although those not at work due to illness or a disability only account for a small proportion of those in poverty, their experience of poverty is high. Furthermore, given the nature of this group *Social Justice Ireland* believes there is an on-going need for targeted policies to assist them. These include job creation, retraining (see chapter 5 on work) and further increases in social welfare supports. There is also a very strong case to be made for introducing a non-means tested cost of disability allowance. This proposal, which has been researched and costed in detail by the National Disability Authority (NDA, 2006) and advocated by Disability Federation of Ireland (DFI), would provide an extra weekly payment of between €10 and €40 to somebody living with a disability (calculated on the basis of the severity of their disability). It seems only logical that if people with a disability are to be equal participants in society, the extra costs generated by their disability should not be borne by them alone. Society at large should act to level the playing field by covering those extra but ordinary costs.

Poverty and education

The *SILC* results provide an interesting insight into the relationship between poverty and completed education levels. Table A3.4 reports the risk of poverty by completed education level and shows, as might be expected, that the risk of living on a low income is strongly related to low education levels. These figures underscore the relevance of continuing to address the issues of education disadvantage and early-school leaving (see chapter 9). Government education policy should ensure that these high risk groups are reduced. The table also suggests that when targeting anti-poverty initiatives, a large proportion should be aimed at those with low education levels, including those with low levels of literacy.[104]

Table A3.4 Risk of poverty among all persons aged 16yrs + by completed education level, 2007-2011

	2007	2009	2011
Primary or below	24.0	18.6	18.6
Lower secondary	20.7	19.7	21.9
Higher secondary	13.8	12.8	18.9
Post leaving certificate	10.9	9.1	14.5
Third level non-degree	8.4	4.9	10.8
Third level degree or above	4.2	4.8	5.4
Total	**15.8**	**14.1**	**16.0**

Source: CSO (2008:15; 2013:9), using national equivalence scale and excluding SSIA effect for 2007.

---

[104] We address the issues of unemployment and completed education levels in chapter 5 and adult literacy in chapter 9.

Poverty by region and area

Recent SILC reports have provided a regional breakdown of poverty levels. The data, presented in table A3.5 suggests an uneven national distribution of poverty. Using 2011 data, poverty levels are recorded as higher for the BMW region compared to the South and East. Previous SILC data (not since updated) demonstrated that within these regions Dublin had less than one in ten people living in poverty while figures were twice this in the Mid-West, South-East and the Midlands. The table also reports that poverty is more likely to occur in rural areas than urban areas. In 2011 the risk of poverty in rural Ireland was 4.6 per cent higher than in urban Ireland with at risk rates of 18.8 per cent and 14.2 per cent respectively.

Table A3.5 Risk of poverty by region and area, 2005-2011

	2005	2009	2010	2011
Border, Midland and West	-	16.2	13.8	20.4
South and East	-	13.3	15.0	14.3
Urban Areas	16.0	11.8	12.5	14.2
Rural Areas	22.5	17.8	18.1	18.8
Overall Population	**18.5**	**14.1**	**14.7**	**16.0**

Source: CSO (2008:15; 2013:9) using national equivalence scale.

Deprivation: food and fuel poverty

Chapter 3 outlines recent data from the SILC survey on deprivation. To accompany this, we examine here two further areas of deprivation associated with food poverty and fuel poverty.

Food poverty

While there is no national definition or measure of food poverty, a number of reports over the past decade have examined it and its impact. A 2004 report entitled *Food Poverty and Policy* considered food poverty as "the inability to access a nutritionally adequate diet and the related impacts on health, culture and social participation" (Society of St. Vincent de Paul et al, 2004). That report, and a later study entitled *Food on a Low Income* (Safefood 2011), reached similar conclusions and found that the experience of food poverty among poor people was that they: eat less well compared to better off groups; have difficulties accessing a variety of nutritionally balanced good quality and affordable foodstuffs; spend a greater proportion of their weekly income on food; and may know what is healthy but are restricted by a lack of financial resources to purchase and consume it.

Recently, Carney and Maitre (2012) returned to this issue and used the 2010 SILC data to construct a measure of food poverty based on the collected deprivation data. They measured food poverty and profiled those at risk of food poverty using three deprivation measures: (i) inability to afford a meal or vegetarian equivalent every second day; (ii) inability to afford a roast or vegetarian equivalent once a week; (iii) whether during the last fortnight there was at least one day when the respondent did not have a substantial meal due to lack of money. An individual who experienced one of these deprivation measures was counted as being in food poverty (2012: 11-12, 19).

The study found that one in ten of the population experienced at least one of the food poverty/deprivation indicators; approximately 450,000 people and an increase of 3 per cent since 2009. Those most at risk of food poverty are households in the bottom 20 per cent of the income distribution, households where the head of household is unemployed or ill/disabled, household who rent at less than the market rent (often social housing), lone parents and households with three adults and children (2012: 29, 38-39).

The results of these studies point towards the reality many household face making ends meet, given their limited income and challenging living conditions in Ireland today. They also underscore the need for added attention to the issue of food poverty.

Fuel poverty

Deprivation of heat in the home, often also referred to as fuel poverty, is another area of deprivation that has received attention in recent times. A 2007 policy paper from the Institute for Public Health (IPH) entitled *"Fuel Poverty and Health"* highlighted the sizeable direct and indirect effects on health of fuel poverty. Overall the IPH found that the levels of fuel poverty in Ireland remain "unacceptably high" and that they are responsible for "among the highest levels of excess winter mortality in Europe, with an estimated 2,800 excess deaths on the island over the winter months" (2007:7). They also highlighted the strong links between low income, unemployment and fuel poverty with single person households and households headed by lone parents and pensioners found to be at highest risk. Similarly, the policy paper shows that older people are more likely to experience fuel poverty due to lower standards of housing coupled with lower incomes.

More recently, The Society of St Vincent de Paul's (SVP) has defined energy poverty as the inability to attain an acceptable level of heating and other energy services in the home due to a combination of three factors: income; energy price and energy efficiency of the dwelling. The 2011 SILC study found that 12.2 per cent of individuals were without heating at some stage in that year; a figure which is 21.7 per cent for those in poverty (see table 3.11). The SVP points out that households in receipt of energy-related welfare supports account for less than half of the estimated energy poor households and over time these payments have been cut while fuel prices and carbon taxes have increased. Clearly, welfare payments need to address energy poverty. Other proposals made by the SVP include detailed initiatives on issues such as: the prevention of disconnections; investing in efficiency measures in housing; education and public awareness to promote energy saving; and the compensation of Ireland's poorest households for the existing carbon tax. [105]

Social Justice Ireland supports the IPH's call for the creation of a full national fuel poverty strategy similar to the model currently in place in Northern Ireland. While Government have made some inroads in addressing low-income household energy issues through funding a local authority retrofitting campaign, progress to date has been limited given the scale of the problem and its implication for the health and wellbeing of many low-income families. Clearly, addressing this issue, like all issues associated with poverty and deprivation, requires a multi-faceted approach. The proposals presented by the SVP should form the core of such a fuel poverty strategy.

The experience of poverty: Minimum Income Standards

A 2012 research report from the Vincentian Partnership for Social Justice (VPSJ) and Trinity College Dublin casts new light on the challenges faced by people living on low incomes in Ireland (Collins et al, 2012). Entitled '*A Minimum Income Standard for Ireland*', the research established the cost of a minimum essential standard of living for individuals and households across the entire lifecycle; from children to pensioners. Subsequently the study calculated the minimum income households required to be able to afford this standard of living. The data in this report has been updated annually by the VPSJ and published on their website.[106]

A minimum essential standard of living is defined as one which meets a person's physical, psychological, spiritual and social needs. To establish this figure, the research adopted a consensual budget standards approach whereby representative focus groups established budgets on the basis of a household's minimum needs, rather than wants. These budgets, spanning over 2,000 goods, were developed for sixteen areas of expenditure including: food, clothing, personal care, health related costs, household goods, household services, communication, social inclusion and participation, education, transport, household fuel, personal costs, childcare,

---

[105] We address these issues further in the context of a carbon tax in chapter 4.
[106] See www.budgeting.ie

insurance, housing, savings and contingencies. These budgets were then benchmarked, for their nutritional and energy content, to ensure they were sufficient to provide appropriate nutrition and heat for families, and priced. The study establishes the weekly cost of a minimum essential standard of living for five household types. These included: a single person of working age living alone; a two parent household with two children; a single parent household with two children; a pensioner couple; and a female pensioner living alone. Within these household categories, the analysis distinguishes between the expenditure for urban and rural households and between those whose members are unemployed or working, either part-time or full-time. The study also established the expenditure needs of a child and how these change across childhood.

Table A3.6 summarises the most recent update of these numbers following Budget 2014 (October 2013). Looking at a set of welfare dependent households, the study found that when the weekly income of these households is compared to the weekly expenditure required to experience a basic standard of living, they all received an inadequate income. As a result of this shortfall these households have to cut back on the basics to make ends meet (Collins et al, 2012:105-107). The comparison between 2013 and 2014 highlights the impact of price increases and budgetary policy over that period. In each case the challenges facing households is increasing as the gap between income and expenditure widens.

Table A3.6 Comparisons of minimum expenditure levels with income levels for selected welfare dependent households (€ per week)

	2A 3C Baby, 3 & 10 yrs	2A 2C 10 & 15 yrs	1A 2C Baby & 3 yrs	1A 2C 10 & 15 yrs	Single Adult	Single Pensioner
2013						
Expenditure	573.28	566.37	366.12	445.81	344.90	255.56
Income	494.11	438.17	317.60	323.37	278.00	236.70
Shortfall	*-79.17*	*-128.20*	*-48.52*	*-122.44*	*-66.90*	*-18.86*
2014						
Expenditure	582.93	575.94	372.32	453.45	350.59	262.13
Income	494.12	438.17	317.60	323.37	278.00	236.70
Shortfall	*-88.81*	*-137.77*	*-54.72*	*-130.08*	*-72.59*	*-25.43*

Source: VPSJ, 2013:2
Notes: 2A 3C baby, 3 10 yrs = 2 adults and 3 children where the children are an infant aged below 1 year, aged 3yrs and 10 years.

These results, which complement earlier research by the VPSJ (2006, 2010), contain major implications for government policy if poverty is to be eliminated. These include the need to address child poverty, the income levels of adults on social welfare, the 'working poor' issue and access to services ranging from social housing to fuel for older people and the distribution of resources between urban and rural Ireland.[107]

Ireland's income distribution: trends from 1987-2011

The results of studies by Collins and Kavanagh (1998, 2006), Collins (2013) and CSO income figures provide a useful insight into the pattern of Ireland's income distribution over 24 years. Table A3.7 combines the results from these studies and reflects the distribution of income in Ireland as tracked by five surveys. Overall, across the period 1987-2011 income distribution is very static. However, within the period there were some notable changes, with shifts in distribution towards higher deciles in the period 1994/95 to 2005.

Table A3.7 The distribution of household disposable income, 1987-2011 (%)

Decile	1987	1994/95	1999/00	2005	2011
Bottom	2.28	2.23	1.93	2.21	2.05
2nd	3.74	3.49	3.16	3.24	3.64
3rd	5.11	4.75	4.52	4.46	5.14
4th	6.41	6.16	6.02	5.70	6.39
5th	7.71	7.63	7.67	7.31	7.82
6th	9.24	9.37	9.35	9.12	9.18
7th	11.16	11.41	11.20	10.97	11.10
8th	13.39	13.64	13.48	13.23	13.32
9th	16.48	16.67	16.78	16.35	16.50
Top	24.48	24.67	25.90	27.42	24.85
Total	100.00	100.00	100.00	100.00	100.00

Source: Collins and Kavanagh (2006:156), CSO (2006:18-19) and Collins (2013:2)
Note: Data for 1987, 1994/95 and 1999/00 are from various Household Budget Surveys. 2005 and 2011 data from SILC.

---

[107] Data from these studies are available at www.budgeting.ie

Using data from the two ends of this period, 1987 and 2011, chart A3.1 examines the change in the income distribution over the intervening years. While a lot changed in Ireland over that period, income distribution did not change significantly; the decile variations are all small. Compared with 1987, only two deciles saw their share of the total income distribution increase - the fifth decile and the top decile. However, the change for the former is small (+0.11 per cent) while the change for the latter is larger (+0.37 per cent). All other deciles witnessed a small decrease in their share of the national income distribution with the bottom two deciles recording the largest falls.

Chart A3.1: Change in Ireland's Income Distribution, 1987-2011

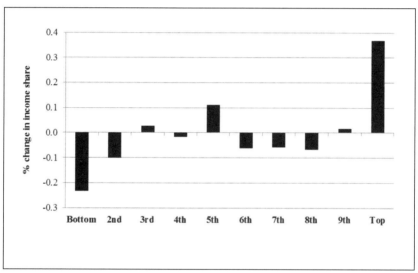

Source: Calculated using data from Collins and Kavanagh (2006:156), CSO (2006:18-19) and Collins (2013:2)

The most recent data also allows as assessment of the overall level of income inequality has grown using the Gini coefficient, which ranges from 0-100 with higher scores indicating greater inequality. The CSO reports that Ireland's inequality levels grew from 29.3 in 2009 to 31.1 in 2011. Furthermore, the 2011 data indicates that the share of the top 20 per cent of households climbed further to reach 4.9 times the share of the bottom 20 per cent. The comparable ratio in 2009 was 4.3 times.

Looking at the last seven available SILC surveys (2005-2011), the data shows a small decline for the bottom decile, small gains for all others and a decrease of 2.5 per cent for the top decile (see Table A3.7). It is likely that the top deciles decline reflects the transition from boom to recession over those years; although the share of the top 10 per cent remains more or less the same as the share of the entire bottom 50 per cent of households.

Benchmarking Social Welfare Payments, 2001-2011

While Chapter 3 considers the current challenges associated with maintaining an adequate level of social welfare, here we examine the transition to benchmarked social welfare payments.

The process of benchmarking social welfare payments centred on three elements: the 2001 *Social Welfare Benchmarking and Indexation Working Group* (SWBIG), the 2002 *National Anti-Poverty Strategy (NAPS) Review* and the *Budgets 2005-2007*.

Social welfare benchmarking and indexation working group

In its final report the SWBIG agreed that the lowest social welfare rates should be benchmarked. A majority of the working group, which included a director of *Social Justice Ireland*, also agreed that this benchmark should be index-linked to society's standard of living as it grows and that the benchmark should be reached by a definite date. The working group chose Gross Average Industrial Earnings (GAIE) to be the index to which payments should be linked.[108] The group further urged that provision be made for regular and formal review and monitoring of the range of issues covered in its report. The group expressed the opinion that this could best be accommodated within the structures in place under the NAPS and the *National Action Plan for Social Inclusion* (now combined as *NAPinclusion*). The SWBIG report envisaged that such a mechanism could involve:

* the review of any benchmarks/targets and indexation methodologies adopted by government to ensure that the underlying objectives remain valid and were being met;
* the assessment of such benchmarks/targets and indexation methodologies against the various criteria set out in the group's terms of reference to ensure their continued relevance;
* the assessment of emerging trends in the key areas of concern, e.g. poverty levels, labour market performance, demographic changes, economic performance and competitiveness, and
* identification of gaps in the area of research and assessment of any additional research undertaken in the interim.

---

[108] The group recommended a benchmark of 27 per cent although *SJI* argued for 30 per cent.

National Anti-Poverty Strategy (NAPS) review 2002

In 2002, the NAPS review set the following as key targets:

To achieve a rate of €150 per week in 2002 terms for the lowest rates of social welfare to be met by 2007 and the appropriate equivalence level of basic child income support (i.e. Child Benefit and Child Dependent Allowances combined) to be set at 33 per cent to 35 per cent of the minimum adult social welfare payment rate.

Social Justice Ireland and others welcomed this target. It was a major breakthrough in social, economic and philosophical terms. We also welcomed the reaffirmation of this target in *Towards 2016*. That agreement contained a commitment to 'achieving the NAPS target of €150 per week in 2002 terms for lowest social welfare rates by 2007' (2006:52). The target of €150 a week was equivalent to 30 per cent of Gross Average Industrial Earnings (GAIE) in 2002.[109]

Table A3.8 outlines the expected growth rates in the value of €150 based on this commitment and indicates that the lowest social welfare rates for single people should have reached €185.80 by 2007.

Table A3.8: Estimating growth in €150 a week (30% GAIE) for 2002-2007

	2002	2003	2004	2005	2006	2007
% Growth of GAIE	-	+6.00	+3.00	+4.50	+3.60	+4.80
30% GAIE	150.00	159.00	163.77	171.14	177.30	185.80

Source: GAIE growth rates from CSO Industrial Earnings and Hours Worked (September 2004:2) and ESRI Medium Term Review (Bergin et al, 2003:49).

Budgets 2005-2007

The NAPS commitment was very welcome and was one of the few areas of the anti-poverty strategy that was adequate to tackle the scale of the poverty, inequality and social exclusion being experienced by so many people in Ireland today.

In 2002 *Social Justice Ireland* set out a pathway to reaching this target by calculating the projected growth of €150 between 2002 and 2007 when it is indexed to the estimated growth in GAIE. Progress towards achieving this target had been slow

---

[109] GAIE is calculated by the CSO on the earnings of all individuals (male and female) working in all industries. The GAIE figure in 2002 was €501.51 and 30 per cent of this figure equals €150.45 (CSO, 2006: 2).

until Budget 2005. At its first opportunity to live up to the NAPS commitment the government granted a mere €6 a week increase in social welfare rates in Budget 2003. This increase was below that which we proposed and also below that recommended by the government's own tax strategy group. In Budget 2004 the increase in the minimum social welfare payment was €10. This increase was again below the €12 a week we sought and at this point we set out a three-year pathway (see table A3.9).

Table A3.9: Proposed approach to addressing the gap, 2005-2007

	2005	2006	2007
Min. SW payment in €'s	148.80	165.80	185.80
€ amount increase each year	14.00	17.00	20.00
Delivered	✓	✓	✓

Following Budget 2004 we argued for an increase of €14 in Budget 2005. The Government's decision to deliver an increase equal to that amount in that Budget marked a significant step towards honouring this commitment.. Budget 2006 followed suit, delivering an increase of €17 per week to those in receipt of the minimum social welfare rate. Finally, Budget 2007's decision to deliver an increase of €20 per week to the minimum social welfare rates brought the minimum social welfare payment up to the 30 per cent of the GAIE benchmark.

Social Justice Ireland believes that these increases, and the achievement of the benchmark in Budget 2007, marked a fundamental turning point in Irish public policy. Budget 2007 was the third budget in a row in which the government delivered on its NAPS commitment. In doing so, the government moved to meet the target so that in 2007 the minimum social welfare rate increased to €185.80 per week; a figure equivalent to the 30 per cent of GAIE.

Social Justice Ireland warmly welcomed this achievement. It marked major progress and underscored the delivery of a long overdue commitment to sharing the fruits of this country's economic growth since the mid-1990s. An important element of the NAPS commitment to increasing social welfare rates was the acknowledgement that the years from 2002-2007 marked a period of 'catch up' for those in receipt of welfare payments. Once this income gap had been bridged, the increases necessary to keep social welfare payments at a level equivalent to 30 per cent of GAIE became much smaller. In that context we welcomed the commitment by Government in *NAPinclusion* to 'maintain the relative value of the lowest social welfare rate at least at €185.80, in 2007 terms, over the course of this Plan (2007-2016), subject to available resources' (2007:42). Whether or not 30 per cent of GAIE is adequate to eliminate the risk of poverty will need to be monitored through the SILC studies and addressed when data on persistent poverty emerges.

Annex 4

TAXATION

In this annex, we outline the background data on taxation in Ireland. We first compare the overall level of taxation in Ireland to that of other European countries and then trace how this has changed over time. We then examine trends in income tax levels, outline and compare income tax levels across the income distribution and examine the distribution of indirect taxes on household.

Ireland's total tax-take up to 2011

The most recent comparative data on the size of Ireland's total tax-take has been produced by Eurostat (2013) and is detailed alongside that of 26 other EU states in table A4.1. The definition of taxation employed by Eurostat comprises all compulsory payments to central government (direct and indirect) alongside social security contributions (employee and employer) and the tax receipts of local authorities.[110] The tax-take of each country is established by calculating the ratio of total taxation revenue to national income as measured by gross domestic product (GDP). Table A4.1 also compares the tax-take of all EU member states against the average tax-take of 35.7 per cent.

Of the EU-27 states, the highest tax ratios can be found in Denmark, Sweden, Belgium, France, Finland and Italy while the lowest appear in Lithuania, Bulgaria, Latvia, Romania, Slovakia and Ireland. Overall, Ireland possesses the sixth lowest tax-take at 28.9 per cent, some 6.8 per cent below the EU average. Furthermore, Ireland's overall tax take has notably decreased over recent years with the 2011 value representing a marginal increase from a record low figure in 2010 (see chart A4.1). The increase in the overall level of taxation between 2002 and 2006 can be explained by short-term increases in construction related taxation sources (in particular stamp duty and construction related VAT) rather than any underlying structural increase in taxation levels.

---

[110] See Eurostat (2013:266-268) for a more comprehensive explanation of this classification.

Table A4.1: Total tax revenue as a % of GDP for EU-27 Countries in 2011

Country	% of GDP	+/- from average	Country	% of GDP	+/- from average
Denmark	47.7	12.0	Cyprus	35.2	-0.5
Sweden	44.3	8.6	Czech Rep	34.4	-1.3
Belgium	44.1	8.4	Malta	33.5	-2.2
France	43.9	8.2	Portugal	33.2	-2.5
Finland	43.4	7.7	Estonia	32.8	-2.9
Italy	42.5	6.8	Poland	32.4	-3.3
Austria	42.0	6.3	Greece	32.4	-3.3
Germany	38.7	3.0	Spain	31.4	-4.3
Netherlands	38.4	2.7	**Ireland GDP**	**28.9**	**-6.8**
Slovenia	37.2	1.5	Slovakia	28.5	-7.2
Luxembourg	37.2	1.5	Romania	28.2	-7.5
Hungary	37.0	1.3	Latvia	27.6	-8.1
United Kingdom	36.1	0.4	Bulgaria	27.2	-8.5
Ireland GNP	**36.0**	**0.3**	Lithuania	26.0	-9.7

Source: Eurostat (2013:172) and CSO National Income and Expenditure Accounts
Notes: All data is for 2011. EU-27 average is 35.7 per cent.

Chart A4.1: Trends in Ireland and EU-27 overall taxation levels, 2000-2010

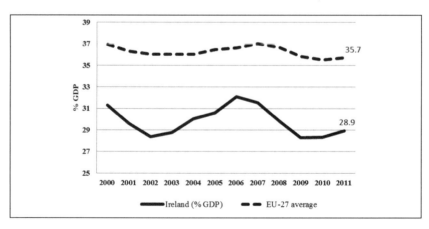

Source: Eurostat (2013:172) and CSO National Income and Expenditure Accounts

Socio-Economic Review 2014

GDP is accepted as the benchmark against which tax levels are measured in international publications. However, it has been suggested that for Ireland gross national product (GNP) is a better measure. This is because Ireland's large multinational sector is responsible for significant profit outflows which, if included (as they are in GDP but not in GNP), exaggerate the scale of Irish economic activity.[111] Commenting on this, Collins stated that "while it is clear that multinational profit flows create a considerable gap between GNP and GDP, it remains questionable as to why a large chunk of economic activity occurring within the state should be overlooked when assessing its tax burden" and that "as GDP captures all of the economic activity happening domestically, it only seems logical, if not obvious, that a nations' taxation should be based on that activity" (2004:6).[112] He also noted that using GNP will understate the scale of the tax base and overstate the tax rate in Ireland because it excludes the value of multinational activities in the economy but does include the tax contribution of these companies. In this way, the size of the tax-take from Irish people and firms is exaggerated.

Social Justice Ireland believes that it would be more appropriate to calculate the tax-take by comparing either GNP or GNI (Gross National Income) and using an adjusted tax-take figure which excludes the tax paid by multi-national companies. As figures for their tax contribution are currently unavailable, we have simply used the unadjusted GNP figures and presented the results in table A4.1. In 2011 this stood at 36.0 per cent. [113] This also suggests to international observers and internal policy makers that the Irish economy is not as tax-competitive as it truly is. This issue should be addressed by Government and appropriate adjustments made when calculating Ireland's tax-take as a percentage of GNP.

In the context of the figures in table A4.1 and the trends in chart A4.1, the question needs to be asked: if we expect our economic and social infrastructure to catch up to that in the rest of Europe, how can we do this while simultaneously gathering less taxation income than it takes to run the infrastructure already in place in most of those other European countries? In reality, we will never bridge the social and economic infrastructure gaps unless we gather a larger share of our national income and invest it in building a fairer and more successful Ireland.

---

[111] Collins (2004:6) notes that this is a uniquely Irish debate and not one that features in other OECD states such as New Zealand where noticeable differences between GDP and GNP also occur.

[112] See also Collins (2011:90) and Bristow (2004:2) who make a similar argument.

[113] The 2011 tax take as a percentage of GNI is 35.6 per cent.

Effective tax rates

To complement the trends and data outlined in chapter 4, it is possible to focus on the changes to the levels of income taxation in Ireland over the past decade and a half. Central to any understanding of these personal/income taxation trends are effective tax rates. These rates are calculated by comparing the total amount of income tax a person pays with their pre-tax income. For example, a person earning €50,000 who pays a total of €10,000 in tax, PRSI and USC will have an effective tax rate of 20 per cent. Calculating the scale of income taxation in this way provides a more accurate reflection of the scale of income taxation faced by earners.

Following Budget 2014 we have calculated effective tax rates for a single person, a single income couple and a couple where both are earners. Table A4.2 presents the results of this analysis. For comparative purposes, it also presents the effective tax rates which existed for people with the same income levels in 2000 and 2008.

In 2014, for a single person with an income of €15,000 the effective tax rate will be 2.7 per cent, rising to 15.1 per cent on an income of €25,000 and 42.9 per cent on an income of €120,000. A single income couple will have an effective tax rate of 2.7 per cent at an income of €15,000, rising to 8.3 per cent at an income of €25,000, 26.6 per cent at an income of €60,000 and 39.3 per cent at an income of €120,000. In the case of a couple, both earning and a combined income of €40,000, their effective tax rate is 9.9 per cent, rising to 33.8 per cent for combined earnings of €120,000.

Table A4.2: Effective Tax Rates following Budgets 2000 / 2008 / 2014

Income Levels	Single Person	Couple 1 earner	Couple 2 Earners
€15,000	13.9% / 0.0% / 2.7%	2.5% / 0.0% / 2.7%	0.8% / 0.0% / 2.0%
€20,000	13.9% / 0.0% / 11.1%	8.3% / 2.7% / 7.6%	6.1% / 0.0% / 2.3%
€25,000	24.0% / 8.3% / 15.1%	12.3% / 2.9% / 8.3%	11.0% / 0.0% / 2.5%
€30,000	28.4% / 12.9% / 17.7%	15.0% / 5.1% / 9.5%	14.6% / 1.7% / 5.6%
€40,000	33.3% / 18.6% / 24.8%	20.2% / 9.4% / 14.9%	17.5% / 3.6% / 9.9%
€60,000	37.7% / 27.5% / 33.9%	29.0% /19.8% / 26.6%	28.0% /12.2% / 17.7%
€100,000	41.1% / 33.8% / 41.1%	35.9% /29.2% / 36.8%	35.9% /23.8% / 30.2%
€120,000	41.9% / 35.4% / 42.9%	37.6% /31.6% / 39.3%	37.7% /27.2% / 33.8%

Source: *Social Justice Ireland* (2013:8).
Notes: Tax = income tax + PRSI + levies/USC
Couples assume 2 children and 65%/35% income division
All workers are assumed to be PAYE earners

While these rates have increased since 2008 for almost all earners they are still low compared to those that prevailed in 2000. Few people complained at that time about tax levels being excessive and the recent increases should be seen in this context. Taking a longer view, chart A4.2 illustrates the downward trend in effective tax rates for three selected household types since 1997. These are a single earner on €25,000; a couple with one earner on €40,000; and a couple with two earners on €60,000. Their experiences are similar to those on other income levels and are similar to the effective tax rates of the self-employed over that period.

Chart A4.2: Effective tax rates in Ireland, 1997-2014

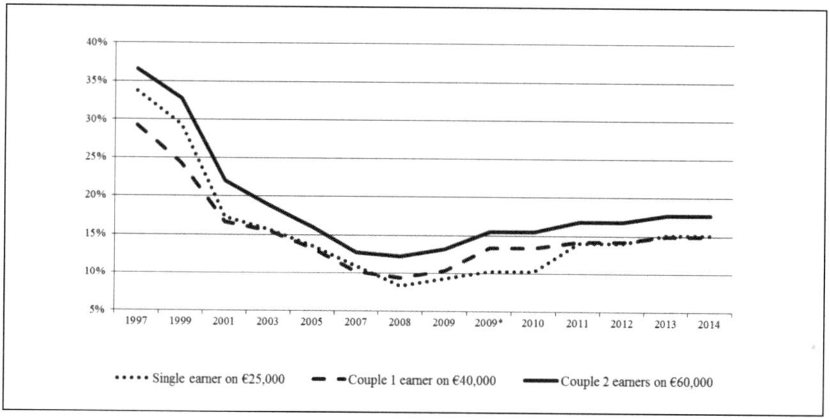

Source: Department of Finance, Budget 2013 and *Social Justice Ireland* (2012:8).
Notes: Tax = income tax + PRSI + levies/USC
Couples assume 2 children and 65%/35% income division
2009*= Supplementary Budget 2009 (April 2009)
All workers are assumed to be PAYE earners

The two 2009 Budgets produced notable increases in these effective taxation rates. Both Budgets required government to raise additional revenue and with some urgency - increases in income taxes providing the easiest option. Similarly, the introduction of the USC in Budget 2011 increased these rates, most notably for lower income earners, The subsequent Budget 2012 provided a welcome reduction for the lowest earners through raising the income level at which the USC applies. Despite that change, the employee PRSI increase in Budget 2013 targeted lowest income earners hardest and increased effective taxation rate for almost all workers.

However, income taxation is not the only form of taxation and, as we highlight in chapter 4, there are many in Ireland with potential to contribute further taxation revenues.

Income taxation and the income distribution

An insight into the distribution of income taxpayers across the income distribution is provided each year by the Revenue Commissioners in its Statistical Report. The Revenue's ability to profile taxpayers is limited by the fact that it only examines 'tax cases' which may represent either individual taxpayers or couples who are jointly assessed for tax. A further disadvantage of these figures is that there is a considerable delay between the tax year being reported on and the publication of the data for that year. The latest data, published in 2012, is for 2010.[114]

The progressivity of the Irish income taxation system is well demonstrated in table A4.3 – as incomes increase the average income tax paid also increases. The table also underscores the issues highlighted earlier in chapter 3; that a large proportion of the Irish population survive on low incomes. Summarising the data in the table, almost 20 per cent of cases have an income below €10,000; 55 per cent have an income below €30,000 and 90 per cent of cases are below €75,000. At the top of the income distribution, 5 per cent of households (almost 100,000) receive an income in excess of €100,000. The table also highlights the dependence of the income taxation system on higher income earners, with 27 per cent of income tax coming from cases with incomes of between €60,000 and €100,000 and 46 per cent of income tax coming from cases with incomes above €100,000. While such a structure is not unexpected, a symptom of progressivity rather than a structural problem, it does underscore the need to broaden the tax base beyond income taxes – a point we have made for some time and develop further in chapter 4.

Indirect taxation and the income distribution

As chapter 4 shows, the second largest source of taxation revenue is VAT and the third largest is excise duties. These indirect taxes tend to be regressive – meaning they fall harder on lower income individuals and households (Barrett and Wall, 2006:17-23; Collins, 2011: 102-103).

An assessment of how these indirect taxes impact on households across the income distribution is possible using data from the CSO's Household Budget Survey (HBS), which collects details on household expenditure and income every five years. Chart A4.3 and table A4.4 presents the results of Barrett and Wall's examination of the 2004/05 HBS data.[115] They show that indirect taxation consumes more than 20 per cent of the lowest decile's income and more than 18 per cent of the income of the bottom five deciles. These findings reflect the fact that lower income households tend to spend almost all of their income while higher income households both spend and save.

---

[114] An update for the 2011 tax year is due in mid 2014.
[115] A subsequent study by Leahy et al (2010) found similar results but provides less data on the income distribution impacts of indirect taxes.

Table A4.3: Income taxation and Ireland's income distribution, 2010

From €	To €	No. of cases	Av. income	Av. Tax	% Total Tax
-	10,000	387,175	€4,399	€12	0.05
10,000	12,000	71,719	€11,026	€35 0.03	
12,000	15,000	109,788	€13,523	€56	0.06
15,000	17,000	72,768	€16,009	€70	0.05
17,000	20,000	122,603	€18,517	€114	0.14
20,000	25,000	200,619	€22,495	€476	0.97
25,000	27,000	74,917	€25,988	€892	0.68
27,000	30,000	102,601	€28,492	€1,196	1.25
30,000	35,000	152,930	€32,454	€1,738	2.71
35,000	40,000	137,680	€37,439	€2,554	3.58
40,000	50,000	198,857	€44,648	€4,242	8.59
50,000	60,000	130,636	€54,645	€6,665	8.87
60,000	75,000	124,574	€66,898	€9,497	12.05
75,000	100,000	102,146	€85,621	€14,659	15.26
100,000	150,000	63,191	€118,783	€25,612	16.49
150,000	200,000	17,101	€170,895	€43,216	7.53
200,000	275,000	9,308	€231,717	€62,667	5.94
Over	275,000	9,830	€522,062	€157,165	15.74
Totals		2,088,443	€37,218	€4,700	100.00

Source: Calculated from Revenue Commissioners (2012).

Dealing specifically with VAT, the study also found that lower income households paid more at the 21 per cent (now 23 per cent) rate than did higher income households. Consequently in our *Analysis and Critique of Budget 2012*, *Social Justice Ireland* highlighted the way that that Budget's increase in VAT was regressive and unnecessarily undermined the living standards of low income households. Other, fairer approaches to increasing taxation were available and should have been taken.

Chart A4.3: VAT and excise duties as a % of household income, by decile

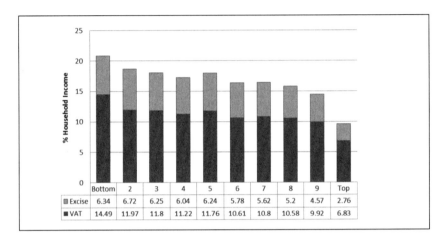

Source: Barrett and Wall (2006:19-20).

Table A4.4 VAT Payments at reduced and standard rates as a % of income, by selected deciles

% income paid in VAT	Bottom	2nd	3rd	8th	9th	Top
@ 13.5% rate (reduced)	3.6	3.0	2.7	2.0	1.8	1.3
@ 21% rate (standard)*	11.5	9.1	9.4	8.9	8.4	5.8

Source: Barrett and Wall (2006:19-20).
Note: * Rate subsequently decreased & increased – latest increase to 23% (Budget 2012)

Annex 5.

WORK, UNEMPLOYMENT AND JOB CREATION

Measuring the labour market

When considering terms such as "employment" and "unemployment" it is important to be as clear as possible about what we actually mean. Two measurement sources are often quoted as the basis for labour market data, the *Quarterly National Household Survey* (QNHS) and the *Live Register*. The former is considered the official and most accurate measure of employment and unemployment although, unlike the monthly live register unemployment data, it appears only four times a year.

The CSO's QNHS unemployment data use the definition of 'unemployment' supplied by the International Labour Office (ILO). It lists as unemployed only those people who, in the week before the survey, were unemployed *and* available to take up a job *and* had taken specific steps in the preceding four weeks to find employment. Any person who was employed for at least *one hour* is classed as employed. By contrast, the live register counts everybody 'signing-on' and includes part-time employees (those who are employed up to three days a week), those employed on short weeks, seasonal and casual employees entitled to Jobseekers Assistance or Benefit.[116]

Labour force trends

The dramatic turnaround in the labour market after 2007 (see chapter 5) contrasts with the fact that one of the major achievements of the preceding 20 years had been the increase in employment and the reduction in unemployment, especially long-term unemployment. In 1992 there were 1,165,200 people employed in Ireland. That

---

[116] See Healy and Collins (2006) for a further explanation of measurement in the labour market.

figure increased by almost one million to peak at 2,169,600 in mid-2007. During early 2006 the employment figure exceeded two million for the first time in the history of the state. Overall, the size of the Irish labour force has expanded significantly and today equals over 2.18 million people, eight hundred thousand more than in 1992 (see chart A5.1).

However, in the period since 2007 emigration has returned, resulting in a decline in the labour force. Initially this involved recently arrived migrants returning home but was then followed by the departure of native Irish. CSO figures indicate that during the first quarter of 2009 the numbers employed fell below two million and that the level continued to fall until achieving some growth in 2013. In that year there were just under 1.9 million people employed (see chart A5.1).

Chart A5.1: The Numbers of People in the Labour Force and Employed in Ireland, 1991-2013

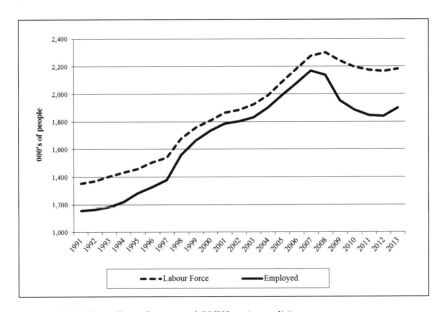

Source: CSO, Labour Force Survey and QNHS various editions

As chart A5.2 shows, the period from 1993 was one of decline in unemployment. By mid-2001 Irish unemployment reached its lowest level at 3.6 per cent of the labour force. Subsequently the international recession and domestic economic crisis brought about increases in the rate. During 2006 unemployment exceeded 100,000 for the first time since 1999 with a total of 105,100 people recorded as unemployed in mid-2006. As chart A5.2 shows, it exceeded 200,000 in early-2009, 300,000 in 2010 and peaked at 328,000 in 2011. Unemployment has since declined, reaching a figure of 280,000 in 2013. The chart also highlights the rapid growth in the number of long-term unemployed (those unemployed for more than 12 months). The CSO reports that there are now over 165,000 people in long-term unemployment and that this figure has increased five-fold since 2007. Quite simply, given the on-going economic crisis many of those who entered unemployment in 2007-2010 have remained unemployed for more than 12 months and have therefore become long-term unemployed.

Chart A5.2: The Numbers of Unemployed and Long-Term Unemployed in Ireland, 1991-2012

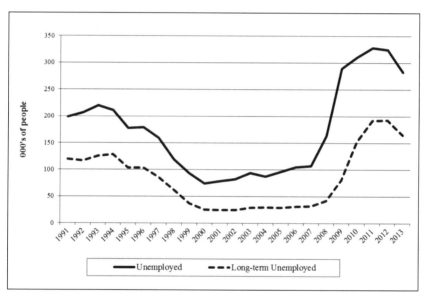

Source: CSO, Labour Force Survey and QNHS various editions

Annex 7

HOUSING AND ACCOMMODATION

The following annex accompanies chapter seven providing data in relation to range of areas already discussed in the chapter. Table A7.1 provides additional information relating to house completions for the period 1993 to 2000.

A7.1 House Completions by Sector for years 1993 to 2000

Year	Local Authority Housing	Voluntary/Non Profit Housing	Private Housing	Total
1993	1,200	890	19,301	21,391
1994	2,374	901	23,588	26,863
1995	2,960	1,011	26,604	30,575
1996	2,676	917	30,132	33,725
1997	2,632	756	35,454	38,842
1998	2,771	485	39,093	42,349
1999	2,909	579	43,024	46,512
2000	2,204	951	46,657	49,812

Source: Department of the Environment, Heritage and Local Government, (2013)

Table A7.2 shows new social housing output for the period from 2007 to 2012. This data provides an overview of the fall off which has occurred in relation to completions and acquisitions across the area of social housing, both within the voluntary and cooperative and the local authority sectors.

A7.2 New Social Housing Output for 2007 to 20012

Year	Local Authority Completions	Acquisitions	Voluntary and Cooperative Completions	Total Completions and acquisitions
2007	4,986	2,002	1,685	8,673
2008	4,905	787	1,896	7,588
2009	3,362	727	2,011	6,100
2010	1,328	850	741	2,919
2011	494	325	745	1,564
2012	363	351	677	1,391

Source: Department of the Environment, Heritage and Local Government, (2013)

Table A7.3 outlines the <u>new</u> RAS units acquired by the local authority for social housing purposes over the corresponding year. In general, data in relation to RAS is provided in cumulative format due to the nature of the scheme, numbers in RAS constantly vary as contracts end, tenants move on to other properties, landlords withdraw from the scheme, new tenancies are allocated or vacancies in contracted units are filled.

A7.3 New RAS Units Acquired under Long Term Lease Years 2007 to 2012

Year	Number of New RAS Units Acquired
2007	796
2008	1,600
2009	1,990
2010	1,783
2011	1,918
2012	1,416

Source: Department of the Environment, Heritage and Local Government, (2013)

Table A7.4 provides an overview in regard to the number of households assessed as being in need of social housing from 1993-2013. The table shows a massive increase from 1993 to 2013 with the total number of households going from 28,200 up to 89,872. This represents an increase of 61,672 households over a twenty year period. When comparisons are drawn between 2008 and 2013, there is an increase of 33,623.

A7.4 Net Household Need 1993-2013

Year	Number of Households	Number of households yearly increase/decrease
2013	89,872	-8,446
2011	98,318	+42,069
2008	56,249	+13,303
2005	42,946	-5,467
2002	48,413	+9,327
1999	39	+11,749
1996	27,427	-773
1993	28,200	

Source: Housing Agency (2013)

A7.5 Breakdown of the Local Authority Waiting List by Major Categories of Need 2005, 2008 and 2011

Category of need	2005[117]	as % of net need 2005	2008	as % of net need 2008	2011	as % of net need 2011
Homeless	1,987	4.5	1,394	3	2,348	2.4
Traveller	1,004	2	1,317	2	1,824	1.9
Accommodation unfit	1,719	4	1,757	3	1,708	1.7
Accommodation overcrowded	4,073	10	4,805	9	4,594	4.7
Involuntary sharing	3,371	8	4,965	9	8,534	8.7
Young persons leaving care	256	0.5	715	1	538	0.5
Medical compassion	3,504	8	8,059	14	9,548	9.7
Older Persons	1,658	4	2,499	4	2,266	2.3
People with a disability	455	1	1,155	2	1,315	1.3
Unable to meet Accommodation Cost	24,919	58	29,583	53	65,643	66.8
Total	42,946	100	56,249	100	98,318	100

Source: Department of the Environment, Heritage and Local Government, Annual Housing Statistics Bulletin (2008) & Housing Agency (2011).

---

[117] These figures are different from the figures reported in the 2005 Housing Needs Assessment as an adjustment was made to the 2005 figures in the 2008 Housing Statistics Bulletin for comparison purposes with the 2008 results.

Socio-Economic Review 2014

Annex 11:

SUSTAINABILITY AND ENVIRONMENT

Ireland: some key environmental facts (CSO 2013, EPA 2013, SEAI 2013))

Greenhouse Gases and Climate Change

• Greenhouse gas (GHG) emissions fell substantially between 2009 and by 2011. The EPA estimates that Ireland will meet its Kyoto Protocol target through the use of Kyoto Protocol credits already purchased by the State and use of unused allowances in the New Entrant Set Aside under the EU Emissions Trading Scheme.

• Agriculture is the largest source of GHG emissions, representing 32 per cent of total national emissions in 2011. The energy industries are the second largest source of emissions, representing 20.8 per cent of total national GHG emissions in 2011.

• The transport sector has been the fastest growing source of GHG emissions, showing a 120 per cent increase between 1990 and 2011, although emissions from this sector have shown decreases on an annual basis from peak levels in 2007.

• Ireland is likely to breach its EU 2020 target and obligations on emissions from 2016 onwards (EPA, 2013). Emissions are projected to be between 1 – 9 per cent higher in 2020[118].

• Forest sinks in Ireland could provide a removal of 4.6Mtonnes of CO2 in 2020 and 32 Mtonnes of CO2 over the 2014-2020 period.

---

[118] This is based on projections using both the 'With Measures' and 'With Additional Measures' scenarios (EPA, 2013:1).

Transport

- Ireland's car density in 2012 was 524 cars per 1,000 adults.

- There has been a substantial increase in the number of low emission vehicles licensed since the introduction in 2008 of motor taxation rates based upon emissions. In 2011, 90% of new private vehicles licensed were in emission bands A and B.

- Two out of three persons drove to work in 2011.

- 61% of children aged 5-12 were driven to school by car in 2011.

- The transport sector accounted for 40.2% of Ireland's final energy consumption in 2011, the highest for any economic sector in that year.

- More women walked to work (96,796) than men (73,714). Men accounted for the majority of those cycling with 29,075 (73%), while the majority of public transport commuters were women (55.5%).

Energy

- Ireland's renewable energy targets for 2020 are to have 40% of electricity, 10% of transport and 12% of heat to be generated from renewable energy.

- In 2012 Ireland generated 19.6% of electricity, 3.8% of transport[119] and 5.2% of heat from renewable energy.

- Ireland's primary energy requirement was 13.23 million tonnes of oil equivalent (t.o.e) in 2012. It rose from 9.5 million t.o.e. in 1990 to 16.5 million t.o.e. in 2008 and has been slowly decreasing since 1990.

- Transport accounted for 39% of Ireland's final energy consumption in 2012.

- Oil accounted for 56.8% of Ireland's total final energy consumption in 2012.

- Renewable energy accounts for 7.1% of Ireland's gross final energy use in 2012. The target set for 2020 is 16%.

- Wind energy accounted for 41% of Ireland's renewable energy in 2012.

- Ireland's overall energy import dependency was 85% in 2012. Overall indigenous energy production decreased by 23% in 2012.

Water

- Food Harvest 2020 proposes a 50% increase in milk production. This will present a significant challenge if Ireland is to meet its Water Framework Directive goals as agriculture is one of the main sources of nitrates in groundwaters and of nutrient enrichment in surface waters. The Food Harvest target for milk

---

[119] Includes weightings for biofuels

production will potentially increase total nitrogen generation by as much as 14% by 2020. The proportion of Irish rivers classified as being unpolluted has declined from 77.3% in 1987-1990 to 68.9% in 1997-2009.

- The percentage of slightly polluted river water has increased steadily from 12% in 1987-1990 to 20.7% in the period 2007-2009.

Table A12.1: Irish River Water Quality 1987 – 2009

Quality	Unpolluted polluted	Slightly polluted	Moderately polluted	Seriously	Total
1987-1990	77.3	12.0	9.7	0.9	100
1995-1997	66.9	18.2	14.0	0.9	100
2001-2003	69.3	17.9	12.3	0.6	100
2007-2009	68.9	20.7	10.0	0.4	100

Source: Environmental Protection Agency 2010, Water Quality 2007 - 2009

Waste

- The amount of municipal waste generated fell from 800 kilograms per capita in 2006 to 618kgs per capita in 2011. Municipal waste sent to landfill was 1.344 million tonnes in 2011 , an improvement on the two million tonnes in 2007.
- By 2011, the recovery rate for packaging waste had reached 79%.
- Almost 20% of household waste is presented at civic amenity and bring centres.
- 91% of Ireland's hazardous waste is exported to four European countries (UK, Germany, Belgium and the Netherlands).

Table A12.2 Ireland: Municipal waste, generated, recovered and landfilled

Year	Waste generated (000 tonnes)	Waste recovered (% of waste generated)	Waste landfilled (% of waste generated)
2003	3,001.0	24.2	61.1
2005	3,050.1	31.6	59.8
2007	3,397.7	34.1	59.3
2009	2,952.9	37.3	58.4
2011	2,832.2	42.6	47.6

Source: Environmental Protection Agency (2013), National Waste Report Series

Land Use

- In 2010, 10.7% of Ireland's land was covered by forestry. This was the second lowest proportion of forest cover in the EU. The EU average forest cover in 2010 was 35.5% of total land area.

- The area of forest owned privately in Ireland increased from 23% in 1980 to 46% in 2010.

- Although the area farmed organically increased by over 150% between 1997 and 2009, Ireland had the third lowest percentage of agricultural land designated as organic in the EU in 2009.

- Ireland had the fifth largest cattle herd in the EU in 2010 with 6.8% of total cattle numbers.

Biodiversity and Heritage

- Only 7% of Ireland's habitats listed under the Habitat's Directive are considered to be in a favourable state.

- The social and economic benefits of Ireland's biodiversity are worth at least €2.6 billion per annum.

- Ireland had the smallest percentage of land in the EU designated as a Special Protected Area, under the EU Birds Directive, at only 3% of total land area in 2010.

- Ireland at 11% had less land designated as a Special Protected Area under the EU Habitats Directive than the EU average of 14% in 2010.

Annex 13

THE GLOBAL SOUTH

UN Millennium Development Goals

The following are the UN Millennium Development Goals and the specific targets attached to each of these goals:

Goal 1: Eradicate extreme poverty and hunger

Target 1:   Halve, between 1990 and 2015, the proportion of people whose income is less than $1.25 a day.

Target 2:   Halve, between 1990 and 2015, the proportion of people who suffer from hunger.

Goal 2: Achieve universal primary education

Target 3:   Ensure that, by 2015, children everywhere, boys and girls alike, will be able to complete a full course of primary schooling.

Goal 3: Promote gender equality and empower women

Target 4:   Eliminate gender disparity in primary and secondary education, preferably by 2005 and in all levels of education no later than 2015.

Goal 4: Reduce child mortality

Target 5:   Reduce by two-thirds, between 1990 and 2015, the under-five mortality rate.

Goal 5: Improve maternal health

Target 6:   Reduce by three-quarters, between 1990 and 2015, the maternal mortality ratio.

Goal 6: Combat HIV/AIDS, malaria and other diseases

Target 7:   Have halted by 2015 and begun to reverse the spread of HIV/AIDS.

Target 8:   Have halted by 2015 and begun to reverse the incidence of malaria and other major diseases.

Goal 7: Ensure environmental sustainability

Target 9:   Integrate the principles of sustainable development into country policies and programmes and reverse the loss of environmental resources.

Target 10:   Halve by 2015 the proportion of people without sustainable access to safe drinking water.

Target 11:   Have achieved by 2020 a significant improvement in the lives of at least 100 million slum dwellers.

Goal 8: Develop a global partnership for development

Target 12:   Develop further an open, rule based, predictable, nondiscriminatory trading and financial system (includes a commitment to good governance, development, and poverty reduction - both nationally and internationally).

Target 13:   Address the special needs of the least developed countries (includes tariff and quota free access for exports, enhanced programme of debt relief for and cancellation of official bilateral debt, and more generous official development assistance for countries committed to poverty reduction).

Target 14:   Address the special needs of landlocked countries and small island developing states (through the Programme of Action for the Sustainable Development of Small Island Developing States and 22nd General Assembly provisions).

Target 15:   Deal comprehensively with the debt problems of developing countries through national and international measures in order to make debt sustainable in the long term

Target 16:   In cooperation with developing countries, develop and implement strategies for decent and productive work for youth.

Target 17:   In cooperation with pharmaceutical companies, provide access to affordable essential drugs in developing countries.

Target 18:   In cooperation with the private sector, make available the benefits of new technologies, especially information and communications technologies.

(UNDP, 2003: 1-3)

REFERENCES

References

Advisory Group on Unfinished Housing Developments (2011) *Resolving Irelands Unfinished Housing Developments.* Dublin: Department of Environment, Community and Local Government.

All Ireland Traveller Health Study Team. (2010) *All Ireland Traveller Health Study: Our Geels Summary Of Findings.* Dublin: University College Dublin.

An Comhairle Leabharlanna (2012) *Public Library Authorities Budgeted Expenditure for 2012, Full Annual Estimates Report.* Dublin: Local Government Management Agency.

An Chomhairle Leabharlanna (2010) *Public Library Authority Statistics Actuals.* Dublin: Department of Environment, Community and Local Government.

Ashe, J. (2014) *Remarks by H. E. Mr. John W. Ashe President of the 68th Session of the United Nations General Assembly.* Available from www.un.org/en/ga/president/68/pdf/statements/02182014TD_Water%20Sanitation %20and%20Sustainable%20Energy_Opening_final.pdf (14 March 2014)

Bank for International Settlements (2013) *Triennial Central Bank Survey of Foreign Exchange and Derivatives Market Activity.* Basel: BIS.

Barrett, A. and Wall C. (2005) *The Distributional Impact of Ireland's Indirect Tax System.* Dublin: Combat Poverty Agency.

Begg, D. (2003) "The Just Society - Can we afford it?" in Reynolds B. and S. Healy (eds.) *Ireland and the Future of Europe: leading the way towards inclusion?.* Dublin: CORI.

Behan, J. (2014) *Occupational Employment Projections 2020.* Dublin: SOLAS.

Bennett M., D. Fadden,. D. Harney, P. O'Malley, C. Regan and Sloyan L. (2003) *Population Ageing in Ireland and its Impact on Pension and Healthcare Costs - Report of Society of Actuaries Working Party on Population Studies.* Dublin: Society of Actuaries in Ireland.

Bergin, A., J. Cullen, D. Duffy, J. Fitzgerald, I. Kearney and McCoy D. (2003) *Medium-Term Review: 2003-2010.* Dublin: ESRI.

Blankenburg, S., L. King, S. Konzelmann and Wilkinson, F. (2013) 'Prospects for the eurozone', *Cambridge Journal of Economics*, 37 (3) 463-477.

Bristow, J. (2004) *Taxation in Ireland: an economist's perspective.* Dublin: Institute of Public Administration.

Browne, D. Caulfield, B. & O'Mahony, M. (2011*)* Barriers to Sustainable Transport in Ireland. *Climate Change Research Programme (CCRP) 2007-2013 Report Series No.7* Dublin: EPA.

Browne, M. (2007) *The Right Living Space, Housing and Accommodation Needs of People with Disabilities*. Dublin: Citizens Information Board/Disability Federation of Ireland

Cahill, S., O'Shea, E., & Pierce, M. (2012) *Creating Excellence in Dementia Care: A Research Review for Ireland's National Dementia Strategy*. Dublin: Department of Health.

Callan, T. (2013) *Distributional impact of Budgets 2009 to 2013: An Update*. Dublin: ESRI.

Callan, T., B. Nolan, C. Keane, M. Savage and Walsh, J. (2013) 'Crisis, Response and Distributional Impact: The Case of Ireland'. *Working Paper No. 456*. Dublin: ESRI.

Carneiro, P and Heckman, J. (2003) 'Human Capital Policy'. *NBER Working Paper Series*. Cambridge MA: National Bureau of Economic Research.

Carney, C and Maître, B. (2012). 'Constructing a Food Poverty Indicator for Ireland using the Survey on Income and Living Conditions', *Social Inclusion Technical Paper No. 3*. Dublin: Department of Social Protection.

Carrie, A. (2005) "Lack of long-run data prevents us tracking Ireland's social health" in *Feasta Review No2 Growth: the Celtic Cancer*. Dublin: Feasta.
Carswell, S. (2013) 'Former IMF chief says Irish authorities were not helpless over EU policy', *The Irish Times,* December 13, 2013. Available from http://www.irishtimes.com/news/politics/former-imf-chief-says-irish-authorities-were-not-helpless-over-eu-policy-1.1625918 (14 March 2014).

Central Bank (2013) 'Central Bank publishes outcome of Mortgage Arrears Resolution Targets', *Press Release* 29 November 2013. Available from http://www.centralbank.ie/press-area/press-releases/Pages/CentralBankpublishesoutcomeofMortgageArrears.aspx (14March 2014).

Central Bank (2013) *Residential Mortgage Arrears and Repossessions Statistics: Q3 2013*. Dublin: Central Bank.

Central Bank (2012) *Residential Mortgage Arrears and Repossessions Statistics: Q2 2012*. Dublin: Central Bank.

Centre for Ageing Research and Development in Ireland (2012) *Future Demand for Long-term Care in Ireland*. Dublin: CARDI.

Central Statistics Office (2014) *Quarterly National Household Survey Quarter 4 2013*. Dublin: Stationery Office.

Central Statistics Office (2014) *Measuring Ireland's Progress 2013*. Dublin: Stationery Office

Central Statistics Office (2013) *Measuring Ireland's Progress 2012*. Dublin: Stationery Office.

Central Statistics Office (2013) *Quarterly National Household Survey, Effects on Households of the Economic Downturn Quarter 3 2012*. Dublin: Stationery Office.

Central Statistics Office (2013) *Statistical Yearbook of Ireland 2013*. Dublin: Stationery Office.

Central Statistics Office (2013) *Sustainable Development Indicators Ireland 2013*. Dublin: Stationery Office.

Central Statistics Office (2013) *Population and Migration Statistics*. Dublin: Stationery Office.

Central Statistics Office (2013) *Survey on Income and Living Conditions 2011 and revised 2010 results,* Dublin, Stationery Office.

Central Statistics Office (2013) *Information Society Statistics.* Available at http://www.cso.ie/en/statistics/informationsociety/ (14 March 2014).

Central Statistics Office (2012) *Census 2011 Profile 6: Migration and Diversity.* Dublin: Stationery Office.
Central Statistics Office (2012) *Environmental Indicators Ireland 2012.* Dublin: Stationery Office.

Central Statistics Office (2012) *Measuring Ireland's Progress 2011.* Dublin: Stationery Office.

Central Statistics Office (2012) *Population and Migration Statistics.* Dublin: Stationery Office.

Central Statistics Office (2012) *Census 2011 Profile 2 – Older and Younger.* Dublin, Stationery Office.

Central Statistics Office (2012) *Census 2011 Profile 8: Our Bill of Health – Health, Disability and Carers in Ireland.* Dublin: Stationery Office.

Central Statistics Office (2012) *Statistical Yearbook of Ireland 2012.* Dublin: Stationery Office

Central Statistics Office (2012) *Census 2011 Profile 4: A Roof Over Our Heads,* Dublin, Stationery Office.

Central Statistics Office (2011) *Quarterly National Household Survey Quarter 3 2010, Health Status and Health Service Utilisation.* Updated, June 2012. Dublin: Stationery Office.

Central Statistics Office (2011) *Quarterly National Household Survey Voter Participation Quarter 2 2011.* Dublin: Stationery Office.

Central Statistics Office (2011) *Population and Migration Estimates.* Dublin: Stationery Office.

Central Statistics Office (2011) *Measuring Irelands Progress 2010.* Dublin: Stationary Office.

Central Statistics Office (2011) *Quarterly National Household Survey, Educational Attainment Thematic Report 2011.* Dublin: Stationery Office.

Central Statistics Office (2010) *Mortality Differentials in Ireland.* Dublin: Stationery Office.

Central Statistics Office (2010) *Statistical Yearbook of Ireland 2010.* Dublin: Stationery Office.

Central Statistics Office (2010) *National Disability Survey 2006 – Volume two. Dublin*: Stationery Office.

Central Statistics Office (2010) *Quarterly National Household Survey: Special Module on Carers Quarter 3 2009.* Dublin: Stationery Office.

Central Statistics Office (2010) *Survey on Income and Living Conditions 2009 Results.* Dublin: Stationery Office.

Central Statistics Office (2008) *National Disability Survey 2006 – First Results. Dublin*: Stationery Office.

Central Statistics Office (2006*) Industrial Earnings and Hours Worked.* Dublin: Stationery Office.

Central Statistics Office (2004*) Industrial Earnings and Hours Worked.* Dublin: Stationery Office.

Central Statistics Office (2004) *Quarterly National Household Survey: Special Module on Disability Quarter 1 2004.* Dublin: Stationery Office.

Central Statistics Office (various) *Quarterly National Household Survey.* Dublin: Stationery Office.

Central Statistics Office (various) *Survey on Income and Living Conditions Results.* Dublin: Stationery Office.

Central Statistics Office (various) *National Income and Expenditure Annual Results.* Dublin: Stationery Office.

Chambers of Commerce of Ireland (2004) *Local Authority Funding – Government in Denial,* Dublin: Chambers of Commerce Ireland.

Children's Rights Alliance (2013) *Report Card 2013.*Dublin: CRA.

Clark C.M.A. (2002) *The Basic Income Guarantee: ensuring progress and prosperity in the 21ˢᵗ century.* Dublin: Liffey Press and CORI Justice Commission.

Clark C.M.A. and Alford, H. (2010) *Rich and Poor: Rebalancing the economy.* London: CTS.

Coates, D., F. Kane, and Treadwell Shine, K. (2008) *Traveller Accommodation in Ireland Review of Policy and Practice (Housing Policy Discussion series 3).* Dublin: Centre for Housing Research.

Collins, M.L. (2013) 'Income Distribution, Pre-Distribution and Re-Distribution: latest data for the Republic of Ireland' *NERI Research inBrief no5,* August 2013. Dublin: NERI.

Collins, M.L. (2013) 'Income Taxes and Income Tax Options – a context for Budget 2014' *NERI Working Paper,* 2013/05. Dublin: NERI.

Collins M.L. (2011) "Taxation". In O'Hagan, J. and C. Newman (eds.) *The Economy of Ireland* (11th edition). Dublin: Gill and Macmillan.

Collins, M.L. (2011) *Establishing a Benchmark for Ireland's Social Welfare Payments.* Paper for Social Justice Ireland. Dublin: Social Justice Ireland.

Collins, M.L. (2006) "Poverty: Measurement, Trends and Future Directions", in Healy, S., B. Reynolds and M.L. Collins, *Social Policy in Ireland: Principles, Practice and Problems.* Dublin: Liffey Press.

Collins, M.L. (2004) "Taxation in Ireland: an overview" in B. Reynolds, and S. Healy (eds.) *A Fairer Tax System for a Fairer Ireland.* Dublin: CORI Justice Commission.

Collins, M.L., B. Mac Mahon, G. Weld and Thornton, R. (2012) 'A Minimum Income Standard for Ireland – a consensual budget standards study examining household types across the lifecycle – Studies'. *Public Policy No. 27,* Dublin: Policy Institute, Trinity College Dublin.

Collins, M.L. and Larragy, A. (2011) 'A Site Value Tax for Ireland: approach, design and implementation' *Trinity Economics Papers Working Paper 1911.* Dublin: Trinity College Dublin.

Collins, M.L. and Walsh, M. (2011) Tax Expenditures: Information and Revenue Forgone – the experience of Ireland. *Trinity Economic Papers Series*, 2011/12.

Collins, M.L. and Walsh, M. (2010) *Ireland's Tax Expenditure System: International Comparisons and a Reform Agenda – Studies in Public Policy No. 24*. Dublin: Policy Institute, Trinity College Dublin.

Collins, M.L. and Kavanagh, C. (2006) "The Changing Patterns of Income Distribution and Inequality in Ireland, 1973-2004", in Healy, S., B. Reynolds and M.L. Collins, *Social Policy in Ireland: Principles, Practice and Problems*. Dublin: Liffey Press.

Collins, M.L. and Kavanagh, C. (1998) "For Richer, For Poorer: The Changing Distribution of Household Income in Ireland, 1973-94", in Healy, S. and B. Reynolds, *Social Policy in Ireland: Principles, Practice and Problems*. Dublin: Oak Tree Press.

Comhar (2002) *Principles for Sustainable Development*. Dublin: Stationery Office.

Commission for Communications Regulation (2012) *The provision of telephony services under Universal Service Obligations.* Available from http://www.comreg.ie/publications/the_provision_of_telephony_services_under_un iversal_service_obligations_- _response_to_consultation__decision_and_decision_instrument.583.104149.p.html (14 March 2014)

Commission for Communications Regulation. (2011) *Provision of Universal Service by Eircom, Performance Data – Q3 2011 (1 July 2011 to 30 September 2011).* Available from www.comreg.ie/_fileupload/publications/ComReg1315.pdf (14 March 2014).

Commission of Investigation into the Banking Sector in Ireland (2011) *Misjudging Risk: Causes of the Systemic Banking Crisis in Ireland Report of the Commission of Investigation into the Banking Sector in Ireland*, Dublin: Stationery Office.

Commission on Taxation (2009) *Commission on Taxation Report 2009*. Dublin: Stationery Office.

Commission on Taxation (1982) *Commission on Taxation First Report*. Dublin: Stationery Office.

Considine, M. and Dukelow, F. (2009) *Irish Social Policy a Critical Introduction.* Dublin: Gill and Macmillan.

Costanza, R., Hart, M., Posner S. and Talberth, J. (2009) *Beyond GDP: The Need for New Measures of Progress*. Boston University: The Pardee Papers.

Coughlan, O. (2007) 'Irish Climate Change Policy from Kyoto to the Carbon Tax: a Two-level Game Analysis of the Interplay of Knowledge and Power'. *Irish Studies in International Affairs*, Vol. 18 (2007) 131–153.

Council of Europe (2011) *Council of Europe's charter of shared social responsibilities.* Brussels: Council of Europe.

Council of the European Union (2011) *Council Resolution on a renewed European Agenda for adult learning*. 20 December 2011. (2011/C 372/01)

Curtin, J and Hanrahan, G (2012) *Why Legislate? Designing a Climate Law for Ireland.* Dublin: The Institute of International and European Affairs.

Daft (2013) *Daft.ie rental report 2013 Q3*. Available at http://www.daft.ie/report/ronan-lyons-2013q3-rental (14 March 2014).

Dalal-Clayton, B. and Bass, S. (2002) *Sustainable development strategies: a resource book.* OECD: Paris.

Daly, H.E and Cobb, J.B. (1987) *For the Common Good: Redirecting the Economy toward Community, the Environment and a Sustainable Future.* Boston: Beacon Press.

De Grauwe, P. (1992) *The Economics of Monetary Integration*, Oxford: Oxford University Press.

De Grauwe, P. (1998) 'The Euro and Financial Crises', *Financial Times*, February 20.

Debt and Development Coalition Ireland (2014) *Submission to the Review of Ireland's Foreign Policy and External Relations.* Available from http://www.debtireland.org/news/2014/02/05/ddci-calls-for-financial-justice-to-be-prioritised/ (14 March 2014).

Delaney, A. (2011) *Árainn Mhór: A Case for Combining Social and Environmental Sustainability in an Irish Island Community.* Denmark: Aalborg University.

Delaney, A. (2012) *Donegal Islands Survival Plan 2012-2015*. Denmark: Aalborg University.

Department of Agriculture, Food and the Marine (2014) *The Rural Development Programme (RDP) 2014-2020 Consultation Paper.* Dublin: Department of Agriculture, Food and the Marine.

Department of Agriculture, Food and the Marine (2012) *Harnessing Our Ocean Wealth – An Integrated Marine Plan for Ireland.* Dublin: Stationery Office.

Department of Agriculture and Food (1999) *Ensuring the Future –A Strategy for Rural Development in Ireland.* Dublin: Stationery Office.

Department of An Taoiseach (2012) *National Reform Programme for Ireland 2012 Update.* Dublin: Stationery Office.

Department of An Taoiseach (2002) *Basic Income, A Green Paper.* Dublin: Stationery Office.

Department of An Taoiseach (2001) *Final Report of the Social Welfare Benchmarking and Indexation Group.* Dublin: Stationery Office.

Department of Communication, Energy, Natural Resources (2013) *Doing More with Digital, National Digital Strategy for Ireland, Phase 1 Digital Engagement.* Dublin: Stationery Office.

Department of Communications, Energy and Natural Resources (2012) *Delivering a Connected Society, A National Broadband Plan for Ireland.* Dublin: Stationery Office.

Department of Education and Skills (2014) *General Scheme Technological Universities Bill.* Dublin: Department of Education and Skills.

Department of Education and Skills (2014) *Review of Apprenticeship Training in Ireland.* Dublin: Department of Education and Skills.

Department of Education and Skills (2013) *Memorandum: Irish Students' Performance in PISA 2012.* Dublin: Department of Education and Skills.

Department of Education and Skills (2013) *Review of ALCES funded Adult Literacy Provision.* Dublin: Department of Education and Skills.

Department of Education and Sills (2012) Address by Minister for Education and Skills, Ruairí Quinn TD, at Nordic Education Seminar. Dublin: Department of Education and Skills.

Department of Education and Sills (2012) Speech by Minister for Education and Skills Ruairi Quinn, TD at the launch of his Junior Cycle Framework. Dublin: Department of Education and Skills.

Department of Education and Skills (2012) *A Framework for Junior Cycle.* Dublin: Stationery Office.

Department of Education and Skills (2012) Press Release *Minister Quinn protects frontline services in Budget 2013.* Dublin: Department of Education and Skills.

Department of Education and Skills (2012) *Report to the Minister for Education and Skills on the impact in terms of posts in Budget measures in relation to The Withdrawal form DEIS Band 1 and Band 2 Urban Primary Schools of Posts from Disadvantage Schemes pre-dating DEIS.* Dublin: Department of Education.

Department of Education and Sills (2011) *2011-2031, Twenty Years of Radical Reform* Speech by Minister for Education and Skills Ruairi Quinn, TD at the MacGill Summer School, Glenties, Co. Donegal.

Department of Education and Skills (2011) *An Evaluation of Planning Processes in DEIS Post-Primary Schools.* Dublin: Stationery Office.

Department of Education and Skills (2011) *An Evaluation of Planning Processes in DEIS Primary Schools.* Dublin: Stationery Office.

Department of Education and Skills (2011) *Comprehensive Review of Current Expenditure.* Dublin: Department of Education and Skills.

Department of Education and Skills (2011) *Information Note regarding main features of 2012 Estimates for Education and Skills Vote.* Available from http://www.education.ie/en/Press-Events/Press-Releases/2012-Press-Releases/PR2012-12-05.html (14 March 2014).

Department of Education and Skills (2011) *Literacy and Numeracy for Learning and Life, The National Strategy to Improve Literacy and Numeracy among Children and Young People 2011 – 2020.* Dublin: Stationery Office.

Department of Education and Skills (2011) *National Strategy for Higher Education to 2030.* Dublin: Stationery Office.

Department of Education and Skills (2009) *Policy Options for New Student Contributions in Higher Education: Report to Minister for Education and Science.* Dublin: Stationery Office.

Department of Environment, Community and Local Government (2014) *Report of the Working Group on Citizen Engagement with Local Government.* Dublin: Department of Environment, Community and Local Government.

Department of Environment, Community and Local Government (2013) *General Scheme of a Climate Action and Low Carbon Development Bill 2013.* Dublin: Stationery Office.

Department of Environment, Community and Local Government (2013) *Homeless Policy Statement* Dublin: Department of Environment, Community and Local Government.

Department of Environment Community and Local Government (2013) *Opportunities for All, The Public Library as a Catalyst for Economic, Social and Cultural Development- A strategy for public libraries 2013-2017.* Dublin: Department of Environment, Community and Local Government.

Department of Environment, Community and Local Government (2013) Latest Social and Affordable Housing Statistics http://www.environ.ie/en/Publications/StatisticsandRegularPublications/HousingStatistics/

Department of Environment, Community and Local Government (2013) *Resolving Unfinished Housing Developments, Annual progress report on actions to resolve unfinished housing developments.* Dublin: Stationery Office.

Department of Environment, Community and Local Government (2013) *Latest House Building and Private rented Statistics.* Available from http://www.environ.ie/en/Publications/StatisticsandRegularPublications/HousingStatistics/ (14 March 2014).

Department of Environment, Community and Local Government (2012) *Putting People First: Action Programme for Effective Local Government.* Dublin: Stationery Office.

Department of Environment, Community and Local Government (2012) *Final Report of the Local Government/Local Development Alignment Steering Group.* Dublin: Stationery Office.

Department of Environment, Community and Local Government (2012) *Our Sustainable Future. A Framework for Sustainable Development for Ireland.* Dublin: Stationery Office.

Department of Environment, Community and Local Government (2012) *Green Tenders – An Action Plan for Green Public Procurement* Dublin: Stationery Office.

Department of Environment, Community and Local Government (2012) *National Housing Strategy for People with Disability 2011-2016, National Implementation Framework.* Dublin: Stationery Office.

Department of Environment, Community and Local Government (2012) *Progress Report on Actions to Resolve Unfinished Housing Developments.* Dublin: Stationery Office.

Department of Environment, Community and Local Government (2011) *A Roadmap for Climate Policy and Legislation.* Dublin: Stationery Office.

Department of Environment, Community and Local Government (2011) *Review of National Climate Policy.* Dublin: Stationery Office.

Department of Environment, Community and Local Government (2011) *2011 National Housing Development Survey Summary Report.* Dublin: Stationery Office.

Department of Environment, Community and Local Government (2011) *Housing Policy Statement.* Dublin: Stationery Office.

Department of Environment, Community and Local Government (2011*) Press release announcing climate policy review.* Available from http://www.environ.ie/en/Environment/Atmosphere/ClimateChange/ClimatePolicyReview2011/News/MainBody,28331,en.htm (14 March 2014)

Department of Environment, Community and Local Government (various) *Annual Report and Annual Output Statement.* Dublin: Department of Environment, Community and Local Government.

Department of Environment Heritage and Local Government (2009) *Annual Housing Statistics Bulletin 2008.* Dublin: Department of Environment, Heritage and Local Government.

Department of Environment, Heritage and Local Government (2008) *Statement of Strategy.* Dublin: Department of Environment, Heritage and Local Government.

Department of Environment, Heritage and Local Government (2008) *Branching Out - Future Directions.* Dublin: Department of Environment, Heritage and Local Government.

Department of Environment Heritage and Local Government (2008) *The Way Home: A Strategy to Address Adult Homelessness in Ireland 2008 – 2013.* Dublin: Stationery Office.

Department of Environment, Heritage and Local Government (1998) *Branching Out - A New Public Library Service.* Dublin: Stationery Office.

Department of Finance (2014) *Revised Estimates for Public Services 2014.* Available from http://per.gov.ie/estpubexp2013/ (14 March 2014).

Department of Finance (2013) *Budget 2014.* Dublin: Stationery Office.

Department of Finance (2013) *Budget 2014: Medium Term Budgetary Framework.* Dublin: Stationery Office.

Department of Finance (2013) *April 2013 Stability Programme Update.* Dublin: Stationery Office.

Department of Finance (2013) *Ireland's International Tax Strategy.* Dublin: Stationery Office.

Department of Finance (2012) *Medium-Term Fiscal Statement November 2012.* Dublin: Stationery Office.

Department of Finance (2010) *National Recovery Plan.* Dublin: Stationery Office.

Department of Finance (2010) *Infrastructure Investment Priorities 2010-2016 A Financial Framework.* Dublin: Stationery Office.

Department of Finance (various*) Budget Documentation – various years.* Dublin: Stationery Office.

Department of Health (2014) *First Annual Progress Report - National Carers Strategy.* Dublin: Department of Health.

Department of Health (2013) *Health in Ireland: Key Trends, 2013.* Dublin: Department of Health.

Department of Health (2013) *Healthy Ireland: A Framework for Improved Health and Wellbeing, 2013-2015.* Dublin: Department of Health.

Department of Health (2013) *Minister Reilly announces free GP care for children aged 5 and under as part of Budget 2014; Progress made in achieving more for less but 2014 will be a challenging year for the health services.* Press Release, 15 October 2013. Available from http://www.dohc.ie/press/releases/2013/20131015.html (14 March 2014).

Department of Health (2012) *Annual Output Statement, 2013 for Health Group of Votes 38-39*. Dublin: Department of Health.

Department of Health (2012) *National Carers Strategy*. Department of Health.

Department of Health and Children. (2000) *National Children's Strategy, Our Children their Lives*. Dublin: Stationery Office.

Department of Justice and Equality (2014) *Immigration in Ireland – 2013 in Review*. Dublin: Department of Justice and Equality.

Department of Justice and Equality (2013) *Immigration in Ireland – 2012 in Review*. Dublin: Stationery Office.

Department of Public Expenditure and Reform (2014) *Focused Policy Assessment of the Rural Social Scheme*. Dublin: Department of Public Expenditure and Reform.

Department of Public Expenditure and Reform (2011) *Comprehensive Expenditure Report, 2012-14*. Dublin: Department of Public Expenditure and Reform.

Department of Social Protection (2013) *Mortgage Arrears Information and Advice Service: Review of the Independent Financial Advice Service*. Dublin: Department of Social Protection.

Department of Social Protection (2012) *Statistical Information on Social Welfare Services Report 2012*. Dublin: Department of Social Protection.

Department of Social Protection (2011) *Annual Report 2011*. Dublin: Department of Social Protection.

Department of Social Protection (2011) *Comprehensive Review of Expenditure*. Dublin: Department of Social Protection.

Department of Social, Community and Family Affairs (2000) *Supporting Voluntary Activity*. Dublin: Stationery Office.

Department of Transport, Tourism and Sport (2014) *Varadkar Announces €332M for Regional and Local Roads*, Press release 23 January. Available from http://www.dttas.ie/press-releases/2014/varadkar-announces-%E2%82%AC332m-regional-and-local-roads (14 March 2014).

Department of Transport, Tourism and Sport (2011) *Statement of Strategy 2011-2014*. Dublin: Department of Transport, Tourism and Sport.

Department of Transport (2009) *A Sustainable Transport Future A New Transport Policy for Ireland 2009 – 2020*. Dublin: Department of Transport.

Donnellan, T., Hanrahan, K., Hennessey, T., Kinsella, A., McKeon, M., Moran, B. and Thorne, F. (2013) *Outlook 2014: Economic Prospects for Agriculture*. Galway: Teagasc.

Dorgan, J. (2009) *Adult Literacy Policy: A Review for the National Adult Literacy Agency*. Dublin: National Adult Literacy Agency.

Dorgan, J.. (2009) *A Cost Benefit Analysis of Adult Literacy Training: Research Report, March 2009*. Dublin: National Adult Literacy Agency.

Drudy, P.J. (2006) "Housing in Ireland, Philosophy Problems and Policies", in Healy, S. Reynolds, B. and Collins, M. (eds) *Social Policy in Ireland: Principles, Practice, and Problems*. Liffey Press: Dublin.

Duffy, D., J. FitzGerald, K. Timoney and Byrne, D. (2013) *Quarterly Economic Commentary Winter 2013*. Dublin: ESRI.

Dunne, T. (2004) "Land Values as a Source of Local Government Finance" in B. Reynolds, and S. Healy (eds.) *A Fairer Tax System for a Fairer Ireland*. Dublin: CORI Justice Commission.

Economic and Social Research Institute (2003) *National Development Plan Mid-Term Review*. Dublin: ESRI.

Economist Intelligence Unit (2009) *European Green City Index Assessing the Environmental Impact of Europe's major Cities*. Munich: Siemens.

Economy for the Common Good (2013) *The Economic for the Common Good – An Economic Model for the Future*. Gemeinwohl Oekonomie. Available from http://www.gemeinwohl-oekonomie.org/en/content/downloads (14 February, 2014)

ECORYS (2010) *Study on Employment, Growth and Innovation in Rural Areas*. Rotterdam: ECORYS.

EEAC (2011) *The "Green Economy" Agenda in the context of SD Institutional framework for SD at National Level*. Brussels: EEAC.

Eivers, E. and Clerkin, A. (2012) *PIRLS and TIMSS 2011: Reading, Mathematics and Science Outcomes for Ireland*. Dublin: Education Research Centre.

Eivers, E. and Clerkin, A. (Ed.) (2013) *National Schools, International Contexts: Beyond the PIRLS and TIMSS test results*. Dublin: Education Research Centre.

Ellmers, B. and Hulova, D. (2013) *The New Debt Vulnerabilities, Why the Debt Crisis is Not Over*. Eurodad: Brussels.

Engineers Ireland (2012) *The State of Ireland 2012: A review of infrastructure in Ireland*. Dublin: Enterprise Ireland.

Enterprise Ireland (2013) *Annual Report and Accounts 2012*. Dublin: Enterprise Ireland.

Environmental Protection Agency (2013) *EPA Releases figures for key air pollutants*. Press release 26 February. Available from http://www.epa.ie/newsandevents/news/previous/2013/february/name,51293,en.html#.UyMV7IUw2E4 (14 March 2014).

Environmental Protection Agency (2013) *Governance and Climate Change: Making the Transition to an Adapted Ireland*. Wexford: EPA.

Environmental Protection Agency (2013) *Ireland's Greenhouse Gas Emission Projections 2012-2030*. Dublin: EPA.

Environmental Protection Agency (2013) *SIMBIOSYS: Sectoral Impacts on Biodiversity and Ecosystems Services*. Dublin: EPA.

Environmental Protection Agency (2013) *Winners and Losers: Climate Change Impacts on biodiversity in Ireland*. Wexford: EPA.

Environmental Protection Agency (2012) *The EU Emissions Trading Scheme. A review of the first six years of operation*. Dublin: EPA.

Environmental Protection Agency (2012) *A Year in Review – Highlights from 2011*. Dublin: EPA.

Environmental Protection Agency (2012) *A Focus on Urban Waste Water Discharges in Ireland.* Dublin: EPA.

Environmental Protection Agency (2012) *Ireland's Climate Strategy to 2020 and beyond - A contribution to the Programme for Development of National Climate Policy and Legislation 2012.* Dublin: EPA.

Environmental Protection Agency (2012*) Ireland's Environment 2012 - An Assessment.* Dublin: EPA.

Environmental Protection Agency (2012) *Ireland's Greenhouse Gas Emissions in 2011 - Key Highlights.* Dublin: EPA.

Environmental Protection Agency (2012) *Ireland's Greenhouse Gas Emissions Projections 2011-2020.* Dublin: EPA.

Environmental Protection Agency (2012) *National Waste Report 2010.* Dublin: EPA.

Environmental Protection Agency (2012) *Biodiversity Action Plan 2011-2013.* Dublin: EPA.

Environmental Protection Agency (2011) *Biochange: Biodiversity and Environmental Change: An Integrated Study Encompassing a Range of Scales, Taxa and Habitats.* Wexford: EPA.

Environmental Protection Agency (2010) *Environmental Protection Agency Biodiversity Action Plan.* Dublin: EPA.

Environmental Protection Agency (2010) *Water Quality in Ireland 2007-200.* Dublin: EPA.

ESRI (various) *Quarterly Economic Commentary (QEC).* Dublin: ESRI.

Eurostat (2012) *Population and Social Conditions, Asylum applicants and first instance decisions on asylum applications: third quarter 2012.* Brussels: Eurostat.

Eurofound (2012) *Third European Quality of Life Survey - Quality of Life in Europe: Impacts of the crisis.* Publications Office of the European Union: Luxembourg.

European Centre for the Development of Vocational Training (2009) *Future skill supply in Europe: Medium-term forecast up to 2020 - synthesis report.* Luxembourg: European Centre for the Development of Vocational Training.

European Commission (2014) *Social Europe: Many ways, one objective - Annual Report of the Social Protection Committee on the social situation in the European Union.* Luxembourg: Publications Office of the European Union.

European Commission (2014) *A Policy Framework for Climate and Energy in the period 2020-2030.* Brussels: European Commission.

European Commission (2013) *A Decent Life for All: Ending Poverty and Giving the World a Sustainable Future.* Brussels: European Commission.

European Commission (2013) *Digital Agenda Scoreboard 2013-1. SWD (2013) 217 Final.* Brussels: European Commission.

European Commission (2013) 'Vade mecum on the Stability and Growth Pact', Occasional Papers, *European Economy,* 151. Brussels: European Commission.

European Commission (2013) Economic Adjustment Programme for Ireland Autumn 2013 Review, *European Economy, Occasional Papers, 167.* Brussels: European Commission.

European Commission (2013) *Proposal for a Council Directive implementing enhanced cooperation in the area of FTT*. Brussels: European Commission.

European Commission (2012) *A View of Employment, Growth and Innovation in Rural Areas*. SWD 2012/44. Brussels: European Commission.

European Commission (2012) *The CAP towards 2020: Meeting the food, natural resources and territorial challenges of the future*. COM(2010) 672. Brussels: European Commission.

European Commission (2012) *Current account surpluses in the EU: European Economy 9*. Brussels: European Commission.

European Commission (2012) *The 2012 Ageing Report: Economic and budgetary projections for the EU27 Member States (2010-2060)*. Brussels, European Commission.

European Commission (2011) A *resource-efficient Europe – Flagship initiative under the Europe 2020 Strategy*. Brussels: European Commission.

European Commission (2011) *Early Childhood Education and Care: Providing all our children with the best start for the world of tomorrow*. Brussels: European Commission.

European Commission (2011) *Our life insurance, our natural capital: an EU biodiversity strategy to 2020*. Brussels: European Commission.

European Commission (2011) *Roadmap to a Resource Efficient Europe. COM(2011) 571*. Brussels: European Commission.

European Commission (2011) *Strategic framework for European cooperation in education and training (ET 2020)*. Brussels: Brussels: European Commission.

European Commission (2011) *The Social Dimension of the Europe 2020 Strategy A report of the Social Protection Committee*. Luxembourg: Publications Office of the European Union.

European Commission (2011) *Commission Staff Working Paper Accompanying the White Paper - Roadmap to a Single European Transport Area –Towards a competitive and resource efficient transport system*. Brussels: European Commission.

European Commission (2010) *Digital Agenda for Europe, Digital Scorecard*. Brussels: European Commission.

European Commission (2010) *Eurobarometer 74 Autumn 2010 Report*. Brussels: European Commission.

European Commission (2010) *Europe 2020: A strategy for smart, sustainable and inclusive growth*. Brussels: European Commission.

European Commission (2008) *Staff working document - Digital Literacy Report: a review for the i2010 eInclusion Initiative Digital Literacy: High-Level Expert Group Recommendations*. Brussels: European Commission.

European Network for Rural Development (2010) *Climate Change and Renewable Energy measures in EU RDPs 2007-2013 Member State profile - Ireland*. Available from http://enrd.ec.europa.eu/themes/environment/climate-change/en/climate-change_en.cfm (14 March 2014).

Eurostat (2013) *Taxation Trends in the European Union*. Luxembourg: Eurostat.

Eurostat (2013) *Internet access and use in 2013 More than 60% of individuals in the EU28 use the internet daily,* News release 18 December. Available from http://europa.eu/rapid/press-release_STAT-13-199_en.htm (14 March 2014).

Eurostat (2012) *'In 2010, 17% of employees in the EU were low-wage earners'* Statistics in Focus 48/2012 Population and Social Conditions. Luxembourg: Eurostat.

Eurostat (2008) Satellite accounts sharpen the focus. *Sigma – The bulletin of European Statistics, 2008.03.* Luxembourg: Eurostat.

Eurostat (2008) *Taxation Trends in the European Union.* Luxembourg: Eurostat.

Eurydice Network (2012) *Key Data on Education in Europe 2012.* Brussels: European Commission.

Expert Group on Future Skills Needs (2007) *Tomorrow's Skills: Towards a National Skills Strategy. 5th Report.* Dublin: Expert Group on Future Skills Needs.

Expert Group on Future Skills Needs (2012) *Addressing High Level ICT Skills Recruitment Needs Research Findings.* Dublin: Expert Group on Future Skills Needs.

Farrell, C., H. McAvoy, J. Wilde and Combat Poverty Agency (2008) *Tackling Health Inequalities an All-Ireland Approach to Social Determinants,* Combat Poverty Agency/Institute of Public Health: Dublin.

Financial Inclusion Working Group (2013) *Report of the Financial Inclusion Working Group on the Standard Bank Account pilot project June 2013 (Updated November 2013).* Dublin: Department of Finance.

Flannery, D. and O'Donoghue, C. (2011) 'The Life Cycle Impact of Alternative Higher Education Finance Systems in Ireland'. *The Economic and Social Review, Vol. 42, No.3. (Autumn, 2011):pp.237-270* Dublin: UCD.

Forfas and National Competitiveness Council (2012) *Ireland's Competitiveness Scorecard 2012.* Dublin: Stationery Office.

Forfás and National Competitiveness Council (2011) *Ireland's Competitiveness Challenge 2011.* Dublin: Stationery Office.

Forfás (2013) *Annual Employment Survey 2012.* Dublin: Forfás.

Forfas (2011) *Ireland's Advanced Broadband Performance and Policy Priorities.* Dublin: Forfás.

Friedman, M. (1951) 'Neo-Liberalism and its Prospects', *Farmland*, February 17, pp. 89-93.

Fuentes-Nieva, R. and Galasso, N. (2014) *Working for the Few.* Oxfam International: Oxford.

Glynn, I., Kelly, T., and Mac Éinrí, P. (2013) *Irish Emigration in an Age of Austerity.* Cork: Emgire.

Godley, W. (1992) 'Maastricht and all that', *London Review of Books*, Vol. 14, No. 19.

Goldberg, F.T., L.L. Batchelder and P.R. Orszag (2006) *Reforming Tax Incentives into Uniform Refundable Tax Credits.* Washington: Brookings.

Government of Ireland (2013) *A Strategy for Growth: Medium Term Economic Strategy, 2014-2020.* Stationary Office: Dublin.

Government of Ireland (2013) *Stability Programme Update.* Dublin: Stationery Office.

Government of Ireland (2012) *Programme for Government and National Recovery 2011-2016*. Dublin: Stationery Office.

Government of Ireland (2012) *Ireland's National Reform Programme 2012 – Update*. Dublin: Stationery Office.

Government of Ireland (2011) *Towards Recovery: Programme for a National Government 2011-2016*. Dublin: Stationery Office.

Government of Ireland (2007) *National Action Plan for Social Inclusion 2007-2016*. Dublin: Stationery Office.

Government of Ireland (2007) *National Climate Change Strategy*. Dublin: Stationery Office.

Government of Ireland (various) *Action Plan for Jobs*. Dublin: Stationery Office.

Government of Ireland (various) *Jobs Initiative*. Dublin: Stationery Office.

Government of Ireland (various) *Pathways to Work*. Dublin: Stationery Office.

Growing Up in Ireland (2013) *Growing Up in Ireland - Key Findings: Infant Cohort (at 5 years) No. 3 Well-being, play and diet among five-year-olds*. Dublin: ESRI/TCD.

Gutmann, A. and Thompson, D. (2004) *Why Deliberative Democracy?*. Princeton University Press: Princeton.

H.M. Treasury (2004) *Financial Statement and Budget Report, 2004*. London: H.M. Treasury.

Hämäläinen, T. (2013) *Towards a Sustainable Well-being Society version 1.0*. Helsinki: Sitra.

Health Insurance Authority (2013) *Newsletter: December 2013 Edition*. Available from www.hia.ie/assets/files/publications/Press_Releases/Dec_Newsletter_final_2013.pdf (14 March 2014).

Health Service Executive (2014) *Mental Health Divisional Operational Plan*. Dublin: HSE.

Health Service Executive (2013) *National Performance Assurance Report*. Dublin: HSE.

Health Service Executive (2013) *National Service Plan, 2014*. Dublin: HSE.

Health Service Executive (2012) *December 2012, Performance Report, National Service Plan, 2012*. Dublin: HSE.

Health Service Executive (2012) *December 2012 Supplementary Report, National Service Plan, 2012*. Dublin: HSE.

Health Service Executive (2011) *December 2011 Performance Report on NSP, 2011*. Dublin: HSE.

Health Service Executive (2010) *Annual Report and Financial Statement, 2010*. Dublin: HSE.

Health Service Executive (2010) *Performance Report on NSP, 2010*. Dublin: HSE.

Health Service Executive (2009) *Performance Report on NSP 2009*. Dublin: HSE.

Health Service Executive (2008) *Performance Monitoring Report, National Service Plan 2008*. Dublin: HSE.

Healy, S. and Reynolds, B. (2011) 'Sharing Responsibility and Shaping the Future: Why and How?' in Healy. S. and Reynolds, B. eds. *Sharing Responsibility and Shaping the Future*. Dublin: Social Justice Ireland.

Healy, S and Reynolds, B. (2003) "Christian Critique of Economic Policy and Practice" in Mackey, J.P. Mackey and McDonagh, E. eds. *Religion and Politics in Ireland at the turn of the millennium*. Dublin: Columba Press.

Healy, S. and Collins, M.L. (2006) "Work, Employment and Unemployment", in Healy, S., B. Reynolds and M.L. Collins eds. *Social Policy in Ireland: Principles, Practice and Problems*. Dublin: Liffey Press.

Healy, S., M. Murphy, S. Ward and Reynolds, B. (2012) '*Basic Income – Why and How in Difficult Economic Times: Financing a BI in Ireland*' Paper to the BIEN Congress 2012, Munich.

Healy, S. and Reynolds, B. (Eds.). (2009) *Beyond GDP: What is prosperity and how should it be measured?*. Dublin: Social Justice Ireland.

Healy, T. (2013) *Banks, Governments & Citizens*. NERI inBrief Research.

Hennessy, T., Buckley, C., Dillon, E., Donnellan, T., Hanrahan, K., Moran, B., and Ryan, M. (2013) *Measuring Farm Level Sustainability with the Teagasc National Farm Survey*. Galway: Teagasc.

Higgins, M. D. (2013) '*Toward an ethical economy*', Public Lecture 11th September. Available from http://www.president.ie/uncategorized/ethics-for-all-public-lecture-series-toward-an-ethical-economy/ (14 March 2014).

Higher Education Authority (2013) *Completing the Landscape Process for Irish Higher Education*. Dublin: HEA.

Higher Education Authority (2013) *What Do Graduates Do? The Class of 2012*. Dublin: HEA.

Higher Education Authority (2012) *10/11 Higher Education Key Facts and Figures*. Dublin: HEA.

Higher Education Authority (2012) *Springboard 2011 First Stage Evaluation*. Dublin: HEA.

Higher Education Authority (2012) *Towards a Future Higher Education Landscape*. Dublin: HEA.

Higher Education Authority (2011) *Report on the Social and Living Conditions of Higher Education Students in Ireland 2009/2010*. Dublin: HEA.

Higher Education Authority (2010) *A Study of Progression in Irish Higher Education*. Dublin: HEA.

Higher Education Authority (2010) *National Plan for Equity of Access to Higher Education 2008-2013 Mid-Term Review*. Dublin: HEA.

Higher Education Authority (2010) *Review of Student Charge*. Dublin: HEA.

Hoegen, M (2009) *Statistics and the quality of life. Measuring progress – a world beyond GDP*. Bonn: InWent.

Homelessness Oversight Group (2013) *Homelessness Oversight Group 1st Report 2013*. Dublin: Department of Environment, Community and Local Government.

Honohan, P. (2010) *The Irish Banking Crisis: Regulatory and Banking Stability, 2003-2008*. Dublin: Stationery Office.

Housing Agency (2013) *Review of Housing Grants for Older People and People with a Disability*. Dublin: Housing Agency.

Housing Agency (2013) *Summary of Social Housing Assessments 2013 Key Findings*. Dublin: Housing Agency.

Housing Agency (2011) *Housing Needs Assessment 2011*. Dublin: Housing Agency.

Houston, M. (2013) 'Cuts Post Additional Threats to Safe Patient Care'. *Irish Times*. 19 December 2013. Available from http://www.irishtimes.com/news/health/cuts-pose-additional-threat-to-delivery-of-safe-patient-care-1.1632329 (14 March 2014).

Human Development Report (2013) *The Rise of the South: Human Progress in a Diverse World*. New York: UN Development Programme.

Hyland, A. (2011) *Entry to Higher Education in Ireland in the 21st Century*. (Discussion Paper for the NCCA/HEA Seminar 2011) Dublin: HEA.
Irish Council for Social Housing (2013) *Social Housing Newsletter of the Irish Council for Social Housing Winter 2013*. Dublin: Irish Council for Social Housing.

Irish Council for Social Housing (2013) *Scale of waiting list figures show increased supply of new social housing essential to avoid supply crisis- Housing Federation Warns*. Press release 18 December. Available from http://www.icsh.ie/content/icsh-news/scale-waiting-list-figures-show-increased-supply-new-social-housing-essential (14 March 2014).

Irish Council for Social Housing (2013) *Press Release-Non Profit housing associations could help find homes for 5,000 families*. Press release 20 November. Available from http://www.icsh.ie/content/icsh-news/press-release-non-profit-housing-associations-could-help-find-homes-5000-families (14 March 2014).

IDA Ireland (2013) *IDA Ireland Annual Report and Accounts 2012*. Dublin: IDA Ireland.

IMD (2007) *IMD World Competitiveness Yearbook*. Lausanne: IMD.

Indecon (2005) *Indecon Review of Local Government Funding – Report commissioned by the Minister for Environment, Heritage and Local Government*. Dublin: Stationery Office.

Indecon (2010) *Assessment of Economic Impact of Sports in Ireland*. Dublin: Stationery Office.

Institute for Public Health (2007) *Fuel Poverty and Health*. Dublin: IPH.

Inter-Departmental Mortgage Arrears Working Group (2011) *Report of the Inter-Departmental Mortgage Arrears Working Group*. Dublin: Department of Finance.

Intergovernmental Panel on Climate Change (2013) *Climate Change 2013: The Physical Science Basis*. Switzerland: IPCC.

International Energy Agency (2011) *World Energy Outlook 2011*. Paris: International Energy Agency.

International Monetary Fund (2013) *Greece: Ex Post Evaluation of Exceptional Access under the 2010 Stand-By Arrangement*. Washington DC: International Monetary Fund.

International Monetary Fund (2013) *Ireland: Twelfth Review under the Extended Arrangement and Proposal for Post-Program Monitoring*. Washington DC: International Monetary Fund.

International Monetary Fund (2012) *Ireland: Eighth Review Under the Extended Arrangement; Staff Report; Staff Supplements; and Press Release on the Executive Board discussion.* Washington DC: International Monetary Fund.

International Monetary Fund (2010) *Ireland: Request for an Extended Arrangement—Staff Report; Staff Supplement; Staff Statement; and Press Release on the Executive Board Discussion.* Washington DC: International Monetary Fund.

International Monetary Fund (2008) *World Economic Outlook.* Washington DC: IMF.

International Monetary Fund (2004) *World Economic Outlook.* Washington DC: IMF.

Department of Foreign Affairs and Trade (2013) *One World, One Future: Ireland's Policy for International Development.* Dublin: Stationery Office.

Irish Aid (2012) *Annual Report 2012.* Dublin: Department of Foreign Affairs and Trade.

Irish Fiscal Advisory Council (2012) *Fiscal Assessment Report September 2012.* Dublin: Stationery Office.

Irish Sports Council (2013) *Irish Sports Monitor 2013 Interim results from first six months of data collection.* Available from http://www.irishsportscouncil.ie/Research/The_Irish_Sports_Monitor/Irish-Sports-Monitor-2013.pdf (14 March 2014).

Irish Sports Council (2009) *Building Sport for Life: The Next Phase The Irish Sports Council's Strategy 2009-2011.* Dublin: Irish Sports Council.

Irish Sports Council (2011) *Irish Sports Monitor 2011 Annual Report.*Dublin: Irish Sports Council.

Joint Oireachtas Committee on Arts, Sport, Tourism, Community, Rural and Gaeltacht Affairs (2005) *Volunteers and Volunteering in Ireland.* Dublin: Stationery Office.

Joyce, C. and Quinn, E. (2014) *The Organisation of Facilities for Asylum Seekers in Ireland.* Dublin: European Migration Network/ESRI.

Kelly, E., S. McGuinness and O'Connell, P. (2012) 'Literacy and Numeracy Difficulties in the Irish Workplace: Impact on Earnings and Training Expenditure'. *Research Series Number 27,* September 2012. Dublin: ESRI.

Kelly, E., S. McGuinness and O'Connell, P. (2012) 'Literacy, Numeracy and Activation among the Unemployed'. *Research Series Number 25,* June 2012. Dublin: ESRI.

Kelly, R. and McQuinn, K. (2013) 'On the hook for impaired bank lending: Do sovereign-bank inter-linkages affect the fiscal multiplier?', *Research Technical Paper, 1/RT/13.*

Kitchen, R. Gleeson, J. Keaveney, K. & O' Callaghan, C. (2010) *A Haunted Landscape: Housing and Ghost Estates in Post Celtic Tiger Ireland Working Paper Series no. 59.* National Institute for Regional and Spatial Analysis: NUI Maynooth.

Krugman, P (1994) *Peddling Prosperity.* London: W.W Norton & Company.

Larragy, A. (2013). 'A Universal Pension for Ireland', *Social Justice Ireland Policy Research Series,* September 2013. Dublin: Social Justice Ireland.

Leahy, A., M. Murphy, S. Mallon and Healy, S. (2012) *Ireland and the Europe 2020 Strategy – Employment, Education and Poverty.* Dublin: Social Justice Ireland.

Leahy, E., S. Lyons and Tol, R. (2010) 'The Distributional Effects of Value Added Tax in Ireland' *ESRI Working Paper 366*. Dublin: ESRI.

Legal Aid Board (various) *Annual Reports*. Dublin: Legal Aid Board.

Local Government Management Agency (2011) *Public Library Authority Statistics: Actuals 2011*. Dublin: Department of Environment, Community and Local Government.

Lucas, K., Grosvenor, T. and Simpson, R. (2001) *Transport, the Environment and Social exclusion*. Joseph Rowntree Foundation: York.

Lunn, P. and Layte, R. (2009) *The Irish Sports Monitor Third Annual Report*. Dublin: Irish Sports Council.

MacDonald, L. (2012) *A New Chapter Public Library Services in the 21st Century*. Dunfermline: Carnegie UK Trust.
Martin, M.O., I.V.S. Mullis, P. Foy, P., and Stanco, G.M. (2012) *TIMSS 2011 International Results in Science*. Chestnut Hill, MA: TIMSS & PIRLS International Study Center, Boston College.

McDaid, S. and Cullen, K. (2008) *ICT accessibility and social inclusion of people with disabilities and older people in Ireland: The economic and business dimensions*. Dublin: NCBI.

McCoy, S, Byrne, D, O'Connell, P, Kelly, E and Doherty, C. (2010) *Hidden Disadvantage? A Study on the Low Participation in Higher Education by the Non-Manual Group*. Dublin: HEA. McDonagh, J., Varley,T., and Shortall, S. (Eds.). (2009) *A living countryside?: the politics of sustainable development in rural Ireland*. Ashgate: England.

McGee, Harry (2012) 'IFSC lobby group powerful in shaping policy', *The Irish Times*, October 8, 2012.
McGinnity, F. and Russell, H. (2008) *Gender Inequalities in Time*. Dublin: ESRI.

McGrath, B., Rogers, M. and Gilligan, R. (2010) *Young People and Public libraries in Ireland: Issues and Opportunities*. Department of Health and Children: Dublin.

McGuinness, S., A. Bergin, E. Kelly, S. McCoy, E. Smyth and Timoney, K. (2012) 'A Study of Future Demand for Higher Education in Ireland'. *Research Series Number 30*, December 2012. Dublin: ESRI.

Mental Health Commission (2009) *From Vision to Action? An Analysis of the Implementation of A Vision for Change*. Dublin: Mental Health Commission.

Meredith, D. and Van Egeraat, C. (2013) 'Revisiting the National Spatial Strategy ten years on', *IPA Administration Journal*, 60 (3) pp. 3-9. Dublin: IPA.

Morrone, A. (2009) "The OECD Global Project on Measuring Progress and the challenge of assessing and measuring trust" in Reynolds, B. and Healy S. (eds.) *Beyond GDP: what is progress and how should it be measured*. Dublin: Social Justice Ireland.

Mullis, I.V.S., M.O. Martin, P. Foy, and Arora, A. (2012) *TIMSS 2011 International Results in Mathematics*. Chestnut Hill, MA: TIMSS & PIRLS International Study Center, Boston College. Mullis, I.V.S., M.O. Martin, P. Foy, and Drucker, K.T. (2012) *PIRLS 2011 International Results in Reading*. Chestnut Hill, MA: TIMSS & PIRLS International Study Center, Boston College. National Anti-Poverty Strategy Review (2002) *Building an Inclusive Society*. Dublin: Stationery Office.

National Anti-Poverty Strategy (1997) *Sharing in Progress*. Dublin: Stationery Office.

National Competitiveness Council (2012) *Irelands Competitiveness Scorecard 2012*. Dublin: NCC.

National Disability Authority (2006) *Indecon Report on the Cost of a Disability*. Dublin: NDA.

National Economic and Social Council (2012) *Ireland and the Climate Change Challenge: Connecting 'How Much' with 'How To'. Final Report of the NESC Secretariat to the Department of Environment, Community and Local Government*. Dublin: NESC.

National Economic and Social Forum (2006) *Improving the Delivery of Quality Public Services*. Dublin: Stationery Office.

National Office for Suicide Prevention (2013) *Annual Report, 2012*. Dublin: HSE.

National Office for Suicide Prevention (2011) *Annual Report 2010*. Dublin: HSE.

National Suicide Research Foundation (2013) *Statistics: Suicides in Republic of Ireland, 2001-2011*. Available from http://nsrf.ie/suicides-in-republic-of-ireland-from-2001-2011/ (29 January 2014).

National Transport Authority (2013) *Consideration of applications to increase monthly and annual fares from Dublin Bus, Bus Éireann and Iarnród Éireann for 2014*. Dublin: NTA.

National Transport Authority (2013) *Strengthening the Connections in Rural Ireland: Plans for Restructuring the Rural Transport Programme*. Dublin: NTA.

NERI (2013) *Quarterly Economic Facts – Winter 2013*. Dublin: NERI.

Niestroy, I. (2005) *Sustaining Sustainability*. Brussels: EEAC

Nolan, B. (2006) "The EU's Social Inclusion Indicators and Their Implications for Ireland", in Healy, S., B. Reynolds and M.L. Collins eds., *Social Policy in Ireland: Principles, Practice and Problems*. Dublin: Liffey Press.

O'Hara, P. (2013) 'What Future for the Regions?'. In: Healy, S. and Reynolds, B. eds. *A Future worth Living For: Sustainable Foundations and Frameworks*. Dublin: Social Justice Ireland.

O'Siochru, E. (2004) "Land Value Tax: unfinished business" in B. Reynolds, and S. Healy eds. *A Fairer Tax System for a Fairer Ireland*. Dublin: CORI Justice Commission.

O'Siochru, E. (Ed.). (2012) *The Fair Tax*. Dublin: Smart Taxes Network.

O'Sullivan, E. (2008) *Researching Homelessness in Ireland Explanations, Themes and Approaches* in, Downey, D. (eds) *Perspectives on Irish Homelessness, Past Present and Future*. Dublin: The Homeless Agency.

O'Toole, F. and N. Cahill (2006) "Taxation Policy and Reform", in Healy, S., B. Reynolds and M.L. Collins eds., *Social Policy in Ireland: Principles, Practice and Problems*. Dublin: Liffey Press.

O'Brien, D. (2013) 'Ireland ill-served as President becomes increasingly partisan and political', *The Irish Times*, 20th September 2013. Available from http://www.irishtimes.com/business/economy/ireland/ireland-ill-served-as-president-becomes-increasingly-partisan-and-political-1.1533632 (14 March 2014).

OECD (2013) *Education at a Glance 2013: OECD Indicators*. Paris: OECD Publishing.
OECD (2013) *Health at a Glance, 2013. OECD Indicators*. Paris: OECD Publishing.

OECD (2013) *Health Statistics 2013, online database* Available from http://dx.doi.org/10.1787/health-data-en (accessed 9 February 2014).

OECD (2013) *OECD Health Data, 2013. How Does Ireland Compare?* Paris: OECD Publishing.

OECD (2013) *OECD Skills Outlook 2013: First Results from the Survey of Adult Skills.* Paris: OECD Publishing

OECD (2013) *PISA 2012 Results: Ireland.* Paris: OECD Publishing

OECD (2013) *Action Plan on Base Erosion and Profit Shifting (BEPS).* Paris: OECD.

OECD (2013) *Revenue Statistics*. Paris: OECD.

OECD (2012) *Equity and Quality in Education: Supporting Disadvantaged Students and Schools Spotlight on Ireland.* Paris: OECD.

OECD (2012) *Health at a Glance, Europe 2012.* Paris: OECD Publishing.

OECD (2011) *How's Life? Measuring well-being.* Paris: OECD Publishing

OECD (2011) *OECD Factbook 2011: Economic, Environmental and Social Statistics.* Paris: OECD.

OECD (2008) *Economic Survey of Ireland.* Paris: OECD.

OECD (2006) *The new rural paradigm - policies and governance.* Paris: OECD.

OECD (2004) *OECD Factbook.* Paris: OECD.

OECD (2000) *Literacy in the Information Age: Final Report of the International Adult Literacy Survey.* Paris: OECD.

Office of Minister for Children and Youth Affairs (2010) *State of the Nation's Children Ireland 2010.* Dublin: Stationery Office.

Office of Social Inclusion (2008) *Guidelines for Poverty Impact Assessment, March 2008.* Dublin: Department of Social Protection.

Office of the Refugee Applications Commissioner (2013) *Statistical Report December 2013.* Dublin: Office of the Refugee Applications Commissioner.

Office of the Refugee Applications Commissioner (2012) *Statistical Report December 2012.* Dublin: Office of the Refugee Applications Commissioner.

Office of the United Nations High Commissioner for Refugees (2013) *Global Trends 2012.* New York: United Nations.

Office of the United Nations High Commissioner for Refugees (2013) *Statistical Yearbook 2012, 12th Edition.* New York: United Nations.

Office of the United Nations High Commissioner for Refugees (2012) *Global Trends 2011.* New York: United Nations.

Oxfam (2013) *Media Brief 07 : Inequality massively undermining progress on poverty goals.* London: Oxfam.

Pavee Point (2011) *Irish Travellers and Roma, Shadow Report, A response to Ireland's Third and Fourth Report on the International Convention on the Elimination of all Forms of Racial Discrimination (CERD).* Dublin: Pavee Point Travellers Centre.

Perkins, R., G. Sheil, B. Merriman, J. Cosgrave and Moran, G. (2013) *Learning for Life: The Achievements of 15 year olds in Ireland on Mathematics, Reading Literacy and Science in PISA 2012*. Dublin: Educational Research Centre.

Pfizer (2012) *The 2012 Pfizer Health Index*. Pfizer Healthcare Ireland.

Pickett, K and Wilkinson, R. (2009) *The Spirit Level: Why Greater Equality Makes Societies Stronger*, London: Bloomsbery Press.

Pope Francis (2013) *Evangelii Gaudium, Exhortation on the Joy of the Gospel*. Vatican City: Rome.

Pope John Paul II. (1981) *Laborum Exercens, Encyclical Letter on Human Work*. Catholic Truth Society: London.

Pope Paul VI. (1967) *Populorum Progressio*. Vatican City: Rome.

Private Residential Tenancy Board (2012) *Annual Report and Accounts 2012*. Dublin: PRTB.

Private Residential Tenancy Board (2010) *Annual Report and Accounts 2010*. Dublin: PRTB.

Public Health Alliance for the Island of Ireland (2007) *Health inequalities on the Island of Ireland – the facts, the causes, the remedies*. Dublin: PHAI.

Public Health Alliance for the Island of Ireland (2004) *Health in Ireland – an Unequal State*. Dublin: PHAI.

Rapple, C. (2004) "Refundable Tax Credits" in B. Reynolds, and S. Healy eds. *A Fairer Tax System for a Fairer Ireland*. Dublin: CORI Justice Commission.

Reception and Integration Agency (2012) *Monthly Statistics Report November 2012*. Dublin: Reception and Integration Agency.

Reception and Integration Agency (2013) *Monthly Statistics Report December 2013*. Dublin: Reception and Integration Agency.

Regling, K. and Watson, M. (2010) *A Preliminary Report into the Sources of Ireland's Banking Crisis*. Dublin: Stationery Office.

Repetto, R., W. Magrath, M. Wells, C. Beer and Rossini, F. (1989) *Wasting Assets, Natural Resources in the National Income Accounts*. Washington: World Resources Institute.

Revenue Commissioners (2012) *Statistical Report 2011*. Dublin: Stationery Office.

Revenue Commissioners (various) *Analysis of High Income Individuals' Restriction*. Dublin: Stationery Office.

Revenue Commissioners (various) *Effective Tax Rates for High Earning Individuals*. Dublin: Stationery Office.

Robertson, J. (2007) *The New Economics of Sustainable Development report to the European Commission*. Brussels: European Commission.

Russell, H. Maitre, B. and Donnelly, N. (2011) *Financial Exclusion and Over-indebtedness in Irish Households*. Dublin: Department of Community, Equality and Gaeltacht Affairs.

Safefood (2011) *Food on a Low Income*. Safefood.

Schwab, K. (Ed.). (2013) *Global Competitiveness Report 2013-14*. Geneva: World Economic Forum.

Schwab, K. (Ed.). (2011) *Global Competitiveness Report 2011-12*. Geneva: World Economic Forum.

Schwab, K. and Porter, M. (Eds.). (2008) *Global Competitiveness Report 2008-09*. Geneva: World Economic Forum.

Schwab, K. and Porter, M. (Eds.). (2003) *Global Competitiveness Report 2003-04*. Geneva: World Economic Forum.

Scott S. and Eakins, J. (2002) *Distributive effects of carbon taxes,* paper presented to ESRI conference entitled "The sky's the limit: efficient and fair policies on global warming" December: Dublin.

Shucksmith, M. (2012) *Future Directions in Rural Development?* Dunfermline: Carnegie UK Trust.

Simonazii, A., Ginzburg, A., and Nocella, G. (2013) 'Economic Relations between Germany and southern Europe', *Cambridge Journal of Economics, 37* (3) pp653-675.

Social Justice Ireland (2010) *Building a Fairer Taxation System: The Working Poor and the Cost of Refundable Tax Credits*. Dublin: Social Justice Ireland.

Social Justice Ireland (2013) '*What Would Real Recovery Look Like*', *Socio-Economic Review, 2013*. Dublin: Social Justice Ireland.

Social Justice Ireland (2013) *Analysis and Critique of Budget 2014*. Dublin: Social Justice Ireland.

Social Justice Ireland (2013) *Policy Briefing: Budget Choices*. Dublin: Social Justice Ireland. Society of St. Vincent de Paul, Combat Poverty Agency and Crosscare (2004) *Food Poverty and Policy*. Dublin: Combat Poverty Agency.

Stahel, W. (2010) *The Performance Economy*. London: Palgrave-Macmillan.

Stedman Jones, D. (2012) *Masters of the Universe: Hayek, Friedman, and the Birth of Neoliberal Politics*, Princeton University Press: Princeton.

Steering Group on Financial Inclusion (2011) *Strategy for Financial Inclusion Final Report*.

Stiglitz Commission (2008) *Report by the Commission on the Measurement of Economic Performance and Social Progress*. Paris.

Stiglitz, J. (2013) *The Price of Inequality: How Today's Divided Society Endangers Our Future*, New York: W. W. Norton & Company.

Stockholm International Peace Research Institute (2013) *Trends in International Arms Transfers, 2013*. Available from http://portal.sipri.org/publications/pages/transfer/splash (14 March 2014).

Sustainable Energy Authority of Ireland (2013) *Energy in Ireland Key Statistics 2013*. Dublin: SEAI.

Sweeney, P. (2004) "Corporation Tax: leading the race to the bottom" in Reynolds, B. and Healy, S. eds. *A Fairer Tax System for a Fairer Ireland*. Dublin: CORI Justice Commission. Szélsky, István P., and Miroslav, F. (2013) 'Social developments in Ireland at the time of fiscal consolidation and challenges ahead', in Reynolds, B. and Healy, S. cds.*A Future Worth Living For: Sustainable Foundations and Frameworks*. Social Justice Ireland: Dublin.

United Nations Programme on HIV/AIDS (2013) *UN AIDS Global Report 2013*. New York: United Nations.

UNEP (2011) *Decoupling natural resource use and environmental impacts from economic growth, A Report of the Working Group on Decoupling to the International Resource Panel.* Paris: UNEP.

UNEP (2011) *Keeping track of our changing environment from RIO to RIO +20 1992-2012.* Nairobi: UNEP.

UNEP (2011) *Towards a Green Economy: Pathways to Sustainable Development and Poverty Eradication.* Norway: UNEP.

United Nations General Assembly (2014) *Progress Report of the Open Working Group of the General Assembly on Sustainable Development Goals A/67/941.* United Nations.

United Nations General Assembly (2012) *Future We Want Resolution 66/288.* United Nations.

UN High-Level Panel on Global Sustainability (2012) *Resilient people, Resilient planet: A Future Worth Choosing.* New York: United Nations.

Vatican Council II. (1966) *Gaudium et Spes.* New York: Orbis.

Vincentian Partnership for Social Justice (2013) *Budget 2014: Minimum Essential Budget Standards: Income Briefing.* Dublin: VPSJ.

Vincentian Partnership for Social Justice (2010) *Minimum Essential Budgets for Households in Rural Areas.* Dublin: VPSJ.

Vincentian Partnership for Social Justice (2006) *Minimum Essential Budgets for Six Households.* Dublin: VPSJ.

Von Hagen, J. and Eichengreen, B. (1996) 'Federalism, Fiscal Restraints, and European Monetary Union', *The American Economic Review*, 86 (2) pp. 134-138.

Wall, M. (2014) *"HSE Chief raises prospect of further cut-backs in health".* Irish Times, 14th January. Available from http://www.irishtimes.com/news/health/hse-chief-raises-prospect-of-further-cutbacks-in-health-service-1.1655133 (14 March 2014).

Walsh, K. and Harvey, B. (2013) *Employment and Social Inclusion in Rural Areas: A Fresh Start.* Dublin: Pobal.

Watson, D, and Maître, B. (2013). 'Social Transfers and Poverty Alleviation in Ireland: An Analysis of the CSO Survey on Income and Living Conditions 2004 – 2011', *Social Inclusion Report No. 4.* Dublin: Department of Social Protection/ESRI.

Weir, S and Archer P (2011) *A Report on the First Phase of the Evaluation of DEIS.* Dublin: Educational Research Centre.

Whelan, C.T., R. Layte, B. Maitre, B. Gannon, B. Nolan, W. Watson, and Williams, J. (2003) 'Monitoring Poverty Trends in Ireland: Results from the 2001 Living in Ireland Survey', *Policy Research Series No. 51.* Dublin: ESRI.

Wijkman, A. and Rockstrom, J. (2012) *Bankrupting Nature: Denying our Planetary Boundaries.* Stockholm: Routledge.

Wilkinson, R. and Marmot, M. (eds) (2003) *Social Determinants of Health, The Solid facts (2nd ed).* Denmark: World Health Organisation.

World Commission on Environment and Development (1987) *Our Common Future (the Bruntland Report)*. Oxford University Press.

Thomson, S., M. Jowett and Mladovsky, P. (Eds.). *Health System responses to pressures in Ireland: Policy Options in an International Context.* World Health Organisation/ European Observatory on Health Systems and Policies.
World Health Organization Regional Office for Europe (2013) *Review of social determinants and the health divide in the WHO European Region: Final report.* Copenhagen: WHO.

World Health Organization (2011) *World Conference on the Social Determinants of Health 19-21 October 2011: Rio Political Declaration on Social Determinants of Health.* Rio de Janeiro: WHO.

World Hunger (2013). World Hunger and Poverty Facts and Statistics. Available at http://www.worldhunger.org/articles/Learn/world%20hunger%20facts%202002.ht m (Accessed 18 March 2014).

Online databases

AMECO Online Database, web address: http://ec.europa.eu/economy_finance/ameco/user/serie/SelectSerie.cfm

Eurostat online database, web address: http://epp.eurostat.ec.europa.eu

CSO QNHS online database, web address: http://www.cso.ie/en/databases/

CSO Live Register online database, web address: http://www.cso.ie/en/databases/